THE REMEMBERED EARTH

The Remembered Earth

An Anthology of Contemporary Native American Literature

Edited by

GEARY HOBSON

UNIVERSITY OF NEW MEXICO PRESS
Albuquerque

ISBN 0-8263-0584-9 (cloth)
ISBN 0-8263-0568-7 (paper)

Library of Congress Cataloging in Publication Data
Main entry under title:

The Remembered earth.

Originally published by Red Earth Press, Albuquer-
que, N.M.
Includes bibliographical references.
1. American literature—Indian authors.   2. American
literature—20th century.   3. Indians of North America—
Literary collections.   I. Hobson, Geary.   II. Title.
[PS508.I5R4   1981]   810'.8'0897   80-54561
ISBN 0-8263-0584-9
ISBN 0-8263-0568-7 (pbk.)

Many poems, works of fiction, and essays in *The Remembered Earth* have previously appeared
in the following publications, and we gratefully acknowledge permission to reprint them.

ACKNOWLEDGMENTS:

A: a journal of contemporary literature: Story from Bear Country by Leslie Marmon Silko. © 1976, Leslie Marmon Silko, reprinted with permission.

Academic Squaw: Reports to the World from The Ivory Tower by Wendy Rose: *To Some Few Hopi Ancestors; For the white poets who would be Indian* and *Three Thousand Dollar Death Song.* Blue Cloud Press, 1977.

Akwesasne Notes: Bear by Peter Blue Cloud. Reprinted by permission.

Americans Before Columbus: Pottery Maker by Laura Watchempino and *"We Shall Endure"* by Simon J. Ortiz.

Beloit Poetry Journal: After Fish and *Mosquitoes* by Linda Hogan, reprinted with permission.

Bidato: Ten Mile River Poems by Duane BigEagle: *My Father's Country.* © 1975, Workingman's Press, reprinted with permission.

Blue Cloud Quarterly: Bronze Tablets! by John F. Kerr, reprinted with permission.

Calyx: A Northwest Feminist Review: Soalt' in Tleeyaga and *Indian Blood* by Mary Tall Mountain. © 1977, 1978, Calyx, reprinted with permission.

Carriers of the Dream Wheel, edited by Duane Niatum: *Girl with the Green Skirt* and *Untitled* by Dana Naone. © 1975, Harper & Row, reprinted with permission.

Chicago Review: Wolf Hunting Near Nashoba by Jim Barnes. © 1975, *Chicago Review,* Vol. 27, No. 1; *Notes for a Love Letter from Mid-America* and *Lost in Sulphur Canyons* by Jim Barnes. © 1977, *Chicago Review,* Vol. 28, No. 4.

Chokecherry Hunters and Other Poems by Joseph L. Concha: *Grandmother; Chokecherry Hunters; August* and *Leaf.* © 1976, The Sunstone Press, reprinted with permission.

Chouteau Review, Fall 1977: *on the banks of black bear creek* by Anna L. Walters, reprinted with permission.

Cimarron Review: Ritual to Insure Long Life by Raven Hail, reprinted with permission.

College English, Vol. 39, No. 3, November 1977: *men tell and talk* and *i have sat through sunlight* by Nia Francisco. © 1977, the National Council of Teachers of English, reprinted with permission.

Come to Power, edited by Dick Lourie: *i breathe as the night breathes* by Suzan Shown Harjo. © 1974, The Crossing Press, reprinted with permission.

Conversations from the Nightmare by Carol Lee Sanchez: *The poster invites me to take a trip to the Museum* and *They have disappeared me.* © 1975, Casa Editorial, reprinted with permission.

Coyote and Friends by Peter Blue Cloud. *For Rattlesnake.* © 1976, Blackberry Press, reprinted by permission.

Coyote's Daylight Trip by Paula Gunn Allen: *Tucson: First Night* and *Madonna of the Hills.* La Confluencia Press, 1978.

Cutbank, number 8: *Autobiography, Chapter IV* and *Autobiography, Chapter IX* by Jim Barnes, reprinted with permission.

Dacotah Territory, 6: anniversary poem (for the Cheyennes who died at sand creek) by Lance Henson: *Vickie Loans-Arrow; John Knew-the-Crow* and *Bessie Dreaming Bear* by Marnie Walsh, reprinted with permission.

Distant Visions (formerly *Newborn): Acoma* by William Oandasan and *Inspiration (for Indin Artists)* by Karoniaktatie.

Entering Onondaga by Joseph Bruchac: *Ellis Island; The Remedies; Birdfoot's Grampa* and *The Geyser.* © 1977, Cold Mountain Press, reprinted with permission.

The Face of Poetry, edited by Laverne Harrell Clark and Mary MacArthur: *Self-Portrait: Microcosm, or Song of Mixed Blood* by Robert J. Conley. © 1977, Gallimaufry Press, reprinted with permission.

First Annual Women's Poetry Festival Anthology: Indian Anthropologist by Wendy Rose. New World Press Collective, 1977

The First Skin Around Me, edited by James L. White: *moving camp too far* by nila northSun. © 1976, Territorial Press, reprinted with permission.

Flow by Joseph Bruchac: *Elegy for Jack Bowman.* © 1975, Cold Mountain Press, reprinted with permission.

Four Indian Poets edited by John R. Milton: *Snowgoose; Rain for Ke-waik Bu-ne-ya; The Hoop Dancer* and *Ikce Wichasha* by Paula Gunn Allen. Dakota Press, 1974, reprinted with permission.

Going for the Rain by Simon J. Ortiz. *The Boy and Coyote; Yuusthiwa; Juanita, Wife of Manuelito; Significance of a Veteran's Day; My Father's Song* and *Dry Root in a Wash.* © 1976, Harper & Row, reprinted with permission.

A Good Journey by Simon J. Ortiz. *Heyaashi Guutah; Time to Kill in Gallup* and *A San Diego Poem: January-February 1973.* © 1977, Turtle Island Foundation, reprinted with permission.

The Gourd Dancer by N. Scott Momaday: *Headwaters; The Fear of Bo-talee; The Story of a Well-Made Shield; The Horse That Died of Shame; The Gourd Dancer; Rainy Mountain Cemetery* and *Krasnopresnenskaya Station.* © 1975, Harper & Row, reprinted by permission.

Greenfield Review: To Insure Survival by Simon J. Ortiz; *Barbara's Land—May 1974* by Geary Hobson; *Blessings* and *Heritage* by Linda Hogan. Greenfield Review Press, reprinted with permission.

Indian Historian Magazine: Travels in the South by Simon J. Ortiz, reprinted with permission.

Indian Mountain by Joseph Bruchac: *First Deer* and *Three Poems for the Indian Steelworkers in a Bar Where I Used to Drink.* © 1971, Ithaca House, reprinted with permission.

Indian Thoughts: The Children of God by Norman H. Russell: *Old men climbing* and *a great mosquito dance.* Native American Series. Kenneth R. Lincoln (editor) Los Angeles: American Indian Culture Center, UCLA, 1975, reprinted with permission.

Indian Thoughts: I am Old by Norman H. Russell: *i do not wish to be old.* San Marcos Press, 1975, reprinted with permission.

Indian Voices: The Man Made of Words by N. Scott Momaday. © 1970, Indian Historian Press, reprinted with permission.

Kayak: Thought of Going Home by Dana Naone, reprinted with permission.

La Confluencia: Buffalo Poem #1 by Geary Hobson and *Honest John's Seven Idols Pawn Shop* by Luci (Beach) Abeita. Reprinted with permission.

Laguna Woman by Leslie Marmon Silko: *Slim Man Canyon; When Sun Came to Riverwoman* and *Horses at Valley Store.* Greenfield Press, 1974, © 1974, Leslie Marmon Silko, reprinted with permission.

The Last Song by Joy Harjo: *Too Far into Arizona; the last song* and *3 AM.* Puerto del Sol Press, 1975.

Like Spirits of the Past Trying to Break Out and Walk to the West by Minerva Allen: *Returning from scouting for meat; A warm sunny day; Dog soldier renounced life* and *In the lodge where no one lives.* Wowapi Productions, 1974.

The Magazine of Fantasy and Science Fiction: Rite of Encounter by Russell Bates. © 1973, Mercury Press, reprinted with permission.

Margarine Maypole Orangoutang Express. Number 24: *Round Valley Song #3* and *Round Valley Song #4* by William Oandasan.

Message Bringer Woman by Carol Lee Sanchez: *La Tienda; More Conversations from the Nightmare* and *Prophecy.* © 1977, Taurean Horn Press, reprinted with permission.

Mestizo: An Anthology of Chicano Literature: Dragon Mountain by Robert L. Perca. Pajarito Publications, Albuquerque, NM, 1978. Reprinted with permission.

Mississippi Valley Review, Volume 6, Number 3: *Summer night* by William Oandasan.

Muted War Drums by Adrian C. Louis: *The Pseudo Shaman's Cliché.* Blue Cloud Press, 1977. Reprinted with permission.

Naming the Dark: poems for the Cheyenne by Lance Henson: *the leaving; love poem; portrait in february; snow song; old country* and *seeing.* © 1976. Point Riders Press, reprinted with permission.

The Nation: The Last Chance by Jim Barnes; *My People* and *Flowers of Winter* by Duane BigEagle. © The Nation, reprinted with permission.

Native Colours by Karoniaktatie: *i lost the song.* © 1974, Akwesasne Notes, reprinted with permission.

New America. Vol. 2, Number 3, (Special Native American Issue) edited by Geary Hobson: *Untitled Journey* by Veronica Riley; *Jicarilla in August* by Ronald Rogers; *Gallup* by Larry Emerson; *squash blossom shit and heishi horrors* by Luci (Cadzow) Abeita; *Blowing Wind* by Genevieve Yazzie; *the words* and *two circles* by Norman H. Russell and *Mickey, To Nilinigli,* and *Shighan—The Navajo Way* by Bernadette Chato.

New Mexico Magazine. January 1951: *Echo from Beyond* by Joe S. Sando; reprinted with permission.

North: Poems of Home by Maurice Kenny: *Akwesasne; Cold Creek; Home (for Rick)* and *North (in memory of my father).* Blue Cloud Press, 1977.

Northwest Passage: The Last Wolf by Mary Tall Mountain, reprinted with permission.

Northwest Review. Volume 13, No. 2: *Long Person* by Gladys Cardiff, reprinted with permission.

Ocean Mountain: Hair Poem by Dana Naone, reprinted with permission.

The Only Good Indian (unpublished novel manuscript) by Janet Campbell. © 1977, Janet Campbell, reprinted with permission.

Pembroke Magazine: indian dancer by nila northSun, reprinted with permission.

Plucked Chicken: The Old Man Said: Two and *Powwow* by Carroll Arnett, reprinted with permission.

The Poet's Analyst by Rokwaho (Daniel Thompson): (unpublished book manuscript) *i dream; blue deep; Poem for a stone* and *"Innocence Returned."* © 1977. Rokwaho (Daniel Thompson).

Prairie Schooner: impression of strong heart song by Lance Henson and *When you talk of this* by Elizabeth Cook-Lynn, reprinted with permission.

Puerto del Sol: Storyteller by Leslie Marmon Silko. © 1976, Leslie Marmon Silko, reprinted with permission.

The Raven Speaks. Vol. 2, No. 11: *Danaga Echodiya* by Raven Hail. © 1970. Raven Hail, reprinted with permission.

River Styx: Ponca War Dancers by Carter Revard, reprinted with permission.

*Scree: **Deer Hunting*** by Geary Hobson; ***The Rattlesnake Band*** by Robert J. Conley and ***What Eagle Saw in the West*** by Duane BigEagle, reprinted with permission.

*South Dakota Review: **Woman Singing*** by Simon J. Ortiz. Reprinted with permission of John R. Milton, editor.

*Southwest Women's Poetry Exchange: **Someone Talking*** by Joy Harjo and ***Conversations*** by Luci Tapahonso, reprinted with permission.

*The State: **Legend of the Cherokee Rose*** by Raven Hail, reprinted with permission.

*Strawberry Press: **Muted War Drums*** (broadside) by Adrian C. Louis; ***Natural Law*** (broadside) by William Oandasan. Reprinted with permission of Maurice Kenny, editor.

*Sun Tracks: **The Bare Facts*** by Elizabeth Cook-Lynn; ***The Last Dream*** by Ray A. Young Bear; ***Wazhazhe Grandmother*** by Carter Revard; ***The Witch of Goingsnake*** by Robert J. Conley; ***Sionima*** and ***The Bee Hunt*** by Refugio Savala; ***Cry of Nature*** by Geraldine Keams; ***Happening*** and ***Bel Woman*** by Roman C. Adrian; ***The Snakeman*** by Luci Tapahonso; ***what gramma said about how she came here, what gramma said about her grandpa,*** and ***what gramma said about her kids*** by nila northSun. Reprinted with permission from *Sun Tracks*.

Taking Off by William Oandasan: ***Who Am I?*** and ***Silent Afternoon.*** © 1977, A Press, reprinted with permission.

A Taste of the Knife by Marnie Walsh: ***Angelina Runs-Against; June the Twenty-second*** and ***The Red Fox.*** © 1977, Ahsahta Press, reprinted with permission of Thomas Truskey, editor.

Then Badger Said This by Elizabeth Cook-Lynn. *Not Everything in the world; There was a Sisseton Woman . . . ; When the Dakotapi . . . ; "Wichinchila waste . . . ";* Vantage Press, reprinted with permission.

Third World Women (Third World Communications: ***i Clouding Woman*** by Suzan Shown Harjo. © 1977, Suzan Shown Harjo, reprinted with permission.

Tsalagi by Carroll Arnett: ***Uwohali; The Story of My Life; Tlanuwa; Early Song; Homage to Andrew Jackson*** and ***Roadman.*** © 1976, Elizabeth Press, reprinted with permission.

Voices of the Rio Grande: ***Old Man for His People*** by Harold Littlebird. © 1977, Rio Grande Writer's Association Press, reprinted with permission.

War Games (unpublished novel manuscript) by Opal Lee Popkes. © 1977, Opal Lee Popkes, reprinted with permission.

*The Wormwood Review: **how my cousin was killed*** by nila northSun, reprinted with permission.

Y'Bird (formerly *Yardbird Reader*): ***The Rise of the White Shaman as a New Version of Cultural Imperialism*** by Geary Hobson and ***An Old-Time Indian Attack Conducted in Two Parts*** by Leslie Marmon Silko. Reprinted with permission of Yardbird Publishing Co., Berkeley, CA, 1976, 1977.

Dust jacket and paperback cover design by HSI Editype

Dust jacket and paperback photograph by Diane Reyna

Title page drawing by Aaron Yava

Once in his life a man ought to concentrate his mind upon the remembered earth, I believe. He ought to give himself up to a particular landscape in his experience, to look at it from as many angles as he can, to wonder about it, to dwell upon it. He ought to imagine that he touches it with his hands at every season and listens to the sounds that are made upon it. He ought to imagine the creatures that are there and all the faintest motions in the wind. He ought to recollect the glare of noon and all the colors of the dawn and dusk.

— N. Scott Momaday
(from "The Man Made of Words")

The Remembered Earth is dedicated to the Native American people of the Western Hemisphere. More particularly, it is dedicated to all other Native American writers, unpublished and striving, whose work will come after this book.

A Special Note of Thanks is due to the staff of the Native American Studies program at the University of New Mexico, with whom I worked and served from 1976 to 1978 — Junella Haynes, Robert Mondragon, Betty Ojaye, Pierre Shield, Elouise Chicharello, D.C. Cole, and most particularly, Agnes Lucero, the program secretary.

TABLE OF CONTENTS

1. Continuance

In 1969 the Pulitzer committee for fiction awarded its annual prize to a young professor of English at Stanford University. The writer receiving the award was N. Scott Momaday and his novel was *House Made of Dawn*. The fact that Momaday's book dealt almost entirely with Native Americans did not escape the attention of the news media or of readers and scholars of contemporary literature. Neither did the novelist's Kiowa Indian background. Several news stories pointed out that not since Oliver La Farge received the Pulitzer Prize for *Laughing Boy* exactly forty years before had an "Indian" novel been so honored. The writers of the stories also pointed out that while La Farge was a white man writing about Indians, Momaday was an Indian — the first to be acclaimed as a Pulitzer laureate.

The same year, another young writer, a Standing Rock Sioux attorney named Vine Deloria, Jr., published *Custer Died for Your Sins,* which was subtitled "An Indian Manifesto." It was indeed a manifesto. Part of its importance was its incisive examination of current American attitudes towards Native American issues, and it came at a time when the American conscience seemed ready to be jolted by Indians again. Also within the same year, John R. Milton edited a special Native American issue of the *South Dakota Review.* Especially noteworthy was the inclusion of work by Simon J. Ortiz, James Welch, Grey Cohoe, Phil George, Janet Campbell, Ronald Rogers, and Norman H. Russell, all of whom had been up until then little published, but who were already known in Indian circles as young writers of promise. Milton's special issue proved so popular and so completely adaptable as a text that he soon issued it through Dakota Press as an anthology entitled *The American Indian Speaks.* Few anthologies following it in the next few years would be so thorough and pioneering, though many "borrowed" liberally from it through reprinting.

Partly responsible also for America's new interest in contemporary Native American writing was the appearance at about this time of two works of "pop" scholarship — Peter Farb's *Man's Rise to Civilization* (1968) and Dee Brown's *Bury My Heart at Wounded Knee* (1970). Both struck a responsive chord in the American popular taste, and by the signs of it — paperback reprints widely available in supermarkets and newsstands — their popularity has still not abated. Both books stimulated interest in American Indians from historical and anthropological viewpoints, and while there are many other books much more precisely written and scholarly researched, *Bury My Heart at Wounded Knee* and *Man's Rise to Civilization* have contributed a great deal to America's new concern for contemporary Native American cultures and literature.

Where does this brief summary of a flurry of literary activity, in the years 1968-1970, bring us? Simply, it brings us to the point where we must begin to view this activity, particularly as it continued with published works of Leslie Marmon Silko's *Ceremony,* James Welch's

Winter in the Blood, Duane Niatum's *Ascending Red Cedar Moon* and *Carriers of the Dream Wheel,* the poetry of Paula Gunn Allen, Ray A. Young Bear, Robert J. Conley, Simon J. Ortiz, Carol Lee Sanchez and many others as well, as a renascence and not just simply as a "boom" — both of these things contemporary Native American literature certainly is. It is indeed much more than a "boom," or a "fad," — to echo what certain literary scholars have said. It is renewal, it is continuance — and it is remembering.

I believe I can best illustrate the phenomenon of renascence in a couple of ways. First, I remember a remark made by a student of mine in class more than a year ago. We had been reading xeroxed poems by Peter Blue Cloud, Rokwaho, and Maurice Kenny — Mohawks from the upper-state New York and southern Quebec area — and the subject turned to all the various Native Americans — in other portions of the country. Yes, we all agreed, there did indeed seem to be a lot of Indian writers around today. The student marvelled, and I'm sure most of us were thinking generally along the same lines: "Isn't it amazing how Native American literature has just burst so suddenly upon the scene?"

The question is itself marvelous, especially since I've heard variations of the same thing articulated by many other people — particularly reviewers of books of poetry by Native Americans. While I would not deny there has been a virtual boom in Native American literature in the past ten years, I am also aware that the Native American literature itself has not merely "just sprung up." Native American literature, like the life and culture of which it is a part, is immeasurable centuries old — perhaps 30,000 years or more as Leslie Marmon Silko and Simon J. Ortiz say in their poems — and its roots are deep in the land — too deep, I would venture to say, for a mere five centuries of European influence to upturn in any lasting, complete and irrevocable way.

As I mentioned before, it has to do with remembering, continuance, renewal. Traditionally, certainly long before the Europeans came to the Western Hemisphere and even long after their arrival, Native American people have been accustomed to remembering their histories and their ways of life through intricate time-proven processes of storytelling. It is only recently that these ways of storytelling have become designated by scholars as oral tradition. For millenia Native American people carried on their traditions in this fashion. Never more than a generation from extinction, as N. Scott Momaday says in "Man Made of Words," it is all the more to be cherished by the people because of this tenuous link. In remembering, there is strength and continuance and renewal throughout the generations.

It was when things became forgotten and lost, when the chain of generations were broken by European invaders, that many Native American people became lost and forgotten. The Europeans came like a flight of locusts — a handful, another handful, then another, then hundreds, then thousands, until there were millions. The Indian people, particularly those along the Atlantic Coast, were overwhelmed without having had much chance of learning how to live within the influx. In search of a new world in which they could live and exercise their religious freedom, the Europeans came upon the Native

American people and rapidly undertook to deny them theirs. Every American knows from the elementary school history books that Europeans brought with them guns, horses, steel tools, whiskey, disease, but rarely do those history books discuss Christianity as the one element brought by the newcomers that caused the most effective and irrevocable devastation to the lifeways of Indians. Yet I do not think even the most devout Christian would deny this as a fact of history. Europeans, like farmers in a hurry to get a late crop in, plowed under tribal religions with zeal as they sought to make the Indian into their own image as Christian brother. Within a century after the settling of Plymouth Rock, the Bible had been translated into several Algonquoin dialects, and many Puritan missionaries, as well as Moravians and Jesuits, had penetrated the interior of America with a mission to make Christians out of the Indians.

With this replacing of long-held tribal religious values, the Indians lost the basis of their old ways of life and, just as importantly, their traditional ways of remembering. It was also a natural correlative, at least to the white man, that for Indians to give up the tribal religions, they were also expected to relinquish their way of life and, of course, their land.

All of this would be an old story, known to most Americans in that part of the psyche that makes up the public mind and certainly to every Native American, if it were merely something that had once occurred in early American history and from which America had benefitted, but sadly, that is not the case. What is disturbing is that while it is indeed an old story, it is not just a "yesterday" story. Today, Native American people face perhaps the greatest threat ever to their continued existence as a people. They are still being threatened by the exploitation of their land, at least that which still remains to them, from a blind, profit-motivated and apparently self-serving dominant society. It can be seen in nearly every quarter of Indian country — in the Navajo Four Corners region, the coal strip-mining operations on Cheyenne and Crow lands in Montana, Pyramid Lake in Nevada, the Arkansas River-bottom ripoff in eastern Oklahoma.

In terms of religious exploitation, Protestant and Mormon missionaries still appear to be working overtime to eradicate native tribal religions, by seeking to subvert the long-honored wisdom of medicine-makers and elders of tribes. Rare these days is the non-Indian who accords the same degree of seriousness, of respect, to the medicine man of an Indian community that would be given to a psychiatrist working, say, for some industrial firm's personnel department, or some Baptist minister, newly transferred in to, say, Muleshoe, Texas, from a central office in Dallas or Austin. Yet the functions of both these types of persons would approximate some of the duties of an Indian community's medicine-maker, and they would still not be as deeply an essential part of the community as their Native American counterpart. Therefore, since the continuing threat of western dominance still looms heavily over Indian people, there is all the more reason for rediscovering, and in doing so, cherishing, Indian ways of remembering.

One looks back over American history and finds the pages of the nation's book — or the tombs in its graveyard — strewn with the names of long-past tribes — Narragansett, Wampanoag, Nipmuc, Huron, Cayuga, Ofo, Biloxi, Yazoo, Natchez, Chakchiuma, Yuchi, and scores more. While the total of all tribes and the numbers of people lost during European expansion on the continent is staggering, the really amazing thing is not a question of how many peoples and cultures were eradicated, and by whatever means, but how great a number of people and how much of their traditional beliefs and values are yet retained by them. Brewton Berry's *Almost White* is an excellent though general study of the enclaves of Indian communities which continue to exist in states east of the Mississippi. It is encouraging to realize that there are countless communities of generally landless, certainly "reservation-less," Indian people — or people of primarily Native American origin — all over the continent, particularly in areas where no Indians are thought by the average American to be. Lumbees, Waccamaws and Person County Indians in North Carolina, Chickahominies in Virginia, Nanticokes in Delaware, Creeks in Alabama and Florida, Cherokees and Quapaws in Arkansas. They exist without benefit of the largesse of the federal government, especially the B.I.A., and most often without recognition by other more legitimate Indian or white communities. Yet they endure.

It is well enough to discuss how the Navajos, the Pueblos, the hill country Cherokees, have retained much of the culture — language, religion, old ways — but we must honor the "forgotten Indians" as well, those who survive as Native Americans despite the myriad pressures of the dominant culture all around them. We learn, just as Simon J. Ortiz says in "Travels in the South," that "Indians are everywhere," and when we know this to be true, we ought to answer as he does: "Goddamn right."

2. Strength

"Indians are everywhere." Enduring, surviving, continuing. This can be seen in the contemporary literature of Native Americans. From Refugio Savala of Sonora to Mary Tall Mountain of the Alaska Koyukon tribe; from the Navajo country of Geraldine Keams and Larry Emerson to the northeastern Maine of Joseph Bruchac, Native Americans are writing about themselves and their people and their writings are based on firm ground, nurtured by strong roots, and are putting forth indomitable flowers. Thinking for a moment of the wide dispersal of current Native American writers, I am brought back to another part of the question posed by my student. Granted that contemporary Native American literature is founded on strong traditional grounds, the tribal beliefs and ways of living, the oral tradition — what of literature in its written form? Isn't it new, and hasn't it rather lately "sprung-up?"

The answer is again, quite simply, no. Even in its written form, in the English language, Native American literature is quite old within the framework of American literature. Daniel G. Brinton, in an essay entitled "Aboriginal American Authors and Their Productions" published in 1883, catalogued the numerous works by Native American writers in the early nineteenth century. Most of those early writers discussed by Brinton — William Apess (Pequod); George Copway, or

Kah-ge-ga-gah-bowh (Ojibway); Peter Jones (Ojibway); David Cusick (Tuscarora); Peter Dooyentate Clark (Wyandott); Chief Elias Johnson (Tuscarora) — published books relating to their tribal cultures; but they were generally Christian converts. Though their books usually contain a condescension towards their formerly held tribal religious beliefs, they are nevertheless extremely important as contributions to an understanding of their tribes in the early days.

Although it is a debatable point, I believe it can be posited with some validity that many tribes had variants of written language long before Sequoyah developed the Cherokee syllabary and made his people literate virtually overnight. Certainly, the "Walum Olum," or "Red Score," of the Delawares and the *Book of Rites* of the Great League of the Iroquois Confederacy were handed down orally for many generations, but at an early date the people reproduced them in various written ways. It is also a contention held by many Cherokees that Sequoyah merely elaborated on the ancient system of communicative symbols, previously the sole domain of medicine-makers and keepers of the old ways, which he made widely available to every Cherokee. Even while American Indians were being written about and stereotyped by American writers from Cooper and Longfellow to Helen Hunt Jackson and Oliver La Farge, Native American writers were writing books, developing a literature. The poems of John Rollin Ridge (Cherokee), Alexander L. Posey (Creek), Pauline Johnson (Mohawk) were greeted as if they were curios, things to be marvelled at rather than be examined critically. Their works are extremely dated by today's standards, but they are at least as noteworthy as the productions of Edward Rowland Sill and Joaquin Miller, their white contemporaries who were not quite of the first rank occupied then by Ralph Waldo Emerson, Walt Whitman, and Edgar Allan Poe.

Little known today is *Poor Sarah; or the Indian Woman* (1833), the first novel written by a Native American in a Native American language. It was published six years after the founding of the *Cherokee Phoenix,* the first tribal newspaper to print in both the native language and in English, and its editor Elias Boudinot, was the author.

However, some of the best of Native American literature began to come about following the end of the Plains Wars. With the beginning of the reservation system in the 1870s and 1880s the peoples' lives underwent great changes which were not always for the best. For well over a half-century — and it still continues to a great extent — Native American literature became primarily the productions of autobiography and biography. Recently, the Western Writers Series, out of Boise State College, published Lynne Woods O'Brien's pamphlet entitled *Plains Indian Autobiographies*. Given the established pattern of brevity which dictate the series' pamphlets, most of which run from 40 to 48 pages in length, Ms. O'Brien could scarcely more than scrape the surface of her subject. However, her essay is an important and informative examination of several valuable books that have as yet received very little critical attention. In the period 1880-1940 — the Era of the Vanishing American to many scholars and historians of Indian culture — scores of autobiographies were issued and they constitute an important genre in the body of Native American literature. To continue to ignore them is to deny a whole panorama of fairly recent history, let alone an important link between the generations of people making the adjustment from oral tradition to the written word.

The autobiographies were usually "written" by anthropologists or poets recording and editing the life-stories of old Native Americans who were seen as individuals standing at the crossroads of the 19th and 20th centuries. It is common to find the autobiographies listed by the subject's name in the title, and a "as told to" or "recorded and edited by" note attached to the white writer's name. Probably the most famous of these autobiographies is John G. Neihardt's *Black Elk Speaks* (1932). As Neihardt informs us, Black Elk's story was told in Oglala Lakota to his son who then translated it into English to Neihardt, who then rewrote it. Others of this sort include *Plenty-Coups, Chief of the Crows* (1930) and *Pretty-Shield, Medicine Woman of the Crows* (1932), both recorded and edited by Frank B. Linderman; *Wooden Leg, A Warrior Who Fought Custer* (1931), told years later by a Cheyenne who was eighteen when he fought at Little Big Horn and edited by Thomas Marquis; *Two Leggings, The Making of a Crow Warrior* (1967), edited by Peter Nabokov; *Cheyenne Memories* (1967), by John Stands in Timber, with editorial help from Margot Liberty and Robert M. Utley; *Mountain Wolf Woman: Sister of Crashing Thunder* (1961), edited by Nancy O. Lurie; *Crashing Thunder: The Autobiography of a Winnebago Indian* (1920), with Paul Radin; and *Lame Deer: Seeker of Visions* (1972), with Richard Erdoes.

During this time a number of Southwestern Indians contributed to the autobiographical form: *Sun Chief: The Autobiography of a Hopi* (1942), Don Talayesva, with Leo W. Simmons; *Son of Old Man Hat: A Navajo Autobiography* (1940), edited by Walter Dyk; *Geronimo's Story of His Life* (1906), in which the famed Apache war chief told his story to Stephen M. Barrett; and *Flaming Rainbow's People* (1932) by James Paytiamo of Acoma Pueblo. There are dozens more. Clearly, the area of the Indian autobiography is a rich and virtually untapped field for future literary scholars. I would invite students of Native American literature from The Modern Language Association, who all too often concern themselves with the problems involved in translating Native American languages into English even while by and large knowing nothing of the Indian tongues (an exercise in futility, like rattling bee-bees around in a boxcar; or as Lame Deer might say, like trying to pour a handful of sand into a flying duck's ass) to turn their attention in this direction.

Another kind of autobiography, rather than the "as told to" or "recorded and edited by" variety, was the individual author sort, in which no colloborators were involved. Some of these include: *Indian Boyhood* (1904), *The Soul of the Indian* (1911), *From the Deep Woods to Civilization, Chapters in the Autobiography of an Indian* (1916), all by Charles A. Eastman, a Santee Sioux who was also a university trained medical doctor; Chief Luther Standing Bear's *My People The Sioux* (1928), *My Indian Boyhood* (1928), and *Land of the Spotted Eagle* (1933). Recently, N. Scott Momaday wrote a book in this genre: *The Names* (1975).

Native American literature in the early decades of this century did not find itself being expressed only in forms of autobiography. There were also novelists, newspaper columnists, and at least one playwright. John M. Oskison (Cherokee) published three novels in the 1920's and 1930's: *Wild Harvest* (1925), *Black Jack Davy* (1926), and *Brothers Three* (1935). John Joseph Matthews (Osage) wrote a novel, *Sundown* (1934), in addition to two scholarly works about his tribe entitled *Wah' Kon-Tah* (1932) and *The Osages* (1961).

By far the best of the early twentieth century Indian novelists was the late D'Arcy McNickle (Salish - Kootenai), whose *The Surrounded* (1936) was recently reprinted through The University of New Mexico Press' Zia series of neglected western classics. Two other McNickle novels are *Runner in the Sun* (1954) and the posthumous *Wind from an Enemy Sky* (1978). Like his colleague, Oliver La Farge, about whom he wrote a book, *Indian Man* (1971), McNickle was also extremely active as a proponent of Indian Affairs and his rightful due as a novelist of stature has yet to be appreciated.

It may come as a surprise to most Americans to learn that Will Rogers (Cherokee) was an Indian, but he most certainly was. Justly famous as a show business personality and a social critic, he was also widely known as a newspaper columnist of great social concern, whose incisive down-home humor cut through the stale wind of politicians like a butcher knife through hot butter. His writings have been collected in *Roger-isms, The Cowboy Philosopher on the Peace Conference* (1919), *Ether and Me* (1936), *The Illiterate Digest* (1936), and *The Autobiography of Will Rogers* (1949). Dan C. Madrano (Caddo) also wrote humorous columns and they have been collected in *Heap Big Laugh* (1955).

Lynn Riggs (Cherokee) was a playwright of great sensitivity. In his plays *Big Lake* (1927) and *The Cherokee Night* (1931), he created a brooding sense of tragedy, a darkness, that is found in at least one other Cherokee writer whose work I know — Robert J. Conley and his short stories, "The Witch of Goingsnake" and "Wili Woyi." Riggs is probably best known today for his play *Green Grow the Lilacs* (1931) from which the popular Broadway musical *Oklahoma!* has been taken. Needless to say, *Oklahoma!* is a great deal modified from *Green Grow the Lilacs*.

3. Renewal

In the past decade Native American literature has flourished. In addition to older established periodicals, such as the *South Dakota Review* and *Cimarron Review,* the emergence of several new small presses and magazines — *Sun Tracks,* out of the University of Arizona; *Blue Cloud Quarterly* of South Dakota; Indian Historian Press, with both a quarterly magazine and a monthly newspaper, *Wassaja; Akwesasne Notes* of upstate New York; *Greenfield Review; Scree; Pembroke;* Strawberry Press; and A Press — have been instrumental in publishing most of the new and primarily young Native American writers. From the pages of these journals first appeared the poems of William Oandasan, Joy Harjo, Linda Hogan, and many others. These publications have offered a forum for Indian writers that might not have been so easily obtainable any place else. Many of us who are now publishing in other places, particularly more non-Indian oriented as well as "Indian" journals, realize the great debt to editors and publishers like Rupert Costo, Lawrence Evers, Joseph Bruchac, Maurice Kenny, Brother Benet Tvedten, and John R. Milton. They have indeed been like midwives to a rising generation of writers.

The writers in *The Remembered Earth* come from all quarters of the North American continent — Mexico as well as Canada, Hawaii as well as Alaska. In fact, the inclusion of Dana Naone, a young and gifted native-born Hawaiian writer, serves to honor those of us "mainland" Native Americans since we are increasingly becoming aware that while Hawaiians are not, properly speaking, American Indians, they are also, in just as real a sense, "Native Americans." It should not be surprising that Dana's poems contain some of the same themes and concerns that are to be found in those of, say, Paula Gunn Allen or Leslie Marmon Silko.

Who are Native American writers anyway? In compiling the work for *The Remembered Earth* I decided early that I would try to include as broad a spectrum of definition as possible. I wanted to include writers of mixed-blood, even those who would probably have difficulty producing a Certificate of Indian Blood or a tribal enrollment number, as well as those who were born full-bloods and raised on reservations. Attempting to define *who* is a Native American writer also necessarily entails considering the question of *who/what* is an Indian — something on which there is apparently still no universal agreement. In terms of politics and sociology it appears there are several ways of defining Indians: 1) the Indian tribe's, or community's, judgment, 2) the neighboring non-Indian communities' judgment, 3) the federal government's judgment, and 4) the individual's judgment. There are obvious pitfalls involved when anyone assumes an absolute position in terms of any of these viewpoints, though I must admit that I am partial to believing the first of these definitions is the most essential.

Anthropologists and historians have had a go at defining Native Americans also. Charles Hudson in *The Southeastern Indians* (1977) discusses three criteria essential for "Indian-ness" — 1) genetic, 2) cultural, and 3) social. In the days before Columbus stumbled into the neighborhood, there was no question about it: everyone in the Western Hemisphere were clearly and soundly definable as Native Americans in all three categories. With the intermingling of European and Native American blood, as the generations passed, the definitions began to lose their erstwhile clear lines for many of the people involved, especially those tribes in closest continued contact with Europeans.

Today, Native American people fall into one or more of these categories. People are classified by their tribe, the family, or the government as "full-bloods," "half-bloods," "one-fourths," "one-eighth," and so on. This is the genetic distinction. Culturally, a person is characterized in terms of where he or she is from, who his or her people are and what their ways of life, religion, language, are like. Socially (I believe there is a rather fine line between this and the cultural criterion), a person is judged as Native American because of how he or she views the world, his or her views about land, home, family, culture, etc. There are, I think, no easy answers. I do believe, however, that John Ross, the one-eighth blood Cherokee chief (with seven-eighths Scottish blood), who fought arduously against the removal of his people into Indian Territory, was more "Indian" than John Ridge, the seven-eighths Cherokee, who collaborated with Andrew Jackson's henchmen, selling out his people. Though both were genetically part Indian, of differing degrees, it was clear to the Cherokee people of the 1830s that John Ross was more "one of themselves" than was John Ridge.

The same standard applies to Hispano-American, or Chicano, peoples. While they are undeniably of Indian blood, and genetically Indian, they are nevertheless culturally and socially Spanish. Because of centuries of Catholicism, they are for the most part irrevocably alienated from the Native American portion of their heritage. Thus, to most Native Americans today, it is not merely enough that a person have a justifiable claim to Indian blood, but he or she must also be at least somewhat socially and culturally definable as a Native American.

However, I feel that in the final analysis the most important concern is not whether one is "more" Indian than his fellow-Indian; it is much more imperative that both recognize their common heritage, no matter to what differing degree, and that they strive to join together for the betterment of Native Americans — as well as other people — one-eighth bloods as well as full-bloods, "unenrolled" as well as "enrolled." I believe all the writers in The Remembered Earth recognize and share this sense of affirmation. After all, when all is said and done, the writing we leave behind us will be there for the people. But granted that Native American writers share a deep sense of obligation to Native American people, I also believe that it is the individual writer's duty to write about those things he or she feels to be important, regardless of whether the subject of the writing deals exclusively with Native American concerns. If Native Americans were manacled in such a way as to be limited to write only "Indian" poems or stories, then we would not have Momaday's "Krasnopresnenskaya Station," the two short poems about outer space by Aaron Carr, the excellent science fiction stories and television scripts of Russell Bates, much of Ronald Rogers' fiction, William Oandasan's translations from the French; and our literature would be the poorer. I have often heard the complaint voiced that certain Native American writers are not writing "Indian" poems. This is similar to the blasts by certain black critics thirty years ago against Willard Motley, a black novelist who wrote several first-rate novels that do not have blacks as central characters. Motley knew he was black, but since he did not feel compelled to explore that aspect of his experience, he should not have been castigated but rather valued for the artistry and insight he possessed as a different kind of novelist. It so happened that he found other ways than writing novels of affirming his heritage as a black man.

To insist that Indians write only "Indian" poems or books is as myopic as wishing Joseph Conrad had written "Polish" novels. Just as non-Indian writers have found it profitable writing about Indians, so should Native American writers have that same freedom. Indeed, non-Indian writers should continue in the freedom of writing about

Native Americans, but given the past three hundred years of American literary history, considering the nauseating stereotypes of Indians as "red devils" and "noble savages' which date back all the way to Captain John Smith, they must recognize that they have two strikes against them. Native American people are today more aware of what is being said and written about them than in Cooper's day, and the tired old truisms, the stereotypes, the too-easy satire, and even the too-easy adulations, will not hold up anymore. This is something that many contemporary non-Indian poets, particularly the neo-romantics "playing Indian" and "shaman" up around the Berkeley Hills, have yet to learn. So does Hollywood.

Native American writers, then, are those of Native American blood and background who affirm their heritage in their individual ways as do writers of all cultures. Some write of reservation life; others of urban Indians trying to make it in the white man's world. Still others write of war, of work far away from home, of old traditions threatened by the clash with new ways of living, of historical days. Though emphases may differ, themes are basically the same, since contemporary Indian people are essentially not any different from, say, Jewish people, blacks, Chicanos, or Anglos from midwestern America. "Literature is a facet of a culture," Paula Gunn Allen says in "The Sacred Hoop," and as the contemporary Native American writer manifests this in poems and stories, he or she is doing the same thing as Saul Bellow and Leroy Quintana, Ernest J. Gaines and Wright Morris — giving something of value back to the people of whom they are a part.

4. Remembering

Earlier in this essay I mentioned that in the remembering of heritage there is strength, continuance, and renewal. Remembering is all. Anna L. Walters says the same thing in "Come, My Sons":

> It is in remembering that our power lies,
> and our future comes
> This is the Indian way.

In Grant Foreman's *Indian Removal* there is a passage quoted from a letter by Col. George S. Gaines to the *Mobile Commercial Register* (November 12, 1831). Gaines was in the Choctaw country of central Mississippi, assisting some of the people in the tribe who were making preparations for removing to Indian Territory. Gaines noted:

> The feeling which many of them evince in separating, never to return again, from their long cherished hills, poor as they are in this section of country, is truly painful to witness; and would be so for me, but for the conviction that the removal is absolutely necessary for their welfare (Foreman, 56).

Another observer along with Gaines later told of "seeing the departing emigrants (Choctaws) touching the tree trunks, twigs and leaves about their homes in token of farewell to these old friends (Foreman, 56)." This scene, in which the Choctaws stored away memories of their homeland, is a deeply poignant illustration of what it is to remember the earth.

Heritage is people; people are the earth; earth is heritage. By remembering these relationships — to the people, the land, the past — we renew in strength our continuance as a people. Literature, in all its forms, oral as well as written, is our most durable way of carrying on this continuance. By making literature, like the singers and storytellers of earlier times, we serve the people as well as ourselves in an abiding sense of remembrance.

Land is people. We have come far from this correlation, but return is not impossible. In many Native American languages the words "people" and "land" are indistinguishable and inseparable. In the name of "Oklahoma," for instance, that land of exile for great numbers of eastern tribes and people, the word taken from the Choctaw and Chickasaw tongues, we find the words enveloped in synonymity. In these Muskhogean languages, Oklahoma is literally "red people's land." In many high school classes in Oklahoma, over the past decades since statehood, non-Choctaw-and-Chickasaw teachers charged with dispensing Oklahoma state history have had difficulties sometimes as they attempt to translate "Okla-homa" (more literally, "ogula homma") into the three-word phrase, "red people's land." Sometimes they will correctly label "homa" as *red,* then have trouble in deciding if "Okla" means *people* or *land,* and then decide, as if washing their hands of the matter, that *Oklahoma* translates to either *Red land,* or *Red People.* There should be no difficulty (*Okla, Ogula, ogla, okala, goula, cola* — whatever the variant) means *both* people and land. There is no separation; they are one.

And in another full meaning of how the terms *land* and *people* and also *red,* intermingle, the Chickasaw poet Linda Hogan evokes a striking correlative in "Celebration: Birth of a Colt." The act of bringing forth a new colt into the world, is shown in the redness of the life-sustaining membrane as it is reflected in the early morning sun:

> The sun coming up shines through,
> the sky turns bright with morning
> and the land
> with pollen blowing off the corn,
> land that will always own us,
> everywhere it is red.

The morning sun, the corn pollen, the new colt, the people attending the birth, the land itself — all come together in an epiphany of prayer and celebration.

These are the kinds of relationships we must never forget. Our land is our strength, our people the land, one and the same, as it always has been and always will be. Remembering is all.

Geary Hobson

Maurice Kenny

ADOWE:
WE RETURN THANKS

Lastly, we return thanks to the Great Spirit, in whom is embodied all goodness, and who directs all things for the good of his children.

From "Iroquois Prayer"
IN THE TRAIL OF THE WIND

Indian poetry has always been basically a ceremony of thanks to the Great Spirit, to Mother Earth, to the grasses and the various creatures, a song. Indian poetry across the long travel of time has been essentially spiritual. Though a young man sings and plays his flute for the love of a young woman, he is thanking the Great Spirit for his love's existence. Though a poet studies a milkweed-pod's flight across the air, he is thanking the Great Spirit for the milkweed's existence. While he sings of the hunt, he blesses the deer or moose for giving its flesh so that the hunter may continue, and he thanks the Great Spirit that the deer exists. Though he is praying for victory over his enemy, he is praying to the Great Spirit that the best warrior survive, and he is thankful for his prowess and for his safety. There are thankful songs for growth, maturity; songs for the smoke of the holy pipe; for the sun that warms the field and grows corn within that field, and rain which nourishes the corn's roots; for the moon that comforts sleep, and of the evil of the witches of the forest for keeping his walk in balance. There is a song of thankfulness for every deed and thought, for every creation of the Great Spirit.

Greek tragedy rose from a religious background. So too has Indian poetry risen from, and continues to be sustained, by a traditional religious fervor. Greek tragedy was quickly turned into Roman propaganda under the various pens of Latin poets, eventually resulting in the blather of television comedy and totally alienated from that Greek altar. Indian religion has kept its strength in observance, partially at least, through prayer and poetry. For thousands of years, verse-prayer has not been far from the Great Spirit. It has gathered together in ceremony not only its thanks to the Great Spirit, but composed the chronicle of time itself, the calendar of events of an historical culture, and includes love songs, victory songs, healing songs, the joy of creation, the surety of death and reunion with one's ancestors.

"Dawn is a praise of silence to be respected . . ."

From "Autumn Morning"
TURTLE, BEAR & WOLF

13

Peter Blue Cloud has rendered into poetry the beginnings of creation and its continuation through respect. If one has respect for the eastern dawn, he will have thankfulness for all creation, including the western sunset.

Though Adrian Louis may write of drunken Indians inebriated more from despair than rum; or Karoniaktatie sings a troll song of growth; or Joseph Bruchac of the flight of hawks, or any poet speaking of wild strawberry plants creeping through the thawing snows of April . . . there is a touching, teaching, often practical, more often significantly religious, a gratefulness and, possibly, a warning. Indian poetry and story may contain the pleasures of entertainment, the beauty of the imagination and the magic of language, but poetry and story has the extra dividend of praise and usually instruction. The humor of the often delightfully erotic "coyote stories," the "trickster stories," is meant to teach through the means of entertainment. Though delightful telling, they are morally sound. It has always been and remains essential, to circle the family, the clan, the tribe and the Nation together. As the hunter and warrior has duties to the people, as the wife and mother has her prescribed duties as well, as the leaders and holy people have duties, so too do the poets and story tellers have duties, a function and a place in the community. Prayer, teaching and song have as valid a position in the community as do war, the hunt, and housekeeping. They are links in the circle.

MAGIC FORMULA

You have no right to trouble me,
Depart, I am becoming stronger;
You are now departing from me,
You who would devour me;
I am becoming stronger, stronger,
Mighty medicine is now within me,
You cannot now subdue me —
I am becoming stronger,
I am stronger, stronger, stronger.

From the Iroquois
IN THE TRAIL OF THE WIND

Exhortism on the one hand; invocation on the other. The translation of this poem lacks the beauty of the original Iroquois and while its choice of words does not convey the depth of the "medicine" or "magic," it does express the universal truth of a religious experience of strength and freedom of the confining bands of 'evil.' This adowe is a teaching poem with an inherent thankfulness that the poet is growing stronger. Using the English language Karoniaktatie expresses it more succinctly:

a troll song

i am growing
Look! i am growing
        i am growing
        my moccasins
        i can't fit
        my leggings
        i can't fit
        my kastoweh
        it fell off
        my hair dances
        in the wind new
naked, i am growing
yes   only naked will i grow

From NATIVE COLOURS

Self exhortism! Inverted invocation! Growth is synonymous with strength.

marvelous is the miracle of spring
and also the weight of winter:
the plum which ripens
. . .
incredible is the force of April
and the lust of January;
in the summer of the second year
mulleins grow another branch,
chicory spreads to another field

From "mulleins are my arms"
NORTH: POEMS OF HOME

Again an inherent thankfulness, an invocation, to the Great Spirit and to Mother Earth for the new year, the rejuvination of living things: "the rabbits that sleep,/ and the bear," etc. . . . As though mulleins and chicory copulated in the heat of "lust" to produce their kind. Procreation remains a/the important act of creation. These lines equate the spring creation with the original miracle of the Creator who "directs all things for the good of his children."

"sometimes
  i dream
of a place
    where you
can whisper
    with the wind

From "shaman star dancer"

Rokwaho speaks of the time and place of silence . . . perhaps within the "dawn" of Peter Blue Cloud's poem . . . in which, and where, a

15

human can envision the silence of communication with the "wind," the Great Spirit, his Creation, his cosmos. No Indian poet stands too far from this place, this movement, this wishful awareness of place on the planet. The poet's suggestion is to find that quietude, silence and speak to the winds, speak to the hornet, speak to the iris, the trout; speak to creation, bless it for survival, and, in thankfulness, *adowe*, pray for its continuation within the powerful miracle.

Rarihokwats has written that "It is in the hearts of the people that . . . poetry is placed to live."

SONG OF A MAN ABOUT TO DIE IN A STRANGE LAND

If I die here
In a strange land,
If I die
In a land not my own,
Nevertheless, the thunder
Will take me home.

If I die here, the wind,
The wind rushing over the prairie
The wind will take me home.

The wind and the thunder,
They are the same everywhere,
What does it matter, then
If I die here in a strange land.

Reexpressed from the Ojibway by Mary Austin
From THE BELLY OF THE SHARK

The Indian is home in the creation of the Great Spirit. Poetry speaks of this home and is thankful for this place, the thunder, the wind. The poet will continue the ceremony.

then a chanting, a song
and far back
from a cavern back
(whisper)
    "Grandfather,
        I am home."

From "Sweat Lodge - The Afterwards"
TURTLE, BEAR & WOLF

Bierhorst, John: IN THE TRAIL OF THE WIND: American Indian Poems And Ritual Orations; Dell Paperback, 1975

Blue Cloud, Peter: TURTLE, BEAR & WOLF; Akwesasne Notes Press, 1976

Karoniaktatie: NATIVE COLOURS; Akwesasne Notes Press, 1974

Kenny, Maurice: NORTH: POEMS OF HOME; Blue Cloud Quarterly Press, 1977

Lowenfels, Walter: FROM THE BELLY OF THE SHARK; Random House-Vintage, 1973

Rokwaho: shaman star dancer, A Broadside; Strawberry Press, 1977

Peter Blue Cloud (Aroniawenrate)

BEAR
A Totem Dance As Seen by Raven
(for Ranoies)

The black bear does a strange and shuffling dance
foot to foot slowly, head back, eyes closed
      like that of a man.
Beneath a loosely falling robe,
mouth sewn shut upon protruding tongue
      of red-stained cedar shreddings.
Foot to foot slowly in lumbering
                shadow dance
within the fog and rain of high, thick ferns,
beneath a dripping, tapping spruce,
      echo of raven
morning cry of night visions unwanted.

A heavy, leaning snag it seems at first
the sound of crashing fall
             suspended
      between ground and lowered sky.
then swirl of fog unveils
           a huge head
carved atop the pole, a silver-grey of cedar.

Gnashing of angry teeth at driftwood shore
and killer whale spews up
            a wreckage
      of pock-infested sailors.

Foot to foot slowly, the totem dance continues,
sky to earth the leaning weight
            of pole
      and people and bear
      and now the drum,
rectangular and fringed with clacking claws.

A chant begins of deep-voiced rumbling,
of the black slate carved
            into bowls now broken
with fragments scattered in despair
      of a death not prophesied.

Great cedar poles in moist earth,
these dwellings speak with dark passages,
      (the rib of a tribe is a brittle section
                  of a dugout

or what is left
of a stolen house post,
vast heritage dragged
into strange museums)

and still, and forever, foot to foot slowly
the strange and shuffling dance continues.
And day after day the mourning chants
and keening voices silence all else
as dugouts
with quiet paddles
convey the dead to sacred islands
in endless procession.

And soil seeps thru roof cracks to fill
the huge and silent dwellings.
And totems lean from which
great eyes
gaze either up to sky or down to earth,
And the death of a village is a great sorrow,
and the pain of the survivors
is a great anguish
never to heal.

Slowly and gently
foot to foot balanced
and awkward in beauty
the child dances.
And grandfather taps,
delicately taps
the drum and his voice is very, very low,
and the song is a promise
given a people
in the ancient days of tomorrow.

And grandmother's stiff
and swollen fingers
weave cedar and fern and spruce,
and occasionally
in a far away closeness
her eyes seek the dancing child.

The bear pauses in his quest for food
to stand and sniff the air
then in a dream like a fasting
he begins
to shuffle
foot to foot slowly
as the dance continues.

berkeley, california
nov. 25, 1973

fire/rain (dedicated to the California drought)

Long before the last
rainfall gave as a promise
flowers still sleeping,

in yesterday lived
fire in the core of cedar,
of lightning stepping,

among, within the
forests of dry decaying
rootlets and the fall-

en spark of painful
fire rolling, walking thunder
seasons like anger.

A nation it was
who would burn the underbrush
for deer and acorn,

nesting, fat field mice,
squirrel chatter, coyote bark
naked, keening voice

of story teller
pleading sun and moon to birth
walking stick stamping

a light beating pat-
ter, ter, pat,ter pat, chanting
chanting a prayer,

mortar filled with dirt
now, kneel ear to ground listening,
all are near, close by,

the moon whimper is
a child within the fir stump,
smoldering ember,

listen close-ly now
the tap-ping lightness deer walk,
deep grunt of black bear,

bubbling acorn mush
sinewy strips of meat drying for the winter.

I sing you blood of
a tribe, a nation dancing
rattlesnake as guide,

bear his scent pungent
berry-eater and silent
dreamer of dreams gone

into night camp fire
singing again the people,
the oak, the cedar,

madrone and buckbrush,
manzanita and pine nut
blackened in thinking

of fire, of raining
torrents of surging waters
sung into being,

heart blood the painful
pumping clouds of thunderheads
Creation's power.

Stars are fire vessels
the universe happening
regardless of man,

(who was granted song
and chose the winding passage
of mind-games instead),

come on now, come on,
dance bloody your feet stomping
dust puffs of raindrops,

sing raw your voices
calling, calling, falling stars
and join the deer run,

and climb the sky path
of realities sought for
atop the mountain,

send your thought waves out
and let the earthworm fashion
compost to thinking

that long before the
beginning we were nothing
if not the guardians,

of earth, her wond'rous
birth Creation fashioned once,
    and never again.

For Rattlesnake: a dialogue of creatures
(A Voice Play)

(Each speaker introduced by -----)

Snow Plant; child of winter:
  See now the curving browness emerging
      from snow
  as earth her winter robe begins to fold,
  a trickle of moisture
  a gurgle   then   sand
      rolling,
  so like a pebble-filled gourd
  clasped between hands
  to mute to gentle murmur.

  Then freshets sigh the hillsides
  and stones to roundness tumble
      their praise.

Cedar; oldest of trees:
  Yes, my friend,
  and dawn breezes lend me voice
  my branches whisper
  and sweet
              my scent
  mingles your own breath
  as we await the others.

Woodpecker:
  It seems then a short night and day
  that berries sweet have mantled
  the mountain's greenness.
  Then Bear-who-used-to-be, would . . .
(Long pause)

Oak Tree:
  Yes, brothers and sisters
  Bear no more his soft and heavy walk,
  Bear no more
              his strange and sacred manner.

Flicker: (Quickly)
  Are we about to speak of THEM
                              again?

Fox: (As a chanting)
  I remember the last of Bear's tribe
      dragged
      by fear-sweating horse
  Foaming from whip and bear smell
      eyes rolling
      and Bear
              great clots of blood

and the human   a most awful smell
   of hate
and fear and lust
and the thought-pictures
   of his mind   hurting all,
and we wondered at such cruelty
for his thought-pictures
   were of himself
   torn and devoured
by the others of his likeness.

Squirrel:
  Wasn't this get together supposed to be
    for Rattlesnake?
  Hey, Coyote, what of you,
  your silence is like a burr
    beneath my tail.

Coyote: (In old long coat, floppy hat, stroking tail)
  Yes, well, Rattlesnake
  is on his way
  and should be here soon.
  And don't forget
             it's said,
  that we are here to stay
  as long as one of us remains,
                  and . . .

Bluejay: (Interrupting)
  Who said that?

Coyote: (Innocently)
  Why I guess I just did.

Lizard: (Stamping his or her foot in agitation)
  You know, this is beginning to sound
  like a made-up lie and the liar
  don't know what to say next.

Rattlesnake: (Just the voice)
  I am a manner
           a custom
    a tribal creature.

Coyote:
  He's here! (She's here!)

Rattlesnake: (Emerging from concealment, carrying its head)
  I come to you cut in half
  and cut again   headless
  with strong heart beating a
    constant pulse
  I crawl to you bloody
    a nightmare   of man's genius.

I too am Springtime
like my brother Bear
for together   we emerge
from sleep
to the dancers pounding feet
    and the wormwood smell.
I rattle them a music of my nearness
but they fear song
and axe, or knife, or gun, is the feast
    I am given.

I tell again of the Creation
and beg the peace of their council
and name the many clans and tribes
    of man and all Creation
    that none be omitted.
I teach them the necessary lesson
of alertness
of mind and body ever ready
for the tribal will
    but
they have forgotten the allness
    of the Creation
in their eager quest of vanity.

I lie headless and bloody at their feet
    who am
    their former brother.
(Begins to chant)
    I dream Bear
    I vision Bear
    I call Bear
        we must all become Bear.

Bear: (A dark mass, slowly shuffling in dance, four times in circle slowly,
    humming, as to himself, then pauses to speak)
    They kill my body
        they
    skin me and leave my body
        as in shame,
    let us
            then
    begin again the praise
    forgotten by man.
    Snow Plant, please begin again.

Snow Plant: (As at the beginning)
    See now the curving browness emerging
        from snow
    as earth her winter robe begins to fold.
    A trickle of moisture
    a gurgle   then   sand
        rolling,
    so like a pebble-filled gourd
    clasped between hands
    to mute to gentle murmur.

Then freshets sigh the hillsides
and stones to roundness tumble
    their praise.

Cedar:
    Yes, my friend,
    and dawn breeze lends me voice
and my branches whisper
    a weeping as from an evil dream
    of creatures born of hate.

    Let us again
                then
    chant the evil back
    into earth's womb
    to be re-born
                or not
    as will be.

All the voices: (A chorus in chant)

    Man no more
      look
    he is fading,
    man no more
      see
    he lies dreaming,
    man no more
      forever
    let us forget the pain,
    man no more
      forever
    his bones of dust
    the wind is taking
      to scatter
            to scatter
                    to scatter
                            to scatter.

Adrian C. Louis

MUTED WAR DRUMS

A brown woman
with bleached hair
murmurs into paper against comb
like a wounded owl
her warm breath bent
into sobbing notes

Her man is beside her
like a baby at dry breast
"Mary Lou," he says
"we need more beers . . . ."
words blur in the bar scent
of tinkling bottles

These wooden Indians
in a gin mill crevice
sit at a fiberglass table
muddling over a Hamm's Beer sign:
the 3-D neon painting of
a land of sky blue waters

It ripples in azure light
and speeds across the cool dark
of their empty heart
like muted war drums

THE PSEUDO SHAMAN'S CLICHE

I sit in lotus position
on a throne of dandelions
in the early spring park.

Slightly discernible
through the cawing of crows
the ever muted   ever present
whisper of OM
from roots of grass
stuck in spinning Indian earth
it courses through my
calloused fingertips
quickly   quietly
the connection is soldered
before OM is regenerated
drearily reincarnated into the drone
of city cars chasing factories
where this illusion is fertilized
by electrical sperm:
A man should build pyramids
and not talk to flowers.

Maurice Kenny

AKWESASNE

partridge drum in the land of the elm
Akwesasne
partridge drum in the land of white roots
Akwesasne

wampum
wampum is carried, the runner carries
the wampum
        for the still of the forest
        for the quiet of the valleys
wampum
partridge drum in the land of the elm

Dekanawidah broke arrows
        in the land of the elm
Akwesasne

morning raised clear and blue
as the sun poured into the mountain
the runner carried the wampum
from village to village, from sachem to sachem
in the land of the north
        the land of the elm
        where the partridge drum

the Wolf and the Bear and the Turtle
dance in the land of the Mohiks
the Deer and the Snipe and the Heron
dance in the land of the Seneca
the Beaver and Eagle dance in the land of the Onondaga
        in the land of the younger brothers
        Cayuga, Oneida
where the partridge drums
as the runner carries the wampum
from Dekanawidah to the sachems
in the land of the north and the elm
and the sky remained clear

Hiawatha spoke to Atotarho
where the partridge drums

one morning the sky burst red
like the early star that so often frightens
the hunter and the women taking water
one morning the sky burst red
and the arrows were fitted together
as the runner carried the wampum
from village to village, from sachem to sachem
in the land of the north and the elm
where the partridge drums

words spilled over hills, spread over cedar
rolled onto paper, folded for draws, weapons, for fat judges
who never heard the partridge drum
never heard Dekanawidah
nor saw him break the arrows
never spoke with Hiawatha
as he walked through the land of the elm
never heard Handsome Lake
nor saw him break the arrows
as he walked through the land of the elm
where the partridge drums
Akwesasne

rolled into paper, folded into draws,
weapons for fat judges
who never spoke with Dekanawidah
in the land of the north
in the land of the elm
where the strawberry ripens
under the sun, under the sky
                              blue and clear
by the running rivers of the valleys
where the partridge drums
the runner carries the wampum
Akwesasne

COLD CREEK

trout speckled in April dawn
slivered with silver of early spring . . .
song poured to the willows of daylight
over the sandy banks of the creek
cold to the toe, cold to the boy
caught like rainbow trout
by the hook in the jaw;
song poured to the grass, minnows
burnished in the leaping of noon
over and down the hills, quarried
and crushed in the fist of the pimple
that would claim me to manhood,
manhood shied like rats
in the haybarn seeking blood
not the hen's eggs mama said;
song poured to the flowing creek,
jumping rocks, staggering down dams,
thrusting weight against stones;
song poured to the winds
that bristled my cowlicks and burnt
goosepimples into the flesh of my thighs;
song poured into the night willows
with only shadows under

then words crept out like mice in the dark,
and Cold Creek, that had leaped from a hill
a spring, turned and entered the wide river
with my song

27

moma and nessa

HOME
For Rick

North
       north by the star
hills under, cows, brush
river broken by spring
men broken by harvest and stone
fields and fields of stone
stone tall as a boy
boys tall as crabapple
spruce weighted with moonshine

north
       north by the star
starlight that parts the corn
starlight that glimmers on autumn
squash and beans
apples caught by the frost
frosty women hanging clothes
balloon in the tight sharp air
pine-stove melts those figures, fingers

north
       north by the star
old men smoke in a circle
north by the village
men smoke in a circle
over the feathers of a partridge
that drummed on the floor of the forest
deviled in the ambush of the wind

north
       north by the star
we go home, we go . . .
to the pheasant, woodchuck, muskrat
the last deer standing the summer
of flies on the blood of the wolf
howled in the north
                  north by the star
starring the Adirondacks
forgotten in the rush for camp-sites
brown bear mussled to honey-
cookies tourist tease
to the crackling of their arms
and the butchery of the bear
who will not share the berry picking
with the girls of June this year
in the north, north
                  by the north star
hills under, brush, cabins, towns
rivers broken by spring

we go home to the north
                  north by the star

NORTH
In Memory of My Father

sun rises over mountain lakes
the fox breakfasts in the berry patch
mice tug grains into the burrow
grass has a way of growing

north by the old trail
north by the Susquehanna
north by the Freeway
north by the Alleghany or Mohawk
airlines that sweep you into north country,
deerland, Thousand Islands;
north by semis that scoop up the north
and wrap its aluminum soil about
your Thanksgiving turkey
and freeze your pudding in the refrigerator

north by any path would be north
north . . . by north star, northern
northern country of villages and cowpens
cheese factories and crabapples, trout
diseased elms and sick roots
fenced meadows slit by snowmobiles
sky cracked by television wires,
and hunters blizzard to cabins
by dead deer . . . the last kept
them abandoned in the north snow
from home in Staten Island

north of strawberry fields, milkweed
north of maples running sap to boil
north, north country, northern New York
where corn grew to the table and squash
and bean covered the valleys
north of strawberry fields, north of sumac
north of smoke, north of tomorrow, today
of yesterday that was and is and will be
for strawberries grow forever
and wolves will cross the frozen river
under the flight of geese

sun humps over hills and horses
muskrats in the stream
swimming to shore with a mouthful of mud
the bee sipping honey
minnows in the creek

grass has a way of growing
north, north along the old trail

guard the eastern gate

Rokwaho (Daniel Thompson)

                    i dream
                         still
                    of the
                         magical
                    forests
                         that
                    on a
                         rain
                    heavy
                         day
                    perched
                         the
                    eagle
                         within
                    reach
                         of the
                    land
                         of the
                    thunder
                         people

                    i taste
                         still
                    the haze
                         scented
                    afternoon
                         and the
                    feel
                         of
                    nothing
                         in
                    particular
                         i want
                    to do
                         until
                    hermit
                         thrush
                    pipes
                         of
                    heaven's
                         visit

                    i am
                         passenger
                    pigeon . . .

Poem for a stone

New leaves breathe the morning ending
Time passes unblinking, the shadows close
My eyes are the stars cast at midnight bending
A breeze remembers me sitting, a rooster crows . .

blue deep
metal haze
tints evergreen
skyline
feels like
rain rising

winds wet draught
down crusted
channel silent
of stirs & ripples . .

father awaits
midwinter rain

"INNOCENCE RETURNED"
(for Peter Blue Cloud)

The stars at morning rising
erode by glances, ending between.
Climbs to morningside, burning,
bathing clean the crimes of midnight's keen.
Innocence returned to wing
to the light lit by mysteries gleaned.

The son of all stars is born(e)
dream by dream to the star of all stars.
Glance by glance the dreams adorn
eternity's wayside avatars.

World to world the dreams are dreamed
and somewhere between, dreams the dreamer . . .

Joseph Bruchac

ELLIS ISLAND

Beyond the red brick of Ellis Island
where the two Slovak children
who became my grandparents
waited the long days of quarantine,
after leaving the sickness,
the old Empires of Europe,
a Circle Line ship slips easily
on its way to the island
of the tall woman, green
as dreams of forests and meadows
waiting for those who'd worked
a thousand years
yet never owned their own.

Like millions of others,
I too come to this island,
nine decades the answerer
of dreams.

Yet only one part of my blood loves that memory.
Another voice speaks
of native lands
within this nation.
Lands invaded
when the earth became owned.
Lands of those who followed
the changing Moon,
knowledge of the seasons
in their veins.

FIRST DEER

I trailed
your guts
 a mile through snow
before my second bullet
 stopped it all.
Believe me now,
there was a boy
who fed butterflies sugar water
and kept hurt birds
in boxes in his room.

BIRDFOOT'S GRAMPA

The old man
must have stopped our car
two dozen times to climb out
and gather into his hands
the small toads blinded
by our lights and leaping,
live drops of rain.

The rain was falling,
a mist about his white hair
and I kept saying
you can't save them all,
accept it, get back in
we've got places to go.

But, leathery hands full
of wet brown life,
knee deep in the summer
roadside grass,
he just smiled and said
*they have places to go to
too.*

THE REMEDIES

Half on the Earth, half in the heart,
the remedies for all the things
which grieve us wait for those who know
the words to use to find them.

Penobscot people used to make
a medicine for cancer from Mayapple
and South American people knew
the quinine cure for malaria
a thousand years ago.

But it is not just in the roots,
the stems, the leaves,
the thousand flowers
that healing lies.
Half of it lives within the words
the healer speaks.

And when the final time has come
for one to leave this Earth
there are no cures,
for Death is only
part of Life, not a disease.

Half on the Earth, half in the heart,
the remedies for all our pains
wait for the songs of healing.

THE GEYSER

There is a story
some people tell
of how they came
from a world beneath
this world through a hole in the Earth.

And here, through a hole in the Earth,
there rises a fine clear plume
of mineral water, a Geyser
which lends its name to the brook
which flows about the red stone cone
that has formed from the iron
of its waters.

Drink its water, as the Wind
wraps the mist about you
and feel the life that rises here
like people coming out of the darkness
of a world with no Sun
to this place of light.

One winter I drove
past the Geyser and saw
a White-Tailed Deer standing on the cone,
the cold morning air as clean and new
as it must have been on that first day
when we saw this place
where the magic of waters
rises up from old Earth
to join with the Wind and the Sun.

THREE POEMS FOR THE INDIAN STEELWORKERS
IN A BAR WHERE I USED TO DRINK

I
This place is cold
as the soul of a hundred winters
bottles glitter from tables
bright as markers of polished marble

My greeting lifts the faces of my friends
like furrows of dark soil
turned by a plow to fall again
& I have only come in to
be out of the winter night

There are no songs we can teach each other

But John Last-Walking-Bear
holds a lantern wavering before my eyes
it brightens the dark corners
Tilting it slightly he ripples
effervescent light into our glasses

II

These days I drink in another bar
Only the young and beautiful come here
They toss their long hair
with the lovely abandon of horses
They can walk out into the streets
They can return to familiar houses
not washed away by the river of a hundred years
& when they sleep their bodies float
above their beds, light as Ariel

III

Driving home at night
through the Onondaga Reservation
headlights strike empty white fields
& tired houses with back broken roofs

At the bend in the road are the hills
the Holder Up of the Heavens dropped
on the Stone Giants

& I remember
that this is a land
which has been bright with magic

ELEGY FOR JACK BOWMAN

This afternoon as I sat
on my grandfather's porch,
Thunderer's bolts crackling
across the close sky,
you lay in a room
where doctors tried in vain
to plug an aorta less strong
than your will to live
calmly and in love
with the land and the woman
you shared long life with.

As I closed my eyes,
hearing a heavy summer rain
and *He-noh's* feet walking
across the heavens,
your eyes closed for a last time
thirty miles from this hill
where you and your brother
drove teams with lumber.

You were my grandfather
come to life again
when I saw you at his funeral
and in your face
which was his and your own
I read the stories
of logging and horses and knowing
how to fit the ground to plant.

You never lived more
than a step from the soil.
My last memory
is of you kneeling
to dig with your hands
new potatoes you'd planted.

Old Man, the last of my old men.

Karoniaktatie [Alex Jacobs]

i lost the song
the song
i had
we sang
at winter forage
the song
that a lazy
crow copied
the song
i had
it was blue
as the mountain berries
it was
red
as the pipestone
it had
deer hooves
when we walked
laughing children
when we walked
we sang
the song

i had
i lost the song
O Creation
all around
O what i did
to lose a song
i burn
Tobacco
O Creation
for the song
i had
we sang

we sing!

INSPIRATION (for INDIN ARTISTS)

Andy Warhol
$ power
fame position
yer teacher
competition bia
rocknroll alcohol
drugs grades school
yer teachers job
a new car new stereo
live amerikan
sell amerikan
talk amerikan
die amerikan

sacred pipe   sacred tobacco
sweat lodge   round dance
animal/teachers
plants/medicines
tree of peace
language of dreams
smiles of drum, song, flute
grandparents
children
sundance kiva medicine people
prophecies teachings
earth lodge skin lodge wood lodge

turn my eyeholes to face the east

Kirk Garcia

TRAIL OF STRAW

The trail is made of straw
and cows watch   as cows
will always watch   peacefully
from nearby   through windragged
cottonwoods   as their winter
bedding is packed into bales.

Missouri bluffs shimmer
95 degrees bright and hot
and the dreamer   gets
to ride the woody skid sliding
over furrows and rock
to stack the golden bedding
in piles of ten   cursing
dust   wind   cows   guards
bales   and self   doing
hard time baling   bluffs
beautiful   high cottonwoods
lush in any field of time
but prison time is hard time.

The field's cruel fantasies
and dreams in correctional
barracks have shown
us how   our blond hero
did it   through swamps
under and over   barbed wire
twanging   his hearty theme
song   eluding dramatic dogs
lover waiting not with brown
coweyes of the desperate
but laughing cheering
promising her breasts will
burst   prairie roses
from pink cotton.

Doing   hard time baling
no bravado now   only
time to know   *them* that got
can never be got   revenge
cannot equal in its payment
the hard currents of time
done in a field of rocky
emotion   time done not softly
baling
while dustdevils arise
the westwind drives
through the cottonwood
shelterbelt   leaves glitter
branchtips weave   the tempo
for prisoners   is beat by wood
on an invisible fluid drum
hot and cold
for scalp and temple   pulse
and strain   for blood and heart
bright and clouded   for eye
and hear   accompaniment
by a tractor's rods and baler's
piston   following the straw
trail while dustdevils   arise
teasing   escape
is for skypilots and screenheroes
who know the glitter

how to fade   like celluloid
or vanishing cirrus
not prisoners   eating straw
and dirt   eyes like cows
bewildered by windy satans
dancing   down to the wide
Missouri   slipping maniacally
between waves of cold
water rushing muddy
furious across the brown
carrying sweat   of unwilling
farmers   escaping the prairie
flatland of fantasy done
hard baling   past rocks
round a rock that stands
sentinel near blackhaired women
whose eyes have always been   turned
to the river by hard white hands
to search   for captured lovers past
farmers and daughters   on sunset
porches free   content   marking
time's passage   comparing
the rains of '74 to rains
of childhood   seen in wonder
rains of youth seen at the side
of laughing farmgirls   oh jimmy
jimmy isn't it lovely   wet
rains of life and growth and grainy
abundance   watching Missouri cottonwoods
weave a tempo of life   with floss
and free   leaves rippling yellow
amid clouds pink and red in   arid
sunset   oblivious to the river's burden
of sweat pouring   hard
in time   baled and packed
as some secret   and personal
winter bedding of fantasy
of lovers   waiting   laughing   promising
success   promising   waiting   laughing
home laughing promising   waiting
fantasy   promising   sweat of fill
a river   drift unsoftened
down a river   down from
frowning brows   of balers
daydreaming among trees of bondage
or sleepdreaming in July night   near   miss
August   or miss June
dreams bringing
raw and lumpy throats   acidy
bile and bitter   fantasy   to sour
in mouths and minds   when time
is done hard   baled.

DOUBLE CLUTCH TSOTSIE

Joy Harjo

OKLAHOMA: THE PRAIRIE OF WORDS

Oklahoma — the red earth gives meaning to the name. Oklahoma is derived from a Choctaw word which means "red people." It is a place which has come to mean home to many tribal peoples. The word dances over our tongues like the bottomless sky that rolls over the curving prairie land. Oklahoma means a center of life to her people, a whole spirit of being. It is a place that comes clear in the voices of her people, who are of many languages and of many parts of the Oklahoma landscape. Kiowa, Creek, Comanche, or Pawnee — their names are these and many more. The sounds of these names fill the Oklahoma landscape. They mean alive and living communities, and signal the roots of many of the singers of the word. These words have a resonance, even on an Oklahoma state map. They begin stories, whole histories of tribal peoples who may have originated thousands of miles away north into Canada, or as close as Spiro Mound in the center of Oklahoma.

As the word Oklahoma gives birth to meaning and creates an energy, it has also given birth to many native poets and writers who call Oklahoma *home*. Those of us who originate from there celebrate the life in her which is the life in ourselves as a part of the red earth. It is as Jim Barnes poignantly says:

> You've got to leave this land again before it hurts you into a sin the years will not ease: a constant fear swells in your groin, and there's a singing in the trees your blood wants to beat time to.

> from "Autobiography, Chapter IX:
> Leaving, Again"

In a sense, we never leave Oklahoma, or maybe it would be better said that Oklahoma never leaves us. The spirit is alive in the landscape that arranges itself in the poems and stories that are created and the spirit takes many forms and many voices.

> The earth is wounded
> and will not heal.

> Night comes down like a blackbird
> with blue flame that never sleeps
> and spreads its wings around us.
> from: "Oil", by Linda Hogan

What is breathing here is some sort of dangerous anger that rises up out of the Oklahoma landscape. The earth is alive with emotions, and will take action on what is being felt. This way of seeing is characteristic of most native poets and writers of Oklahoma. That which has happened to the earth, has happened to all of us as a part of the earth.

We, as the tribal peoples of Oklahoma, bear a responsibility to that place, to the community of earth and language that has formed us. When we write we inadvertently tell who we are and where we came from. We also know our histories and tell even the most painful but true parts, because after all, these are a part of us, too. Carter Revard writes with this strong sense of history when he writes of his people, the Osage, and of his family's particular piece of alloted land near Bird Creek — and the changes that occur.

> . . . built in a timbered hollow where deer came down
> at dusk with the stars
> to drink from the deep pools
> near Timber Hill
> and below . . .

is how he sings it. The poem, called "Wazhazhe Grandmother," is circular and whole. The history is revealed within this circle of time, where clear pools of Bird Creek become piped water for municipal pools. And in a poem by a Cherokee writer, Carroll Arnett, Andrew Jackson is soundly cursed, and justly so, for he is a painful part of history that has affected all of Oklahoma's tribal people. Duane Big Eagle gives a more personal narrative of history in "Oklahoma Boyhood." All of these histories are a part of who we are.

What Oklahoma becomes, in a sense, is a dream, an alive and real dream that takes place inside and outside of the writer. It shimmers and has a rhythm, a heartbeat of its own.

> Mammedaty saw to the building of this house. Just there, by the arbor, he made a camp in the old way. And in the evening when the hammers had fallen silent and there were frogs and crickets in the black grass - and a low, hectic wind upon the pale, slanting plane of the moon's light - he settled deep down in his mind to dream. He dreamed of dreaming, and of the summer breaking upon his spirit, as drums break upon the intervals of the dance, and of the gleaming gourds.
>
> from: "The Gourd Dancer"
> N. Scott Momaday

Our words begin inside of the dream and become a way of revealing ourselves within this landscape that is called Oklahoma. Language becomes all of the people that we are. Living voices surround us and speak from the diverse and many histories that we have been, the ones we have become, and most of all, how we will continue. There are those voices among us who assume the cadence of an ancient and living chant. Carroll Arnett in "Early Song," says:

> for this good brown
> earth; for all
> brothers and sisters,
> for the dark blood

that runs through me
in a great circle
back into this
good brown earth.

He has become a continuing part of the older voices and acknowledges those who guide him. His voice is a part of the circle that his song/prayer rides within. But Arnett also survives within this circle with a voice that urgently asks:

Unelanvhi save us
from
The Whiskey People

from: "Roadman"

It's another kind of invocation. The Whiskey People are those we are asked to be saved from. They are a part of the voices within the landscape, but also a part of us, a more recent part.

And we continue. There is a timelessness present within the voices coming out of Oklahoma, a belief in continuance. The stories and poems are in motion within the red earth — which has the boundaries that dreams have.

it is not the words of the chant
that make the prayer
it is the way they are said
that reaches gods ear
from: "The Words"
Norman H. Russell

All of the people, all of the voices who are from Oklahoma, remain a part of that spirit. Even if they move away they always return. They return, even if they have been sent miles away to school or leave to find jobs, and then come back with families and settle down. Some return only during the moist, humid summers to the dancing, warm drum nights near towns named Anadarko, Henryetta, Miami, or to numerous other grounds. And some return only in their hearts and voices, singing, again and again — to Oklahoma red earth, a curving wind plain — to creeks and rivers that cross over and through the land. No one has ever left.

when the morning comes
i will continue to dream
and when i am killed
my soul will soar like the eagle

from: "before me in white blood . . ."
Susan Shown Harjo

Jim Barnes

LOST IN SULPHUR CANYONS

All the stones
unturned say
you are alone.

Not even a sun
cracks
the lead sky.

The deer
you thought
you tracked
has never known
the stones
you step on.

Stone by stone
you follow
the small water
down through
sulphur springs
rank as the fear
you try not
to taste.

For such descent
as this, you need
a guide, someone
to lean a word
or curse on.

Only the stones
know your breath
is wrong.

An absence
of wind grays
the pines
and your hair.

You stoop
to drink
your face.

The sweet, white
bite of water
leaves you stunned.

You smile to see
a face pale
against the sky,
a smile
you never knew
was there at all.

With all the hell
of sulphur and pitch
you know somehow
you couldn't be
happier, lost
as a stray dog
among the stones.

Wolf Hunting Near Nashoba

for Paul Deer and Leo Smith

Nights you wake to sudden stars
and wind that's always on the run.
Hard hills hugging sulphur springs
make echoes leap past your tuning ears.

You turn your collar up and square
your butt into the stone-dead earth
to better feel the oblique sounds at first,
a thirst of bones no mountain waters clear.

The hounds are scaling up their mouths.
The beagle beat is a bit irregular,
but sweet as madrigals in a greening air.
A comet splits the sky from north to south.

You hear yourself yell the bluetick straight
to hell with *go*. Two other dead stars fall.
You count the losing hounds over a hogbacked hill,
eject a cartridge you've lately come to hate.

Times like this you'd like to end it
all. Kill wolf and dogs and shoot the stars.
The thought passes with the chase. The fire
at your feet is out you forgot you ever lit.

Notes For a Love Letter From Mid-America

There is no death. Only a change of worlds.
—Chief Seattle

1.
No horizon promises a mountain
Cornfields hide sparse trees
like snow the stone.

Mid-America in dead November
lies glacial
in the wake of this
a season come too soon.

I miss your eyes
in my eyes.
I miss my breath
in your hair.

A season of no promises
& a season of long regret:
we gave up our sense of place
for a sojourn in Mid-America
& you are gone in these
our elliptical days.

2.
We were happy in our mountains.
But roll them out
like unruled paper
& memory hangs like a pale woman
rocking on a wall.

Without a horizon
there is no land
worth the moment shared
when hills flung back
the best half of your name.

A sense of place
allowed us room to love.
No wonder salmon
take to falls.

I could die
where hills know
how to reach. Not here:
landscape will not allow
an *I protest.*

Wind breaks corn
that seldom sees the sun.

3.
Lost River. I remember it
by white water sounds
& salmon mad with love
& rainbows dead,
rotting in the weir
my brothers made.

We swam the rapids
to love where moss
claimed rocks smooth with years.

You know it all too well:
image is idea.
My eyes are full of you.

I will write runes
when letters fail.
For any part of you
that calls me fool
I'd give all mountains
I have left.

4.
But mountains do not last
where wind turns faces
hard as glacial drift.

Your name sinks
into the frozen offing

& only the taste
of crying it
hangs like an icicle
in my throat

& this alone I have left
from our sojourn in Mid-America.

Autobiography, Chapter IV: The Mirage

Out of Yuma and heading west, you feel the lift of air: a thermal
    dares you to try your wings.

There is a dance of heat way down the road, a swaying atmosphere,
    and suddenly you see the dance turn clear as ice and above
    the ice, a mountain that is not there.

A floating island and a cold inland sea: too much for the mind
    to take in such a heat. You bat your eyes and caves of wind
    take form. The island undulates in dance. You think you see
    a ship.

The desert dips, and your mind is slow to follow your body down.
    Heading toward the end of sky, the bus realizes the road. You
    see the mirage with another set of eyes. You see the mountain
    real as the wind against the window you count your own eyes in.

Autobiography, Chapter IX: Leaving, Again

You've got to leave this land again before it hurts
    you into a sin the years will not ease: a constant
    fear swells in your groin, and there's a singing
    in the trees your blood wants to beat time to.

Easy it would be to stay and dream, to walk wolf these
    woods and fields, to play what you've always been
    and are afraid to be. You know there's a crescendo
    building in your blood, a raging conquistador, wild
    sailor, part pilgrim looking for a Mecca he'll never
    find. Or find and lose and find again.

Dreams you once had in a bad time come back to haunt
    your ears: sounds of music too sensual for light
    drum dark in the soft trees, and the leaves begin
    again to dance and shapes take form, lovely and
    green.

You see the muddy river clear, sirens naked on its banks.
    A wild urge silent on their lips tells you plain this
    land will always sing you back, quick with dream, your
    hands always poised for overture.

THE LAST CHANCE

The myna bird speaks
of love. His whistle
cuts into the bone
ears of a white-tail's
head stuffed above
the bar.

Fifty miles the county's
dry. You stop here
to tell yourself
go home, but hear
the black experience
of a goddamned bird

whose hello sucks
at the marrow
of your bones.
You wonder how a soul
can pass from
his beak and break

upon your face, split
the whiskers you grew
to be wise in. You wonder
at his avalanche of words,
the last drink you took,
the dance on your skin

you can't beat time to.
You wonder, but you
do not ask. You
listen hard with
your cracking eyes.
He asks about your life.

You tell him lies
while he prunes
a feather, lets it drop.
Your life is sour
in the glass. Crow
made the earth and all

things therein, brought fire.
This bird's a ghost
you tell your sins.
Nobody is listening.
Outside, the sun falls
into the brittle grass.

Linda Hogan

HERITAGE

From my mother, the antique mirror
where I watch my face take on her lines.
She left me the smell of baking bread
to warm fine hairs in my nostrils,
she left the large white breasts that weigh down
my body.

From my father I take his brown eyes,
the plague of locusts that leveled our crops,
they flew in formation like buzzards.

From my uncle the whittled wood
that rattles like bones
and is white
and smells like all our old houses
that are no longer there. He was the man
who sang old chants to me, the words
my father was told not to remember.

From my grandfather who never spoke
I learned to fear silence.
I learned to kill a snake
when you're begging for rain.

And grandmother, blue-eyed woman
whose skin was brown,
she used snuff.
When her coffee can full of black saliva
spilled on me
it was like the brown cloud of grasshoppers
that leveled her fields.
It was the brown stain
that covered my white shirt,
my whiteness a shame.
That sweet black liquid like the food
she chewed up and spit into my father's mouth
when he was an infant.
It was the brown earth of Oklahoma
stained with oil.
She said tobacco would purge your body of poisons.
It has more medicine than stones and knives
against your enemies.

That tobacco is the dark night that covers me.

She said it is wise to eat the flesh of deer
so you will be swift and travel over many miles.
She told me how our tribe has always followed a stick
that pointed west
that pointed east.
From my family I have learned the secrets
of never having a home.

52

GOING TO TOWN

(For Donna)

I wake up early while you sleep,
soft in that room whose walls
are pictures of blonde angels,
and set loose the fireflies.
Their lights
have flickered all night
on our eyelids.

Already you have a woman's hip bones,
long muscles
you slide your dress over
and we brush each other's hair
then step out into the blue morning.
Good daughters,
we are quiet
lifting empty milk cans,
silver cans into the wagon.
They rattle together
going to town.

We ride silent
because the old man has paid us
dimes not to speak
but the wheels of the wagon
sing and we listen,
we listen to ourselves singing
the silence of birds
and dust that flies up in our hair.

The dust moves closer to us,
the place is dark
where we have disappeared.
Our family returns to us
in the bodies of children, of dogs
stretched across the road,
cats who ran away from home.

What do we have left
except the mirage of sound,
frogs creaking over the night land.
The black walnut trees are gone,
stolen during the night
and transformed
into the handles of guns.

That song, if you sing for it
and pray it to come,
in the distance
it grows nearer.
Close your eyes and it comes,
the music of old roads
we still travel together, so far
the sound is all that can find us.

BLESSINGS

Blessed
are the injured animals
for they live in his cages.
But who will heal my father,
tape his old legs for him?

Here's the bird with the two broken wings
and her feathers are white as an angel
and she says goddamn stirring grains
in the kitchen. When the birds fly out
he leaves the cages open
and she kisses his brow for such
good works.

> Work he says
> all your life
> and at the end
> you don't own even a piece of land.

Blessed are the rich
for they eat meat every night.
They have already inherited the earth.

For the rest of us, may we just live
long enough
and unwrinkle our brows,
may we keep our good looks
and some of our teeth
and our bowels regular.

Perhaps we can go live places
a rich man can't inhabit,
in the sunfish and jackrabbits,
in the cinnamon colored soil,
the land of red grass
and red people
in the valley
of the shadow of Elk
who aren't there.

> He says the damned earth is so old
> and wobbles so hard
> you'd best hang on to everything.
> Your neighbors steal what little you got.

Blessed
are the rich
for they don't have the same old
Everyday to put up with
like my father
who's gotten old,
> Chickasaw
> chikkih asachi, which means

they left as a tribe not a very great while ago.
They are always leaving,
those people.

Blessed
are those who listen
when no one is left to speak.

MOSQUITOES

To keep them from you,
paint yourself
red as the natives.
They will not drink
blood exposed to air
only pure blood
embedded deep in flesh.

If you hate them,
hum D minor, the breeding song.
They will be drawn to you,
forgetting to mate
and loving only the sound
of your voice.

Or when one lands
drinking at the rivers of your arm,
make a fist, clenched and
pulsing blood into the thin needle
of mosquito until it swells
with your life and bursts
red into air.

I will not sleep with nets,
burn a yellow light
or citron candle.
When one hums silently
around my ears,
bends its knees upon my arm,
I will be as still as a stone
at the edge of water,
watching my blood carried into air.
I will not scratch the white welt
that grows where one has fed.

CELEBRATION: BIRTH OF A COLT

When we reach the field
she is still eating
the heads of yellow flowers
and pollen has turned her whiskers
gold. Lady,
her stomach bulges out,
the ribs have grown wide.
We wait,
our bare feet dangling
in the horse trough,
warm water
where goldfish brush
our smooth ankles.
We wait
while the liquid breaks
down Lady's dark legs
and that slick wet colt
like a black tadpole
darts out
beginning at once
to sprout legs.
She licks it to its feet,
the membrane still there,
red,
transparent
the sun coming up shines through,
the sky turns bright with morning
and the land
with pollen blowing off the corn,
land that will always own us,
everywhere it is red.

SUMMER AGAIN

What does he think about,
that man staring at the coffee cup,
rubbing out another cigarette.
He plants onions
that make me cry as I undo them.

Under his shirt the skin is white,
small clumps of shadow
that look like hair. He polishes his boots,
saying we're going to move to the country,
keep chickens, have money.
But the kitchen gets painted
which means we'll stay.

Money,
I could taste it
run my tongue along the rough edge of a coin,
salt off some banker's hands,
perfume from a woman
that cold metal taste.

It's summer again
and June bugs fly through the torn screen.
Time to move to another place
where my purse with its dark
sweet smell of tobacco
is going to get fat with dollars
lined up back to back
rubbing each other
telling where they've been.

AFTER FISH

Between gills
I stabbed the knife
spilling eggs from catfish bellies
masses of pearl
emptied before eyes
going cold.
The cats come from nowhere
come on the road of fish smell
and they are as strange in this dry place
as tulips growing among dead weeds.

The sun bakes and bleaches the land
fish belly white.
Night is a blessing
and the moon passes over thirsty ground
like a star over fire.

The fish are gone now
driven by summer,
having worked their silver bodies
into mud, caked
and waiting for rain.

Hooked on old habits
and seeing the moon
float by in daylight,
I catch the knife
and slit the pale crescent.
Its bowels trail down.
The sun beats with blades of fire
glinting over metal.
The heat throbs my temples.
The cats come from nowhere.

THANKSGIVING

Turkey, blue head on the ground
body in a gleaming white tub
with lion claw feet.
Heat rises in the yard
melting crystals of ice
and there are feathers, bronze,
metallic blue and green
that were his strong wings
which never flew away.

And we give thanks for it
and for the old woman
shawl pulled tight around her
she sits
her teeth brown
her body dry
her spoons
don't match.

Some geese, last stragglers
trickling out of Canada
are flying over.
Noisy, breaking the glass sky
grey
they are grey
and their wings are weightless.

OIL

Men smile like they know everything
but walking in slant heel boots
their butts show they are tense.
Dark shirts.
Blue fire
puts out the sun. Rock bits
are clenched metal fists.

The earth is wounded
and bleeds.
Pray to Jesus.

An explosion could knock us all
to our knees

while the bosses stretch out,
white ridge of backbone
in the sun.

We're full of bread and gas,
getting fat on the outside
while inside we grow thin.

The earth is wounded
and will not heal.

Night comes down like a blackbird
with blue flame that never sleeps
and spreads its wings around us.

WHITE WOLF AND THE BLUE RACER

Every day White Wolf filled the river. Every night he took the water out.
Friday night he headed home, one leg after the other, one leg after the other. He
stopped at an empty well. He pushed the wood cover aside and peered down the
stone-smooth walls. From the dark stones, a forked tongue jagged out lightning
fast, the tongue of a blue racer.

The Blue Racer said it lived in the well because it was waiting for moisture. He
said he lived there because the sun was hot all day and all night the light beat
down on its blue scales. It lived there because it was home. It lived there because
there was no place else to go.

White Wolf charmed the snake and it followed him, winding sideways, opening
the dry grass into a path behind them. The path opened like the dry craking of
locusts. The snake told White Wolf, keep the wind on your left cheek, I am
Pathfinder. You must find the way to water.

White Wolf went with the snake to a pond but the pond was always dry. They
went to the river but it was night and there was no water. He carried the snake
home.

White Wolf's grandfather, Black Wolf, came out of the den. Gray Wolf came
out. They chopped off the snake's head. It writhed, twisting tighter than a spring.
The head grew back. Black Wolf shot the head off. Another head grew and it
began to glow. From every wound a head grew, each bigger than the last, each
more bright than the others. The land began to shine and the light was feared in
the night of no water.

Salt came from the ocean to see the light but brought no water with it. Horses
whose ribs wedged out like broken sticks came. They had no blood. Salt flowed in
their veins until they broke and salt fell out like white sand. A moth came to see
the light and burned in it. Fish came up from the hard earth looking for moths. A
bear came to find the fish.

White Wolf sat on the sand, invisible, white in the light near the moth, near the
white blind fish that had come up from beneath the earth. His grandfather could
not see him. Gray Wolf could not see him. He could not see himself. He looked in
the water when he filled the river but only white was reflected. He looked in the
river at night when there was no water. He was sorry he was not the color of
other wolves. He was sorry he was not a red fox against the white snow.

But yellow is coming. When White Wolf saw yellow, he hid his head in the river
at night. Yellow came down to the river. It burst over him like the sunflowers
growing up and leaning hard into the light. Yellow made the blue snake turn
green. Now it was invisible in the new grass. The grass opened up before them in
many paths. Yellow turned the salt to pollen and the bees swarmed down, coming
to life on the first of the moon. Yellow made the horses fly back together and their
blood was sap running life into their manes and their manes were gold. They
floated out like water. Yellow made the moth turn to melted butter. The fish
swam in the butter. The bear reached in and when he brought his hand out,
daffodils were growing between his claws.

The blue racer said, Now there will never be water. White Wolf. White Wolf.
White Wolf. Go back to the well and start again.

Robert J. Conley

The Witch of Goingsnake

Bill Brown was what most of the town Cherokee of the Western Cherokee Nation in the 1890's called a conservative Cherokee. There were those of the People back in the hills, of course, who thought differently. They were the real conservatives — the ones who did their best in spite of the whites and their own "progressive" people to live in the old ways according to the ancient teachings of *Keetoowah*. They would have called Bill Brown a progressive, and they would not have meant it as a compliment. Those others, those town Cherokees, the ones who called him a conservative, didn't mean it as a compliment or as an insult. It was just fact as they saw it. Bill Brown was a conservative Cherokee. He was a tall and powerful man who worked a little farm in the Goingsnake District of the Cherokee Nation West. (That is, of course, part of northeast Oklahoma now.) The farm Bill Brown worked was not far from a small town called Baptist. It was not far from Goingsnake Courthouse. Bill Brown did not own his farm, for all Cherokee People, officially all Cherokee *citizens*, held the land in common. The progressive Cherokee and the traditional Cherokee agreed on at least this one point. The traditionalists did not, however, think of themselves in terms of citizenship, and that's another reason Bill Brown's tag of conservative can be accepted only from a specific point of view. Bill Brown worked his farm, voted in national elections, (another activity the real conservatives — the traditionalists — kept away from), he read the newspapers (*the Cherokee Phoenix* written in the Sequoyah syllabary), he sent his oldest son to Tahlequah to attend the Cherokee Male Seminary, and he dressed himself up in his best suit and tie to attend church every Sunday — the Baptist Church at Baptist, of course — services held in the Cherokee language.

But Bill Brown was a conservative. What made him a conservative was the fact that with all the trappings of "civilization" he had acquired, he for some reason held on to certain of the old beliefs — the superstitions, some would say. He had been known on more than one occasion to pay for the services of a *didahnuwisgi*, a conjurer, shaman, witch doctor to some. He steadfastly clung to the Cherokee language, refusing to learn English — or at least, refusing for the most part to use it. And he retained his belief in witches. Yes, witches. *Sgili*. Bill Brown had great fear of a *sgili*, but to no avail. He would not be convinced that they did not exist — that they were mere superstition. Not his best friends, not the most respected politician of Goingsnake District, not the Principal Chief of the Cherokee Nation, not, in fact, the Baptist Church itself could convince Bill Brown that his belief was false and childish. Bill Brown was a conservative Cherokee.

Down the road a short distance from the Browns' house lived an old woman called *Tewa*, the flying squirrel. *Tewa* was known to be a conjuring woman; people often took their troubles to her and paid her to make a charm for them or to cure their ills. Some of the more progressive Cherokee simply chuckled at *Tewa* and her customers; a few of them went to her on the sly with their own problems. Bill Brown was convinced that *Tewa* was a *sgili* — a witch. And he lived in almost constant fear of her proximity to his own home.

One spring morning Bill was just walking out the front door of his house to go into his field to work. He looked up as he was about to step off his front porch, and there walking down the road that wound by his farm and on down into the woods was *Tewa*. She said nothing. She didn't stop. She was simply walking down the road on the way back to her own house from somewhere. But as she passed by his house, and just as he looked up and noticed her, *Tewa* shot a quick glance at him that sent a shudder through his entire huge frame. She went on. He caught his breath and went on out of the house and around to the back. About an hour later Bill was walking behind his big brown mule guiding the plow when the blade struck a large rock in its path, and as Bill lunged forward, his weight on the handles of the plow, the right handle snapped, and he was sent sprawling in the dirt on his face.

"God damn," said Bill Brown. (There were a few words of English which Bill knew and used on certain occasions — occasions when there were simply no Cherokee words that would fit the need.)

He was getting back to his feet and dusting himself off when he heard a commotion in the patch of woods to his rear. He got on up to his feet and loped over to the edge of the woods. There was a loud rustling of leaves almost at his feet, and his heart skipped a beat. He looked around quickly and saw the squirrel scamper up the trunk of the tall oak nearest him. It reached a branch of the oak well above Bill's head but not so far that he could not still see it well, and it stopped. Its tail twitched very quickly six or seven times, then in almost imperceptible movements, it turned around on the branch and looked down into his eyes. Beads of sweat appeared on the brow of Bill Brown as he stood transfixed to the spot returning the gaze of the squirrel.

Tewa," he said in a barely audible voice.

Then suddenly, perhaps it ran, its movements were so very quick, but to Bill Brown the squirrel just disappeared. Bill stood still for a few seconds more, then he backed up three, four steps, turned and ran back into the field to his plow and mule. He unhitched the mule and, leaving the broken plow there in the field, drove the mule hurriedly back to its corral behind his house. He went inside and dropped the bar across the door. He was standing there, his back against the barred door, the sweat running down his face which was as pale as it could possibly get. His wife, Sarah, looked up from the table where she was mixing the meal for her cornbread. Bill's condition was both visible and unmistakeable.

"*Wil,*" said Sarah, "what's wrong with you? What's happened?"

"*Tewa,*" Bill said, "*Tewa* passed by here this morning."

"So."

"She gave me a look as she passed, and it made me shiver, but I went on to work anyway."

"Is that all?" said Sarah. "You must stop worrying so over *Tewa*. She is just a poor old woman."

"No," said Bill, "that was not all. In the field my plow broke, and I was thrown. And there was this squirrel watching me. It was the *sgili*."

"Sit down, *Wil*," said Sarah. "Let me get you some coffee."

"Where is *An*?"

"She is at school, of course. Where should she be on a school day?"

Sarah brought Bill his coffee. He took a quick sip and, finding it too hot to drink, slopped some into his saucer and blew on it.

"Something bad will happen," he said, and he slurped the coffee from the saucer.

Then he got up from his chair and put his cup and saucer on the table. He went to the chest of drawers across the room and took a pistol from the top drawer, then a box of shells, and began to load the pistol.

"*Gado haduhne?* What are you doing?" asked Sarah.

"I'm going to the school to get *An*."

"Why? Why will you do that?"

"Something bad will happen. I must have her here at home where I can watch over both of you."

Bill jammed the pistol into the waistband of his trousers and hurried out the door. In less than an hour he was home again with *An*, his nine year old daughter. He pounded on the door and shouted to his wife to let them in for he had ordered her to replace the bar after him when he left. Sarah let them in, and Bill again barred the door. Only then did he sit down and have a cup of hot coffee. It settled his nerves a bit; however, he kept the loaded pistol in his lap. Sarah and *An* finished mixing the cornbread.

"I'm going out to the field for my plow," said Bill, again tucking the pistol into his pants. "I must mend it this afternoon so I can work tomorrow. Already I've lost one day. The corn won't wait forever — *Tewa* or no. You two stay inside. I won't go far, and I won't stay long."

Halfway to the field Bill stopped and rubbed his eyes. *No*, he thought, *it can't be*. But the plow was not to be seen. He ran to the spot where he had abandoned it earlier that day, and there he found the piece of handle which had broken off but nothing else. He had picked that up and was looking helplessly at it when he heard the rustling leaves in the oak tree. He looked, and there staring at him again from the same branch was the squirrel.

"God damn you," he shouted in English, and he jerked the pistol from his trousers and fired five shots. The first one struck the squirrel in the center of the face and tore most of its head off. The second hit its soft belly as the body flopped backward through the air. The other three went wild.

"That's all of that," Bill said nervously to himself, and, pistol in one hand, broken plow handle in the other, he walked back to his house.

"That's all of that," he said again.

Nevertheless, Bill Brown did not sleep well that night.

The following morning Bill got up early. Although he felt reasonably certain that he had killed the *sgili*, he yet bade Sarah keep little *An* home from school one more day and cautioned her to keep inside the house and keep the door barred during his absence. He hitched the mule to his wagon and drove in to Baptist where he had the storekeeper order him a new plow. On his way back home he stopped by the farm of his friend, George Fox. Bill and George often rode together on posses for the sheriff of Goingsnake District when he needed their help. George was plowing.

"Well, farmer Brown," said George, "have you gotten so rich that you don't need to work any more now?"

"My plow was broken yesterday, and then it disappeared," said Bill. "I had to go to town and order a new one. I'm afraid that it will be too late this year when the new plow comes."

"When I am done with my plowing," said George, "you can take this one to use."

"Wado," said Bill. "Thank you."

"But what do you mean your plow disappeared? Is it stolen?"

"I wish it had been stolen," said Bill. "I think it was taken by the sgili."

Then he told George of the events which made him suspicious of Tewa; he did not, however, tell of the killing of the squirrel. Something made him hold back the telling of that part.

"My friend," said George when Bill had finished his tale, "I believe that you are too superstitious. Perhaps Tewa is a sgili. I do not know, but I rather doubt it. I know that many believe in her conjuring, but I think she just takes clever advantage of their foolishness. I think that she's just a shrewd old woman. I think that you've been frightened by a series of coincidences — rather strange ones, for sure, but coincidences nonetheless, and because of your superstition you have imagined that Tewa is after you. Your plow has been stolen, I think."

Bill shook his head slowly.

"I hope that you're right," he said, "but I fear not."

"When I finish with my plowing, I'll bring this plow to your house. Don't worry about Tewa. It's all in your head. I'm sure of it."

Three nights later Bill Brown was awakened from a sound sleep by a terrible commotion in back of house. There was the sound of scuffling and of snorting and squealing. He hurriedly got out of bed, lit the kerosene lamp, secured his pistol and ran out into the night. The commotion was coming from his corral, and when he rounded the house he discovered a large wild hog just in the process of finishing off his mule. The mule had put up a valiant fight, but he was no match for the wild hog. Its throat had been ripped open, and it hardly had strength enough left to even try to defend itself. Bill fired his pistol into the thick hide of the hog. The hog snapped its head back as if it thought that something had bitten it there where the bullet struck. Bill fired again, running toward the battle and screaming at the hog. When the second bullet struck the hog, and he realized that Bill was there, he abandoned the kill and ran into the darkness. It was too late. The wretched mule was done for. It was in dreadful agony, and Bill could tell that it would only be a matter of time before the poor animal would be dead. He took careful aim with his pistol, and with one shot put the mule to rest.

Two days later George Fox showed up at the Brown's farm with his plow in a wagon.

"Bill," he said as Bill came out the front door of his house to see who was there, "I've brought you this plow to use."

"Thank you, friend," said Bill, "but it is too late. My mule is killed now. It's too late for my corn."

"*Aiee,*" said George, "that's too bad about your mule. How did it happen?"

After Bill had told him about the wild hog, George said, "I'm sorry about your mule, and I know it's late for the corn, but it's not yet too late. Here is a plow for you to use. Put out your corn. Perhaps it will be all right yet."

"But I have no mule to pull the plow."

"I will leave my horse here for you to use until you get your plowing done. I can manage without him for a few days."

"You're a good friend," said Bill, "but I am not going to plow. It's too late. Besides, if you leave your horse there something may happen to it. Then you would have no horse because of my troubles."

"Nonsense," said George. "You're still thinking that old *Tewa* is doing this to you, I see. You've had some bad luck is all. Listen. I'll stay and help you to plow your field. That way it will be done more quickly, and your corn will have a better chance."

Finally Bill was persuaded, and he and George both went immediately to the field and set to work. They plowed the rest of that day, and George took his plow and horse back home for the night only to return with them the following morning early. The two men worked together all that day too. They finished the plowing, and they planted the seed. George Fox's horse was once more hitched to the wagon standing in the road before Bill's house.

"*Wado,* my friend," said Bill. "Without you I would not have done it."

"All will be well, Bill. You'll see," said George.

Just then the two men heard shuffling footsteps in the dirt road. Someone was approaching from beyond. They waited in silence until they could see the approaching figure amble around the bend. When it came into sight, Bill Brown's heart stopped for an instant. George Fox, in spite of himself, was also stunned briefly, but he quickly regained his composure.

"*Siyo, Tewa,*" said George as cheerfully as he could manage.

The old woman nodded and grumbled something under her breath as she came closer. Without saying anything more or even looking in the direction of the two men, she slowly made her way past the house and on down the road. George went on home and Bill went inside the house feeling very ill at ease.

It was two days later when little *An* fell ill. Bill was afraid to leave Sarah and *An* alone for very long, so he rushed to the home of George Fox who readily agreed to go for the doctor. When the doctor arrived he examined the child and administered some medication, but he was not hopeful. He could not be sure, he said, what was wrong with her. He told the worried parents to continue to give her the medicine he left with them and said that he would be back to check on her, but he was not hopeful. Two days passed, and little *An's* condition only grew worse. In desperation, Bill went into the hills and sought out an old shaman. The old man returned to the house with Bill and examined *An*. He sang over her and gave her some medicine made from herbs. He went outside and drew a ring of tobacco around the house chanting the whole time. He stood in the road for some time smoking and blowing smoke down the road, singing the while. When he was finished, he told Bill and Sarah that he had done all he could do. His medicine, he was afraid, would not be very effective, because some other medicine person had cast a spell upon the Browns' house. The spell, he said, was very strong. He had done all he could do. Three days later *An* was dead.

Bill and Sarah buried their daughter back behind their house under a large oak tree. Bill built a small wooden frame like a house over the grave. He built a roof over the house. The Baptist preacher came and offered a prayer for the child's soul. When all was done and the friends and relatives had gone, Bill took out his pistol again.

"Wil," said Sarah, "what are you doing?"

"I am going to kill that *sgili*," he said. "I will take no more of this from her. She has done this to us — this and all the rest. Now I am going to kill her for sure."

He took the pistol, checked its load and left the house. In a few minutes he had walked the distance to *Tewa's* cabin. It stood under the trees on the edge of the woods just a few yards back from the winding road. Bill Brown was terribly afraid, but he was also determined. Nervously, he checked his pistol again. He could see a thin column of smoke rising from the chimney of the cabin there before him. Holding the pistol in his right hand, he drew himself up to his full height and started toward the cabin. When he stepped onto the front porch his shoes made a clomping sound and the boards of the porch creaked loudly. He hesitated. Then he heard the voice of the hated old woman from inside the cabin.

"Who is there?" she asked in a creaky voice.

"Tewa," Bill shouted, "sgili, ayuh Bill Brown."

He held out the pistol ready for firing, drew himself back and with all his might kicked the door. It flew open swinging all the way back and smashing into the wall. The old woman was at a pot on the fire. She looked up startled just in time to see Bill level his pistol at her. She began to scream, and Bill Brown emptied his gun into her body.

The force of the shots had thrown *Tewa* away from the fire and back against the far wall of the small room. She lay there in a crumpled heap looking very small — too small, indeed, for the rivers of blood that kept pouring from the horrible fresh wounds. Bill stood still staring at the body for a few seconds, his eyes wide. Finally he took two long and hurried steps to the fireplace and, shifting the empty pistol to his left hand, seized with his right the cold end of a flaming hickory faggot from the fire. He raced about the room touching flame to anything that would catch fire quickly — the drab and dirty curtains on the windows, the worn tablecloth, the bedclothes. Then he hesitated, flames all about him, and stepped to the center of the room. He looked again at the old woman's body. The flames began to crackle. Bill tossed the burning hickory on top of the body and watched until the ragged dress which covered it began to smolder, then he turned and ran from the cabin. He ran across the road and sat down beneath a tree where he stayed to watch until the cabin had burned to the ground.

The evening of the following day the sheriff of Goingsnake showed up at the Brown house and arrested Bill Brown for *Tewa's* murder. Bill did not resist. He did not deny the killing. He bade his wife farewell and went peacefully to jail. Bill spent some time in jail awaiting his trial, and during that time Sarah visited him regularly, but when the day of trial came she was not there at Goingsnake Courthouse. Bill looked nervously about. He saw his friend, George Fox.

"George, my wife is not here," he said.

"She is ill today, Bill," said George. "I have just now come from your house. I'm sorry, but I'm sure she'll soon be over it. Don't worry. I'll watch over her for you. Right now my wife is with her."

The trial was brief. Bill admitted having done the deed. His only defense was that *Tewa* was a witch and that she had cast a spell upon him and his whole house. She had begun by breaking his plow and making it disappear. She had then sent a wild hog to kill his mule, and finally she had done her worst — she had sent a mysterious illness to take his only daughter from him. The court refused to accept Bill's steadfast belief in witchcraft as grounds for justifiable homicide or to see the killing as one done in self-defense, and he was found guilty of murder and sentenced to die by hanging. A date was set. As Bill was being led from the courtroom, George Fox put a hand on his shoulder.

"Don't worry, Bill," he said. "Your friends haven't given up on you yet. Some of us are going to go to Tahlequah to see the chief. Maybe we can get him to pardon you. We'll explain the circumstances to him. I'm sure that when we've shown him that you're no murderer, he'll understand and issue the pardon."

"Don't bother about all that," said Bill. "I know that I'm doomed, but if you want to go to Tahlequah for me, go to the school and get my son. I want to see him once more before I die, and when I'm gone his mother will need him at home."

I'll tell him, Bill, but we'll also talk to the chief."

Bill did not see George again until the day which had been set for his hanging had arrived. The sheriff came with his two deputies to the cell. They tied Bill's hands behind his back, and they led him out to the hanging tree — a huge oak out behind the courthouse. They helped Bill to climb into the bed of a wagon which was parked beneath the tree. Dangling above the wagon bed was the noosed hanging rope. Bill stood just beneath the noose. A deputy climbed into the driver's seat with a whip in his hand. The other deputy climbed into the wagon beside Bill and placed a black sack over his head. Then he began to adjust the noose around Bill's neck. Bill did not mind dying. The day before, Martha Fox, George's wife, had come to visit him in his cell. She had told him that his Sarah was dead. Bill no longer felt that he had anything to live for. He would have liked to have seen his son one more time, but then he would have been perfectly content to die. He was not at all certain since having heard about Sarah that the killing of *Tewa* had put an end to the curse of the *sgili*. He might as well die. He would have liked to have seen his son once more, but perhaps it was better, he thought, that he had not come. Perhaps as he was away at school when the curse had been put on the Brown family it had missed him, and with Bill's death, surely it would come to an end.

The sheriff was reading the death warrant and the deputy had finished adjusting the noose when Bill heard the approach of a fast running horse.

"Stop it. Stop it. Wait," someone was shouting.

The rider pulled up his horse somewhere very near and began to speak rapidly. Bill recognized the voice of George Fox.

"Wait, sheriff, I've got a pardon here for Bill."

"What?" said the sheriff, "a pardon?"

"I've just ridden as hard as I could all the way from Tahlequah. I was afraid that I wouldn't get here in time."

"You've got a pardon for Bill Brown?"

"Yes, right here."

"How'd you get that?"

"Well, sheriff, you know, politics. The chief realizes that a good many of the People still hold fast to many of our old traditions. Anyhow, it's signed and legal."

"Keep your foot on that brake," said the sheriff, "and you — turn loose the prisoner."

At long last the sack was removed from Bill's head and he was untied. He climbed down from the wagon, and George ran to hug him.

"Bill," said George, "It's over now. *Tewa* is dead and you are free."

"*Wado*, George," said Bill, "but where is my boy? I suppose you rode so fast that he could not keep up with you."

George's face grew long.

"Bill," he said, "I'm so sorry. You've had so much misfortune lately. He's dead, Bill. Killed in Tahlequah by a stray bullet in a gunfight. He was just standing in the wrong spot."

For the next two years of his life, Bill Brown lived alone. He continued to live in his old house with all its painful memories. He continued to plant his field. He seldom left the farm to go to town or to visit friends. In fact, had George Fox not made it a point to drive over to visit him every couple of weeks, Bill would almost have been a hermit. After the first year, he did start attending church in Baptist again, but even then he would not pause following the service to chat with his old friends. About eighteen months had passed before he again agreed to ride with the special posses when he was asked. When he went out with the posse the first time, George had been worried, but Bill did his part without any problems. George began to think that perhaps after all Bill would be all right.

Bill was forty-two years old the night the posse rode up to his house for the last time. He had just finished his evening meal. The sheriff had come up to the door and knocked. Bill opened the door to the sheriff, and he could see the posse members on horseback waiting on the road.

"We're riding tonight?" he asked.

"Yes," said the sheriff. "Four men robbed the store on the road to Tahlequah. We've tracked them out this direction. They're armed, and they're pretty mean. We can use your help."

"Of course, I'll go," said Bill, and he got out his pistol.

The posse rode down the road past the spot where old *Tewa's* cabin had stood and Bill felt his heart begin to pound. He suppressed an urge to stop his borrowed mount and inspect the spot. They rode on. It was an hour later when the posse was met on the road by a lone rider.

"Who's that coming?" asked Bill.

"One of us," said George. "We sent him ahead to scout the outlaws."

The sheriff called the posse to a halt, and the rider trotted his mount up to meet them.

"Sheriff," the scout said, "I found them just up ahead. There's an old cabin just on the other side of that hill there. It faces this direction. They're in there. Looks like they're settled in for the night. They've got a fire going, and their horses are unsaddled."

The posse rode up the hillside to just below the crest, and there they dismounted and were divided into four small groups by the sheriff. One group was sent around behind the cabin in case anyone got out that way. One group each was sent to the two sides of the cabin. The fourth group stayed in front. In this group were the sheriff, George Fox and Bill Brown. The sheriff's group would give the others time to get into place, and then they would move in on the men in the cabin. When everyone was in position, the group in front crept up very close. The sheriff, George and Bill went quietly up onto the porch of the cabin. The sheriff got on one side of the door, George Fox on the other. Bill stood directly in front of the door but a couple of steps back. All three had their guns in hand.

"You inside," shouted the sheriff in English, for he did not know just who the men were, "you inside, come out one at a time with your hands up."

Someone inside shouted, "The law," and another one, "God damn."

Just then Bill kicked in the door. He saw a man go for a rifle, and he dropped him with one shot. A second outlaw quickly raised a shotgun and fired both barrels full into Bill's chest. Bill went flying back out onto the porch. The sheriff rushed into the house and, dodging to one side of the door, shot the man who had fired the shotgun in the side. The outlaw dropped screaming to the floor. A third man was trying to open a back door, but just as he got it unlatched, George Fox sent a bullet smashing into the door over the man's head.

"Hold it," he shouted.

"Don't shoot. Don't shoot," screamed the outlaw, darting his hands up over his head. The fourth man was seen to be hugging his knees to his chin behind a table in a corner of the room. As soon as he could see that things were under control, George turned from the room to see about Bill out on the porch. The quiet after the holocaust was almost eerie. Just as George stepped across the threshold to go out the door, something flew by him right in front of his face. He screamed involuntarily and stepped back, his heart pounding. Then he looked in the direction the thing had flown. He saw a squirrel running madly for a nearby oak.

"*Tewa*," he whispered harshly and in spite of himself.

And Bill Brown breathed his last breath.

SELF-PORTRAIT:
MICROCOSM, OR, SONG OF MIXED-BLOOD

1.

In me the Cherokee
wars against *yoneg* (white)
I have college degrees (2)
all major credit cards
pay my bills on time each month
on my wall is a photograph
of the Great Spirit

2.

Because the meat I eat
comes wrapped in cellophane
I do not understand
the first facts of life

I have never drunk blood
and I hunt
with the channel selector
in front of my tv

3.

When I go to the supermarket
and buy some meat
pre-cut and wrapped
how do I apologize
to the spirit of the animal
whose meat I eat
and where shall I build my fires?

4.

My poems are my fires.
oh gods forgive me all
the things I've failed
to do. the things I should
have done. forgive the meat
I've used without a prayer
without apology forgive
the other prayers I haven't
said those times I should
but oh ye gods both great
and small I do not know
the ancient forms. my poems
are my fires and my prayers.

The Rattlesnake Band

"don't wear that snake
for a hatband, boy,
you'll get struck by lightnin', sure."

      In the house of Thunder,
      Thunder's Son, the Lightning Boy,
      wound a rattlesnake round his neck
      to make a pretty necklace.

he walked with a swagger
& when he did, the rattles would sound.
ignore old superstitious men. be cool.

      The Lightning Boy
      flashed here and there
      around the ballfield—
      played circles all around
      his brothers—
      outnumbered two to one
      he won the game.

      There was once a time
      a hunter in the woods
      found himself surrounded
      by rattlesnakes
      the Chief—a very large one—spoke.
      "Your wife," it said, "just now
      has killed my brother.
      when you go home," it said,
      "make her go outside for water.
      And I will kill her."
      The hunter, though he loved his wife,
      did what the rattler said,
      and she was killed.

At the carwash
the boy with the rattlesnake band
was washing his car
when Lightning struck
the metal roof overhead

      One time in Cherokee country
      Lightning struck a house.
      a family of six
      lies cold in a single grave
      their names are listed there.
      "Killed by Lightning," it says.

On a shelf in the house
the hat with the rattlesnake band
is gathering dust.

from

Poems From the Wisdom of Swimmer Snell

(for Evelyn, his daughter)

You told me that
your Daddy would have liked me.
You even know
the words he would have used:
"You make my daughter happy,"
he'd have said.
And you've told me
things about him
and passed on to me
knowledge that he
had passed to you.
But most of all,
I love you,
and you loved him,
and still you love his memory
(or soul), and he
helped make you
what you are.
I wish that I had known the man.

They scratched his legs
when he was little,
and the old men
in and about Little Kansas
say that Swimmer Snell
could really run.
When he got up to bat
and he got an RBI,
they say that he'd get home
before the guy he batted in.

His greatest pleasure
in his later years
was to sit with friends
and talk in Cherokee.

The Cedar tree
stays green throughout the winter.
Don't cut one down,
and if you move one,
and it lives and grows,
when the span of its boughs
equals your height,
then you will surely die.
That tree is Sacred.

WE WAIT

1. White Blight

Crookneck Whiteblight, anthropologist,
Bermuda shorts & tennis shoes,
spectacles on nose,
in radiant pomposity rares back
in his chair, feet on desk.
Of course, the songs themselves have small
value for the serious scholar, though I, myself, should probably acknowledge a certain
indebtedness to the savage for filling out
my biblio. But the real thrill is getting
the stuff they think in their childlike
simplicity is sacred. The successful anthro.
must be not only well-informed but *clever*.
And in the *cleverness*—ah, therein lies the
thrill. For instance, it's amazing what
the waving of a dollar bill can do; spirit-
uality goes up in smoke, so to speak, and
you've got yourself an article. I've had
not a few successes with the Amerinds.

2. The Earth

the earth is my mother
the grass is her hair
with your plows you are ripping her breast
I will not use a plow
nor will I cut the grass
nor herd and pen up my little brothers
the various animals
I cannot stop you
but I will not follow you.

3. (to be sung to the tune of "A Mighty Fortress is Our God")

Is it not wonderful to think
What God has done for man?
He's sent the white to save the red,
To take him by the hand,
To take his hand and lift him up
From darkness and from Sin,
To teach him how to work and pray,
Speak English and drink gin,
To cut his hair a decent way,
Wear pants and shirts and shoes,
To eat his food with knife and fork
And gracefully to lose.

4. USA

the cities are overcrowded
with people who are going crazy
streams are polluted
a man cannot swim in them
nor drink from them
neither can he eat with safety
the fish that swim in them
the air is not fit to breathe
there is violence on campus
violence in the streets
the crime rate soars and
a senseless immoral war drags on
the government is corrupt
and does not even know it
and the English language is degenerating
on all fronts into Madison Avenue drivel
we have maybe 30 yrs. (they say)

5. the old prophecy

it came in various forms
from the Creek
& the Navajo
but the message is always clear
white men will come
(they did)
they will take the land
(they did)
they will nearly destroy the People
(they tried)
they will waste the land
(they have)
then they will go away
(we wait).

WILI WOYI

Illinois District, Cherokee Nation,
summer, 1886

Wili Woyi sat in the small clearing behind his cabin. The great rocks rose sharply just behind, and above and beyond the rocks, the hills, covered with woods. In the small clearing *Wili Woyi* sat, and he burned tobacco. *Tso laga yun li.* And as the smoke from the burning *tso laga yun li* rose upward toward the rocks, toward the hills, toward the clouds rolling overhead, *Wili Woyi* repeated in Cherokee seven times the following charm.

> *Listen.*
> *They will speak well of me today*
> *there at Illinois.*
> *Those who would do me harm*
> *will be wandering about.*
> *Today I will ride back home again.*
> *Ha.*

Later that same morning *Wili Woyi* rode toward the Illinois Courthouse in the Illinois District of the Cherokee Nation where he was to stand trial for having killed a man. He was going in alone. He had given his word that he would appear, and his word had been accepted. He was known as a man of honor. *Wili Woyi* was not only a man of honor, he knew that he had nothing to fear, for the killing had been done in self defense and, as such, was provided for in the Cherokee National Constitution. *Wili Woyi* knew that the Cherokee courts were fair, and he knew that Benge, the judge for the Illinois district, was a fair, honorable and intelligent judge. The trial would be brief, and he would be on his way back home soon. He rode with confidence.

Then from ahead on the road he heard the noise of fast hoofbeats. He could not see the rider for the bend in the road, but as he rounded the bend he recognized his friend, Turtle Brashears. When Turtle saw *Wili Woyi* he called out to him in Cherokee and reined in his mount.

"*Wili Woyi. Wili Woyi.* Go back."

Wili Woyi, too, stopped his horse.

"What is it, Turtle? Why should I go back? You know that I have given my word to appear in court today because of that man I killed. I cannot go back now."

"It is because of that man that I ask you to go back, *Wili Woyi*. You will be hanged if you do not go back."

"I am no murderer, Turtle, and our courts are just. They will not hang me. Come. Ride in with me."

"No. Wait. There will not be a trial. Not today and not in Illinois Court House. That is why I have ridden out here to meet you and to stop you from going into court. Judge Benge knows that I have come out here to meet you, though he must keep that a secret."

"Perhaps you should tell me what is going on at Illinois Court House, Turtle."

"Yes. There is a United States marshal waiting there to take you to Fort Smith for trial. There is nothing that Benge can do anymore. That man you killed — he was not of our Nation."

"Ai," said *Wili Woyi*, smacking himself on the forehead, "then you are right. I will not be taken to Fort Smith to the hanging judge, Parker. It is part of his divine purpose, it seems, to hang Indians in order to bring the law of the *yoneg*, the white man, to our country. He would hang me for sure. I will not go in now."

"What will you do, *Wili Woyi*?"

Wili Woyi looked up at the sky.

"*U-lo-gi-la*," he said. "It's cloudy. Come on, Turtle, let's go to my house."

"*Uh, inena,*" Turtle said.

At Illinois Court House a crowd had gathered. There were a number of Cherokees standing about, not waiting to see if *Wili Woyi* would show up for they knew that once Turtle had intercepted him on the road and told him the news he would not, but to see what the white law man from Fort Smith would do when he had realized that Billy Pigeon was not going to arrive. The white law man was pacing about nervously in front of Illinois Court House. The Cherokee were standing calmly with crossed arms leaning against the side of the court house or sitting idly about under the great walnut trees and cottonwoods which stood nearby. Benge stood in the doorway to the court house. Then the white law man, who was called Glenn Colvert, took a watch from his vest pocket and looked at it.

"He's forty minutes late, now, God damn it. I knew he wouldn't come in here by hisself like you said he would. I never heard of such Goddamn foolishness."

"You have no patience, Mr. Colvert," said Benge. "We Cherokee have a different way of looking at time than do you whites. If a Cherokee promises he will be somewhere then he will be there. He may not be there on time, for we have never lived our lives according to clocks as you do. But *Wili Woyi* - uh, excuse me, Bill Pigeon - is a man of honor."

"Yeah," said Colvert, "So you told me. Look, Benge, ain't you got no deputies here you can send out after 'im? I can't stand around here all Goddamn day. I got other things to do, too, y'know?"

"The case is out of my hands now, Mr. Colvert. You should know that. The man that *Wili Woyi* killed was not a Cherokee citizen, and, as you know, your law will not allow us jurisdiction over such cases. Otherwise, why should you be here? If *Wili Woyi* has not broken Cherokee law, how can Cherokee law take any action against him?"

"Damn it, Benge, I know all that, but you know as well as I do that that's just a Goddamn technicality. He's killed a man, and I got a legal warrant for his arrest right here in my coat pocket."

"And it's your job to serve that warrant. I have no intention of interfering with you in the line of your duty. Serve the warrant, Mr. Colvert, any time you please. I, however, will not break the laws by arresting a man outside of the jurisdiction of my court."

"Aw, son of a bitch!"

"Mr. Colvert, I suggest you go inside and relax. I believe it's going to rain any minute now. I'm sure that if you'll just be patient, *Wili Woyi* will show up, and then you can arrest him."

"You people think you're pretty Goddamn smart, don't you? You think you've made a fool out of a duly appointed officer of the law of the United States government. Well, it ain't gonna work. I can tell you that. Maybe I ain't got Bill Pigeon right now. Maybe I ain't gonna get him today, but I'll be comin' back, and I'll get the sonafabitch, and I'll have him at Fort Smith in the court."

Colvert stalked to his horse which was tied nearby. He jerked the reins loose from the hitching rail, mounted up hurriedly, and started to ride off immediately, but an afterthought made him turn back to shout over his shoulder to Benge and all the other Cherokees within hearing.

"And I'll see to it personal that you all get a invitation t' the hangin'."

When *Wili Woyi* and Turtle Brashears arrived at the cabin below the great rocks, they took the saddles from their horses' backs and turned the animals out to graze. *Wili Woyi* invited Turtle into his house.

"*Da na tlas da yun ni.* We will eat," he said.

He poured coffee grounds into a pot, picked up a heavy iron skillet and handed pot and skillet to Turtle. He found half a cake of cornbread left from earlier in another pot and, taking it up, he led the way back outside and around behind his cabin. There he soon built a small fire, filled the coffee pot with water from a bucket, and set it on to boil. He walked to the small smokehouse he had built up against the great rocks and returned with several medium sized perch, cleaned previously, and put them in the skillet to fry.

"Ha," said Turtle, "are these the largest you could catch in the Illinois?"

"I caught one very large," said *Wili Woyi*, "this long," and he held his hands apart so far that Turtle raised his brows.

"It was the first one," said *Wili Woyi*.

Turtle chuckled. He knew that *Wili Woyi*, according to tradition, always threw back into the water the first fish he caught no matter what the size, and upon throwing it back said to the fish, "It was the Fishinghawk." This was, of course, a ruse intended to misdirect any vengeful spirits who might seek restitution for violence done to the fish by sending into the body of the fisherman some dread disease.

Later, fish fried and eaten, coffee drunk, the two friends settled back. Now is the time for talk—after eating. Turtle stared up at the grey clouds.

"This thing is not over, *Wili Woyi*," he said.

"No," answered the other, "it will not be over. With Parker's men after me, it will not be over."

"What will you do?"

Wili Woyi had been rolling cigarettes. He finished, handed one to Turtle, picked a faggot with a glowing end from the fire and held it out while Turtle lit his smoke. Then he lit his own. He leaned back again on his elbows drawing deeply on the cigarette.

"I will live, Turtle," he said finally. "What should I do? As usual, I will

76

live my life. These men from Parker, they must simply become a part of my life."

Wili Woyi felt the first few drops of rain fall against his cheek.

"*A ga sga,*" he said. "It's raining."

They gathered up the pots and went back inside the cabin.

Horse Jackson had a bad pain in his stomach. He had had it for three days. On the morning of the fourth day of his misery he awoke still in pain. As he moaned audibly, his wife, *Quatie*, said, "Your insides still hurt you?"

"Ahhh," Horse groaned, "yes, as much as ever."

"Some angry spirit has gotten inside you because of something you have done—or have neglected to do," said *Quatie*, who was a good Baptist, as was her husband, but saw no reason why the spirits should not attack Baptists as anyone else.

"*Ayo,*" said Horse, "it is three whole days now."

"Today will be four," answered his wife. "Four is a good day. Go to *Wili Woyi*. If anyone can find the cause of your pain and drive it away, *Wili Woyi* can."

"Perhaps you're right. There is no wiser *didahnuwisgi* in our Nation than *Wili Woyi*. He has more charms for healing than anyone else, but how can I pay him? We have no money."

"Take these tobacco seeds," said *Quatie*. "I was saving them for our own use, but what good will even this good Georgia tobacco do us when you are ill if we do not know the charms with which to use it? *Wili Woyi* has much use for good tobacco. Take the seeds."

Deputy Marshal Glenn Colvert squinted his eyes through the rain and through the stream which was running off the brim of his hat. There before him was what, according to directions he had been given, should be the house of Bill Pigeon. The sharp rise of the hills behind the cabin would make a quick escape to the rear, if not impossible, at the least, slow and difficult.

"That's good," thought Colvert, "first damn thing all day. That's good."

He climbed creaking down out of his saddle and slapped the reins of his mount twice quickly round the trunk of a nearby *bois d'arc* sapling, removed the rifle from the saddleboot and started slowly toward the cabin keeping well in under the trees. His boots squished with each step.

"God damn rain," he thought.

He was headed for a large boulder which was nestled just beside the trees in front of and slightly off to the left, Colvert's left, of the cabin of Billy Pigeon.

Inside, *Wili Woyi* and Turtle Brashears drank coffee and smoked the cigarettes which *Wili Woyi* had rolled.

"It is a good rain," Turtle was saying. "It will be good for my corn."

"And for everything else," added *Wili Woyi*, "It was much needed."

Outside, Colvert cranked a shell into the chamber of his rifle. He aimed above *Wili Woyi's* house and fired. Then he yelled at the top of his lungs, "Pigeon. Bill Pigeon."

Wili Woyi was up, rifle in hand, at his front window in an instant, and Turtle was not much slower. He, too, held a rifle.

"Pigeon."

"Who's that?" shouted *Wili Woyi* in English. "Who are you?"

"This here's Depitty Yewnited States Marshal Glenn Colvert, Pigeon, an' I've got a warrant f'r y'r arrest right-chyear in my coat pocket. Now, I don' want no trouble from you. I don' wanna kill nobody if I don' hafta. My orders is to take you in f'r trial."

Turtle asked *Wili Woyi*, "How many with him, do you think?"

"I do not know, Turtle. He is alone, I think. I am not sure."

"We two can kill him."

"No, Turtle. Then there would be warrants for two."

"We can go out the back way into the hills."

"And maybe then we would get shot in our backs, too."

Colvert called again. "Pigeon. Whattya say?"

Wili Woyi turned to Turtle.

"Turtle, the time is not right to fight or to run. Later will be the right time, maybe. Right now I will go with this deputy. Take my rifle and do not show your face. I do not think he knows that anyone is with me."

Turtle Brashears took the rifle. He did not say anything.

"Deputy," called *Wili Woyi*, "I am coming out. I will go with you."

"No Goddamn guns. No funny stuff," said Colvert.

"No guns, deputy."

Wili Woyi kicked open the front door of his cabin and walked out into the rain, hands held high.

Deputy Marshal Glenn Colvert made *Wili Woyi* saddle his own horse at gun point, then he put handcuffs on him and told him to mount up. He tied the Indian's feet together underneath the belly of the horse and led them to the *bois d'arc* to which he had tied his own mount, then they headed toward Muskogee and the nearest railroad depot. *Wili Woyi* had not spoken a word since coming outside. They rode most of the rest of that day—as long as there was much light, and because of the heavy rain the light did not last as long that day as was usual for a summer day. On the west bank of the Grand River Colvert ordered *Wili Woyi* to stop at the mouth of a small cave. There was enough overhanging rock above to give the horses some shelter. Colvert staked them out, untied *Wili Woyi*'s feet in order to allow him to dismount, tied them again, and then prepared a camp for the night. He built a small fire, made some coffee, and heated a can of beans. *Wili Woyi* refused the beans but accepted a cup of the hot coffee. Still, he did not speak.

When Colvert had finished his beans and coffee, he unlocked the cuffs from one of *Wili Woyi*'s wrists and locked them again with the Indian's hands behind his back. He checked the ropes binding his prisoner's feet together. Satisfied, he tossed a blanket over *Wili Woyi* and crawled into his own bedroll with a loud fart. Soon he was snoring peacefully. *Wili Woyi* was still awake, still sitting upright. It was not yet quite dark. It was no longer light. It was the next best time of the day for speaking to the spirits, the best time of all being the similar time between dark and light in the morning. *Wili Woyi* turned his eyes toward the clouds. He spoke out loud but in a very low voice. He spoke, in Cherokee, the following words.

> *Hey, you spirits on high,*
>> *you anidawe,*
>> *you who dwell*
>> *in umwadahi,*
>> *come down at once.*
>> *go into the brain of that man —*
>> *that man who thinks evil of me.*
> *Hey, instantly you have come down.*
>> *you have gone into that man.*
>> *he will not hear me.*
>> *he will not see me.*
>> *he will not even awaken*
>> *until well past dawn*
> *Hey, you anidawe*
>> *who dwell on high,*
>> *I will escape from that man. Yu.*

Wili Woyi spat four times toward the sleeping Colvert and repeated the charm four times, spitting again at the end of each recitation. By the time he had finished his ritual, total darkness had set in, and the hard rain had diminished to a light but steady drizzle.

While the heavy rain was still falling, before the light of day had fully disappeared, Turtle Brashears still sat in the house of *Wili Woyi* pondering what to do when he heard the sounds of an approaching wagon. The events of the day had made Turtle a bit jumpy, and he ran to the window with his rifle in hand. As he looked out into the rain, he recognized the wife of Horse Jackson sitting on the driver's seat. He put down the rifle and ran out into the rain.

"Quatie, osiyo," said Turtle.

Then he saw that Horse Jackson was lying in the bed of the wagon wrapped up in blankets, the hard rain pouring over him. Horse did not speak. He did not even show any sign that he had seen or heard Turtle.

"We must get him inside, quickly," said Turtle.

And quickly, he and *Quatie* Jackson carried the ailing man inside where they undressed and dried him and wrapped him in dry blankets. They made him a pallet beside *Wili Woyi's* fireplace, and Turtle built the fire up. Then he went back out into the rain to care for the Jacksons' horses before returning to the fire to make coffee. He and *Quatie* drank coffee. Then *Quatie* spoke.

"My husband has been very ill these four days," she said. "We said that he should go to *Wili Woyi* and take tobacco. Then he became worse and could not even drive, so I had to bring him here."

"Ahh," replied Turtle, "*Wili Woyi* is not here. I do not know when he will return. You know, he killed that man awhile back, and there was to be a trial today at Illinois courthouse with Judge Benge. *Wili Woyi* was not worried as that man needed killing and Benge is a fair judge. But then they discovered that the man was not of our Nation, and so the trial could not be held at Illinois Courthouse. A lawman came from Fort Smith, and arrested *Wili Woyi* today. I wanted to kill the lawman, but *Wili Woyi* would not let me. He said it was not the time."

Turtle paused.

"I do not know when he will be back."

Quatie stared at the floor.

"I do not know what I should do."

"Wait here," said Turtle. "Wait a little. Perhaps *Wili Woyi* will return, and Horse needs to rest and stay dry anyway. Wait here. *Wili Woyi* will come back maybe."

He poured more coffee.

The sun had been up and the rain had stopped for about thirty minutes before Glenn Colvert opened his eyes. He yawned and stretched. He propped himself up on one elbow, hacked and spat, then he looked over toward where he had left his prisoner. All he could see was his blanket lying there in a wad.

"God damn," he said as he threw his cover back from over him. He jumped to his feet and started for the blanket. His left foot became entangled in his bedroll, and he dragged it a couple of hopping steps with him before he managed to get it loose. Running in his sock feet, he reached the blanket and jerked it up from the ground. There were the handcuffs, still locked, and there, too, were the ropes with which he had tied Bill Pigeon's feet, his knots still in them. He picked up the ropes and the cuffs, looking hard at them as if they might tell him something. He looked around himself at the rocks and the trees. His horse still stood where he had hobbled it, but Bill Pigeon's mount was gone. There were no tracks to be seen, neither human nor animal. The rain had seen to that.

"God damn it," he thought, "he could be anywhere out there. He could be long gone or he could be layin' for me."

Another thought occurred to Colvert, and he hurriedly checked his weapons. Bill Pigeon had not touched them. Then he was still unarmed, and the chances were that he was as far away as time had allowed him to be. Colvert considered going after him, but could not decide where to look. Bill Pigeon would surely not return to his cabin so soon after having been arrested there, not with the same man who had arrested him likely to be on his trail. If he was not returning to his own home he might be going in any direction, and with the tracks having been washed away by the rain, Colvert could only guess at a direction in which to look. Pigeon likely had Cherokee friends and relatives all through the hills. He might be anywhere. Colvert thought a moment, and then forced himself to admit that he had simply lost his prisoner. He picked up the ropes and cuffs once more and looked at them.

"God damn it," he thought, "it just ain't possible. There just ain't no way."

The rain was still falling when *Wili Woyi* rode up to his cabin, and neither Turtle Brashears nor *Quatie* Jackson heard the sound of the approaching horse. When *Wili Woyi* walked through the front door the other two jumped quickly to their feet.

"*Wili Woyi,*" said Turtle, "I am glad to see you back. That lawman. .."

"I left him snoring, Turtle. But what is this? *Quatie?* Your man is ill?"

"For four days now, *Wili Woyi.* In his stomach it hurts, and now his head is hot. We have tobacco seeds from Georgia."

"*Wado,*" said *Wili Woyi.* "Thank you, the seeds will wait. We do not know if Horse will wait."

Wili Woyi removed his wet hat and coat and knelt beside the sleeping Horse Jackson. He looked long at his patient. He felt the head, the chest, the stomach. He looked at *Quatie.*

"Four days?"

"Yes."

"How long has he been this way?"

"He was awake when we left our home, but he was in much pain. Sometime on the way here he went to sleep."

Wili Woyi poured himself some coffee from the pot which Turtle had kept fresh and hot and took a long sip. Then he went back to Horse Jackson.

"Horse," he said, "Horse. This is *Wili Woyi.* Do you hear me?"

"Ahh," Horse struggled to comprehend.

"How do you feel, Horse?"

"*Ag wes da ne ha,*" said Horse, "I am in pain."

"We will fix it, Horse. It will go away."

When Glenn Colvert stepped off the train at Fort Smith, he headed directly for the office of his immediate superior, United States Marshal Moss Berman. Colvert desperately wanted a glass of whiskey, but he knew Berman well enough to know that the drink had better wait until he had made his official report — a report which he, by the way, did not relish making. He had failed, and Moss Berman did not take failure lightly. He, himself, seldom failed to accomplish his purpose, and he expected the same from the men who rode for him—for the law. Colvert took a deep breath and knocked on the door.

"Come on in."

He did.

"Moss."

"I heard the train pull in, Glenn. You got your prisoner turned in already?"

"Well, no, Moss, . . ."

"Where is he? You hafta kill 'im?"

"No, but, damn it, I shoulda. Hell, Moss, I ain't got 'im."

Colvert stood shuffling his shoes on the floor like a teenager waiting for a scolding, but he was waiting rather for an explosion from Moss Berman—an explosion which never came. That was much harder on the deputy's nerves than if it had. Moss Berman took a long, black cigar from inside his coat pocket, bit off an end spat it out, took his time wetting down the cigar, and finally struck a match on the front of his desk and lit it.

"What happened?" he asked in a quiet voice.

"Well, you know, Moss, that there Pigeon, he was lined up for a trial in the Cherokee courts. He was s'posed to show up at that Illinois Courthouse, so that's where I went to fetch 'im. The injun judge an' a whole mess a injuns was standin' around there a waitin' f'r 'im, an' they kept swearin' to me that Pigeon 'uld be there most any time, but he never showed. So I went on out t' his house, an' he was there jus' bigger'n shit, and he never even give me no trouble. I hollered out for 'im t' come on out, that he's under arrest, an' he come. I tied 'im up, an' we tuck out. Well, come nightfall I bedded us down. Now, Moss, God damn it, I know how to hogtie a prisoner. You know I know. I tied that son-of-a-bitch up good. I tied his feet, an' I cuffed his hands. There wasn't no way nobody coulda got outta them ropes an' arms. Nobody."

"But Bill Pigeon did?"

"Yessir. God bless me, Moss, he did. When I woke up come mornin', his horse was gone, an' he was, too. Right there where I left the son-of-a-bitch, there on the ground, there was my blanket that I'd throwed over 'im, an' under the damn blanket—Moss, this here next is crazy, but I swear, Moss, them cuffs was layin' right there still locked, and them ropes was layin' right there with my knots still tied in 'em. Right here they is. I ain't done nothin' to 'em but jus' bring 'em along to show you."

Colvert pulled the ropes and the cuffs out of the pocket of his yellow slicker and held them out to Moss Berman. Berman took them, and Colvert continued to stare accusingly at them.

"Well," he went on, "I looked around, but I never seen no sign of no kind. If Pigeon left any, the rain wiped 'em on out."

Moss Berman tossed the ropes and cuffs back across his desk toward Glenn Colvert, and puffed on his cigar.

"Glenn, go on over an' get y'se'f a drink an' a good meal an' a bath. You need all of 'em. Then you get y'se'f a good night's sleep. In the mornin' round up Monk an' Estey. The three of y're takin' the first train outta here f'r Muskogee t'morra. That warrant you're carryin's for murder. I want it served, and I want it served now."

Wili Woyi had given him the specially prepared drink and had sung over him, and Horse Jackson was resting. *Wili Woyi* and Turtle Brashears were outside in back of the cabin smoking.

"*Wili Woyi,*" said Turtle, "what will you do about this lawman? I think you should have killed him. Or you should have let me kill him for you when I wanted to. He did not follow you back here when you escaped from him probably because he did not expect you to be so foolish to return straightaway to your own home, but he will come back here looking for you one day. Will you kill him then? Perhaps there will be more of them with him that time. It will not be so easy as it would have been before."

"He will come here again, of course," answered *Wili Woyi*, "and most likely he will have others with him, but this time I will be prepared for him. There are ways, you know, to protect one's home from intruders."

"So I have heard, but I have never seen it done."

"Nor will you, Turtle. Some kinds of magic must be worked alone or the power will be lost. You know, for instance, that I cannot allow you to look upon my tobacco—that which I have prepared."

"Yes, I know."

"As soon as Horse Jackson is ready to move, I want you to go with them to help *Quatie* get him home safely. He will be ready soon. When I am alone again I will prepare my home. I will be ready from now on. The lawmen will not enter my house."

Horse Jackson slept the rest of that morning. At noon *Quatie* fed him some stew which *Wili Woyi* had prepared. About the middle of the afternoon the Jacksons, having given over the Georgia tobacco seeds to *Wili Woyi*, left for home accompanied by Turtle Brashears. *Wili Woyi* undressed and slept. He slept soundly until just before dawn the next morning. Then he arose and went to a corner of his room where he kept a leathern pouch. He untied the thongs with which the pouch was bound and withdrew from inside a small handful of tobacco. He was still naked. He did not bother to put on any article of clothing. It was dawn.

Off to the left side of *Wili Woyi's* cabin, coming from the rocks behind, ran a small stream. The water in the stream was cold and clear. To the edge of this stream *Wili Woyi* walked taking with him tobacco. He faced the east and held the tobacco before him in his left hand. With the four fingers of his right hand he stirred the tobacco in his palm in a motion counter-clockwise as he repeated four times the following words.

> *Ha.*
> *From the four directions*
> *they are bringing their souls.*
> *Just now*
> *they are bringing their souls.*

After each repetition *Wili Woyi* blew his breath upon the tobacco, and when he had finished, he held the tobacco up toward the rising sun. He returned to his cabin, wrapped the tobacco in a piece of newspaper, and placed it under the pouch in the corner of the room. Then he dressed and made his morning coffee.

When he had finished a leisurely breakfast and had plenty of coffee, he rolled and smoked a cigarette. Then he went back to the spring where he was keeping a bucket of crawdads to be used for fishing. He took the crawdads and disappeared into the woods.

Wili Woyi returned home just in time for sundown. He set aside his catch of fish for cleaning later. Then he took up his pipe. It was only a handmade, corncob pipe, but it was serviceable, and it would do. He retrieved the tobacco which he had that morning prepared, and then, pipe in one hand, tobacco in the other, he went outside and to the east of his house. He filled the bowl of the pipe and lit it. Puffing slowly but steadily, *Wili Woyi* began to walk around his house. In a counter-clockwise direction he walked in a huge circle. He paused to blow smoke toward the south, and again toward the west, the north, and finally the east when he had arrived back at his starting point. This circling he repeated four times, making each circle larger than the last. Then he returned to the cabin to clean his fish, confident that he would not be disturbed in his home for at least six months.

Turtle Brashears was driving the wagon for the Jacksons. Horse was lying in the back, but he was awake and was feeling much better.

Quatie Jackson rode on the seat beside Turtle.

"*Wili Woyi* is a marvelous doctor," Horse was saying. "I cannot begin to tell you how much better I feel already. He has much power."

"Indeed he has," answered his wife. "You could not have known, of course, but when we arrived at his house, *Wili Woyi* was not there. He was carried off by some lawman."

"What?"

"Yes," said Turtle, "I was worried about him, but I shouldn't have been. *Wili Woyi* escaped from that man, and he did not even have to kill him. His magic is very great."

"This lawman," said Horse, "what was he?"

"He was from Parker," said Turtle. "Recently, as you may know, *Wili Woyi* was forced to kill a man who was trying to rob him. He reported this killing as any good citizen would do, and there was to be a trial at Illinois Courthouse, but before the trial happened, they discovered at Fort Smith that this man, the thief, was not of our Nation. He was a *yoneg*. So a lawman came from Parker to arrest *Wili Woyi*, and he got him. I was there, and I wanted to kill the lawman. *Wili Woyi* said that I may not, and he went with him, but as you know he came back later. He escaped by magic. He did not need to fight with the fool."

"Turtle," said Horse Jackson, "if *Wili Woyi* has escaped from a white lawman, there will be more of them. They will not stop looking for him, and since he has made a fool of one of them, they will not be so careful next time just to arrest him. They will maybe kill him. Maybe we should go back there with our guns and help him. *Wili Woyi* is a great man, and it would not be right to let those dogs from Fort Smith get him."

"I agree with you, Horse," said Turtle, "but *Wili Woyi* sent me away with you just now. He is working some magic—I think against the lawmen. I think *Wili Woyi* will not be so easy for them to catch or to kill."

"I have heard that *Wili Woyi* is not only a great *didahnuwisgi*," said *Quatie*, "but that he is also a master of *didisgahlidhodhiyi*."

"Ah, yes," said Turtle, "indeed, he can make himself invisible, and not only that, but if he wishes to, he can put his soul into the body of something else. Sometimes he will go into an owl. I have seen these things."

"Well," said Horse, "perhaps you are right then. Perhaps *Wili Woyi* will be all right. Perhaps he does not need us."

"Perhaps," added *Quatie*, "he will be even better off without you."

Glenn Colvert was approaching the home of *Wili Woyi* for the second time in less than a week, but the second time he was not alone. With him rode Harper Monk and Birk Estey, both deputies from Fort Smith assigned by Moss Berman to ride with and assist Colvert in the arrest of Billy Pigeon. Berman considered a man who was wanted for murder and had already escaped once from an experienced deputy to be a serious enough threat to merit the additional manpower. It had been a source of embarrassment to Colvert, but as he had lost his prisoner there was not much he could say. Usually a loud talkative man, Colvert had been amazingly quiet the whole of the trip from Fort Smith to Muskogee by rail and thence on horseback with Monk and Estey.

Just before the point in their journey at which *Wili Woyi's* cabin would become visible to them, Colvert reined in his mount and called a halt.

"Now, boys," he said, "'course, we ain't got no way a knowing if Pigeon's at home 'r not, but let's not take no chances. He's sneaky as hell. B'lieve me. I know. Now, what I suggest we do is I think you two had oughta spread out 'n' go th'ough the woods so's one of you comes up on each side a the house. You c'n cover the back as well as the front thataway. I'll give you time t' git in position, then I'll move in on the front. I'll call out to 'im first. Give 'im a chance t' come on out peaceable. But if he takes out the back, you all cut down on 'im right quick. If he don't come out neither door, then I'll move on in."

It took only a few minutes for Monk and Estey to position themselves, and when Colvert was sure that they had had enough time, he stepped out in the open, facing the front of *Wili Woyi's* cabin, rifle in hand.

"Pigeon," he shouted. "Bill Pigeon."

Then aloud but only to himself he muttered, "Seems as how I've been here before, an' not too God damn long ago."

"Bill Pigeon. You in there?"

The only sounds to answer him were the gentle rustling of the breeze through the giant oaks and walnuts, the scamperings of busy squirrels, the flight of some crows, and off in the distance the rapid rat-tat-tat of a woodpecker hard at work. Colvert began moving toward the cabin. Slowly. Cautiously. About half way across the clearing which lay before the cabin he let his eyes dart rapidly from one side of the cabin to the other. There were no out-buildings in sight. The only place that looked as if it might be used to shelter animals was a depression in the rock behind the cabin and off to Colvert's left. It looked as if it might accomodate two or three horses, but that was about all. It was not too deep, and although it was heavily in shadow, Colvert could see that *Wili Woyi's* horse was not there.

"Shit. He ain't home," Colvert muttered.

He stopped when he reached the door, paused for an instant, then called out again.

"Pigeon, you in there?"

There was no answer.

Colvert, his heart pounding, tried the door. It opened easily. He pushed it just a few inches, peering inside. There was dim light inside the cabin.

"Anybody home?"

Still no answer. Colvert shoved the door all the way inside to the wall to be sure that no one could be lurking behind it. Then, with one foot across the threshold, he poked his nose inside and slowly looked around. He stepped back outside quickly with a strange and eerie sense of relief.

"Monk. Birk. Come on out, boys. Ain't nobody here. God damn it."

As the three riders from Fort Smith disappeared back down the road by which they had come, inside the cabin, *Wili Woyi* uncrossed his legs and rose to his feet. He walked straight across the room to the still open door, leaned with his left hand on the doorframe and stared after his departing visitors. With his right hand he raised to his lips the cup of steaming coffee which he held and took a long and satisfying sip.

Glenn Colvert, Monk and Estey had spent the entire day riding in circles in the woods around *Wili Woyi's* house—counter-clockwise. Colvert thought that *Wili Woyi* would not have gone far from home, and he was determined that if they searched long and hard enough in the area they would be certain to find some sign of the fugitive. When darkness fell and they could no longer search effectively, the three deputies began to look for a good camp site. As things worked out, they made their camp in the woods along the bank of the same stream which flowed by *Wili Woyi's* cabin. They built a small fire, made coffee and supper, and ate. When they had finished off all the coffee and cleaned their dishes in the stream, Glenn Colvert told the other two men to get some sleep.

"I'll stay up for a couple a hours an' keep watch," he said. "Pigeon might be onto us by now, an' there ain't no sense in bein' careless. In a couple a hours I'll wake you up," (he gestured toward Birk.), "then you c'n watch for two hours, an' then wake up Monk. OK?"

The other two crawled into their bedrolls and were soon asleep. Colvert made more coffee. He built the fire up just a little for there was a slight chill in the night air. Then he sat down near the fire with a cup of coffee, his rifle across his knees. The two hours dragged slowly by with about the only break in the monotony the eerie hoot of a near-by night owl. When his time had passed, Colvert jostled Birk with his foot.

"Two hours is up, Birk," he said, "you're on."

As Birk yawned, stretched and moaned, crawled out of the sack, Glenn Colvert laid aside his weapons and pulled off his boots. Soon Colvert was snoring, and Birk was sitting beside the small fire with his rifle. Birk yawned and rubbed his eyes. His head fell forward, and he jerked it back upright.

"Shit," he muttered to himself, "cain't fall asleep on watch. Cain't do that."

He laid aside his rifle and poured himself a cup of coffee from the pot which Colvert had brewed. The owl hooted. Birk jumped.

"Just a hootowl," he said. "Goddamn hootowl."

Even having thus reassured himself, Birk found that each time the owl hooted, he jumped. He began to feel that the owl knew that it was startling him and was taking delight in the fact. He thought about trying to locate the villain to shoot it, but immediately realized that such a course of action would bring Monk and Colvert rapidly to their senses and almost certainly put them in a very bad humor. But the owl hooted again, and Birk jumped again, and he knew that he must do something. He put aside his rifle once more and began to look about on the ground for a stone just the right size. He found and hefted two or three before he settled on one. It was smooth, nearly round, and was not quite a fistfull. It should do nicely.

Birk stood up slowly with the rock in his right hand and faced in the direction from which the hoots had seemed to come. He strained his eyes into the darkness but could see nothing. Suddenly he heard it again, and he threw the rock with all his might in the direction of the sound. There was a rustling of leaves and the sound of the rock falling to the ground—then silence. Glenn Colvert snorted and rolled over in his sleep but did not wake up. Monk showed no sign of having been in the least disturbed. Birk went back to the fire and squatted. He took up his cup and sipped from it. As he reached to place the cup back on the ground, he stiffened. He heard what he would have sworn was the sound of footsteps, and it was very near. He reached for his rifle and was astonished when he saw that it was not there where he had left it. He drew his revolver, clumsily in his haste, and looked around the camp in all directions. There was no one to be seen. Nothing moved. Poised, ready to shoot, he continued to look. He thought about waking Colvert but did not know what he would tell him. Then he saw his rifle lying beside Colvert's where Colvert slept. He retrieved it.

"I know I left it over here," he muttered, "I know it. But there ain't no one here. I musta moved it over yonder when I'us gettin' after that damn hootowl. I musta moved it an' never knowed it. Too damn jumpy."

He picked up his coffee and lifted it to his lips to drink. It was empty.

"Glenn. Glenn," he yelled. "Get up. Monk?"

Glenn Colvert came out first. He had a pistol in each hand. Monk was reaching for his rifle and trying to get his legs out from under his blanket at the same time.

"What is it?" said Colvert.

"Glenn, they's somebody here."

"Where?"

"Here."

"Well, didja see 'im?"

"No, I never."

"Where'd the sound come from?"

"Right by God here. Right here."

Birk was stamping and pointing to the ground just back of the campfire from where he had been sitting.

"Come on, Birk," said Colvert lowering his guns. "You mean he 'us right here behind you, an' you never seen 'im? You been sleepin', Birk?"

"No, Glenn. Goddamnit, I swear it. I never went to sleep. I was settin' here with a cup of coffee in my hand, and I heard footsteps right here. I looked around, and they wasn't nobody there, so I got up to look around somemore. Then I seen my rifle was gone. I found it over yonder. Right beside yours. I swear, I never put it there. Well, I figgured I must be gettin' spooky, so I went back t' the fire, an' I found m' cup empty, an', Glenn, I hadn't tuck but a sip out of it. I don't know who 'r what it is, but Goddamnit, they's somebody here."

Again Birk stamped the ground around the fire.

"All right, all right," said Colvert, "you go on an' get some sleep. Monk, you awake? You take on over your watch now. It's a little early, but Birk's too . . ."

Colvert didn't finish what he was saying, for just then there was a loud splashing, followed by a hissing and a clank. All three deputies turned at once and raised their weapons. The fire was almost out, steam was coming up from the ashes, hissing still, and the coffee pot was on its side rocking a tiny bit in the dirt.

*   *   *   *   *

*Three miles southeast of
Illinois Courthouse, near the
Illinois River. Winter 1891.*

"Looks like he's been here for sometime," one of the men in the group was saying. There were about a dozen of them gathered around to get a good look at the body so recently discovered.

"Yeah," said another. "Hogs 'r somethin's been after 'im. Bet his own mother couldn't recanize 'im now."

Glenn Colvert shoved his way through the crowd.

"Make some room here, fellas. This here's the law comin' through. Make some room."

A path to the body was more or less cleared, and Moss Berman followed Glenn Colvert through it.

"God damn," said Colvert, "that's a hell of a sight."

Moss Berman turned and walked away again. He paused a few feet distant under a large walnut tree to light a cigar.

"Reckon who it is?" said one of the men.

"Who it was, you mean," said Colvert.

Berman spoke out in a strong voice.

"It was Bill Pigeon," he said. "I recognize him, even like that."

There were murmurs of surprise and disbelief. Glenn Colvert hurried over to Berman. He spoke in a harsh whisper.

"How c'n you tell, Moss? I mean, the shape he's in? I had Pigeon under arrest that time, an' I can't tell. Fact a the matter is, I don't recall him bein' as big as this here feller looks to a been."

Berman sucked at his cigar. Slowly an expression of great puzzlement came over Colvert's face.

"Moss?" he said. "Whenever did you set eyes on Bill Pigeon?"

Berman reached out and took hold of Colvert's necktie. He gave it a gentle tug as if to straighten it. The crowd of spectators was still milling about the body as if they could not get their fill of the gruesome sight—all but one who seemed to be more interested in the two lawmen than in the body. Turtle Brashears, though being careful not to be too obvious about it, was watching Berman and Colvert with great interest.

"We been after this son-of-a-bitch for goin' on six years now, Glenn," said Moss Berman, his voice still low. "I got a damn good record, an' all I been gettin' from you is a bunch of hoodoo stories. Now, that there body over there looks a hell of a lot like Bill Pigeon t' me."

Just then one of the crowd spoke out.

"Hey, how the hell's he know who this is?"

Glenn Colvert turned to face the man.

"Fellas," he said, "this here's United States Marshal Moss Berman. You've all heard a him. I reckon he oughta know Bill Pigeon when he sees 'im. Even in that shape."

Berman turned to walk back to his horse, and Colvert followed him. As they mounted up they could hear the conversation continuing behind them.

"That there's Moss Berman?"

"Bill Pigeon, huh?"

"Well, I be God damned."

As Moss Berman and Glenn Colvert rode away from the scene, they heard a loud screech from the top of a tall cottonwood which was standing nearby. They paid it no mind, but back in the crowd Turtle Brashears turned his head toward the tree, and his keen eyes found, sitting on one of the topmost branches, a great horned owl, and he smiled.

Geary Hobson

MARLENE

I guess Frances and I have been going to Okies for about three years now and in all that time a lot of changes have taken place. For a corner beer-joint near the university, that's saying a lot, since places like Okies generally don't change at all. We've watched it go from being a place once patronized by university students and Indians to a biker bar. Yeah, for a while, when the bikers started coming in and the Wigwam Club opened up — that's an Indian bar over on North 4th Street — we stopped going to Okies and started going to the Wigwam Club. Then when the drinks started getting higher at the Wigwam Club, we started going back to Okies. By then the bikers didn't hang out there any more and it had turned into something of a hippie bar, except for the few Indians who still went there all along, preferring the cheaper prices of beer to Indian company.

Then a lot of black guys started patronizing the place and soul music seemed to be about all that would get played on the jukebox, but that was okay most of the time, because the blacks never bothered Indians. Now all of a sudden, the 'Skins have started coming back to Okies in droves, especially on Tuesday nights. It's gotten to be that on Tuesday nights the place literally busts open at the seams, it gets so crowded. Somehow or another, Tuesday night has become an almost unofficial 'Skin night at Okies and the Wigwam Club even closes up then. So it ought not be a surprise for you to learn that Frances and I were down there at Okies last Tuesday, starring around with all the other 'Skins, when what I'm going to tell you about happened.

You know, the thing about Okies, you go down there, you buy a draft and then walk towards the back of the place and kind of stand around like everyone else. People are there, standing around in little groups, talking and laughing and drinking, and pretty soon they sort of start drifting towards the back booths as they empty out. A lot of the white people who've been sitting there start moving up to the front of the bar or go home, kind of like they're worried we might massacre their wagon train or something. Pretty soon, the whole back area of Okies — the booths, the dance floor, the aisle, — will be crowded with 'Skins. For about two hours or so, until closing time, the place jumps, and then afterwards there will almost always be a party at somebody's house and it will generally continue on until the daylight hours. Not many people make it to work or classes on time the next morning, saying that for Wednesday they'll just hang it up.

Anyway, as I was saying, it was no surprise that Frances and I were in Okies last Tuesday, but it was sure one hell of a surprise for us to see Marlene Little Cloud there. I was up at the bar, getting another beer, when I saw Marlene sitting there at the bar all alone. About six weeks ago her husband died and I hadn't seen her since before it happened. She's a Navajo woman, about thirty-five years old.

"Hey, Marlene. How's it going?"

She looked around and seemed pleased to see me.

"Hey, Wayne. How are you?"

"What're you doing sitting up here all by yourself. We're all in the back."

"Oh, I'm doing okay. Is Frances with you?"

"Yeah, she's in back. We're sitting in a booth."

Just then, I got one of the bartender's attention and got my beer. It was crowded as hell right there at the bar. It made me feel like the thirteenth pig at the trough. People were bumping into each other like bugs in the water, it was so packed.

I thought that Marlene might be feeling lonesome since Mike died so I asked her again to come back and sit with us.

"Okay. Lead the way."

We made our way through the crowd to the back room. When Frances saw her, she greeted Marlene pretty enthusiastically, since she hadn't seen her for a long time, and everyone in the booth moved over so she could sit down with us. Ron Romero and a San Juan girl whose name I can never remember were sitting with us. I was about to slide into the booth when Tommy Atencio, who works with me down at the BIA office, came over. I stepped back to the aisle and we stood near the booth and small-talked about office things while Frances and Marlene talked about their classes and work.

Ron and his snag got up to dance and Tommy and I sat down in their places. As usual, Tommy flirted a little bit with Frances. It don't bother me any, because I know it don't mean anything. I was about to introduce him to Marlene when I heard her telling Frances about Mike's death. Well, I sort of dreaded that, because the last thing I wanted was to have Marlene feeling real bad. I think we were all trying to avoid even mentioning anything about Mike, but now that she was talking about him I told her I was sorry to hear about his death. Frances asked her how he had died. I had heard rumors about him being killed, but I didn't know how to ask her about it.

". . . they found his body near the railroad tracks in Flagstaff. His head was beat in. They didn't know whether he fell out of a freight car or if somebody hit him with something. I don't know much about it, myself, other than that. They sent his body up to Montana for burying and I didn't get to see it."

We listened quietly while in front of us, on the dance floor, people were dancing to some Mo-Town music. Some real jivey stuff.

"Well, we're sure sorry to hear about it," Frances said.

"Thanks, but you know, Frances, I think it was bound to happen sooner or later," Marlene said.

We nodded, not knowing what to say. Just then, Marlene asked to get by so she could slide out of the booth to go to the john. After she left, Tommy asked us about her husband.

"Mike Little Cloud? He's that Cheyenne guy who used to come down here all the time. He was the only 'Skin that got kicked out of here that night when the bikers started picking on people. You oughta remember him. A real big guy. Weighed about two-ten."

"No. Beside, I was on vacation in California when the famous

Biker—'Skin fight took place," Tommy said, grinning. "I missed that great event." He looked at the place on my chin where I've got just the smallest scar from where one of those hairy mother-fuckers hit me with a fist that must've had a dozen rings on it. Sonofabitch hit me when I wasn't looking.

"Anyway, Mike's one of the guys who used to come in the office every once in a while, hoping that we could help him find a job," I said. "In fact, I did get him a job a couple of times, but he either lost them or didn't show up for work."

"Well, with the horseshit jobs they make available for 'Skins, could you blame him?"

"But one of the jobs was working with Barney Edwards."

"Oh." Tommy said, pausing thoughtfully. "Well, what happened?"

"Mike just didn't show up. Barney was real put-out with me after that."

Barney Edwards is the very prestigious director of the City maintenance operations division for Indians. He has more contacts than Carter has Little Liver Pills. They say he might be Commissioner of Indian Affairs some day.

"Well, you never know," Tommy said.

"Mike was so far into the booze by that time that I guess nothing could help him," I said. "He would stay away from it for a couple weeks then he would go on a toot that would last for a week."

"I don't remember him. I might know him if I saw him, but I don't know the name," Tommy said.

"Wayne, you and Tommy ought not say anything to Marlene about Mike when she comes back," Frances said.

"Yeah, I know. I was just thinking that. But she's the one that started talking about him." I said.

"I know, but maybe we ought to cool it," she said.

"Could be she wants to talk about him. Maybe do her some good," Tommy said. "I remember when my niece's little boy got run over by a truck, she wouldn't say anything to anybody for weeks. She'd just stay in her room and cry steadily, real quiet-like, and then one day, after about a month, she was calm as everything and she began talking about him again and she took up her normal life. It was like it was okay then and that she'd passed through it all okay."

"You might be right, but let her talk about it only if she wants to."

"It could be too, that she didn't really care for him anymore by the time he died. You know, he put her through a hell of a lot of shit."

"Don't be too sure about that," Frances said. "Women love a different way than men."

"Well, after the way he treated her — beating her up, taking her car, getting drunk so much — I don't see how there could have been much love left," I said.

"Love's a funny thing. You never know," Tommy said, and we nodded. Tommy's a hell of a philosopher.

"She's sure had a hard time. I don't know very many nicer people than Marlene," Frances said.

"Yeah, but you know what they say about good guys catching all the shit," I said. They nodded, as just then Marlene came back from the john and so we played musical chairs with the seating arrangements for a moment. She had gotten a fresh drink—it looked like a whiskey-sour. Just as she sat down, Ron and the San Juan girl came back from dancing and the shifting around started all over again.

"I hear there's a party over at Bob Benally's," Ron said as he sat down.

"Who's Bob Benally?" Frances asked.

"He's a student at the U. He's a Navajo guy from Farmington," Ron's snag said. She looked at Marlene and asked, "Do you know him?"

"No, I don't know him. I know a lot of Benallys, but I don't think I know him," Marlene said.

"I also heard that Frank Barton is having a party, too," Tommy said.

"Just like those Navajos—having parties all the time," Ron teased, looking at Marlene.

"Ay-eeh. That's what you Taos guys say," Marlene kidded him back. We laughed. It was good to see that Marlene was in a good mood.

Some more people came over that Ron and his snag knew and they began to talk to each other. Tommy asked Frances to dance and they got out and went to the floor. Marlene and I watched them.

"You guys doing okay?" Marlene asked me.

"Oh yeah, sure. We're probably going to go to Anadarko for the fair next week. Maybe get to meet a lot of each other's relatives there."

"Is that something you guys from the Paralyzed Tribes celebrate every summer?" she asked, smiling as she kidded me in the age-old way about being from one of the Five Civilized Tribes.

"No, not really. It's just an annual event in western Oklahoma—mostly for western Oklahoma tribes—but we go there anyway."

"You *paralyzed* Indians," Marlene said. It didn't sound like kidding now, though. I laughed, then I changed the subject by asking her about her classes.

"Oh, they're okay, I guess. But, you know, they just don't seem important to me now."

I nodded.

"I'm working under this one professor in Education this summer in a bi-lingual reading project. I've got all the research work done, with some tapes and all, but I just don't seem to care about getting it all written up to turn in. You know what I mean?"

"Yeah. I know. I've been in that boat before, too." I said.

Frances and Tommy came back then and Tommy asked if anybody needed another drink. I said I did and so did Marlene. He got everybody's orders and Ron's snag went with him to help him carry them back. Ron asked me a question about the new housing deal for the Eight Northern Pueblos so we got into a discussion about that. I was aware of it when Marlene and Frances started talking about Mike after a couple of minutes and Ron and I both began listening to them. Or, actually, listening to Marlene, since she was doing all the talking.

". . . in the nine years we were married he took jewelries that I had and he sold them for money to drink with. He wrecked four different cars I had. He sold or hocked about eight different TV sets throughout all that time. We used to argue and fight about it. He'd always be real sorry about it afterwards and would try to pay me back. But then it's happen all over again." She stopped talking for a moment and drank the rest of her whiskey-sour. "He would even go down to Sears or Wards and get the money for the stuff I'd put on layaway, telling them that I'd changed my mind and didn't want it after all. But I'd never see a penny of that money."

Frances patted her on the hand. We could see that Marlene was getting a little loaded. She didn't seem real sad or angry, though, just kind of quiet and gentle.

"I don't know how many times I had to come into this place and get him. Most of the time he wouldn't be here when I got here. People would tell me that he had been in a little earlier, but that he'd bought himself a quart bottle of whiskey and had left. Most of the time I wouldn't find him and he wouldn't come home that night. He would, though, after a couple of days, looking real bad and feeling real sorry about everything." She stopped for a moment when Tommy came back to the booth.

"Yeah, I can remember Mike here sometimes," I said. "We even got loaded together a couple of times."

"But it was different with him, Wayne. He wouldn't know when to stop, but you do," Marlene said.

"Not always, he doesn't," Frances said, giving me a sharp look. I tried to ignore it, or at least to try to pass it off with a shrug. She's been on my case for a month, just because I didn't come in from my night out with the boys when I'd said I would. You know, once you get in the dog-house, you never really ever get out of it, do you?

"No, Frances, but Mike would get started and he wouldn't stop until he'd run out of money or booze or ground himself down to a frazzle. The times I tried to get him to A.A. or in an antibuse program—it didn't do no good. It seem like he only got worse."

"I remember one time Mike was real loaded and was in here yelling that he was a full-blood Cheyenne Indian, the great-grandson or something of Dull Knife, or somebody like that. And that he could beat up everyone here—including Indians," Ron Romero said. "He was sure getting out of hand. Some of us tried to get him to quiet down. After a while we got him to shut up when we said we were going off to a forty-nine. He said he wanted to go with us, he got a bottle, and then when all of us got in our cars to go, he just up and walked the other way. You know, come to think of it, he never would go to any of the parties or forty-nines with us."

"I wish he had, maybe it would of been better for him," Marlene said.

"Well, you never know about those things," Tommy said. I could sense he was getting a little bummed out by Marlene. Pretty soon, he asked Ron's snag if she'd like to dance and they got up and did their thing on the dance floor. Tommy's a good dancer—a hell of a lot better than me, and Ron's snag was something else to watch, and that's just what we did for the next few minutes.

I looked up at the clock and saw that we had ten minutes before the lights were supposed to come on, announcing last call, so I got out of the booth and went to the bar and ordered us all another round. When I got back, with Ron helping me carry everything, Marlene was talking about Mike again.

"Come on, Marlene. Let's go dance," I said, hoping that would get her mind off her problems.

"Okay." She got up. I halfway expected her to say no, and I was sort of surprised by how passive she was. We went ahead and danced. She wasn't really much of a dancer, kind of heavy-set and slow, but hell, I'm no one to criticize anybody else—me with my over-thirty beer-gut and two left feet. The record ended and we went back to the booth. Just then the lights came on and, like always, a lot of people yelled for them to turn them off. Might as well yell for the buffalo to come back as to have them turn those damned lights back off, I remember Ed Raushel, a Kiowa guy, say one night.

"You know, Frances when Mike went off that last time, I had a strong feeling that something was going to happen. Oh, he'd been gone before, but this was different. I don't know why. He left and I didn't hear from him for about two weeks. Then he called me from Flagstaff, saying that he was working and playing softball with a team. He said everything was okay and he wanted me to send him his clothes. I told him I would. But, you know, I thought to myself: he'll probably come back home in a few days and so I won't send them. Then I got a call from him again about a week later. He was in Phoenix then. He told me he'd lost his job. I asked him if he was drinking again and he got mad at me. He told me if I was serious about getting a divorce this time and I said, no, I guess not. Because I'd thought about it a lot and I figured that a divorce wouldn't solve our problems because I knew we'd always get back together again. I told him I didn't know what to do."

She paused and took a drink as one of the bartenders came by picking up empties from the tables. "Last call, folks. Can you all move up to the front so we can clean up back here?" He asked. We said we would. Frances touched Marlene's shoulder and said: ''It's okay. You don't have to talk about it.''

"No, it's all right," Marlene said as we moved toward the front of the bar. "Anyway, Mike asked me if I'd come get him. I asked him if that's what he wanted and he said yes. So the next day I withdrew my tuition money and caught a plane to Phoenix. I went to this address there but they said he'd moved out and hadn't left a forwarding address. I knew something was wrong, so I spent two days going around all the Indian bars—The Ponderosa, the Can-Can, the Esquire—but I couldn't find him. Nobody had seen him. I thought to myself: I'd better call the police. Everytime I called the police number, it was busy. I called four times until I finally got someone, but they said he wasn't in the jail. I was running out of money and I had to get back to Albuquerque so I left that Sunday night. I was back here for two days when I got word that he was dead. And you know what? He *was* in that jail that Sunday. And while I was there. They'd probably picked him up for being drunk on the weekend sometime. I found out they let him out of jail on Monday morning and the next morning after that he was found dead by the railroad tracks in Flagstaff. The police wouldn't tell anything more."

"It's okay, Marlene. There was nothing you could do," Frances said. I agreed. We were up at the package liquors now and Ron and Tommy were talking about going over to Frank Barton's party. I asked Frances if she wanted to go and she nodded yes. We got a couple of six-packs to go.

"Well, it's all over with now. There wasn't anything anybody could've done. It seems to me now like that was the only thing that could of happened and I think sometimes that maybe it was for the best, him dying like that," Marlene said as she went up to the package counter. She bought a quart of Jim Beam which the clerk placed in a tall brown paper bag. "But it's over now and I have to live. I know that. I want to get out and have some fun for a change."

"You're right, Marlene. Why don't you come go to Frank's party with us?" Frances said.

Marlene looked at us as we all went out the front door. She smiled kind of sad-like and said:

"No, you guys go on without me. I think I'll just go on home tonight."
Last we saw she was walking alone down the sidewalk toward her car.

DEER HUNTING

1.

"God dammit, Al. Are you gonna help me
cut up this deer, or
are you gonna stand there all day
drinking beer and yakking?"
Knives flash in savage motion
flesh from hide quickly severs
as the two men rip the pelt tail downwards
from the head. The hide but not
the head is kept. Guts spew forth
in a riot of heat and berries and shit,
and is quickly kicked into the trash hole.
Hooves are whacked off,
and thrown also to the waste hole—
a rotted hollow stump.
But the antler rack is saved,
sawed from the crown with a hand-saw,
trophy of the hunt,
like gold teeth carried home
from the wars
in small cigar boxes.
Men stand around in little groups,
bragging how the deer fell to their rifles
and throw their empties into the stump-hole.
Al walks to the stump, unzips his pants.
"Hell, Bob, you're so fucking slow,
I could skin ten deer while you're doing one
and I'll show you up just as soon
as I take a piss."
The hounds,
tired from the slaughter,
watch the men. They whine
for flesh denied them
and turn to pans filled with Purina.

2.

"Now, watch me, *ungilisi*, grandson,
as I prepare this deer
which the Great Spirit has given to us
for meat."
    The old man hangs the carcass
feet-first from the pecan tree
with gentleness
like the handling of spider-webbing
for curing purposes.
    Slow cuts around the hooves,
quick slices of the knives as
the grandfather and father
part the hide from the meat.
The young boy—now a man—
stands shy and proud,
his initiating kill before him,
like a prayer unexpected,
his face still smeared
with the deer's blood of blessing.
    The hide is taken softly,
the head and antlers brought easily with it,
in a downward pull by the two men.
    Guts in a tumbling rush
fall into the bucket
to be cooked with the hooves
into a strength stew
for the hunting dogs
brothers who did their part in the chase.
    The three men share the raw liver,
eating it to become
part of the deer.
    The older man cuts
a small square of muscle
from the deer's dead flank,
and tosses it solemnly into the bushes
behind him, giving back part of the deer's
swiftness
to the place from which it came.
    Softly, thankfully, the older man
breathes to the woods,
and turns and smiles at his grandson,
now become a man.

BARBARA'S LAND — MAY, 1974

Driving across your people's old homeland
I pull into Claude, Texas
2 o'clock in the afternoon
Hottern the hinges of hell
                              as they say here.

Dry panhandle wind
sifts through the red land
Buffalo clouds in the distance
herd up in the afternoon heat.

A chocolate milkshake at the tastee-freeze:
—Are there Comanche people here anymore?
—Huh? Naw, Naw.
The tastee-freeze lady's eyes
describe a suspicion
                              as if to say:
Another one of them damned
Indian trouble-makers.

The wind shifts the heat
around in circles and
dust-devils dance along the interstate.

The historical marker
on the outskirts of town
said something about Comanches
in the year 1874
Adobe Wells   Quanah Parker   Palo Duro.

Well, Barbara,
I celebrate the Comanche centennial
with the milkshake
(a piss-pore substitute)
and think of those days
                              of buffalo,
of winter camps, blood, plains,
horses, wind, raids, scalps, and hardships.

This land is your bones.
You are stronger than concrete.
You are stronger than steel.

BUFFALO POEM #1

(or)

ON HEARING THAT A SMALL HERD OF BUFFALO
HAS "BROKEN LOOSE" AND IS "RUNNING WILD"
AT THE ALBUQUERQUE AIRPORT --- SEPTEMBER 26, 1975

---roam on, brothers . . .

THE RISE OF THE WHITE SHAMAN AS
A NEW VERSION OF CULTURAL IMPERIALISM

Recently, at a poetry reading at one of the universities in the southern part of a southwestern state, a middle-aged, Anglo poet, after referring to himself as a "shaman," began reading poems in which he identified himself with several historical Indian personae. He had made it clear at the outset that he wasn't merely a poet — as if that weren't enough in itself — but he was a "shaman," a man who was going to recreate the world through the power of his words. I wasn't present at this reading, though a friend of mine, a well-known Chicano poet, was there, and it was he who later told me about it. The "shaman," at midpoint in his reading, began another sequence of poems by suddenly inveighing the audience with the salutation "I AM GERONIMO!" in a squeaky falsetto, causing the handful of Indians among the listeners to laugh out loud. I am told that the "shaman" appeared perplexed for a moment, as though at a loss to understand why someone should rudely laugh at such a dramatic moment.

I have seen variations of this moment repeated many times in the past several years. Sometimes it occurs in art galleries, when little old ladies from Boston or Kansas City interrupt the Indian artist, there also on exhibit along with his works, to tell whoever happens to be listening what Indian art — and perhaps even that particular artist's work — is all about. Or, when the visitor to Acoma Pueblo or Taos Pueblo begins to tell the residents there of his or her grandmother back in Syracuse who was a Cherokee, or Sioux, or Blackfoot (it's surprising how popular Blackfoot is becoming these days) princess — (always *Princess*, not merely an Indian *woman* — and certainly *never*, a *squaw*, although they will refer to other Indian women as squaws, but not their own mythical Indian grandmothers). Or, the Junior Chamber of Commerce-types who explain the new housing project designed for a low-rent district as being "simply constructed" like an "Indian pueblo," and, one assumes, with all the comforts of the reservation. Or, in certain university departments whose liberal members sit dreaming up new grant proposals and programs for Indian students without even bothering to consult the Indians themselves; of course, the grant money is available: big corporate industry wants not just to absolve its part in the national guilt, but, more importantly, is slobbering for the tax write-offs that are involved in their Santa Claus-like gestures. In short, it is still the same old ballgame: Indians are still being exploited, both materially and culturally, but the forms now employed are much more subtle than the forms used a century ago by the mountain men and the Seventh Cavalry.

So, in the same spirit as Leslie Silko's two-part old-time Indian attack, I would like to examine some things that are happening on the literary scene today — things that I feel are detrimental to both Indian people, not only of the past but of the present as well, and to non-Indians, whose knowledge of Indian cultures has, unfortunately, been formed too often by the romantic (and now the neo-romantic) writers/artists/ethnologists who have avidly and imperiously staked out their claims as unequivocal experts on our Indian cultures.

It seems a foregone conclusion of non-Indians that the great store of wisdom "collected" from Indian cultures by these same "friends" is *their* property and no longer that of the Indians' — that this body of knowledge and consciousness, like the land and water and the sky itself, now belongs to them by dint of appropriation. Leslie has already touched on this, but it bears repeating that the same attitudes implicit in the bullying "guests" of this continent in the past — the Captain John Smiths, the Custers, and other Great White Fathers — are equally as prevalent today as they were then; and they are even present when such well-meaning hot-shots as Elsie Clews Parsons, D.H. Lawrence, and Mabel Dodge invaded Taos Pueblo in the 1920's (to cite only one tribe and its own particular set of "friends") and claimed it as their own. The assumption seems to be that one's "interest" in an Indian culture makes it okay for the invader to collect "data" from Indian people, when, in effect, this taking of the essentials of cultural lifeways, even if in the name of Truth or Scholarship or whatever, is as imperialistic as those simpler forms of theft, such as the theft of homeland by treaty.

I find it amusing that hippies who are now glutting the market with tons of bogus "Indian" jewelry get uptight when an Indian asks them why *they* are making jewelry copied after the Indian forms and designs. One has only to spend a day or so here in Albuquerque or in Gallup to see the extent to which this form of Indian art has been cheapened and bastardized and taken over by non-Indians. In fact, it has recently been reported that the increase of non-Indian exploitation of the silver, turquoise, and heishi market here in New Mexico has raised serious speculation concerning the future survival of these ancient crafts. The Santo Domingo smith, for example, who spends weeks working on a single silver bracelet, can't compete with the assembly-line, machine-produced, or non-Indian-made, or even foreign-made, *junk* that is marketed here and in the East as "authentic" Indian-made. The rationale of the non-Indian who makes Indian jewelry, even when he calls it "imitation" Indian jewelry, is a 20th century counterpart of the buffalo hunters of the last century, the Buffalo Bills and the Billy Dixons, who, even as they killed off the great herds for economic reasons, were aware of the immensity of their exploitation. When the non-Indian jewelry maker is confronted with questions of why he is selling his silver gimcracks and gee-gaws on the mall of the University of New Mexico campus, becomes defensive and usually answers with "I've got a *right* to do it; besides, *my* jewelry is not Indian-imitated!" or "*Everybody* else is doing it, so why pick on just me?" or "I've got to make a living, *too*, haven't I?" He knows what he is doing, but he continues doing it anyway. And so the rip-off continues.

The current fad in some small magazines of poets calling themselves "poet-shamans" or even "shamans" is another counterpart of the Indian crafts exploiters, the imperious anthropologists, and the buffalo hunters. Writing from what they generally assume to be an Indian point of view, calling their poems "shaman songs," posturing as "shamans," and pontificating about their roles as remakers of the world through the power of their words, they seem to have no particular qualms about appropriating the transliterated forms of American Indian songs and poetry and then passing off their own poems based on those transliterations, as the pronouncements of "shamans." Thus, they "become" Indian by equating their poems with what they feel to be the intentions of the original singers. Anyone who has the slightest familiarity with an American Indian language, and is aware of the wide gap between the original work and the transliterations, can readily perceive the differences. But, unfortunately, non-Indian readers, who are used to seeing the transliterations, accord these newer productions as works of an authentic Indian consciousness.

What do I mean by a "white-shaman?" These are the apparently growing number of small-press poets of generally white, Euro-Christian American background, who in their poems assume the persona of the shaman, usually in the guise of an American Indian medicine man. To be a poet is simply not enough; they must claim a power from higher sources. As Gene Fowler says in a "shaman song" from his book *Fires* (Thorp Springs Press, 1972):

> My ancestors were shamans.
> But I am not my ancestors.
> I am shaman
> to a tribe recently come.

> * * * * *

> A tribe with fear of the Other.
> I wear animal skins
> and cast huge shadows on the wall.

Despite the remonstrations of several of the "white shamans" (including Fowler) that their usage of "shaman" is Siberian and not American Indian, the implication that they are modelling themselves after Indians seems clear in the excerpt from the above poem. I doubt very seriously if there is anything in their own cultural environments that really affords them such power, or even the access to such power, to say nothing of the spuriousness of their ancestors being shamans. Even the various dictionary definitions concerning the shaman or shamanism illustrates that there is little in the Euro-Christian American traditions to lend them ready access to shamanistic power.[1] Yet the second-rate efforts continue to pour forth:

> 1
> Come
> 2
> People of this place
> 3
> Come
> 4
> People of this place
> 5
> To the River
> 6
> To the place of the Bear
> 7
> To the place of the Snake

etc., etc., for another tedious forty-eight "stanzas."[2]

Non-Indian readers with little knowledge of American Indian cultures reading the foregoing poem are left with the impression that Indians, as they have always heard, are a people with a "simplistic" way of life. Such readers look at the "simple" phraseology and are further confirmed in that particular stereotype of the Indian — that of the Native American as a "child-like savage." The "white shaman," like other romanticists of the past, quite clearly sees the Indian as something exotic, and he oversimplifies in his efforts to extoll and imitate; unfortunately, when he views the Indian more closely, seeing the everyday occurrences, the prosaic and undramatic elements of small things conducted in almost unnoticeable ritual, he then refurbishes it all into more vivid productions. Pretty soon he has rewritten *Hiawatha* all over again, calling it now perhaps *Seven Arrows* or *Winterhawk* or one of the godawful Billy Jack movies — or "white shaman" poetry. Thus the resurrection of Romanticism, or the beginnings of Neo-Romanticism.

A serious problem involved here for Indian writers, as I see it, is the stone wall of public knowledge confronting them when they begin to put forth their own works based on what they know of their own particular tribal and cultural matrix. Since the American public has already become accustomed to seeing the Jerome Rothenberg "translations," the poetry of the "white shamans" such as Gary Snyder, Gene Fowler, Norman Moser, Barry Gifford, David Cloutier, to name a few, and other neo-romantic writers posing as Indians and/or Indian experts/spokesmen, such as Carlos Casteneda, Hyemeyohsts Storm, Tony Shearer, Doug Boyd, the Baha'i influenced "Indian" works of Naturegraph Publications,[3] contemporary Indian writers are often discounted or ignored since they are not following or conforming to the molds created by these "experts." Just as the "experts" at the turn of the century — the Bureau of American Ethnology writers (Boas, Swanton, Densmore, etc.), Clark Wissler, Theodore Roosevelt, Edward S. Curtis, Oliver LaFarge, etc. — were genuinely concerned with the "Vanishing American," as the American Indian was called then, so too, I believe, are these modern writers likewise concerned. But what is distressing is the fact that these contemporary writers, like the turn-of-the-century people, are often blind to actuality — that Indian cultures *still* exist, and most often, are in far different forms than those which they project in their writings and preachments. Strangely, the contemporary writers, especially the "white shamans," too often perceive Indian cultures through not only the rose-colored glasses of a white, Anglo-Saxon Protestant viewpoint, but the day-glo spectacles of a hastily assumed Oriental (Buddhist, Taoist, etc.) outlook.[4] My concern is not merely the cultural borrowing from Oriental cultures, which I suspect has been as imperialistically bowdlerized as the American Indian conscience (but I'll leave this to Alex Kuo, Frank Chin, and Lawson Inada to examine), but the manner in which outsiders presume to define Indian people and lifeways in an authoritative way. My concern, also, is for the great need which Indian people have of being the ones to speak for themselves, of being the ones to define themselves and their cultures. Quite simply, I believe Indian people are growing tired of the Oliver LaFarges and jerome Rothenbergs speaking for them — and making reputations and money at their expense — however honorable and sensitively felt the original intentions of these outsiders may have been.

Part of the "white shaman" thing is due largely, it seems, to the traditional American way of viewing Indians. Ten to fifteen years ago, white Americans, concerned about the rise of the Black Power movement, were asking the question, sometimes quite earnestly — "What do you people *want,* anyway?" or "Why all this rebellion and dissatisfaction?" Very few non-Indian Americans have bothered to ask these questions of Indian people today — if they have had occasion to reflect on our particular discontent at all. The reason for not asking us these questions, or at least comparable ones, seems to be that since Indians continue to exist almost totally in the minds of most Americans as an *idea* rather than a reality, it is therefore not essential to deal with Indians as people. As *idea,* everyone from early childhood, thanks to elementary school and Hollywood, has known about Indians, and thus all Americans are "experts" about Indians. The fact that these ideas are merely stereotypes is beside the point: nobody has to be told about Indians; everyone knows everything about them already! Indeed, it would be "un-American" not to know about Indians!

When Indian writers/scholars have sought to answer and correct the misconceptions about their people, they have often been smiled at rather patronizingly and then ignored. After all, most of them don't have Ph.D.'s or other academic credentials, and some, Heaven forbid, have only the barest elementary grade schooling[5] But the condescension hasn't come only from the academics and the Ph.D.'s. The self-appointed "white shamans," who incidentally make it part of their posture to sneer at Academia in their "return to the earth" nostalgia, also condescend in their recognition of "things Indian." In various letters and public readings, "white shaman" poets have scorned the bookishness and pedantry of the university-trained scholars — people for the most part, for good and for bad, who have at least gone into the field for their researches. These modern poets tend to scoff at this, using instead the arcane, exotic, half-baked works by non-Indian people published by other small presses. In reality, since the "white shaman" attains his knowledge totally from books, he is probably more "academic" than the BAE people at any rate.

An example of the imperious way of discounting what Indians relate about themselves and their cultures can be seen in how various non-Indian writers reacted to Rupert Costo's negative review of *Seven Arrows* (in *The Indian Historian,* Vol. 5, No. 2; Summer, 1972), and to what the Northern Cheyenne people themselves had to say about how they were offended by the book (*Wassaja,* Vol. 2, No. 4; April-May, 1974, and in *Wassaja,* Vol. 2, No. 7; August, 1974). Many non-Indians were so eager to defend *Seven Arrows* that what Costo and the Cheyennes had to say somehow became lost in all the noise. Since *Seven Arrows* seems to be so very much what the counter-culture wants to hear about Indians — full of peppermint and saccharine, Tantra-like day-glo art superimposed on traditional Plains Indian shield designs, and almost Kahlil Gibran in its message and tone — it is natural to expect the New Age hippies to yell loudly in its behalf, and to hell with how Indians feel about it.

It is interesting to note that two people who are allied with the "white shaman" fad—Gene Fowler and Jim Cody—have discounted the Cheyennes' complaints about the book. Cody, in particular, shrugged off Cheyennes as being "typical" of a Plains Indian tribe, "whose members generally don't agree on anything anyway."[6] Fowler, in a section of *Fires*, entitled *Shaman Songs*, seems to be the most vociferous in his claim to be a "shaman," but he is by no means the only one. In a series of incoherent letters in *Wood Ibis* and *Greenfield Review*, Fowler has proclaimed his "shamanism." In fact, he even begins one of his letters rather chummily by saying "Everyone of us is part Indian, yeh know. Some can trace that through a grandmother or grandfather to the Amerindian. Others across Europe to the Phoenicians (red men). In my case, it goes back to the owl in FOWLer. Magician in the workshop, as it were, hidden there, the skeleton of the shop."[7] Which does nothing to endear him to Indians, and certainly creates no sense of relationship with Indian people whatsoever.

The "white shaman" fad seems to have begun inadvertently with Gary Snyder in his "Shaman Songs" sections of *Myths and Texts*, in which the poet speaks through the persona of an Indian shaman, and his words become calls to power, of a sort, which in and of itself is innocuous enough, since poetry of this kind does seek to transcend the mundane in such a way that people's lives are revivified. The poems contain great vitality and are, I believe, sincere efforts on Snyder's behalf to incorporate an essential part of American Indian philosophy into his work. Importantly, nowhere does Snyder refer to himself as a "shaman." But, along came the bastard children of Snyder who began to imitate him, especially in the Shaman Songs section, and not being content with that, began to call themselves shamans—which, as I understand it, Snyder still refuses to do. Not so with Fowler, Cody, Norman Moser, and Barry Gifford—these are only a few with whose posturings I am familiar.

There have been various other literary fads which exploited Indians. Just as white liberals have their "dilemmas," and Blacks have their "problems," Indians have their "plight"—not the least of which has been the white American writer. Most of the stereotyping of Indians has been perpetuated by well-meaning writers in every century since America's "discovery." One of the silliest fads, before the current one, was the "death song" fad of the Romantic period in the early days of the American Republic. People such as Philip Freneau, Mrs. John Hunter, and Royall Tyler, in the period between 1780 and 1810, wrote gobs of these embarrassingly sentimental poems written from the viewpoint of a "dying" Indian chief or "maiden." That these poems had more in common with Greek and Latin orations and 18th century English drama, than the actual speeches of genuine Indians, is not surprising; nor is it surprising that few of these poems possess any literary merit at all. The fatuousness and pretentiousness of these lofty elegies have, I feel, much in common with the "white shaman" songs that are oozing onto the literary scene today—and have nothing in common with the actual Indian conscience.

The Southwestern and western tribes' most prevalent trickster persona—the coyote—has become a favorite guise for white writers to assume. These writers, like the hippie movement of which they are an unacknowledgeable part, are obsessed with Coyote now—writing "Tantras" about him, renaming him "Charle Kiot" in cutesy misspelling, finding him in every shadow of their lives. I'd be willing to bet that most of these guys, growing up in the 1950's, were once walking around, bored and sulking and pissed because they couldn't go to a Saturday matinee, carrying their .22's and taking potshots at coyotes—this their only association with coyotes—if they had any association with them at all. Nowadays, though, they are deifying Him, and, as with their understanding of Indian things, are calling themselves Coyote, just as some call themselves "Indians"—as though the greatest compliment that can be paid to Indians is to become Indians or Coyotes. I understand that the New Mexico poet John Brandi and fellow hippie communards up around Guadalupita are now calling themselves the "Coyote Tribe." It is also significant to note, as Lawrence Evers[8] has, that Gary Snyder, in his "Incredible Survival of Coyote," totally ignores what modern Indian writers such as Simon Ortiz, Leslie Silko, and Scott Momaday have done with Coyote in their works, and instead praises certain "white shamans" who have suddenly discovered Coyote.[9]

Shamanism, at least in the Indian way of using and making medicine, is a much larger thing than the poet who all of a sudden *decides* he is one. To be a medicine-maker in the tribes of my parents, the Cherokee and the Chickasaw, one — both men and women — has to be something of an apprentice for twenty years or more. Obviously, one can't simply and all of a sudden decide to be a shaman or a medicine-maker. He or she must have confirmation of the community, a great sense of the community, a profound knowledge of animals and plants, a knowledge of pain and suffering, and a sense of power that can be found only in an adherence to the old things. I know I do not have these powers, and I am Indian. Nor do most of the younger Indian writers that I know, nor would we call ourselves "shamans." For Leslie Silko, Joy Harjo, Simon Ortiz, Bill Oandasan, Joseph L. Concha, Ron Rogers, Goweitduweetza (Veronica Riley), Luci Cadzow, Larry Emerson, Gerald Wilkinson — any number of other Indian writers in the Southwest today—to suddenly declare themselves to be shamans would constitute an embarrassment both to themselves and to their friends and family. When an Indian is learning the medicine of his or her tribe, he or she is darned well not going to prance around spilling his guts about it, since (or at least in the Indian way that I know about) to tell about something to outsiders while it is in the process of being made, lessens both its value and its potential power, and cheapens it for the maker. White men seem to have a hard time understanding this.

The desire of "white shaman" poets to remake themselves into new personae seems to be an aspect of the "New Age" philosophy which posits that one can recreate one's karma, that one can assume a totally new consciousness. Missionaries such as Baba Ram Dass and Maharaji-Ji gleefully exhort the true believer-types to accept such a philosophy, but, I think it is absurd to think that if one has grown up in Oakland, California or Topeka, Kansas of Euro-Christian American heritage, has been weaned on and inured to American Bandstand and the Mickey Mouse Club, that one can, all of a sudden, through enlightenment, become Hindu boddhisatvas, Zen masters, or even

American Indian shamans. Thus, the shaman-singing of these poets becomes the cries of the culturally crippled. They are drowning men clutching at the straws of convenient cultures, as though to save themselves from their history. And I don't think it can be done. Such efforts to become new personae, replete with new racial or cultural backgrounds, not only cheapens the cultures which these true believers seek to join, but cheapens as well the culture from which they are fleeing. It should go without saying that the evasion of a culture's history and destiny, by those within it, is not a realistic way of understanding the past — or even the world. As Santayana said, (with a bit of paraphrasing) those who do not know their history, acknowledging and accepting it for what it is, are then doomed to repeat it — all good intentions to the contrary.

What, then, should be the roles for "white shamans?" Or for non-Indians who continue to have a genuine and sincere regard for Indian peoples and Indian cultures? First, obviously, is the need for them to restore themselves to their own houses—by learning and accepting their own history and culture. If it has become a tired stereotype to depict the Indian variously as a "red devil" or a "noble savage," it is likewise tedious for Indians to constantly lay guilt-instilling trips on whites. I am not suggesting that we, whites and Indians alike, turn our backs on history, pretending that that which happened did not happen, but, I am hoping that we can all learn to accept our histories— and our ancestors—for what they are and were.

Secondly, white men writing as Indian medicine-makers, whether as shamans or coyotes, must not continually denigrate their own cultural traditions. If one, then, is not a shaman, but nonetheless feels deeply the dictates of his calling as a poet — he should content himself with being a poet. (Anyway, I've yet to see the various shenanigans of ''white shamans'' at poetry readings or on the printed page do the things that Indian medicine-makers can do.) Or, if one is not content to be called a poet, if he is from the white Euro-Christian American tradition, he might consider calling himself a bard, or a skald, or a scop, or a troubadour, or even a minstrel![10] These terms were in usage in the early centuries of the emerging European nations; they were used to describe the poet or singer in ways which the continual impoverishment of modern English makes difficult for us to understand today. As a matter of fact, Bob Dylan has been referred to recently as a bard — and I, for one, would certainly accord him that title. Shakespeare, Blake, Ronsard, Villon, Dylan Thomas, Keats — all have been called bards, or troubadours, or even singers. To me, Gary Snyder — one of the finest poets in America today when he is not pontificating about Indian things — is a bard. Shaman, he is not. Nor are Fowler and Moser and company. But, I suppose as long as second-raters continue to name themselves ''shamans,'' to bless themselves mightily through their efforts to become something they are not and can never hope to be, then Indians will still have a ''white problem'' to deal with — another aspect of our ''plight.''

ENDNOTES

1. For example, in *Webster's New Collegiate Dictionary* (1968), *Shaman* is shown to have evolved from Russian, and from Tungusic *samān*, and perhaps, even ultimately from Sanskrit *sŕamana* — meaning beggar monk. Its current meaning seems to be "a priest or conjurer of shamanism; loosely, a medicine man." Shamanism, in the same dictionary, is defined as "primarily, the primitive religion of the Ural-Altaic peoples of northern Asia and Europe, in which the unseen world of gods, demons, and ancestral spirits is conceived to be responsive only to the shamans. Hence, any similar religion, especially that of the American Indians." Funk & Wagnall's *Standard College Dictionary* (1963) confirms these definitions, adding only the word "wizard" in regard to the shaman.

2. Laurence S. Fallis. "The Mississippi River; Effigy Mounds National Monument, Marquette, Iowa. (The Shaman's Song)." *Wood Ibis 2*, Summer, 1975.

3. Castaneda's Don Juan books are, of course, "in" right now, and everyone looks toward the missionary-like Don Juan persona for ways to get turned on, another aspect of instant enlightenment, convinced that all Indians are spending their time getting spaced-out on exotic drugs. It seems to be only Indians who are seriously asking: what's Indian about these books? And non-Indians are asking: why have you Indians kept this *pi-yote* to yourselves all these years? Doug Boyd's *Rolling Thunder* is the bastardized testament of a supposed Cherokee medicine man which I would recommend the reader take with a salt-shaker; it also appears to be Random House's attempt to cash in on Simon & Schuster's good fortune with Don Juan. Tony Shearer's works, *The Lord of the Dawn* and *The Praying Flute,* are extremely eccentric in their hippie-like sweetness. Many of Naturegraph's Indian writers have had their works rewritten from a Baha'i point of view. Read a few and you will see what I mean.

4. For instance, Tom Tarbet's "The Hopi: At the Heart of the World," (*East-West Journal,* Vol. 5, No. 7: July 15, 1975) is a typical myopic view of an Indian culture. He says at one point in the essay: "I know of no books on 'Indians' that adequately explain the Hopi way of life. Perhaps the best clues available are in the *Tao Teh Ching* and the *I-Ching,* from ancient China." To an Indian, this statement and attitude is not radically different from the early Christian missionaries who saw the Indians' "Great Spirit" only in terms of their own "Almighty God." The point, of course, is for the outsider to look at the culture at hand without cluttering it up with his own strongly held religious principles—to see it on its own terms.

5. Helen M. Bannan's trenchant article in *Christian Science Monitor* (November 10, 1975; page B-9) entitled " 'New Kind of Indian History' Disturbs Academia" examines the phobia and uneasiness of university "experts" as they are now being confronted with histories and tribal accounts written by the peoples of the tribes concerned.

6. See *Wood Ibis 1,* (Spring, 1975), Cody's letter to Gene Fowler. *Wood Ibis* seems to have become a favorite nesting-ground for "white shaman" writers. It is subtitled "A Journal of Contemporary Shamanism" and, so far, its two issues have included several made-to-order "shaman songs."

7. From *Greenfield Review* (Vol. 4, Nos. 3 & 4), 1975.

8. Lawrence J. Evers. "Further Survivals of Coyote," *Western American Literature* (Vol. 10, No. 3), pp. 233-236.

9. Gary Snyder. "Incredible Survival of Coyote," *Western American Literature* (Vol. 9, No. 4), pp. 255-272.

10. From Funk & Wagnall's *Standard College Dictionary* again. *Bard*—1. a Celtic poet and minstrel. 2. A poet. Synonym: 1. Bard, skald, scop, trouvere—denotes poets who, at different times and in different lands, wrote and sang of historical and legendary events. The bards were ancient Welsh and Irish poets, but the word has now been extended to include all who write verses to be recited or sung. The skalds were ancient Scandinavians, the scops Anglo-Saxons, and the trouveres roamed northern France from the 11th century to the 14th century. (Compare minstrel, troubadour, poet.)

Joy Harjo

3 AM
in the albuquerque airport
trying to find a flight
to old oraibi, third mesa
TWA
        is the only desk open
bright lights outline new york,
                                chicago
and the attendant doesn't know
that third mesa
is a part of the center
of the world
and who are we
just two indians
at three in the morning
trying to find a way back

and then i remembered
that time simon
took a yellow cab
out to acoma from albuquerque
a twenty five dollar ride
to the center of himself

3 AM is not too late
to find the way back.

TOO FAR INTO ARIZONA

they found him
crumbled in a dusty boxcar
several miles into Arizona
        at the end of a Santa Fe track
stale wine and blood
were his last bed
        the yellow vultured sun
        had circled for ten years
        but had smelled the death
                in a broken man's song

the last song

how can you stand it
he said
the hot oklahoma summers
where you were born
this humid thick air
is choking me
and i want to go back
to new mexico

it is the only way
i know how to breathe
an ancient chant
that my mother knew
came out of a history
woven from wet tall grass
in her womb
and i know no other way
than to surround my voice
with the summer songs of crickets
in this moist south night air

oklahoma will be the last song
i'll ever sing

SOMEONE TALKING

Language is movement.
They watch the glittering moon
from the front porch in Oxford, Iowa.
Which reservation
in this river of star motion?
The man of words sits next to
Nonnie Daylight,
listening this time.

> Tequila, a little wine, and she
> remembers some Old Crow, yellow
> in a fifth on the drainboard. She
> thinks of Hobson in Oklahoma. And
> how he ducked behind the truck with
> her the summer powwow for a drink.
> Where is the word for a warm night
> and how it continues to here, a
> thousand miles from that time?

Milky Way.
And there are other words
in other languages. Always
in movement. He touches
her back where her hair
reaches to the middle. There
is that gesture and the
crickets voice beginning.
All in the same circle of space.
Maybe the man of words speaks
like the cricket.
Nonnie Daylight
hears him that way.

> It is along the Turner Turnpike
> between Tulsa and Oklahoma City, she
> tells him,
> where they have all those signs,
> Kickapoo, Creek,
> Sac and Fox.
> Dating the beginning and end
> of the United States recognition
> of tribal histories.
> And hell,
> where is Hobson now
> when she needs and tastes
> the Old Crow.
> Yellow fire all the way into
> her belly.
> The way they meant it.

They have maps
named after Africa and the blue oceans.
Sky circles the other way
but she doesn't feel dizzy.
Stars in the dark are clear
not blurred, and the earth's movement
is a whirring current in the grass.
The man of words outlines wet islands
with his lips
on Nonnie Daylight's neck.

> She got stopped outside
> of Anadarko once.
> Red lights.
> You must be Indian, said
> the Oklahoma Highway Patrol.
> Of course they knew the history
> before switching on the lights.
> And when they rolled open the truck
> in the moist night,
> Was only going home,
> She said.

What voice
in the warm grass of her belly,
What planet?

Raven Hail

DANAGA ECHODIYI
(The War Woman of Chota)
NANCY WARD

In the year 1738 in the heart of the Cherokee Country, there was much excitement in the small village among the Wolf Clan. A new baby girl had just arrived, and the Grandmother was deciding on a name—with, of course, suggestions from all the female members of the Clan. This child was the sister of Tuskeegeeteehee (Creek Warrior Killer—sometimes called Longfellow) and the niece of the famed Attakullakulla. Because it was the Season of Many Leaves, a time when the flowers appear; and because her father was an Officer in the British Army, it was decided that she should be called "The White Rose".

She grew up a long-stemmed American Beauty Rose, and Chadlv (Kingfisher) of the Deer Clan laid the deer before her lodge. She responded with the customary ear of corn; and soon presented him with a daughter, Catherine, and a son, Hiskyteehee (Fivekiller).

During the long bloody war with the Creek Indians, she fought alongside her husband. He was killed at the Battle of Taliwa in 1755; she took up his rifle and led the charge that brought about the defeat of the Creeks. At the Victory Dance following this battle she was given the new name of DANAGA (War Woman). She was also privileged to share in the spoils of war, and upon distribution of the prisoners she became one of the first slaveholders in the Cherokee Nation.

She was a close relative of Bryan Ward, who was a Trader among the Indians in his youth and who later settled down with his wife and children in South Carolina. She chose the name Nancy Ward for her white name—from the family names of her white relatives; and thus her name has been recorded. For no self-respecting Cherokee would have her real name bandied about in public. She married a second time, and had a daughter, Betsy Ward. She and Betsy often visited the Wards, and were graciously received.

During the Revolutionary War, she remembered that she was half white. When the Iroquois Confederation, headed by Cornstalk, brought the war belts for the British cause, three Cherokee Chiefs accepted, and struck the war pole against the group of White Settlers who had persistently refused to move from the Cherokee lands. Danaga helped prepare the Qualoga (black drink) for the purification of the warriors at the War Dance. She then secretly sent word to the settlers that the Cherokees were planning a surprise attack, thereby turning the expected victory into a bloody rout. For such loyalty, the White-Eyes conferred upon her the title of "Beloved woman" (Ghigau).

The War Woman was the Ambassador of Peace. She was a connecting link between the Cherokees and the Settlers, and was quick to make use of her knowledge of the outside world. She started raising cattle and making use of dairy products; and smoothed the way for trading corn and other native products for manufactured articles. At the Hopewell

Treaty Council she presented gifts of wampum strings and tobacco and she represented the Cherokees at other councils. She at all times admonished The People to hold fast to their lands and to have no part of the "paper talks" which signed away their rights. She firmly believed in the integrity of the president—that he would never knowingly allow The People to be cheated.

She died in 1822 and was buried on the crest of a hill near Benton, Tennessee. The family of Mrs. Wm. Bean, whom she had rescued from burning at the stake, commissioned a statue of her and shipped it down the river on a flatboat; but it went astray along the way and ended up as a marker for an unknown grave. The Cherokees named War-Woman Creek for her, and Benton named a school for her. In October, 1923, The Nancy Ward Chapter of the Daughters of the American Revolution placed a stone marker on her grave with a bronze tablet inscribed to the:

PRINCESS AND PROPHETESS OF THE CHEROKEE NATION
THE POCOHONTAS OF TENNESSEE
THE CONSTANT FRIEND OF THE AMERICAN PIONEER

LEGEND OF THE CHEROKEE ROSE

The Old Ones say that long, long ago in the Year of the Big Harvest, the land of the Cherokees was becoming too densely populated and they realized they must spread out into neighboring lands in order to grow and prosper. The Peace Chief sent out a party of the leading men of the Nation to talk with the neighboring Creeks, who claimed vast areas of land which would be suitable. The Creeks were not as strong as the Cherokees; they had been at war for a long time.

The Cherokees sat in Council with the Creeks to arrange the terms of the exchange of territory. This Council lasted for many days, for there were many amenities to be observed. It is polite to sit in complete silence at the beginning. First the Medicine Man must enact the lengthy Invocation; then the Peace Pipe Ceremony must be performed. The Pipe is passed leisurely around to each member in turn. Some elaborate speeches of greeting and the presentation of gifts must express the good will of the visitors. These must be answered by the hosts. All this must not be hurried, lest it appear that they were eager to get the business over with and go on home. At the end of each day, the Creeks prepared an elaborate feast which was served by the young maidens. The most beautiful maiden of them all was the Daughter of the Chief.

— — —

In the ranks of the Cherokee group was Little Hawk, nephew and heir of one of the powerful Red Chiefs. The first night he sat long around the campfire composing a love song. The next afternoon he did not appear at the Council meeting. He was playing the new song on his flute near the lodge of the Chief of the Creeks.

They met in secret and enjoyed the thrill of a forbidden adventure. They gathered wildflowers; they waded barefoot across the stream following after the shrill cry of the blue jay. He told her of the land of his people, where the sun is always shining and the cold winds never blow. He knew that he was expected to choose a wife from the proper Clan of an important Cherokee Village, thus increasing the power and solidarity of the Nation. But the Redbird Spirit of Love pays no heed to the notions of nations, and fluttered at the breast of the young Muskokee maiden, the Daughter of the Chief.

The young lovers finally agreed that when the Council was ended, and his people went on their way, he would come for her. They planned that if he should be detained, she would hide in the thicket at the bend of the river, and he would come for her there.

— — —

The Creeks agreed to move back past the banks of the Chattahoochee to allow for the expansion of the Cherokee Nation. Some of the Creek Warriors objected to the trading away of their lands and wanted to fight for it, but the Chief could see that there was no chance of saving the land. He argued that it was better to trade it away than to lose it, along with many lives. So when the Cherokees had left, and the Daughter of the Creek Chief was missing, the Creek Warriors joined in the search for her. Unfortunately, they were the first to find her hiding place.

When the Little Hawk arrived, he found her—dead. He buried her there, and, rejoining his own group, started the long journey homeward. He returned the next Spring and found among the bright green leaves that grew over the mound the tender white petals of the wild rose. He knelt beside it and called it *The Rose of the Cherokee*, for he had claimed her for his own. He carried it back to his home and planted it. But long before the long winter was over he grew eager to see the blossoms again; so he went back to her grave and waited until death came.

The flowers spread throughout the land of the Cherokees and to this day, the Cherokee rose is the first flower to bloom—her eager face opening early in Spring to welcome the return of her loved one.

RITUAL TO INSURE LONG LIFE

Hear me!
Now you are drawn near to hear me,
O Long man.
Let the troubled waters be still
And hear me, O Fountain of Life,
Whose flow with the life-blood commingles;
And from whose grasp there is no escape.
Clasp firmly my soul.
From the cataract yonder
Where, I, too, was born,
I reach out to you.
I submerge myself in your body.
The white foam will cling to my head
And the white staff will be at my hand.
The Ancient White will linger beside me
In the journey onward and upward at last
Unto the Seventh Heaven.
Ee-yah!

CHEROKEE INVOCATION

Sge!

Hisgaya Galunlati,
Great Father of Earth-People here,
Mighty Owner of Lands and all Waters
Who sends forth the Harvest each year;

Creator of all the Wild Creatures,
The Willow, the Wren and the Bear,
The Master of Thunder and Lightning,
Of the Wind and the Rain and the Air;

Hear me,

Iya!

Hear my prayer!

THE TIGER

Once there was a Girl-Child,
A slight *Gehyuja*, Girl-Child,
A white and golden Girl-Child,
Who played by the river side.

She was dearly loved by her Mother,
And pampered and spoiled by her Father,
The fair-haired child of all others
That lived by the river side.

One day there came a Tiger,
A sleek *Tladatz*, Tiger,
A bold and brawny Tiger,
To drink at the river side.

The Girl-Child saw the Tiger,
Oh, wild and willful Tiger!
And longed to hold the Tiger
There by the river side.

So she built a snare of brambles,
And caught him fast in the brambles,
In a cage of the strongest brambles,
Bound, by the river side.

Now, you cannot cage a Tiger,
Nor make a pet of a Tiger;
The fierce and fiery Tiger
Is King, at the river side.

But the Tiger loved the Girl-Child,
So fiercely loved the Girl-Child,
That he stayed in the cage by the Girl-Child,
By the river side----and died.

Ronald Rogers

SANDIA CREST

Cloudbanks move like turtles,
Rainswollen and silver, slitted with sunlight.
Mountains, dark with moisture and pine,
Jut massively into the soft grey belly,
The slow-moving belly of the sky.

JICARILLA IN AUGUST

An elk's head, severed and mummified, hangs on the
                    wall above the chairs, the round tables.
His glass eyes watch the lake, the water-cut roads with
                                        mud axle-deep.
He remembers meat and potatoes that swell the belly.
Food, sunset, then dawn.
The day begins.
The country opens. Grasses bend round cedar poles.
The stripped poles cross, thong and nail secured, the
                            shelters yawn vacant.
On metallic noises of coffee at daybreak, the dog barks,
                            and pulls his chain.
His neck bleeds.
Great rocks warm to the sunlight, and hold it.
Day begins with stories, told like trophies, of feast
                        days and dance.

BUS

A highway runs across the desert, a black,
Rulerthin scab. Along it, a bus crawls.
The passengers read, or sing, or take pictures
As they move along on a dog's back
Across the sand and mesquite and silence.

John F. Kerr

Bronze Tablets!

You'd think the Indians
   hadn't lived here
   ten-thousand years!
What of their chipped stones?
Their slivers of worked bone?

There's nothing shabby about
   bronze tablets!
They stand tall in the rain.
Going sixty miles an hour,
   you can see them.
No need to read the words—
Just so you know something
   happened once
On that last curve.

NOTES TO JOANNE, LXI

When my father took me to Caraway
To see the Sunday ballgames,
I was at the limits of the known world.
We always rode in the back of somebody's farm truck,
   a cloud of dust billowing up behind.
I stood on my knees,
Braced against the bumps in the road,
And watched the broad green fields,
The farm houses with tall shade trees
   and big front porches.
Women in print dresses sat in porch swings,
   fanning with palm-leaf fans,
And men hunkered on the doorsteps,
   smoking.
The driver honked his horn at dogs and chickens.

The graveled parking lot outside the ballpark
Was a miracle of cars and trucks.
We sat in the bleachers
And my father always bought me a box of Cracker-Jacks
   from the vendor.
There was always a toy inside,
Like a green tin frog that clicked
   when you squeezed it.

I always became restless
And wandered out to play in the parking lot.
I sat on running boards of A-model cars,
Fingered chrome grills and hood ornaments,
And stood on running boards to look in
At the strange array of dashboards.
Sometimes, if no one was in sight,
I reached in and pushed the horn.

The parking lot was graveled with rocks
    half the size of eggs
Hauled in from gravel pits far to the west
    of our Mississippi Valley world.
I always filled my pockets with rocks
    to take home.
Sometimes I found dogs to pet,
Sometimes other boys to talk to,
And once three teenage girls scared me
    half to death
By offering me a penny to see my peter.

The gravel was cluttered with bottle caps
And crushed cigarettes and popsickle sticks,
And sometimes I found toys thrown away from
    Cracker-Jack boxes.
Once I found a little doll, too big for
    a Cracker-Jack box,
Made of pink-dyed straw.
For a long time, I carried it in my hand,
Loving the beautiful shade of pink
And sad that I was a boy and couldn't keep it.
How I wish now that you were the little girl
    in a pinafore
That I gave it to when the game was over
And people came streaming out into the parking lot.
And how I wish you could have gone home with me
To sit on the front porch after dark
And strike my rocks against an old steel bolt
    to make sparks in the night.

NOTES TO JOANNE, LXIII

Coming out of darkness,
Crossing the continental divide
With the first pink faint glow
    in the eastern sky,
Stopping for gas at a station that a
    black man runs
Here in this Indian country of New Mexico.

Driving on at seventy miles an hour,
Passing swiftly through the black, crumpled
    lava fields
That have baked here in the noon sun
    before man walked the earth.
Watching the sun rise,
The big red glowing ball in the eastern sky
And the black lava on the valley floor
    between the mesas,
Crumpled and buckled where the earth has
Washed from underneath and let it drop.

What a strange climate it must have been
When the hot earth broke open,
Before there was man,
And spewed out its hot liquids.
How the night must have glowed and rumbled
As the red lava belched up
And flowed down this long valley.
And now, after the August rains,
Green grasses grow in the sponge-like
    crevices of black lava,
And the Indian cattle graze in the pink dawn.
And here and there a sunflower stands
With its yellow head facing east
    to the rising sun.

Driving on, seventy miles an hour,
Passing the Indian huts,
The old traditional stone square buildings.
Knowing that the lava fields were here
    before they came to claim them.
And the strange anomalous sight of mobile homes
With the tight, small corrals full of
    spotted Indian ponies.

Then suddenly changing lanes
To avoid the smashed deer,
Smeared in its own red blood,
And knowing that only yesterday
He too saw the bright sun rise
Over these black lava fields
    between the tall mesas.

We call this our land,
But the green grasses found it first,
And then the insects and the lizards
    and the deer.
They were here perhaps a million years
Before men built their baked mud towers
In Babylon to talk to God.

Traveling east at seventy miles an hour
Through these black lava fields
Touched with the green of grasses and the
    pink of the rising sun.
Traveling east between the tall mesas
Through the black lava fields from an
    old, old time
Before the red man came to claim them,
Before the white man came to build his roads,
Before the black man came to sell his gas to travelers.
Traveling east at seventy miles an hour,
I felt like some ancient Hebrew shepherd boy
Standing after a night alone with the bright stars
    to watch the miracle of sunrise.

Passing on out of the valley
And into a land where scrub cedars
Grow between the humpy knolls that
    once were mesas.
And now and again a big green sign
With white letters telling how far it is
    to Albuquerque.
Such a strangely new and unexpected thing
    a city is
When one comes out of darkness
And travels east at sunrise.

After breakfast, I stood at a table of
    "Indian Curios"
While two men at the counter with a small radio
Listened to stock-market quotations.
I held the objects and turned them
And on the backs of some, I found the words,
    made in the Philippines.
I didn't buy them.
I'll leave this Indian country with no souvenirs
Except the bright memory of having once
Traveled eastward out of darkness.

NOTES TO JOANNE, LXIV

When I came out of the package liquor store
Last night in Santa Rosa, New Mexico,
    with my six-pack of Coors,
A guy in a red Mustang was pulling in to park.
He was obviously drunk.
He opened the door and tried to step
    out of the car
But he forgot to unfasten his seatbelt.
He struggled and squirmed and lurched his
    shoulders forward,
And then he began to cry and scream
And tell the world that he was suddenly paralyzed.

NOTES TO JOANNE, LXVI

The world turned green again
A few miles eastward into Oklahoma,
And I saw knee-high cotton with white blooms.
Then I saw a big signboard with bright letters
    that read,
Seven miles ahead to the Cherokee Restaurant.
And then in smaller letters down below,
Hot Mexican Food.
What in the Goddamned Hell are the Cherokees doing
Serving Mexican food, I'd like to know!
I've been part Cherokee for forty-three years,
And just once in my life I'd like to eat
    some Cherokee food.

I stopped at the restaurant,
And the waitress brought me a glass of water
    and said she was Irish,
And the man at the counter beside me said
The place was owned by a New York Jew.
I'm part Jew and part Irish too,
And so I ordered the damned Mexican food
    and enjoyed it.

And on my way out,
I stopped at the curio table
And thumbed through a Cherokee cookbook.
There were all of my mother's old recipes
For squash and cornbread and succotash.

NOTES TO JOANNE, LXXIV

When my daddy turned the land each spring
    with his breaking plow,
He turned up chunks of roots from the giant trees
That stood there tall and full of birds
    when Columbus sailed.
He'd hitch Dan and Nancy to the wagon
And drive across the soft gray loam,
    gathering up the chunks.
He'd drive the wagon to our back yard.
He'd stand in the wagon with his legs wide
And hurl the big yellow chunks to a pile
    of wood
Beside the black, iron wash pot.
They dried out in the summer sunshine,
And my mother burned them under the pot
    to boil our clothes.

After the first rain,
We found arrow heads that he'd turned up
  in the plowing.
Our farm was an ancient hunting ground
  for another people.
The Cherokee blood flows in the veins of all
  my family,
And yet the arrow heads were silent relics
  from an unknown world.
I felt them cold in my palm with a baffled sense
  of kinship.

Not many miles away,
A farmer's plow turned up a strange stone head.
He tied up his team,
And hurried to his back yard,
And pumped water on the gray stone face
  to wash it clean.

Through all the years,
I've paused at unexpected times
And seen the stack of yellow chunks
  by the blackened pot,
Felt the cold stone of arrow heads,
And stared at the changeless features
  of that gray stone face.
I strain my ears,
And I seem to hear the far-off sounds of people
  too faint to understand.

Norman H. Russell

Two Circles

there are two circles
the men make a circle in the center
around the large fire
behind them the women make a circle
in the cold shadows

the men speak much wisdom
they make all the laws
they make all the decisions
then they look behind them to the women

if the women shake their heads
the men must begin again.

The Words

it is not the words of the chant
that make the prayer
it is the way they are said
that reaches gods ear

it is the same with you and me
it is not the words we say
each to the other
it is how we say them

a good chant
grows and grows with the singing
a good talk
comes from a singing heart.

old men climbing

the trees along this high ridge
are like old men climbing
hunched over
their backs to the devil wind
their torn blankets blowing before
and some of them
have fallen to their knees
and then they crawl on a little way
and go no further
but i go on
clinging to rocks
so the wind will not take me away
and i come to the meadow
there are tracks of elk
white birds watch me
yellow flowers bloom
a cloud speaks in a loud voice
snow stings my face
i go down below now
looking back from time to time.

I DO NOT WISH TO BE OLD

this is a hard gettingup morning
this is a falling against trees morning
i am not able to wait the sun anymore
but must rise in the dark before all wakings

my knees are weak my head spins a little
it will pass i am not ready to crawl yet
i fight with stones and shrubs to find the stream
i am even angry with the quiet water

i do not understand this i do not wish to be old
my limbs sleep and will not obey me anymore
but deep within me life still flames
i turn and burn with a terrible quiet sound.

a great mosquito dance

i look down from the high bank
eaten with dirt caves below
close to the crumbling edges
and see that the talking river
is brown and angry and has risen
above the beaver dam and roars
with a low grumbling and eats
great mouthfuls of mud

and skimming sliding over his back
a great cloud of swallows
white and green are dancing
a great mosquito dance
their flying is so swift and true
the air may hold them tightly
and as i look down on them
they become a single great bird.

Gogisgi / Carroll Arnett

THE STORY OF MY LIFE

Down there where I was
born and reared on

Oklahoma red dirt,

a whirling wind came
out of the east, took

me from the land

my grandfather drank
up, gambled away, land

he stole from the Cherokee

woman he married—an
only memory of her in her

near blindness scraping

the floral design on
her dinner plate—that wind

carried me all the way

to California to dive-bomb
cigarette butts, to fight

the Battle of Tiajuana

whorehouses *semper
fidelis, semper*—another

dry wind took me

north to go drunk, go to
school, study long-range

genetic effects of driving

with a cold beer bottle
between one's legs, to think of

waking in the morning

knowing that's as good as
you're going to feel all

day long, knowing

the pure-dee truth of
a friend's saying,

A slave is anyone

who waits for someone
else to set him free—

took me north

to make a name (there stood
Jesus laughing to beat all,

saying, man, you sure

got your work cut out
for you)—sentenced to

upper midwestern land-

grant learneries by
way of Missouri at whose

world's fair Goyathlay

had signed autographs
for 10 cents apiece, being

allowed to keep half

for his own self—then
back east to Maine

where both the land and

those living on it are
too good to be true,

though progress throbs

all through the night—again
north among Ojibwe women

who still tell children,

"If ya don't be real real
good, Grandmother Spider'll

come down from Canada

and put medicine on ya."
Yet further on to Pig's Eye,

Minnesota, where at

the trials of Dennis and Russell
U.S. marshals wear

small green and yellow

diamond-shaped lapel pins
and get a hardon each

time the .357 Magnums

jounce snug against their
hips. Not wanting to

travel, I have travelled.

I have never been
a homeowner, have

always been a tenant,

will always be
a tenant and hold

as much as I can.

POWWOW

Hair the color of
tobacco ash, the fair lady
anthro asked, Excuse
me please, . . . sir
(guess it beats Chief),

does that red patch
on your blanket symbolize
something?

            Yes mam,
it surely does, it
symbolizes that once
upon a time there
was a hole
in the blanket.

uwohali

grandfather eagle
which art in heaven
thou soarest in heaven
thou makest my blood
to sing sing
sing

TLANUWA

for Hawk LittleJohn

When he first walked in
to our camp I thought,
Well he's younger than
I'd expected from the stories
I'd heard. Then for the rest
of the day he told his own
stories, of the deer he
had hamstrung with his
last arrow and had finally
taken with a stick, of
sewing up his killdog
who'd been ripped by a bobcat,
of the Natchez people who left
sacred marks at Paint Rock
on the Long Lady, of our own
people coming from Blue Wall
to Qualla, of his grandmother
who taught him every
thing he knows of women
and of men—all this time,
the whole day (even
when we came to his house
and Rose told us about
the white hill people's
shootout the night before
—four shot, one dead,
another dying)—all
this time his eyes told
another story, one
older than our people or
the Natchez, older
than the Long Lady,
a quiet story that goes
on forever and ever.

THE OLD MAN SAID: TWO

The wisdom of an
animal may be
measured by
the quantity of its
excrement.
       See
how little of his
waste brother deer
leaves behind.

ROADMAN

Unelanvhi save us
from
the Whiskey People

a button instead
of booze

a button
instead

a button
another

button
instead

not the blood
of the lamb

another button
instead

EARLY SONG

As the sun rises
high enough to
warm the frost
off the pine needles,

I rise to make
four prayers of
thanksgiving for
this fine clear day,

for this good brown
earth, for all
brothers and sisters,
for the dark blood

that runs through me
in a great circle
back into this
good brown earth.

HOMAGE TO ANDREW JACKSON

May you, after 140
years, still fry
in your own
coonskin
hell, you
mother
fucker.

Sandie Nelson

RUINS

There is no loneliness
like this. I am surrounded
by these rocks, they are chanting.
They have each other to listen.
What people is it
who would leave me here?
My body is the only light in this night.
Except for that my life is nothing.
I have always belonged
to these walls of bones.

MIGRATION

All I know
is when we
came from
middle earth
our brother
the dog (my father still holds him sacred)
told us where to go next
with the help of a stick.
In the morning
we would follow
the dog in the way
the stick pointed.
We crossed waters
and hills and finally
we stopped. Some of us
went back to where
we'd started -- but some
of us stayed where
the dog took us.

CALIFORNIA POEM

(for Dan Todachine)

Your name means
"bitter water" and oh
the nights we tasted that
making us wash our mouths
for days afterwards.

But there were also nights
I'd braid your hair
for the squaw dance.
I could hear your singing
in The Place Where Trees Circle.

I think you forgot
all that in L.A.
You brought your braids
home in a paper sack -
a curious souvenir.

That last night in Taos
I saw you arched
against interminable sky
your chant floating down
to the springs
where I waited for you
to come home.

Barney Bush

Daylight no longer comes
   it is left in another
   morning
   leaves shudder at the
   coming of frost
Lake--the liquid sky
   waxen darkness but moving
   and in life
   but aware of betrayal
   by midnight eyes
   that have left my
   innocence cold and ashen
I was watching and
   believing in imaginary
   mornings
   hailing them with songs
   and the touch of my
   fingers
   yet the chimook still
   wins at conquering
   my peace
My hands will stay clenched
   at my side
   until I can escape
   for home away from
   lips that purse in lies
   until I feel the morning
   light dawning through
   the forks of my arms--.

The boy of summer
   was the same--
   lightning in
cement darkness
   brought him out
   to watch the rain--
   rain in swirling currents
washing over the edge
washing away darkness
   and the summer
   flowing over the edge
   of autumn
Long hair whipped
   around his face
   stripping his stare
   of many summers ago

and the fleeting images
   that loped through
   fields of sage and
   sundown making prisms
   through raindrops that
   cling to yellow grass
Rumbling thunder
   came back to him
   too often
   Even in his sleep
   he could still hear
the jingles on her dress.

Powwow
and I am in your
   north country again
   great beauty that holds
   the medicine to make
   people crazy
I look for you in the
   early morning cause
   I didn't 49 last night
   they say you will be
   coming--
In the dust around
   the arena or somewhere
   in woodsmoke
   I'll sort of be watching
   --we both know--
   about how nights turn cold
   the leaves fall too soon
   and the grey mystery
   of glancing at each other
over pool tables and
   jukeboxes
It was a good foreign
   feeling   walking up the
   street carrying food
   orange maple leaves falling
   at our feet
and a carload of
   Oklahoma Indians
   pull up--want to know
   what we're doing
   a good feeling the
   cold lake country
   where I keep missing
   you
and hear only rumors
after you've gone------------.

Carter Revard

Ponca War Dancers

1.

When Uncle Gus came to visit
  his nephew Buck's new wife
she was so polite and nice
    he really liked her very much—
but she talked directly to him,
  and that's not right
  in Ponca ways;
still, he just ignored her efforts
  at conversation,
          or spoke to Buck for her to overhear,
until one day with Buck at work
  she asked Uncle Gus to carry groceries
  into the house—
and that was when he quietly
  left Kansas City,
though she could never figure out
  what she had done
till finally Aunt Jewell had to explain.

2.

He was the greatest of Ponca dancers
  yet when he came to see
some of my white uncles
      and they went off to drink
how come I never understood
  he was a champion
 but saw a heavy-bellied
  quick-talking man
that kids swarmed round,
  full of jokes and laughter,
  never seemed to brawl or argue—
till at the Osage dances one June when he
  was sixty-something
 I saw him dance for the first time
and everybody got quiet
  except to whisper
  "the champion"—
and here came Uncle Gus
 potbellied but quick-footed went
  twirling and drifting,
   stomping with the
    hawkwing a-hover then
              leaping

spinning light as
   a leaf in a whirlwind
     the anklebells shrilling, dancing
the Spirit's dance
   in a strange land where
he had gone and fasted
   and found his vision
  to lead his people
but had nowhere to lead them except
   into white ways,
    so here he danced
  in Wahkondah's circle
  drum at the center
 the old songs being sent up
in the brilliant bugfilled light
       among bleachers and tourists
and the grave, merry faces
Osage and Ponca, Otoe and Delaware,
Quapaw and Omaha, Pawnee Comanche and Kaw,
  who saw what he was doing
and how he did it well even when
 to the white eyes watching he was
 an old Indian slowing down
     and between dances going
 to have another slug of
hell, maybe Old Crow or even
        Canadian Club,
 good enough for the Champion.

3.

A year after Wounded Knee
   it was his memorial feast they held
down in Ponca City, in the auditorium
we had to drive around to find
  (White Eagle grounds being used
   for another Ponca funeral then)—
and I drove in to it with the sons and daughters
  of his sister Jewell,
      all strong in AIM,
          and some just back
from a confrontation down in Pawnee trying
  to keep some AIM supporters
   from being evicted out of their own houses,
drove with my cousins Carter and Craig and Dwain and Serena,
  none of them underground yet
   from Wounded Knee, nor the helicopters sweeping
the Okie hills once more for them as they would be
next year, as back in the Thirties the marshals in V-8 Fords
  had swept the backroads hunting
  their dad, Uncle Woody, when he was hiding
out down by Buck Creek on bootlegging charges, catching catfish
  but letting the big bass get away—

                                        Jesus, think
      of that "Gatsby" bunch in the Thirties making bootleg stuff
    up in Canada, and running it down to Boston, making their
              family fortune so big
        while Uncle Woody was facing jail for the same white lightning,
    and think how in the Nineteen Seventies those same "Gatsbys"
          had got so rich they'd be marrying off into
            some British titled family
        about the time when Uncle Woody
                was just thumbing his rides along
    the roads, this time from California
            eastward to join his sons at Wounded Knee—but that's
          American history for you, and here on the way to Uncle Gus's
        memorial feast, *we* weren't in trouble,
            just driving all crowded up
                in my old Dart,
      with Stephanie from Third Mesa and Mickey
                    from Pine Ridge,
          with Geronimo and Jim Jump and Mary Ann
          teaching us Cherokee and all of us singing
        Forty-Nine songs on our way to the feast,
                "Let's all go up to Porcupine,
                Indians dance in the summertime,
                We will dance the Forty-Nine,
                We will have a damn good time,
                Heyeeyoahyo . . . ."
                        but I could never get the
        right number of yo's and hey's and drive straight too,
          besides, that damn state patrolman was tailgating us
          just waiting for a "traffic violation"
        to nail these militant Indians good—
    but we had put the wine in our trunk so they could not
        possibly get us for driving
            with open bottle—
    still, it was getting dark and I of course
      was scared shitless wondering
          if we'd get shot
          by troopers or by FBI
            or maybe by some 'skins that had been
    lied to or bought or blackmailed,
        but Carter and Craig and Buck were cool as
        a hawk looking down
            from riding the wind to where bluejays
        are calling it names—
    "Hey, Mike," Buck said, "Ever time I see you
        somebody's getting ready to shoot us,
            out at Sunset Lake in '52
        up at Wounded Knee last year,
          now here in Ponca country—
    why don't you ever come see us
        when things are peaceful, so
          we can talk about old times?"
    "Aw shit, Buck," I said, watching
      the trooper in the rearview mirror,
        "I only hope we live to talk
                when these times are old!"

But near the auditorium the trooper
    turned off, and we all pulled in safe,
  piled out and went in to Uncle Gus's feast,
where all the Ponca and Osage women
    had fixed the frybread, boiled beef (sure tastes
  like slow elk, we all said), lots of fruit
    and Jello and all,
        and we ate until our bellies
    were fuller than Santa's sleigh.
        They'd brought the Osage drum
out of mourning to honor Uncle Gus,
        and the Osage War Dancers
    had come to dance for him,
      then when the Ponca singers
    sang the McDonald song his
nephews and nieces danced slowly round
    tall and straight and proud.
            It was a good time there and we gave
all that we could away, blankets and
  shawls and canned hams,
      even the big box of groceries
won in the drawing we gave away,
        the only trouble
broke out when Buck's woman got mad at his flirting
    with someone else and she took
      his gun and hid it,
          but she came and told me
  where it was
      and we got it back—
          nobody got shot or busted that night
    and toward the end of the dancing
      an old cowboy wandered over
  to where I stood behind the bleachers
    and watched the war-dancers a while
        then said to me offhand
"They're good
  but they won't ever be as good
      as Gus McDonald."
          I told Carter what he'd said
when we sat later back in a corner
near closing time in a Ponca City bar,
        watching the door
  and wondering who was sober enough
to stay on the right side back to Stillwater that night—
    "How about that," Carter said quietly.
      "Uncle Gus was the best all right.
          —Mike, they'll nail me some time or other
  for Wounded Knee. I know it, I'm prepared long since.
    But I'm back with my people now."
Well, they nailed him next year all right,
    caught him in Chicago finally,
      hell, we were glad when we heard he hadn't been murdered
        even glad when we heard he'd serve
          his three years in a Federal pen.
We laughed about its being in Indiana,

were kind of surprised when they shifted him
over to Springfield Mo., and of course
it was not too bad that he got three years
for disarming (allegedly) a postal inspector
inside Wounded Knee:
neither snow nor sleet nor Ponca warriors
should stay the appointed rounds of those
who bring junk mail to advertise
how to become Horatio Alger on
the Pine Ridge reservation, man.

4.

Shonge Ska—that was Uncle Gus's name.
His niece Serena put it on her Indian Crafts shop
run by her and her husband
for as long as people will buy
and run, by God,
of the people
by the people
and for the people
who shall not perish from the earth,
not even if they have to use
such European words as these
to keep the Ponca ways together:
not being much of a warrior myself,
cousins, Aunt Jewell,
I've set down this winter-count for a kind
of memorial song
to Shonge-Ska, one
of the greatest of Ponca dancers,
to dance once more.
We know that even
where Poncas are in prison
the songs are with them,
how can the bars stop singing
inside their heads?
For those who saw him dance
and learned from him the way,
he is dancing still.
Come to White Eagle in the summer time,
Indians dance in summer time—
he is back with his people now.

"People From the Stars"

(John Joseph Mathews' *The Osages*, Chapter 1)

Wazhazhe come from the stars
by their choice, not by falling
   or being thrown out
     of the heavenly bars like Satan
  into Europe,
    and we are invited back
  whenever we may choose to go;
but we joined the people of death
  and moved to another village
      (we call it, HO-E-GA)
where time began; we made our fire places
  and made our bodies of
the golden eagle and the cedar tree,
  of mountain lion and buffalo,
  of redbird, black bear, of the
great elk and of thunder so that we
  may live to see old age
  and go back to the stars.
Meantime, the Europeans pay us royalties
  for oil that lights their midnight highways
dangling across the land in
  star-strings through the night.
We trade our royalties for time enthroned
  on wings of shining metal
to look down at the stars beneath
  or up at stars above
     before we touch down in the desert
  creation of Las Vegas and wheel off
  to shoot craps at the Stardust Inn
and talk of Indians and their Trickster Tales,
  of Manabozho, and
  of Wounded Knee.

Wazhazhe Grandmother

—i-ko-eh, tha-gthi a tho

(*HO-e-ga*, literally "bare spot": the center of the forehead of the mythical elk . . . a term for an enclosure in which all life takes on bodily form, never to depart therefrom except by death . . . the earth which the mythical elk made to be habitable by separating it from the water . . . the camp of the tribe when ceremonially pitched . . . life as proceeding from the combined influences of the cosmic forces.

—Francis LaFlesche, *A Dictionary of the Osage Language*, 1932)

They chose their allotted land
  out west of the Agency
            at the prairie's edge,
    where the Osage Hills begin they built
      their homestead, honeymooned there
near Timber Hill,
      where Bird Creek meanders in
from the rolling grassy plains with their prairie chicken
                    dancing in spring,
  built in a timbered hollow where deer came down
    at dusk with the stars
  to drink from the deep pools
    near Timber Hill
           and below the
    waterfall that seemed
so high to me the summer
when I was six and walked up near its clearness gliding
  some five or six feet down from the flat
    sandstone ledge to its pools,
      she called it in Osage, *ni-xe ga-thpe*,
where the dark water turning into
  a spilling of light
      was a curtain clear and flowing, under
    the blue flash of a kingfisher's diving
    into the pool above the falls
    and his flying up
  again to the dead white branch of his willow—
the whole place was so quiet,
    in the way Grandma was quiet,
  it seemed a place to be still,
    seemed waiting for us,
  though no one lived there by then
    since widowed during the war she'd moved
    to the place south of Pawhuska,
and why we had driven down there from Timber Hill, now,
    I can't quite remember—

was it a picnic, or some kind
of retreat or vacation time
out of the August heat of Pawhuska?
The pictures focus sharp-edged:
a curtain of dark green ivy ruffled
a bit by breeze and water beside
the waters falling there
and a dirt road winding red and rocky
across tree-roots, along which, carefully,
my mother eased our rumbling Buick Eight
in that Depression year when Osage oil
still poured to float us into
a happy future—

but whether I dreamed, or saw real things in time,
their road, their house, the waterfall back in the
woods are all
at the bottom of Lake Bluestem now,
because Bird Creek,
blessed with a dam,
is all psyched out
of its snaggly, snaky self into a
windsparkling lake
whose deep blue waters, the politicians promise, will soon
come piped into Pawhuska pure and drinkable,
filling with blue brilliance municipal pools
and sprinkling the lawns to green or pouring freshets
down asphalt gutters to cool the shimmering
cicada-droning fevers of August streets
even as
in Bird Creek's old channel under Lake Bluestem big
catfish grope slowly in darkness
up over the sandstone ledge of the drowned
waterfall, or
scavenge through the ooze of
the homestead and along the road where
the bride and groom came riding one special day
and climbed down from the buggy in all their
best finery
to live in their first home.

Duane BigEagle

OKLAHOMA BOYHOOD

There was a place on Cat Creek,
A wide crossing,
Wagons must have rolled past there.
Round stones in the creek bottom
Worn smooth by the clear water.
Trees leaned from each bank
And some must have fallen in
In winter floods.
But in the summer,
The sun a little past midday,
A light shone in the center of that clearing.
It held horseflies and dragonflies
And the profoundest solitude
A boy of eight could ever know.

FLOWERS OF WINTER: FOUR SONGS

Song of the Drowning Man —
   I want to go
   to a place where nothing can hurt me.

Song of the New Wife —
   Everything I touch turns to dust,
   his pleasure is a mystery to me.

Song of the Husband —
   My arrows miss the heart of the deer,
   her desire is not equal to mine.

Song of the Newborn —
   I come from the valley of endings,
   there is no place to go but onward.

MY PEOPLE

Speak you someone

Who knows what to say

When they come in a dream

Masked desperate angels

From the valley of a massacre.

MY FATHER'S COUNTRY

In the morning light
My father's form
Against a mountain on the horizon.
Woolen trousers and smart leather shoes,
At thirty-two, a handsome man
Standing in the backroads
Of a country as open as his shirt collar.
There the silence of moonless night
Had purity and breath
But that is almost gone.
Now the night, never dark nor silent,
Dazzles our certainty,
Rumbles loudly through fading dreams of spacious warmth.

Father, let us walk again
As our grandfathers did.
If need be we will make new bodies of this earth,
Eat only memories,
Drink only the liquid spilt in our dreams,
Take shelter
In our love.
In the vastness of this land
We need only the songs its spirits teach us
And to sing!
Always to sing!

WHAT EAGLE SAW IN THE WEST

Two warriors, Open Hand and Go For Broke,
Went out for a walk.
They walked in desert and forest,
Across mountains and plains.
Finally they came to the Mississippi River.
Open Hand offered to carry his friend
Across the river on his back.
Go For Broke said "sure"
And hopped on.
They both drowned.
There was a drought for ten years.
Eagle skimmed dew
From his tail feathers
Kept alive.

Susan Shown Harjo

i breathe as the night breathes
i live as the forest life lives
the soft leaves and wet grass
are my protectors

above me in the clear night sea
are the torches of the gods
and the eyes of the dead
and the souls of the unborn
they surround my body with darkness
they give my shadowed mission
clear visioned sight
the night is my friend
        my heart's song is to the night

below me in the moist red earth
are the smooth round stones
and the bones of the dead
and the seeds of the unborn
the night worker worms beneath my body
remind me of the living worlds
giving morning birth
        my heart's song is to the earth

behind me in the sleep dead world
is Pipe Woman, my mother time
and Tall Man, my father earth
and Deer Eye, my sister dawn
the village sleepers stand beside my dream
giving comfort through the silent trials
of early rising suns
the sleeping ones are my friends
        my heart's song is to the sleeping ones

before me in the white blood world
are the blue eyed sons of fire
they stand over me
with yellow hair and white faces
wearing laces made of rough skins
of buffalo rotting in the sun
near my village of now starved people
wearing long braided black trophies
from the heads of my people
from the pride of my land

when the morning comes
i will continue to dream
and when i am killed
my soul will soar like the eagle
and from the great windy calm
i will dry the dawn tears
that blinded my sight
i will remember only the night
        my heart's song ends with the night

waking-up thoughts

a small, gentle kicking awakens me at dawn
my little one beside me, tired from the evening's work
chasing fireflies and snakedoctors in his sleep
now breathing in my time, as before birth
now a once, twice smile, shuddering as young ones do
warming my blanket, changing my dreams with his crawling
taking me from cold death-caves to yellow medicine-flower fields

my little son, destiny boy-child
"give me a boy," said my man, "on my father's day"
and it happened that way without effort
but, before his black eyes lost their newborn glaze,
his belly felt the white man's doctor knife
carving an early sterile scarring mark to last a lifetime
soon, after learning to stand on two feet, then to balance on one foot,
his legs began to quiver as the foul air invaded his chest
fumes from the below garage rising in search of young bodies,
leaving one nightworker dead, another mechanic purple-faced and foaming
then, later, the corner city crashing of cars
before he had anything to say for himself

146

last night we grown-ups told stories and new tales of near misses
we drank day-old coffee and watched smoke and sadness fill the air
i saw her dry eyes form the words her mouth could not release
her knowing and forgetting eyes saw a certain kinship
in our shaking, working, living and dying-hard hands

Lakota woman, sister-friend, once-wife of my brother,
i mourn your little one, burning in a closet in Kyle,
putting her clothes out with her hands, too stunned to cry out
i mourn your little one, living for so long after, her tiny body blackened
then dying, just when there was hope, they said

Lakota woman, mother-daughter, once and now family of mine,
i mourn your memories of fire, of charred hands
i mourn your todays of gunfire, of fear and threats
i know you show these midnight tears because they were absent at her feast
your broken nose making tears the more painful, an accident, they said

Lakota woman, sister in sorrow, now and then friend of mine,
it is fortunate for the fine and upstanding,
those masters of cheap shots and shell games,
that flaming bodies and bloody faces leave no traces of fingerprints

Lakota woman, my little ones are yours this hour until you are stronger
or until they no longer need us in that sweet, holding-on way
let's rest today, tomorrow you must find your own way home
to the other small ones, eating beans for breakfast, over half a world away
right under the noses of good fathers and mothers who look out for their own
tomorrow we will have bigger concerns, tonight we will think of ourselves
tomorrow we will worry about a way to find water that is free of tetanus
on the next tomorrow we will worry about how the air will be rationed
then, on the day after that tomorrow, who will have compassion
for my sleeping one, this gift of the sun?

i Clouding Woman, waking from sleep
remember dreams of my other world
as an antlered female deer
on grass and leaves I'd graze
from the mountainside i'd gaze
on the valley i longed to be near

i saw the Shyelas and Blue Clouds
like colored souls of the skies
once i crept near to see
skin as brown as my eyes
and some coats red like mine

i heard the Shyelas scream in pain
after eating smoking twigs
i watched them grow tall and become the fire
moving like flames of the dying red sun

i feared their fire and ran away
but i cannot say they burned
for dawn is brave and i returned
to circles of sleeping eyes
and scents of happy air

then i, too, slept and thought of smiles
one side cool on the ground
one side warmed by the sun

i awoke to the sound of dry cracking leaves
standing fast, i became a tree
the waking Shyelas ate berries and seeds
and never noticed me

i remember no more of my dream
except that it ended with night
but i, Clouding Woman
my man, Howling White
learn that our brothers, Arapahos proud
once kept the land called the Blue Cloud
and now a Shyela, a Cheyenne, draws me near
and speaks a name no one can hear
                "Deer Eye"
                "Deer Eye"
twice he said
now i know Clouding Woman is dead

now
the sky
at dawning and sunset
is streaked with black clouds
clouds made by man

now
our mother
lies open and wounded
drained of her richness
wealth stolen by man

now
few remember
clear, cool waters
and forests of life
where men were guests

now
to see
the earth as she was
we look through the eyes
of our fathers' hearts

now
we see
the cracked, dry earth
surrounded by filth
covered with sores

now
you've used
our home as your junkheap
taken our memories
taken our eyes

now
i ask
where are you going
whose fair mother
is left to discover
now

Russell Bates

RITE OF ENCOUNTER

In the third week of his fasting, Singing-owl found the white men.

The young Kiowa awakened that morning to lilting daybreak calls of birds. Rain had fallen in the night; his buffalo robe was soaked and smelly; his buckskin shirt and leggings were clammy wet. He was miserable. A chill wind blew in under the overhanging rocks. Singing-owl shivered, almost forgetting the receding hunger pangs. Almost . . .

At last the sun warmed the rocks around him. Singing-owl sat up wearily, hoping that this new day would finally bring him the vision. He dried his long black hair and braided it loosely on the left side. Then he stared for a long while downward from the rocky cleft. The hillside was unchanging: scattered clumps of scrub oaks, moss-grown boulders, thick yellow-green grass and black soil. Hillsides beyond bore the same colors and shapes.

Singing-owl had dreamed sometime before dawn. Of deer and clouds and fishes and snow . . . But the dream had not been the vision he was seeking. When that came, he would speak with spirits and come away with pieces of their wisdom. The wisdom, in songs and chants and riddles, would be his power as a warrior and as a man.

At least that was what the medicine man promised to him. But how much longer did he have to wait? The moon had been just past full when Singing-owl started his fast; soon, it would be full once again.

Singing-owl thought of the medicine man who slept warm at the camp and had no want of food or clothing.

That toothless, half-blind old man! I hope he got bloated on the meat I gave him!

The hunger pangs increased at the mention of food. Singing-owl leaned over and pulled a small deerskin parcel from a crack in the rocks. Wrapped inside was a handful of pounded dried meat mixed with suet. He smelled it for a long time, then closed his eyes and tried to swallow. He put the meat away again, feeling very guilty.

At length he forced himself to leave the cleft. When he stood, dizziness and nausea made him stagger. He leaned back against the rocks, momentarily unable to see. His arms and legs tingled and a cramp twisted the muscles in his side. Then the white sparkles faded from before his eyes.

Water. Must get water.

Singing-owl made his way carefully down the hill; the going was harder than the day before. He could no longer jump from boulder to boulder and instead squeezed between them. Sharp rocks hurt his feet through wet moccasins.

The slope leveled off, and Singing-owl sat on the ground to catch his breath. He glanced up the hill; it didn't seem any higher than he remembered. But now he regretted having passed by other, more gentle slopes.

I chose my suffering spot well. But will I be able to climb it again?

He followed a deer trail and walked listlessly among the trees. Twice he stumbled over tree roots. Another time he brushed against a tree and grabbed it desperately to keep from falling. He stopped and looked around.

Is this the right trail to the river? It's so long. I'm lost!

Singing-owl left the trail and headed away across the clearing. The thick grass slowed him to a stumbling pace. Then he smelled water and knew the river was close.

When he reached its muddy bank, he fell to his knees and threw himself forward to drink. The river was cool and slightly muddied. But the water made him feel better. He washed his face, then stripped off his buckskins to wash the many bruised cuts on his arms, chest and back. His frenzied thrashing against the rocks the evening before had gained him nothing but exhausted sleep; the self-tortures had not made him worthy of the vision. At last, Singing-owl slipped into the water and washed himself vigorously. Some of the fatigue, muscle aches, and lightheadedness flowed away with the sandy mud he used for scrubbing.

Then he lay against a log at the water's edge; the river current soothed his body. It was a struggle to stay awake.

A dog barked. Singing-owl sat up and listened. Again. Close by. Upstream.

He crawled out of the water, grabbed his buckskins, and listened again. The barking broke into howls. Singing-owl scrambled up the bank into bushes and made his way toward the sound, at once curious and afraid.

In this isolated land, no other tribes roamed. A dog meant white men.

Singing-owl paused to put on his buckskins. Then he crept ahead through the bushes: cautious, patient, silent. A few moments later, he reached the edge of a clearing and could see the camp, the dog, and the white men.

The dog was tied to a tree. One white man lay beside a long-dead fire. Another sat against a tree, his arms limp, his head fallen forward to his chest. A third lay sprawled on the riverbank, his head and one arm in the water. All were dressed in dirty gray and brown clothes, with boots scuffed and mud-caked.

A breeze fluttered the leaves of cottonwoods around the clearing; it also brought Singing-owl a whiff of decay. The men were dead.

The dog sensed Singing-owl and barked louder, leaping to the limit of the rope. Singing-owl stood up slowly, then walked into the camp. The dog retreated a little but kept up its barking. Singing-owl noticed a broken rope between two trees; horses had long since pulled free and wandered off.

He stopped at the body laying beside the ashes. The dead man lay face-down, a blanket across his legs. Singing-owl bent down, picked up a fine pistol; it was fully loaded, with light, circular tracings along the barrel. Singing-owl looked around carefully. Perhaps there were other weapons.

Singing-owl turned to the dog. It was brown and white spotted; its fur was matted and the mouth was dirty. Starving and dying of thirst, it had been eating mud.

Singing-owl put the gun in his shirt and hunted through the men's packs. He found hardtack biscuits and dried meat. He also found metal cans but discarded them because their markings were meaningless. He looked with longing at the food. But another nudge of guilt made him throw it to the dog.

It sniffed the morsels suspiciously, then began to eat in great gulps.

Singing-owl sighed, then picked up a small pot to get water. He shivered as he passed the man by the tree. At the riverbank he noticed something strange as he bent to fill the pot. The dead man laying there was covered with sores.

He looked closer. The hand that lay out of the water was almost raw; crusted yellow ooze edged what little skin that remained on its back. He looked at the face. The sores there had ragged white strings that waved in the flowing water. Singing-owl filled the pot quickly and stepped away.

The dog drank the water and wagged its tail. Then it looked up at him, expectant. Singing-owl reached out carefully, untied the rope. The dog brushed against him, happy.

"What killed your people, dog?" Singing-owl said, not truly breaking the ban against speaking to anyone.

The dog shook its head and barked. Its tail slapped against Singing-owl's legs.

"That was a bad way to meet death. Maybe I'd better not stay here any longer." He skirted wide of the man sitting at the tree. Yes, the sores were there. He did not bother turning over the man under the blanket.

Singing-owl remembered the pistol; he took it out with a trembling hand and dropped it. The dog walked with him away from the camp, then stopped.

Singing-owl looked back. "Going to stay here, yes? I wouldn't be able to keep you anyway. Hope you find something to eat . . . ." He brushed away the obvious and horrible thought, heading back into the hills.

When evening came, Singing-owl made a small fire and began his chanting prayers. The wind blew warm over the rocky cleft; stars were glistening in the dying film of twilight. Surely the strange events of the day were signs that the vision was coming. The robes that hid things to come would be lifted and . . .

Singing-owl found himself repeating the words of the medicine man and was disgusted. He waited. Nothing. The air turned cool and the fire slowly fell away.

Where is it? The medicine man is a liar! But what of all the other warriors who claim power from a vision?

He sat quietly, then decided to fast for only a few more days. If no vision came, he would go back to the Kiowas. He would have to tell them something; exactly what, he did not know.

But he would repay the medicine man for many days of discomfort. Singing-owl's brow wrinkled as he half-frowned, half-smiled. His reputation for playing pranks and outwitting his tribesmen was to gain yet another distinction. He would do nothing harmful, to be sure, just a few tricks to upset the old man. Such as: giving him skunk bones if he asked for weasel; hawk meat if he asked for prairie bird; or putting green sticks in his firewood. Singing-owl wanted to laugh, but he could not.

He noticed the fire and started to add more wood. But he felt warm enough; in fact, he felt almost too warm. He touched his face: hot.

Perhaps I'm tired. All right. I am tired.

He lay down to sleep. He remembered the white men and their sores, though he really did not want to. Something had killed them. Quickly. Quietly. He tried to think of other things. The vision. The many tricks he had played. Gray Bear's daughters. A running hunt through trees after a deer.

But nothing forced the image of the dead men from the edge of his sight. Finally, he fell asleep, feeling warmer than before.

Singing-owl opened his eyes. The sun was high above the hills. He lay quietly and listened to his body. All was well, apparently. Relieved, he sat up, yawned and stretched. He pushed the buffalo robe away and started to get up.

The thing sat a short distance away, watching him. Singing-owl stared, unable to move further. It was shaped like a man. But it was not a man.

It was a mass of raw flesh. With a body, and arms and legs, and a head. No skin or hair; just endless running sores. It appeared to be looking at him, but its face was featureless, red, open flesh. Yellow fluids trickled from over its entire body; wet streams ran down the rock on which it sat.

Singing-owl crawled backward, pressed himself against the rocks, eyes wide.

A ghost? Is it a white man's ghost? Or is . . . is that the vision?

He choked on the words: "Are you one of the spirits? Have . . . have you come because I am worthy?"

It moved, raised an arm, touched its chest. In a thick, watery voice, it said, "I am Black Smallpox. And I wish to walk with you."

Singing-owl almost fainted. He stared at it, tried to speak.

But the creature spoke first. "Do not be afraid. I will not harm you. I only wish to go with you to the Kiowas." It stood, and the yellow streams ran down its legs. "Yes, we will walk together to your people."

Singing-owl thought quickly, blinking. It surely was not the vision. Or was it perhaps the vision after all, somehow spoiled by white man's evil? Yes, the white men. Their sores. *Death*.

"No!" he said, feeling for a loose rock. "You came with the white men! You killed them! And now you want to kill . . . !" He found a rock and threw it. Smallpox wavered like a reflection in water, then suddenly was standing a short distance further away. The rock clattered harmlessly to the ground.

Smallpox stepped closer. "Come. Let us go."

Singing-owl sprang away suddenly and clambered down the hillside. He ran, stumbled, fell, crawled, slid over boulders, ran again. When he reached flatter ground, he broke into a run and did not look back. He staggered and almost tripped several times. He ran past trees, over hills, down gullies, into grass and bare ground.

At last, he ran, stumbled, ran into a narrow valley. He fell, gasping and crying. He landed on his face and hands at the edge of a rainwater pool. He lay beside a boulder and a small bush. He tried to crawl, but fell back. His body shook and shivered, though sweat coated him. Then his breathing slowed and he raised himself on one arm.

Singing-owl heard wailing and moaning, but very faint. Then he saw people reflected in the pool. They were Kiowas; ragged, wet sores covered their arms and faces. The wailing reflections reached for him, crying louder.

Singing-owl jerked himself backward and pushed dirt into the pool with his feet. Something stood at the limit of his side vision; he turned and saw Smallpox standing beside the bush.

It stepped toward him. "Why did you stop? We are going to the Kiowas, are we not? The sooner we get there, the better it will please me."

Singing-owl scrambled up, backed away in a low crouch. "No! I won't take you! You have no place here! Go away!"

It raised a hand. "We must go. The day grows long."

Singing-owl turned and ran again.

He climbed a cliff. Smallpox walked to the edge above him before he reached the top.

He ran over the plateau and dove from more than tree-top height into a lake. Smallpox stood atop the beaver lodge when Singing-owl swam toward the dam.

He hid in a box canyon. Smallpox was standing behind him near the sheer rock face. Singing-owl quickly set a grass fire by striking stones together. The flames swept into the canyon, swirling with smoke, trapping Smallpox. But when Singing-owl ran into a forest, Smallpox stepped from behind a tree to meet him.

Through the rest of the day, Singing owl ran, set traps, ran again. But he could neither outrun nor outwit Smallpox; it was always there when he stopped. Night fell and Singing-owl found that he could run no more.

He sat on the top of a grassy hill and watched as Smallpox walked slowly toward him. Light from a nearly full moon flashed in sparks from the dripping liquids.

I have lost. I have no more tricks. Yet . . .

Singing-owl thought hurriedly, formed a plan, then hung his head as Smallpox stopped beside him. "All right," he said, "We will go to the Kiowas."

Somewhere, Singing-owl felt a flicker of hope.

The lodges were quiet; moonlight revealed a score or more of them built at the base of a tree-lined hill. The main campfire was low. Camp dogs roamed in the spaces between the lodges. Sentries stood unmoving at long intervals around the village.

At a distance, Singing-owl circled the camp quietly. Smallpox walked with him.

At the far end of the camp, a woman came out of a lodge and threw bones on the ground. The dogs ran toward her and began fighting over the meal.

Singing-owl saw his chance and boldly walked in among the lodges where there was no sentry. Then he stopped and abruptly turned to Smallpox. "We are here. Now will you let me go? I am ashamed."

It stepped forward and regarded the circle of lodges. "Not just yet. There is still something you must do. Come."

He followed it, glancing from side to side, nervous. Smallpox led him to a large deerskin bag that was supported by crossed poles.

"This water," it said, standing very close to him and pointing. "Spit into it."

Singing-owl stared, not understanding.

"I said, spit into this water."

He stepped to the bag, opened a flap near the top, and spat.

"Again. That will do it. You are free."

Singing-owl moved back. "Free?"

Smallpox turned away. "Your usefulness is at an end." It sat down, still with its back to him; the open flesh gleamed wetly in the moonlight. "You will not understand, but I will tell you anyway. There are but a few I cannot kill. You are one. But I still lived inside you and thus was my purpose served. Leave me."

Singing-owl pretended to walk toward a lodge near large shade trees. "Yes," he said, looking back. "I must go to my lodge. My family will be glad to see me."

But when Smallpox was no longer in sight, Singing-owl ran for the trees. Two dogs ran after him, barking. A sentry shouted and more dogs ran after him. Singing-owl reached the shadows and ran out of the camp. He lost his pursuers quickly.

I'm free. I'm free! And the Pawnees are no friends to the Kiowas! They deserve Smallpox!

Dawn found Singing-owl far away from the Pawnee camp. When he was sure no one followed, he trapped a rabbit and ate his first meal in twenty days. His stomach ached a little when he set out again. But he was still happy at finally outwitting Smallpox.

He laughed. What a tale he would tell of his vision when he reached the Kiowas!

He was almost there when he heard wailing. He stopped and looked around frantically. Nothing else could be seen on the rolling plains except grasses moving in the wind. Then the wailing faded to be replaced by a laughing taunt. It was the voice of Smallpox.

"Where are you?" Singing-owl shouted, turning in circles. "You cannot be here! I outwitted you!"

"I told you, but you did not understand. We still walk together. I am part of you. You cannot get rid of me!" And the laughing began again.

Then Singing-owl knew the laughing came from inside him. He clutched at himself, tore at his own flesh, and screamed.

The laugh rolled on, unstopping.

The cleft of rocks offered little protection from the raging thunderstorm. Singing-owl huddled under his buffalo robe and watched the storm. Lightning split trees on far hills and flashed the night away for

155

brief moments. Thunder snapped down from the clouds and shook the ground. Rain splashed on Singing-owl's face and ran in pools under him.

He prayed, asking the mercy of the spirits. Small things came back to him: a boy's game with a willow hoop; his mother and stories and songs and gentle scoldings; the self-tortures that had declared him a man; the smiling, teasing daughter of Gray Bear; how fat quail sizzled when roasted . . .

For days, Singing-owl had considered exile or suicide. But he knew the one would be spent in temptation to see loved ones again. And there was no honor in the other.

Now Smallpox was to be finally outwitted. Singing-owl was fasting once more. But this time the fasting would go on, until there was nothing left.

He smiled faintly and pulled the buffalo robe tighter around him. At least, he thought, the laughing has stopped.

R.M. Bantista

Waiting To Be Born

We have never seen
Thirty feet before us
Except in the village.

We sleep in hammocks
And you bring me beer.

You carry fruit on your head
And a child on your back.

> Your belly intrigues me.
> It is tight and round and
> Sometimes it moves when I touch it.
>
> There is an animal in your belly.
> When the animal comes out
> We will see.

I will play my flute now.
There is something inside me,
Waiting to be born.
It is not an animal.

There is rain coming
And here is my flute.

> When it comes out
> We will see.

Anna L. Walters

Epitaph

because words fall short
the Pawnee cry, say simply
"she went," when she died

the desert is shifting
sifting sands through my fingers
to swirl through an eternity
of hourglass

in youth at dusk
lightning bugs on my fingers
in my hand a fiery orange red moon

in adolescence at dawn
dew in my eyes
in my toes wet grass curls

in womanhood at midday
sunrays on my naked innocence
and desire for redbirds' wings

in old age at twilight
surreal shadows in my face
in my heart I scent a setting sun

on the banks of black bear creek

a summer in oklahoma
is longer than black bear creek

it winds its fingers
in humid days, feeling damp people

then just around the bend
when the water is red high

temperature a hundred ten
summer floods out bridges

leaving drowned sleep
hot wind on everybody's lap

is blowing summer
down the creek

Lance Henson

old country

we are forgotten in the year
resigned to our pale rooms

like stale bread we sit in the damp
familiar to the rain on the roof

on the street in early morning
someone is singing

an old lady in a shawl
with a basket
is calling the name of
a lost cat
come home

come home

seeing

a dry limb
knocks all day
at the wind

and i have been
here before
though the roots of
things flow around
me without
touching

when i look i see
that even
now

i am crossing
the same
endless
bridge

wrapped in
a strange garment

looking for
myself

anniversary poem for the cheyennes who died
at sand creek

when we have come this long way
past cold grey fields
past the stone markers etched with the
names they left us

we will speak for the first time to the season
to the ponds

touching the dead grass

our voices the colour of watching

impression of strong heart song
cheyenne dog soldier

when the sun goes i stand watching its
shadow turn into night
when the light comes i call through my
smoke the new day

in the winter creek at morning i celebrate
with otter and badger
new beginnings

the songs of my life belong to you maheo

nothing between the sun and moon
lasts forever

snow song

i rise before the fires are given
before even the crows can stir from
their visions

bringing its own shadows the snow
passes among tired faces
worn forgotten hands

it is december
all night messengers passed the windows

all night
the song of the stars echoed
on grey white fields

while the ancient race
slept its bitter sleep

the leaving

night is a turning
of hands
a scent of velvet
going into rooms

soon in a vague weather
the wind
will lie down
with any name

and you will hear
the bell of
august

breathing near the
doorway

alone in the bruised
quiet

love poem

the earth
grows darker
like rich meat
in the fog
with the winter
light upon it

voices grown
silent
wander about
in their
worlds

the air
is on the
leaves
like a
shattered
prayer

portrait in february

near chanute kansas
snow with rain splashes the windshield

a barn through evening haze stands alone
in a frozen field

it is the last snow before spring
a redbird huddles on the barnsill

farther on
near an ice edged pond an owl
sits watching
as we pass

on our way home

N. Scott Momaday

THE MAN MADE OF WORDS

I want to try to put several different ideas together this morning. And in the process, I hope to indicate something about the nature of the relationship between language and experience. It seems to me that in a certain sense we are all made of words; that our most essential being consists in language. It is the element in which we think and dream and act, in which we live our daily lives. There is no way in which we can exist apart from the morality of a verbal dimension.

In one of the discussions yesterday the question "What is an American Indian?" was raised.

The answer of course is that an Indian is an idea which a given man has of himself. And it is a moral idea, for it accounts for the way in which he reacts to other men and to the world in general. And that idea, in order to be realized completely, has to be expressed.

I want to say some things then about this moral and verbal dimension in which we live. I want to say something about such things as ecology and storytelling and the imagination. Let me tell you a story:

One night a strange thing happened. I had written the greater part of *The Way to Rainy Mountain*—all of it, in fact, except the epilogue. I had set down the last of the old Kiowa tales, and I had composed both the historical and the autobiographical commentaries for it. I had the sense of being out of breath, of having said what it was in me to say on that subject. The manuscript lay before me in the bright light. Small, to be sure, but complete, or nearly so. I had written the second of the two poems in which that book is framed. I had uttered the last word, as it were. And yet a whole, penultimate piece was missing. I began once again to write.

During the first hours after midnight on the morning of November 13, 1833, it seemed that the world was coming to an end. Suddenly the stillness of the night was broken; there were brilliant flashes of light in the sky, light of such intensity that people were awakened by it. With the speed and density of a driving rain, stars were falling in the universe. Some were brighter than Venus; one was said to be as large as the moon. I went on to say that that event, the falling of the stars on North America, that explosion of meteors which occurred 137 years ago, is among the earliest entries in the Kiowa calendars. So deeply impressed upon the imagination of the Kiowas is that old phenomenon that it is remembered still; it has become a part of the racial memory.

"The living memory," I wrote, "and the verbal tradition which transcends it, were brought together for me once and for all in the person of Ko-sahn." It seemed eminently right for me to deal, after all, with that old woman. Ko-sahn is among the most venerable people I have ever known. She spoke and sang to me one summer afternoon in Oklahoma. It was like a dream. When I was born she was already old; she was a grown woman when my grandparents came into the world. She sat perfectly still, folded over on herself. It did not seem possible that so many years—a century of years—could be so compacted and distilled. Her voice shuddered, but it did not fail. Her songs were sad. An old whimsy, a delight in language and in remembrance, shone in her one good eye. She conjured up the past, imagining perfectly the long continuity of her being. She imagined the lovely young girl, wild and vital, she had been. She imagined the Sun Dance:

There was an old, old woman. She had something on her back. The boys went out to see. The old woman had a bag full of earth on her back. It was a certain kind of sandy earth. That is what they must have in the lodge. The dancers must dance upon the sandy earth. The old woman held a digging tool in her hand. She turned towards the south and pointed with her lips. It was like a kiss, and she began to sing:

We have brought the earth.
Now it is time to play.

As old as I am, I still have the feeling of play. That was the beginning of the Sun Dance.

By this time I was back into the book, caught up completely in the act of writing. I had projected myself—imagined myself—out of the room and out of time. I was there with Ko-sahn in the Oklahoma July. We laughed easily together; I felt that I had known her all of my life—all of hers. I did not want to let her go. But I had come to the end. I set down, almost grudgingly, the last sentences:

It was—all of this and more—a quest, a going forth upon the way of Rainy Mountain. Probably Ko-sahn too is dead now. At times, in the quiet of evening, I think she must have wondered, dreaming, who she was. Was she become in her sleep that old purveyor of the sacred earth, perhaps, that ancient one who, old as she was, still had the feeling of play? And in her mind, at times, did she see the falling stars?

For some time I sat looking down at these words on the page, trying to deal with the emptiness that had come about inside of me. The words did not seem real. I could scarcely believe that they made sense, that they had anything whatsoever to do with meaning. In desperation almost, I went back over the final paragraphs, backwards and forwards, hurriedly. My eyes fell upon the name Ko-sahn. And all at once everything seemed suddenly to refer to that name. The name seemed to humanize the whole complexity of language. All at once, absolutely, I had the sense of the magic of words and of names. Ko-sahn, I said, and I said again KO-SAHN.

Then it was that that ancient, one-eyed woman Ko-sahn stepped out of the language and stood before me on the page. I was amazed. Yet it seemed entirely appropriate that this should happen.

"I was just now writing about you," I replied, stammering. "I thought — forgive me — I thought that perhaps you were . . . that you had . . ."

"No," she said. And she cackled, I thought. And she went on. "You have imagined me well, and so I am. You have imagined that I dream, and so I do. I have seen the falling stars."

"But all of this, this imagining," I protested, "this has taken place — is taking place in my mind. You are not actually here, not here in this room." It occurred to me that I was being extremely rude, but I could not help myself. She seemed to understand.

"Be careful of your pronouncements, grandson," she answered. "You imagine that I am here in this room, do you not? That is worth something. You see, I have existence, whole being, in your imagination. It is but one kind of being, to be sure, but it is perhaps the best of all kinds. If I am not here in this room, grandson, then surely neither are you."

"I think I see what you mean," I said meekly. I felt justly rebuked. "Tell me, grandmother, how old are you?"

"I do not know," she replied. "There are times when I think that I am the oldest woman on earth. You know, the Kiowas came into the world through a hollow log. In my mind's eye I have seen them emerge, one by one, from the mouth of the log. I have seen them so clearly, how they were dressed, how delighted they were to see the world around them. I must have been there. And I must have taken part in that old migration of the Kiowas from the Yellowstone to the Southern Plains, near the Big Horn River, and I have seen the red cliffs of Palo Duro Canyon. I was with those who were camped in the Wichita Mountains when the stars fell."

"You are indeed very old," I said, "and you have seen many things."

"Yes, I imagine that I have," she replied. Then she turned slowly around, nodding once, and receded into the language I had made. And then I imagined I was alone in the room.

Once in his life a man ought to concentrate his mind upon the remembered earth, I believe. He ought to give himself up to a particular landscape in his experience, to look at it from as many angles as he can, to wonder about it, to dwell upon it. He ought to imagine that he touches it with his hands at every season and listens to the sounds that are made upon it. He ought to imagine the creatures that are there and all the faintest motions in the wind. He ought to recollect the glare of noon and all the colors of the dawn and dusk.

The Wichita Mountains rise out of the Southern Plains in a long crooked line that runs from east to west. The mountains are made of red earth, and of rock that is neither red nor blue but some very rare admixture of the two like the feathers of certain birds. They are not so high and mighty as the mountains of the Far West, and they bear a different relationship to the land around them. One does not imagine that they are distinctive in themselves, or indeed that they exist apart from the plain in any sense. If you try to think of them in the abstract they lose the look of mountains. They are preeminently in an expression of the larger landscape, more perfectly organic than one can easily imagine. To behold these mountains from the plain is one thing; to see the plain from the mountains is something else. I have stood on the top of Mt. Scott and seen the earth below, bending out into the whole circle of the sky. The wind runs always close upon the slopes, and there are times when you can hear the rush of it like water in the ravines.

Here is the hub of an old commerce. A hundred years ago the Kiowas and Comanches journeyed outward from the Wichitas in every direction, seeking after mischief and medicine, horses and hostages. Sometimes they went away for years, but they always returned, for the land had got hold of them. It is a consecrated place, and even now there is something of the wilderness about it. There is a game preserve in the hills. Animals graze away in the open meadows or, closer by, keep to the shadows of the groves: antelope and deer, longhorn and buffalo. It was here, the Kiowas say, that the first buffalo came into the world.

The yellow grassy knoll that is called Rainy Mountain lies a short distance to the north and west. There, on the west side, is the ruin of an old school where my grandmother went as a wild young girl in blanket and braids to learn of numbers and of names in English. And there she is buried.

> Most is your name the name of
> this dark stone.
> Deranged in death, the mind to
> be inheres
> Forever in the nominal unknown,
> Who listens here and now to
> hear your name.
> The early sun, red as a hunter's
> moon,
> Runs in the plain. The mountain
> burns and shines;
> And silence is the long approach
> of noon
> Upon the shadow that your name
> defines—
> And death this cold, black
> density of stone.

I am interested in the way that a man looks at a given landscape and takes possession of it in his blood and brain. For this happens, I am certain, in the ordinary motion of life. None of us lives apart from the land entirely; such an isolation is unimaginable. We have sooner or later to come to terms with the world around us—and I mean especially the physical world; not only as it is revealed to us immediately through our senses, but also as it is perceived more truly in the long turn of seasons and of years. And we must come to moral terms. There is no alternative, I believe, if we are to realize and maintain our humanity; for our humanity must consist in part in the ethical as well as the practical ideal of preservation. And particularly here and now is that true. We Americans need now more than ever before—and indeed more than we know—to imagine who and what we are with respect to the earth and sky. I am talking about an act of the imagination essentially, and the concept of an American land ethic.

It is no doubt more difficult to imagine in 1970 the landscape of America as it was in, say, 1900. Our whole experience as a nation in this century has been a repudiation of the pastoral ideal which informs so much of the art and literature of the nineteenth century. One effect of the Technological Revolution has been to uproot us from the soil. We have become disoriented, I believe; we have suffered a kind of psychic dislocation of ourselves in time and space. We may be perfectly sure of where we are in relation to the supermarket and the next coffee break, but I doubt that any of us knows where he is in relation to the stars and to the solstices. Our sense of the natural order has become dull and unreliable. Like the wilderness itself, our sphere of instinct has diminished in proportion as we have failed to imagine truly what it is. And yet I believe that it is possible to formulate an ethical idea of the land—a notion of what it is and must be in our daily lives—and I believe moreover that it is absolutely necessary to do so.

It would seem on the surface of things that a land ethic is something that is alien to, or at least dormant in, most Americans. Most of us in general have developed an attitude of indifference toward the land. In terms of my own experience, it is difficult to see how such an attitude could ever have come about.

Ko-sahn could remember where my grandmother was born. "It was just there," she said, pointing to a tree, and the tree was like a hundred others that grew up in the broad depression of the Washita River. I could see nothing to indicate that anyone had ever been there, spoken so much as a word, or touched the tips of his fingers to the tree. But in her memory Ko-sahn could see the child. I think she must have remembered my grandmother's voice, for she seemed for a long moment to listen and to hear. There was a still, heavy heat upon that place; I had the sense that ghosts were gathering there.

And in the racial memory, Ko-sahn had seen the falling stars. For her there was no distinction between the individual and the racial experience, even as there was none between the mythical and the historical. Both were realized for her in the one memory, and that was of the land. This landscape, in which she had lived for a hundred years, was the common denominator of everything that she knew and would ever know—and her knowledge was profound. Her roots ran deep into the earth, and from those depths she drew strength enough to hold still against all the forces of chance and disorder. And she drew strength enough to hold still against all the forces of change and disorder. And she drew therefrom the sustenance of meaning and of mystery as well. The falling stars were not for Ko-sahn an isolated or accidental phenomenon. She had a great personal investment in that awful commotion of light in the night sky. For it remained to be imagined. She must at last deal with it in words; she must appropriate it to her understanding of the whole universe. And, again, when she spoke of the Sun Dance, it was an essential expression of her relationship to the life of the earth and to the sun and moon.

In Ko-sahn and in her people we have always had the example of a deep, ethical regard for the land. We had better learn from it. Surely that ethic is merely latent in ourselves. It must now be activated, I believe. We Americans must come again to a moral comprehension of the earth and air. We must live according to the principle of a land ethic. The alternative is that we shall not live at all.

Ecology is perhaps the most important subject of our time. I can't think of an issue in which the Indian has more authority or a greater stake. If there is one thing which truly distinguishes him, it is surely his regard of and for the natural world.

But let me get back to the matter of storytelling.

I must have taken part in that old migration of the Kiowas from the Yellowstone to the Southern Plains, for I have seen antelope bounding in the tall grass near the Big Horn River, and I have seen the ghost forests in the Black Hills. Once I saw the red cliffs of Palo Duro Canyon. I was with those who were camped in the Wichita Mountains when the stars fell. "You are very old," I said, "and you have seen many things." "Yes, I imagine that I have," she replied. Then she turned slowly around, nodding once, and receded into the language I had made. And then I imagined that I was alone in the room.

Who is the storyteller? Of whom is the story told? What is there in the darkness to imagine into being? What is there to dream and to relate? What happens when I or anyone exerts the force of language upon the unknown?

These are the questions which interest me most.

If there is any absolute assumption in back of my thoughts tonight, it is this: We are what we imagine. Our very existence consists in our imagination of ourselves. Our best destiny is to imagine, at least, completely, who and what, and that we are. The greatest tragedy that can befall us is to go unimagined.

Writing is recorded speech. In order to consider seriously the meaning of language and of literature, we must consider first the meaning of the oral tradition.

By way of suggesting one or two definitions which may be useful to us, let me pose a few basic questions and tentative answers:

(1) What is the oral tradition?

The oral tradition is that process by which the myths, legends, tales, and lore of a people are formulated, communicated, and preserved in language by word of mouth, as opposed to writing. Or, it is a collection of such things.

(2) With reference to the matter of oral tradition, what is the relationship between art and reality?

In the context of these remarks, the matter of oral tradition suggests certain particularities of art and reality. Art, for example . . . involves an oral dimension which is based markedly upon such considerations as memorization, intonation, inflection, precision of statement, brevity, rhythm, pace, and dramatic effect. Moreover, myth, legend, and lore, according to our definitions of these terms, imply a separate and distinct order of reality. We are concerned here not so much with an accurate representation of actuality, but with the realization of the imaginative experience.

(3) How are we to conceive of language? What are words?

For our purposes, words are audible sounds, invented by man to communicate his thoughts and feelings. Each word has a conceptual content, however slight; and each word communicates associations of feeling. Language is the means by which words proceed to the formulation of meaning and emotional effect.

(4) What is the nature of storytelling? What are the purposes and possibilities of that act?

Storytelling is imaginative and creative in nature. It is an act by which man strives to realize his capacity for wonder, meaning and delight. It is also a process in which man invests and preserves himself in the context of ideas. Man tells stories in order to understand his experience, whatever it may be. The possibilities of storytelling are precisely those of understanding the human experience.

(5) What is the relationship between what a man is and what he says—or between what he is, and what he thinks he is?

This relationship is both tenuous and complicated. Generally speaking, man has consummate being in language, and there only. The state of human *being* is an idea, an idea which man has of himself. Only when he is embodied in an idea, and the idea is realized in language, can man take possession of himself. In our particular frame of reference, this is to say that man achieves the fullest realization of his humanity in such an art and product of the imagination as literature—and here I use the term "literature" in its broadest sense. This is admittedly a moral view of the question, but literature is itself a moral view, and it is a view of morality.

Now let us return to the falling stars. And let me apply a new angle of vision to that event—let me proceed this time from a slightly different point of view:

In this winter of 1833 the Kiowas were camped on Elm Fork, a branch of the Red River west of the Wichita Mountains. In the preceding summer they had suffered a massacre at the hands of the Osages, and Tai-me, the sacred Sun Dance Doll and most powerful medicine of the tribe, had been stolen. At no time in the history of their migration from the north, and in the evolution of their plains culture, had the Kiowas been more vulnerable to despair. The loss of Tai-me was a deep psychological wound. In the early cold of November 13 there occurred over North America an explosion of meteors. The Kiowas were awakened by the sterile light of falling stars, and they ran out into the false day and were terrified.

168

The year the stars fell is, as I have said, among the earliest entries in the Kiowa calendars, and it is permanent in the Kiowa mind. There was symbolic meaning in that November sky. With the coming of natural dawn there began a new and darker age for the Kiowa people; the last culture to evolve on this continent began to decline. Within four years of the falling stars the Kiowas signed their first treaty with the government; within twenty, four major epidemics of smallpox and Asiatic cholera destroyed more than half their number; and within scarcely more than a generation their horses were taken from them and the herds of buffalo were slaughtered and left to waste upon the plains.

Do you see what happens when the imagination is superimposed upon the historical event? It becomes a story. The whole piece becomes more deeply invested with meaning. The terrified Kiowas, when they had regained possession of themselves, did indeed imagine that the falling stars were symbolic of their being and their destiny. They accounted for themselves with reference to that awful memory. They appropriated it, recreated it, fashioned it into an image of themselves—imagined it.

Only by means of that act could they bear what happened to them thereafter. No defeat, no humiliation, no suffering was beyond their power to endure, for none of it was meaningless. They could say to themselves, "yes, it was all meant to be in its turn. The order of the world was broken, it was clear. Even the stars were shaken loose in the night sky." The imagination of meaning was not much, perhaps, but it was all they had, and it was enough to sustain them.

One of my very favorite writers, Isak Dinesen, said this: "All sorrows can be borne if you put them into a story or tell a story about them."

Some three or four years ago, I became interested in the matter of "oral tradition" as that term is used to designate a rich body of preliterate storytelling in and among the indigenous cultures of North America. Specifically, I began to wonder about the way in which myths, legends, and lore evolve into that mature condition of expression which we call "literature." For indeed literature is, I believe, the end-product of an evolutionary process, a stage that is indispensable and perhaps original as well.

I set out to find a traditional material that should be at once oral only, unified and broadly representative of cultural values. And in this undertaking, I had a certain advantage, because I am myself an American Indian, and I have lived many years of my life on the Indian reservations of the southwest. From the time I was first able to comprehend and express myself in language, I heard the stories of the Kiowas, those "coming out" people of the Southern plains from whom I am descended.

Three hundred years ago the Kiowa lived in the mountains of what is now western Montana, near the headwaters of the Yellowstone River. Near the end of the 17th century they began a long migration to the south and east. They passed along the present border between Montana and Wyoming to the Black Hills and proceeded southward along the eastern slopes of the Rockies to the Wichita Mountains in the Southern Plains (Southwestern Oklahoma).

I mention this old journey of the Kiowas because it is in a sense definitive of the tribal mind; it is essential to the way in which the Kiowas think of themselves as a people. The migration was carried on over a course of many generations and many hundreds of miles. When it began, the Kiowas were a desperate and divided people, given up wholly to a day-by-day struggle for survival. When it ended, they were a race of centaurs, a lordly society of warriors and buffalo hunters. Along the way they had acquired horses, a knowledge and possession of the open land, and a sense of destiny. In alliance with the Comanches, they ruled the southern plains for a hundred years.

That migration—and the new golden age to which it led—is closely reflected in Kiowa legend and lore. Several years ago I retraced the route of that migration, and when I came to the end, I interviewed a number of Kiowa elders and obtained from them a remarkable body of history and learning, fact and fiction—all of it in the oral tradition and all of it valuable in its own right and for its own sake.

I compiled a small number of translations from the Kiowa, arranged insofar as it was possible to indicate the chronological and geographical progression of the migration itself. This collection (and it was nothing more than a collection at first) was published under the title "The Journey of Tai-me" in a fine edition limited to 100 hand printed copies.

This original collection has just been re-issued, together with illustrations and a commentary, in a trade edition entitled "The Way to Rainy Mountain." The principle of narration which informs this latter work is in a sense elaborate and experimental, and I should like to say one or two things about it. Then, if I may, I should like to illustrate the way in which the principle works, by reading briefly from the text. And finally, I should like to comment in some detail upon one of the tales in particular.

There are three distinct narrative voices in "The Way to Rainy Mountain"—the mythical, the historical, and the immediate. Each of the translations is followed by two kinds of commentary; the first is documentary and the second is privately reminiscent. Together, they serve, hopefully, to validate the oral tradition to an extent that might not otherwise be possible. The commentaries are meant to provide a context in which the elements of oral tradition might transcend the categorical limits of prehistory, anonymity, and archaeology in the narrow sense.

All of this is to say that I believe there is a way (first) in which the elements of oral tradition can be shown, dramatically, to exist within the framework of a literary continuance, a deeper and more vital context of language and meaning than that which is generally taken into account; and (secondly) in which those elements can be located, with some precision on an evolutionary scale.

The device of the journey is peculiarly appropriate to such a principle of narration as this. And "The Way to Rainy Mountain" is a whole journey, intricate with notion and meaning; and it is made with the whole memory, that experience of the mind which is legendary as well as historical, personal as well as cultural.

Without further qualification, let me turn to the text itself.

The Kiowa tales which are contained in "The Way to Rainy Mountain" constitute a kind of literary chronicle. In a sense they are the milestones of that old migration in which the Kiowas journeyed from the Yellowstone to the Washita. They recorded a transformation of the tribal mind, as it encounters for the first time the landscape of the Great Plains; they evoke the sense of search and discovery. Many of the tales are very old, and they have not until now been set down in writing. Among them there is one that stands out in my mind. When I was a child, my father told me the story of the arrowmaker, and he told it to me many times, for I fell in love with it. I have no memory that is older than that of hearing it. This is the way it goes:

If an arrow is well made, it will have tooth marks upon it. That is how you know. The Kiowas made fine arrows and straightened them in their teeth. Then they drew them to the bow to see that they were straight. Once there was a man and his wife. They were alone at night in their tipi. By the light of a fire the man was making arrows. After a while he caught sight of something. There was a small opening in the tipi where two hides had been sewn together. Someone was there on the outside, looking in. The man went on with his work, but he said to his wife, "Someone is standing outside. Do not be afraid. Let us talk easily, as of ordinary things." He took up an arrow and straightened it in his teeth; then, as it was right for him to do, he drew it to the bow and took aim, first in this direction and then in that. And all the while he was talking, as if to his wife. But this is how he spoke: "I know that you are there on the outside, for I can feel your eyes upon me. If you are a Kiowa, you will understand what I am saying, and you will speak your name." But there was no answer, and the man went on in the same way, pointing the arrow all around. At last his aim fell upon the place where his enemy stood, and he let go of the string. The arrow went straight to the enemy's heart.

Heretofore the story of the arrowmaker has been the private possession of a very few, a tenuous link in that most ancient chain of language which we call the oral tradition; tenuous because the tradition itself is so; for as many times as the story has been told, it was always but one generation removed from extinction. But it was held dear, too, on that same account. That is to say, it has been neither more nor less durable than the human voice, and neither more nor less concerned to express the meaning of the human condition. And this brings us to the heart of the matter at hand: The story of the arrowmaker is also a link between language and literature. It is a remarkable act of the mind, a realization of words and the world that is altogether simple and direct, yet nonetheless rare and profound, and it illustrates more clearly than anything else in my own experience, at least, something of the essential character of the imagination—and in particular of that personification which in this instance emerges from it: the man made of words.

It is a fine story, whole, intricately beautiful, precisely realized. It is worth thinking about, for it yields something of value; indeed, it is full of provocation, rich with suggestion and consequent meaning. There is often an inherent danger that we might impose too much of ourselves upon it. It is informed by an integrity that bears examination easily and well, and in the process it seems to appropriate our own reality and experience.

It is significant that the story of the arrowmaker returns in a special way upon itself. It is about language, after all, and it is therefore part and parcel of its own subject; virtually, there is no difference between the telling and that which is told. The point of the story lies, not so much in what the arrowmaker does, but in what he says—and indeed that he says it. The principal fact is that he speaks, and in so doing he places his very life in the balance. It is this aspect of the story which interests me most, for it is here that the language becomes most conscious of itself; we are close to the origin and object of literature, I believe; our sense of the verbal dimension is very keen, and we are aware of something in the nature of language that is at once perilous and compelling. "If you are a Kiowa, you will understand what I am saying, and you will speak your name." Everything is ventured in this simple declaration, which is also a question and a plea. The conditional element with which it begins is remarkably tentative and pathetic; precisely at this moment is the arrowmaker realized completely, and his reality consists in language, and it is poor and precarious. And all of this occurs to him as surely as it does to us. Implicit in that simple occurrence is all of his definition and his destiny, and all of ours. He ventures to speak because he must; language is the repository of his whole knowledge and experience, and it represents the only chance he has for survival. Instinctively, and with great care, he deals in the most honest and basic way with words. "Let us talk easily, as of ordinary things," he says. And of the ominous unknown he asks only the utterance of a name, only the most nominal sign that he is understood, that his words are returned to him on the sheer edge of meaning. But there is no answer, and the arrowmaker knows at once what he has not known before; that his enemy is, and that he has gained an advantage over him. This he knows certainly, and the certainty itself is his advantage, and it is crucial; he makes the most of it. The venture is complete and irrevocable, and it ends in success. The story is meaningful. It is so primarily because it is composed of language, and it is in the nature of language in turn that it proceeds to the formulation of meaning. Moreover, the story of the arrowmaker, as opposed to other stories in general, centers upon this procession of words toward meaning. It seems in fact to turn upon the very idea that language involves the elements of risk and responsibility; and in this it seeks to confirm itself. In a word, it seems to say, everything is a risk. That may be true, and it may also be that the whole of literature rests upon that truth.

The arrowmaker is preeminently the man made of words. He has consummate being in language; it is the world of his origin and of his posterity, and there is no other. But it is a world of definite reality and of infinite possibility. I have come to believe that there is a sense in which the arrowmaker has more nearly perfect being than have other men, by and large, as he imagines himself, whole and vital, going on into the unknown darkness and beyond. And this last aspect of his being is primordial and profound.

And yet the story has it that he is cautious and alone, and we are given to understand that his peril is great and immediate, and that he confronts it in the only way he can. I have no doubt that this is true, and I believe that there are implications which point directly to the determination of our literary experience and which must not be lost upon us. A final word, then, on an essential irony which marks this story and gives peculiar substance to the man made of words. The storyteller is nameless and unlettered. From one point of view we know very little about him, except that he is somehow translated for us in the person of an arrowmaker. But, from another, that is all we need to know. He tells us of his life in language, and of the awful risk involved. It must occur to us that he is one with the arrowmaker and that he has survived, by word of mouth, beyond other men. We said a moment ago that, for the arrowmaker, language represented the only chance of survival. It is worth considering that he survives in our own time, and that he has survived over a period of untold generations.

Headwaters

Noon in the intermountain plain:
There is scant telling of the marsh—
A log, hollow and weather-stained,
An insect at the mouth, and moss—
Yet waters rise against the roots,
Stand brimming to the stalks. What moves?
What moves on this archaic force
Was wild and welling at the source.

Rainy Mountain Cemetery

Most is your name the name of this dark stone.
Deranged in death, the mind to be inheres
Forever in the nominal unknown,
The wake of nothing audible he hears
Who listens here and now to hear your name.

The early sun, red as a hunter's moon,
Runs in the plain. The mountain burns and shines;
And silence is the long approach of noon
Upon the shadow that your name defines—
And death this cold, black density of stone.

The Fear of Bo-talee

Bo-talee rode easily among his enemies, once, twice,
three—and four times. And all who saw him were
amazed, for he was utterly without fear; so it seemed.
But afterwards he said: Certainly I was afraid. I was
afraid of the fear in the eyes of my enemies.

The Story of a Well-Made Shield

Now in the dawn before it dies, the eagle swings
low and wide in a great arc, curving downward
to the place of origin. There is no wind, but there
is a long roaring on the air. It is like the wind—
nor is it quite like the wind—but more powerful.

The Horse That Died of Shame

*Once there was a man who owned a fine hunting
horse. It was black and fast and afraid of nothing.
When it was turned upon an enemy it charged in a
straight line and struck at full speed; the man
need have no hand upon the rein. But, you know,
that man knew fear. Once during a charge he turned
that animal from its course. That was a bad thing.
The hunting horse died of shame.*

From *The Way to Rainy Mountain*

In the one color of the horse there were many
colors. And that evening it wheeled, riderless, and broke
away into the long distance, running at full speed. And
so it does again and again in my dreaming. It seems to
concentrate all color and light into the final moment of
its life, until it streaks the vision plane and is indefinite,
and shines vaguely like the gathering of March light
to a storm.

The Gourd Dancer

Mammedaty, 1880-1932

1. *The Omen*

Another season centers on this place.
Like memory the blood congeals in it;
Like memory the sun recedes in time
Into the hazy, southern distances.

A vagrant heat hangs on the dark river,
And shadows turn like smoke. An owl ascends
Among the branches, clattering, remote
Within its motion, intricate with age.

2. *The Dream*

Mammedaty saw to the building of this house.
Just there, by the arbor, he made a camp in the old way.
And in the evening when the hammers had fallen silent
and there were frogs and crickets in the black grass—
and a low, hectic wind upon the pale, slanting plane
of the moon's light—he settled deep down in his mind
to dream. He dreamed of dreaming, and of the summer
breaking upon his spirit, as drums break upon the
intervals of the dance, and of the gleaming gourds.

3. *The Dance*

Dancing,
He dreams, he dreams—

The long wind glances, moves
Forever as a music to the mind;
The gourds are flashes of the sun.
He takes the inward, mincing steps
That conjure old processions and returns.

Dancing,
His moccasins,
His sash and bandolier
Contain him in insignia;
His fan is powerful, concise
According to his agile hand,
And holds upon the deep, ancestral air.

4. *The Giveaway*

Someone spoke his name, Mammedaty, in which
his essence was and is. It was a serious matter that his
name should be spoken there in the circle, among the
many people, and he was thoughtful, full of wonder,
and aware of himself and of his name. He walked
slowly to the summons, looking into the eyes of the man
who summoned him. For a moment they held each
other in close regard, and all about them there was
excitement and suspense.

Then a boy came suddenly into the circle, leading
a black horse. The boy ran, and the horse after him.
He brought the horse up short in front of Mammedaty,
and the horse wheeled and threw its head and cut
its eyes in the wild way. And it blew hard and quivered
in its hide so that light ran, rippling, upon its shoulders
and its flanks — and then it stood still and was calm.
Its mane and tail were fixed in braids and feathers, and
a bright red chief's blanket was draped in a roll over
its withers. The boy placed the reins in Mammedaty's
hands. And all of this was for Mammedaty, in his honor,
as even now it is in the telling, and will be, as long as
there are those who imagine him in his name.

Krasnopresnenskaya Station

For Will Sutter

Their faces do not change at their mouths.
They read and look after themselves.
I mean them no harm,
but they are afraid of me.

I sit at the window. I wonder
that they keep so, to themselves,
in their trains, in the deep streets.
I have no prospects here.

One, a girl not yet disappointed, perhaps,
approaches close to me. I suppose
she does not remember herself;
she dreams of the lindens at Arkhangelskoe.

She would speak of ordinary things;
I would listen
for the hard resonances of the river,
the ice breaking apart in the afternoon.

Opal Lee Popkes

CHAPTER ONE FOR *WAR GAMES*

(a novel-in-progress)

"Half hour to dinnertime yet and Pa won't hang out that white dinner flag until the sun says straight up noon. Him and Jim Moore sit at the kitchen table this minute, guzzling that bottle of whiskey I plowed up yesterday. It's not that I'm against Jim burying it in our fields but with the county being dry I could be put in jail for bootleggin. And the white people would say we're drunk as in the days before the Trail." Emma Lotter referred to the Trail of Tears, that exodus of The Five Civilized Tribes from the South that had occurred a century before. Though the white man had forgotten it, the event stayed like fresh blood on the souls of the Indians whose forebears swam the icy waters of the Mississippi and walked barefoot through the winter to their new home.

Emma forced her stiffened back erect and looked up at the summer sun. She retied the strings of the long grey poke bonnet which she wore, not to keep the sun off but to make her feel as white girls who wore them to keep their skins white. It had never occurred to Emma that she was white as anybody. They said — but Emma never knew, not having spoken of it to her father — that Pa Lotter was a white man. Certainly he had a white man's features but the rust accumulating from a bathless life might have discolored his skin permanently. They said Emma's mother was an Indian woman, Choctaw, but Emma never asked her father about that either. People didn't ask Pa Lotter anything.

She flattened a cardboard slat that had fallen loose out of the poke bonnet, then she rested on the hoe handle. She had been hoeing since before sunup. Since way back in March she had been on the tractor, some days planting, cultivating, running go-devils and knife sleds to cut weeds, to loosen the crust on the hot sand in case a little rain did fall.

July came. No rain. Pa Lotter told his daughter to go into the dry fields again and drag the few remaining weeds from around the yellowing, dying broomcorn. There was no sense to the hoeing for it was like filling the ocean a drop at a time; the weeds returned the next day. Hoeing was a habit passed down by Pa Lotter to his daughter, and it was also a habit passed down to Pa Lotter by *his* father and eventually one could trace it back to Mississippi where the Lotters tried to enslave the Indians. They could not and so they took the Indians' land and enslaved the black man, forcing Emma's Indian forebears to go to the Territories where presumably nobody, white at least, would ever want to go.

However, within the span of a man's lifetime, the Lotters, defeated by a Civil War, converged, en masse, upon the same people, now old men and women, and the younger Indians and once more the exodus began as Indians fled into Texas. Once more southern men, among them the Lotters, found Choctaws and enslaved them and since there were no more men, only women, and slavery illegal, they married them and continued the slavery under the guise of marriage.

They learned about the marvelous invention by Benjamin Franklin — broomcorn, which Franklin created by crossing grass with corn. This marvelous plant would grow where cotton wouldn't grow, and with little moisture. Soon all the farmers planted broomcorn and there grew up a small industry complete with brokers and broomcorn futures.

Pa Lotter, his lessons in enslavement handed down from father to son, bought the land of farmers who'd planted broomcorn en masse and as soon as the price of broomcorn went down, destroying the market, causing farmers to go bankrupt, bought up the land. Nobody knew how much he was worth, not even Emma. Especially Emma, for Emma was a descendant of her Choctaw mother. "If I were paid a dollar a day I would have made a lot of money for Pa. That's not counting the cows I milk or the combining or the steers I raise." Emma suffered not only from the hands of her father but also from the hatred of those people whose lands her father now possessed.

Across this hot land, through the low caliche dust drifting in from the highway a quarter mile away the intense New Mexico southwest sun twinkled hot burning lights into the dry sand, the hot dirt, like white fire, casting blazing fiery burning reflections from busy cars on the highway, sparks of fire, into Emma's squinting eyes. "Three years I've been out of high school, waiting . . . waiting for what? Other girls went to college or maybe they married and they have little babies and they drive up and down that highway in cars of their own, or with husbands of their own, and kids of their own, and homes. And I? I've not been held hands with!" She tried to figure up the money she had made for her father but could not. Those Hereford steers; feeding them? The winter wheat?" And they say one day the oil men are going to be putting up oil derricks and Pa's still too tight to buy real whiskey from a bootlegger. He could drive to Four Corners and buy it legal, right over the counter. I even get hit when I break one of Old Man Moore's bottles with the plow point. I ought to have had my head examined for letting Pa turn down that scholarship they offered me. I could have gone to college, free. Why did Pa do that to me? What did he want to keep me home for?"

The heat reflecting from the hard baked sandy ground slapped her in the face, forcing her to lick her dried lips. Salty perspiration lingered on her tongue.

The tennis shoes kicked up hot dirt which crumbled into the cut-out ends of the shoes, hot sand between her toes. The shoes had been cut to make room for her growing feet five years before. Her feet were tanned to the color of saddle leather where the sun hit, but her legs were white and smooth because of the long black cotton dress she wore. It had belonged to her mother, she thought, but wasn't sure.

She glanced at the highway again with hungry eyes. *Everyone that traveled a highway was married to someone else.* Happy women with husbands and children of their own. Twenty-one years old and Pa Lotter said if he ever saw her kissing a man he'd kill them both. *'spect he would.*

"I could work as a maid in somebody's kitchen. That would be nice.

At least I'd have a new dress and maybe every other year a pair of real shoes with leather soles. But I shouldn't have let Pa turn down that scholarship they offered me. How could I have prevented that? He said he would throw me out of the house. What would I have done? Where would I have lived?"

She pushed the poke bonnet up, adjusted the long protective sleeves of the black cotton dress, then watched Pa Lotter's white tea towel tied to the sucker rod of the windmill. The sucker rod pumped briskly up and down, pulling water out of the ground as it fluttered the tea towel in the fast hot wind.

With care, Emma lifted her feet to avoid scraping the ever hottening sand into her open tennis shoes, then she walked toward the house to eat dinner.

She thought bitterly about her father. He was afraid she might leave and therefore he paid her no wages. She had never done anything except go to school and work for her father. She had not been to Corrillo in three years even though the town was clearly visible to her almost every day. *Where would she go?* Nobody in the county would dare go against her father. He owned too many mortgages and too much land. Emma would not have known there was a World War II going on if Pa Lotter had not bought a radio to keep abreast of the broomcorn stock market quotations after the Japanese bombed Pearl Harbor. The price of Hereford steers rose fantastically and he rejoiced.

As Emma stepped into the kitchen to wash up before dinner she knew Jim Moore watched her with a sly, evilish grin and she thought: *dirty old leech, filthy old crud, wearing a pair of pants so dirty they could stand alone, blinking that gotch eye, and the tobacco dripping down the wrinkles of his chin, and dried.* An old friend! He and Pa Lotter grew up together and they were as one together. Neither knew where the other ended nor began. Fellows together, friends. It bothered neither that one was rich and the other poor for money was a game to be played and only one of them wanted to play it.

"What for dinner, Pa?" she asked.

"You know what fer dinner. We eat it ever day."

"I just asked." In her day-dreaming she had forgotten the rules that she should never ask questions. The two old men had established rules that had never been challenged and because they were never challenged, the rules constantly became more extreme. Walk on the balls of your feet when a man casts a shadow lest the man might think a woman was taking over. Children were seen but not heard. A child was always a child to listen to the parent who always knew best. Women lived for men's convenience and pleasure and had no rights to protest. What a woman owned belonged to the husband.

Emma sloshed water over her face and the red sand ran off like bloody rivulets. Pa Lotter contained himself in toothless silence as he hopped like a frog back and forth between the little wood stove and the kitchen table. In his childhood and younger days he had worshipped horses and rode them from morning until night. At the age of twenty-one he discovered his legs had grown somewhat in the shape of the body of a horse; he was bow-legged. His feet had grown in the shape of cowboy boots, with bunions and arches so high as to preclude lengthy walks. Nowadays, however, the pickup truck took the place of the horse. *He had become wheeled.* And with a daughter who did all the work what man needed a work horse?

Emma dried her face. Funny thing about that sand. It looked white when dry, turned pink when wet, and washed off easily without a trace, without soap, as though it might be powdered glass.

Without the long poke bonnet Emma's face was clear and her gray eyes emerged from out of the depths of the poke bonnet. She had light brown hair, now plaited around her head, still caked with sweat and sand, flat against her skull, the warm brown color obscured by sand and dirt. Her cheeks were inclined to dimples but as thin as she was they were only deep creases. She threw the wash water out the back door and shook the sand out of her tennis shoes onto the back stoop where the wind immediately blew it away.

The cornbread and milk was a very nutritious meal because Emma went looking for guinea hen nests almost daily and the little guinea eggs were part of the cornbread. Alongside there was a bowl of cold Mexican beans, brown and thick with a dull dried film covering it.

Before they sat down to the small repast, Pa Lotter hopped over to the radio and turned it on. Nobody objected to the screeching, the unintelligible howling. Jim Moore poured himself some whiskey in a snuff glass. Emma noticed and remembered she had plowed up that jar of whiskey only a couple of days previously. She didn't break many jars and she knew which ones she uncovered and she knew Jim Moore was drinking heavily because she'd plowed up half a dozen in the past week. Jim Moore had a map upon which was catalogued each bottle and its hiding place. Sometimes he followed behind her plow like a chicken searching for worms, yelling at her to be careful as he scavenged his moonshine.

"Bless the men in this house," murmured Pa Lotter; then he crumbled his cornbread into his milk.

"Pa, if you would stir up a little sugar and milk with it we could have pudding instead of cornbread every time." The words were there before she could stop them, lying thickly in the hot, reeking kitchen air like heavy smoke waiting for a fanning breeze to burst a fire into flame.

Silence.

Pa Lotter gummed his cornbread and milk. Though he was rich he had no teeth. He had owned a pair of false teeth at one time but he had forgotten to take them out of his mouth for so long that one day he found a little flower, a tiny bit of moss, growing out between the two front teeth and then he went to the dentist to have the teeth removed and the dentist had broken them getting them out. Pa Lotter stalked out of the dentist's office and from that day forth gummed his food.

Silence.

Pa Lotter's chin met his nose on each bite. He hadn't yet decided in which way to declare his authority as male head of household. It was Jim Moore who sparked the embers. He cleared his throat daintily, his gotch eye bearing down on Emma, glimmering moistly in anticipation of getting on the good side of Pa Lotter by kicking the female child.

Pa Lotter said nothing. Jim Moore cleared his throat again,

disapproving of Emma, disappointed in Pa Lotter. Then Jim Moore said, "Don't know as I'd take anything from any woman."

Pa Lotter's fist hit the table. Spoons in a cup in the center of the table clattered in all directions.

"Guuurl!" screeched Pa Lotter. The radio howled accompaniment. "Telling a man what to do! Under his own roof! Telling a man how to cook when he's doing the cookin' fer you! Eatin' vittles I stirred up myself! Grown woman eat'n offn my own table, beholden to me for every stitch on your back." He grabbed a kitchen knife. She ducked; he hit her over the head with it. "You got them high falutin' idees goin' to high school. I shoulda took you out of school when you was in the fourth grade!"

"Bread pudding is not high falutin'." She didn't care anyway. He'd forgotten to salt it and he'd fried it on top of the stove lids again — just as he used to do when he was a cowboy before he had settled down.

"Don't talk back to your elders!" he shouted, "I heerd you talk about my cookin for the last time. You lernt it in high school. And you talk to me about collich like you was pretendin to go there. You ain't goin to collich! And them boys you want — don't tell me what you want. I seen you look down there at the highway. You shet your mouth about boys!"

"I never mention college, nor boys, not since you wouldn't let me have the scholarship." she whispered, cringing because the noise from the radio cut across Pa Lotter's words and the air trembled.

"I said don't talk back!" he yelled, "And paintin' yoreself up like a mare's hind end! You ain't goin to lie to me. I saw that paint in your drawer!"

"Last year the Raleigh man left a lipstick sample." she protested.

Pa Lotter ignored her, "Ain't no man in this county goin to tell me how I should raise my youngun and I say you look like a mare's hind end turned wrong side out!"

"I do not!" she said stoutly, "Anyway, all you want is a free hired hand to do your work while you and old Jim sport together." She wanted to kill him.

He saw the anger and said, "Jim, git me the horsewhip. Ain't no youngun goin against me. I'll teach you who's boss." The two men arose quickly but Emma also pushed back her chair and the kitchen table jiggled, overturning the fruit jar of moonshine. Emma ran through the puddle of whiskey on the floor and tore the poke bonnet from the nail over the washstand and ran out the back door with Pa Lotter yelling after her, "You ain't goin no place! I got the whole county locked up! You can't walk ten feet without my say-so and ain't no man in the county who'd take you in!" Pa Lotter held a thumb against one side of his nose and blew his nose expertly through the open door as he watched his daughter.

She yelled back, "I'll go to college. You can't control the college."

He answered, "That whorehouse collich ain't open for two more months."

"Then I'll stay in town and work." Her answer was feeble, uncertain. "Somebody will hire me."

"No they won't," he answered.

She believed him as she had always believed him and she had always tried to push that picture of herself defeated from her mind.

"Here's the horsewhip," laughed Jim Moore. Emma ran out into the sunbaked yard. A quarter mile away was the highway that all morning had been filled with gleaming lines of automobiles but which now hummed only with the sound of the electric high-line alongside it.

She bent low, grabbed the hem of her long dress in her hand and her legs skimmed freely over the beargrass and mesquite of the pasture. She knew what Pa Lotter would do. He would let her run to the highway and after she was tired he would go to the barn and get out the new red pickup truck. He'd drive carefully for he wouldn't risk breaking springs driving over mesquites and beargrasses. He would drive around by the road and meet her at the highway. He could drive that far even if he were so drunk he couldn't see out of either eye.

She ducked back and forth around the beargrasses like a frightened jackrabbit, wiping away her tears, feeling humiliated for outwitting dogs dripping hungry saliva. Then she looked back. The two men sat on the front porch with their heads together and the long whip standing between them and they were laughing at her.

"What am I going to do now?" she sniffed and wiped at her tears.

Far down the highway, where earlier there had been an eternal line of cars, now only empty silent heat waves shook the horizon as though all automobiles had evaporated in a hot mirage. She stopped to get her breath. Cats-claw grabbed her around the ankles. Cockleburrs clung to the tight black tops of her tennis shoes but she continued to walk toward the highway. She could see the village of Corrillo ten miles down the highway, the adobe houses looking black, shimmering in the middle of the hot little valley.

Even without Pa Lotter following her in the new pick-up truck, that ten miles to Corrillo was still ten miles, four hours of fast walking under a hot shaking sun — if a car didn't come along and pick her up.

As she turned on to the highway she saw the water jug she had forgotten to take home for refilling at dinner time. She scurried through the tall Johnson grass bordering the field and lifted the water jug and drank, "If I don't come back that Johnson grass will take over the field. Pa doesn't even know it's there." Then, from force of habit, she poured water into the jar lid then from the lid poured it onto the burlap covering the jar, dampening it. Then she rescrewed the lid and tossed the burlap-covered jar under a cat's claw bush where it would now stay cool as the wind blew over the wet burlap. It was all done unconsciously. Then she began to walk down the highway.

She could feel the highway humming under the blazing sunlight and knew that four or five miles away a car was coming but it wouldn't help any if Pa Lotter beat it to the highway and he was already threading his way over the beargrass, the red pickup lurching. He was turning onto the highway and driving for her, the pickup wavering like a drunken hoot owl and the end of the long leather horsewhip hanging out of the truck cab and the metal end of the whip kicking along the asphalt. Emma ran up an embankment as the pickup slid off the highway into the sand as Pa Lotter took his eyes from the road when flicking at her with the quirt.

She started to run but laughed instead. The truck was stuck, its wheels quickly spinning down to the axles in the sand. Pa Lotter shoved the gear into reverse, gunned the motor and the truck dug in more firmly. The wheels spun forward. The truck was as if imbedded in concrete. The next demand would be to Emma to help, to let the air out of the tires so Pa could drive out. She did not listen to him as he yelled epithets and demands.

Then she saw two cars. She stuck out her thumb. What she saw was a welcome escape from tyranny, a shiny black automobile with a bleating horn. What the occupants of the car saw was something entirely different. The car swerved to the opposite side of the highway, swaying as it passed, the laughter within mingling with the now heinous laughter of Pa Lotter. They laughed at Emma, laughed at the dirty grey poke bonnet, the long black dress, and the protruding thumb.

Quickly, she removed her poke bonnet and the second car stopped. She did not see, at first, who was in the car. She saw only that Pa Lotter dropped his whip as if in a panic. Emma stepped into the open door of the car and heard the hearty hello from the driver and she looked up to see a sheriff's badge.

She shouted in triumph, "I'm going to college!"

"Emma Lotter, I didn't recognize you without your bonnet."

"Bonnet? Who are you?" He was a fleshy man wearing a wide black belt like a girdle, with two empty gun holsters, and flesh protruding over the belt being covered by a neat tan shirt.

"Name's Manuel O'Brien. I'm the sheriff over in Contreras County. I pass by here nearly every week, taking prisoners to Santa Fe. In fact, I'm just returning. Every time I go by here somebody in the car points you out and says, "That's Old Man Lotter's daughter."

"Some of Pa's mighty fine friends?" asked Emma. Manuel O'Brien ignored her sarcasm: He asked, "Crops good this year? They say you are a mighty good farmer."

"Yes?" She was surprised to hear somebody say something nice about her.

"Did I hear you say you were going to college? Summer school?"

"No, fall term."

"Kind of early for the fall term, isn't it? Well, always hoped you would make it. Old Man Lotter object very much?"

The sheriff might as well have struck her. She had always thought it to be her own private secret that she was a slave to her father and the fact that somebody else also knew humiliated and embarrassed her.

She said, "My father object to me going to college? Mr. O'Brien!"

"Yeah?" he answered, looking through the rearview mirror, watching Pa Lotter storing the horsewhip away in the back of the truck.

So Manuel O'Brien asked about the price of broomcorn.

"Two hundred a ton." she answered, "I didn't know a war could affect the price of broomcorn or brooms."

"War affects everybody. My son O'Fallohan was in the National Guard when Bataan fell. He's in the Philippines now — prisoner." Oh Lord, thought Emma. What could anybody say to that? He continued, "And my other son, Ezekial, is home on furlough."

"What's he like — Ezekial?" asked Emma.

Manuel O'Brien began to detail the qualities of his son and Emma nestled her head against the plush upholstery to listen and to think about the son being conjured up in front of her. Ezekial would make a nice husband.

Emma decided that sooner she started hunting a man, the sooner she would find him. It did not occur to her that she was trying to transfer to a lesser master than her father rather than solving her problem. Having been isolated all her life from personal contacts she was unaware of the ways other girls went about the job of acquiring husbands. She knew of Moslems in other countries whose fathers and mothers went in search of husbands instead of their daughters doing this. But then other girls had fathers who cuddled kittens and petted dogs and dandled children on their knees. Emma had never had a kitten or a dog and certainly her father was too bowlegged, even when sober, to dandle any child.

Emma knew the townspeople were afraid of her father, not for themselves in a physical sense, but because of his grasping way with the dollar and the mortgages he held on them.

But Manuel O'Brien, Sheriff of Contreras County, wasn't afraid. Then maybe his son wouldn't be either.

Emma could see, as they neared Corrillo, the 'college', a long flat white building which lay nestled against the flat prairie like a docile worm, slightly down into the valley in which Corrillo nestled, yet two miles west of the village itself.

O'Brien said, "You don't look old enough to go to college. You look about sixteen, maybe fourteen."

"I'm twenty-one years of age!" she replied indignantly.

"Oh pardon me. When a man gets to be fifty he kind of forgets how it feels, and looks, to be twenty-one. I didn't have any daughters or I'd have known. Well, girlie, I have a little business with Sheriff Valdez, so I'll drop you off in front of the courthouse."

"Where is Ezekial now?" she asked, "You said he was on furlough."

"Somewhere about town, visiting his friends."

"If I see Ezekial, how will I know him?" asked Emma.

"He's got kind of yellow hair and he's sunburned, but I suspect you'll know him because he's in uniform."

"Yessir. Thank you for the ride, sir." She got out of the car and looked around at the village she had not seen in three years.

The war did affect everybody. In front of the cut stone courthouse big signs marched along the sidewalk, DON'T SPREAD RUMORS! GIVE BLOOD! UNCLE SAM WANTS YOU! JOIN THE NAVY AND SEE THE WORLD! JOIN THE WACS AND LET THE WORLD SEE YOU!

She did not see any thin blonde young men on the streets. In the whole town, spreading out its one square block of stores, encircling the old fashioned courthouse, she saw nobody she knew. A woman spat snuff on the sidewalk and a heavy-faced soldier wearing a lot of stripes down one arm sat dejectedly on the front steps of the courthouse.

Emma started toward the college in a rapid walk. Two miles out of town meant the sun would say four o'clock before she arrived there. But her steps were light and sure as she imagined herself a college graduate. She shook a grassburr from between the toes of one foot.

Being a college girl would be high falutin' indeed. Maybe she should teach. No. Not teach. Something more exciting. She planned. She dreamed. She passed houses that had remained unchanged during her whole lifetime, houses that had never been painted but that looked exactly the same today as they had when she first went to school. They had weathered shining gray, protected by the dry New Mexico air so they would never decay. There was a small adobe house she knew had been built in 1898, yet today looked the same as it had the first day of school. There, another — a house of wood — shining, glossy grey, sanded smooth by the wind to stand forever. People died in Corrillo, but never buildings.

Soon she arrived at the college. She picked one of the red flowers bordering the sidewalk. Such a strange thing — a cultivated flower, not indigenous to Corrillo at all, but brought in by strangers who knew of flowers from other lands.

Once, in elementary school, Emma learned that other parts of the world were not the same as in Corrillo. There were strange stories in books, telling fairy tales, she was sure, when she was little, telling of grass that grew green over hills, of mountains covered with mantles of green, of green forests.

As Emma grew older she learned other people could verify indeed that the world was green. She supposed it to be true and accepted it as true. There were green lawns in Corrillo, watered by people willing to pay for water and Emma supposed forests were the same color.

Someday she would see the things she read about in books, things people said were true. At the drug store she could unscrew the caps of exotic face creams and inhale the beauty of other lands, other people.

Still, Corrillo had its sweetness too, in the winds that blew over wild prairies and smelled as sweet as any dream. She remembered a book in particular, written by a Russian that detailed vast battles, vast countries, and a vast panorama of land so big as to stretch through time. Even though Emma had no first hand knowledge of the depth and size of earth and its people, she realized it was vast. She stuck the red flower into the front end of her bonnet, along one of the cardboard slats and watched it bob up and down. "I'm really going to like it here." she said to herself. Politely she shook sand and grit from her tennis shoes, scraped the bottoms of them on the steps before entering the long hallway extending the entire length of the building called the 'college.'

Open classroom doors admitted oozes of faint light sporadically down the cool dark hall, at the end of which the slanted light brought a blue painted mural into sharp focus. She walked slowly, noting through open doors the empty classroom chairs clustered as though in hurried confusion when college adjourned in June.

She walked along, silently, past the president's office, the business office, the registrar's office, which she entered. This foyer siphoned off into three tiny cubicles and in one of them a grey-haired woman concentrated intensely upon leafing through papers and she did not hear Emma Lotter's noiseless steps.

Emma stood before the woman's desk, watching her silently. The papers rustled in a small breeze entering through a window. A rose fluttered in a vase on the desk and wafted its educated perfume to Emma's nose. The woman said in a thoughtful voice, "How do they ever get out of high school?" and turned the page onto another pile of papers.

Emma watched, envying the woman whose hand reached in, like a lady, at the top of her dress to adjust a satin and lace slip strap. Then the woman pulled up the side of her dress and carefully changed the position of an itchy garter which Emma noticed was the kind that ran down the leg instead of around the leg like the innertube garters Emma had always cut for herself. As Emma grew old it had been necessary to find larger and larger tire tubes. Once a teacher noticed the garters and asked about them. Emma hadn't realized there was anything wrong with innertube garters until then. After that she rolled her stockings.

Grassburrs entangled in the tops of Emma's tennis shoes and scratched her ankles; her bare toes emerged from the shoes like wrinkled turtle heads. She squiggled her toes together, waiting patiently for the woman to notice her.

First, the woman, her head down, noticed the binding twine lacing the tennis shoes, caught with brown cockleburrs all over. Then she saw the long black dress hanging like a rag mop above the turtle heads. Then she looked up at the pale, intent face peering at her like a racoon in the dark.

"What is it?" cried the startled woman.

"I want to go to college." replied Emma patiently, "I'm Emma Lotter."

"You scared me to death. Where did you come from?"

"I came through the door." Emma's voice was happy, soft, friendly.

"To go to college?" asked the woman, incredulously.

"To go to college." repeated Emma, a little louder but still patient. Surely the woman must be deaf.

"Have you been to high school?"

"Graduated three years ago."

"But you don't look as though you've ever been inside a school house."

"You don't wear education." said Emma testily, "And if you don't like this dress, I got another one at home just like it. I would like to enroll for the fall semester."

"Now?" asked the woman. Emma felt that woman was only trying to get rid of her. The woman said, "This is a college. It may be only the size of a peanut but we don't take just any derelict who shows up."

"It's a state college and you do too, and I ain't no derelict. I've lived around Corrillo all my life. I'm honest. I work hard. Everybody knows me. I guess they must. Just ask anybody."

"I wasn't thinking of references. We do have to accept you but only if you are qualified for college. By the way, I'm Dean Brown."

"Emma Lotter."

Emma extended her hand and the dean did not seem disposed to shake it so Emma withdrew it and wiped it on her black dress.

The dean said, "This is a new job for me and I really had no idea the Southwest was so primitive. I'm from the city. Washington, D.C."

"Are there any boys in Washington, D.C.?"

"How do I know? I don't go around looking for boys." She flung all the papers into the top drawer of her desk and fumed, "I'm nothing but a deanlet, just a deanlet for the likes of you."

Emma plowed in, "You have records on me. I had a scholarship. I wanted to go to college three years ago but . . . Pa . . . I couldn't then, but I can now."

Dean Brown walked over to the tall metal filing cabinet and said thoughtfully as she rummaged through records, "They'll laugh you right out of school if you come to college wearing something like that." Then the dean pulled out records and looked up at Emma. Emma had become a human, suddenly, in the dean's eyes, "You were valedictorian of your class and didn't go to college? Well, in a little town like this it is possible. You could be dumb as a doorknob." She turned the papers over and read on the back, then she looked up at Emma with new respect and with surprise, "Your achievement scores were very high. Well, Emma, we certainly do want you to go to college. We need you to raise the grade point average of the new freshmen."

"All right, ma'am. Where do I sign?"

"Not today. We'll have to try to reactivate your scholarship but I don't know how. You come back next week and we'll try to find you a job. You have to earn enough to pay board and room — if you have to make it on your own." The dean looked keenly at Emma and Emma stood her ground, not giving away any family secrets. "There will be a tuition fee of twenty dollars per semester, five dollars for matriculation, five dollars for the yearbook, five dollars for the student union fund and five dollars laboratory fee."

"FORTY DOLLARS!" shouted Emma, "to go to college for one semester! I had a scholarship!"

"Don't worry about it, Emma. We'll try to get another one."

The dean patted Emma's shoulder and pointed her to the door in order to get rid of her because the clock was nearing 4:30, quitting time. "Your father can probably help a little."

Emma silently scrubbed her exposed toes together. She took off her poke bonnet, carefully undid a tangle of hair from around a grassburr above her ear. She was thinking about Pa Lotter helping with tuition.

Dean Brown read her, became irritated and said, "Your mother?"

Emma slowly flipped the grassburr into a wastebasket.

"You do have a mother, don't you?"

"No ma'am."

"When did she pass away?"

"She . . ." Emma didn't know and didn't want to appear ignorant.

The dean snapped, "You do have a belly button, I presume. You must pattern your life after somebody. Every girl has to have a mother-image."

Emma could hear the dean's stomach growling.

Emma didn't know what to answer.

"Where do you live?" asked the dean.

"Ten miles west."

"Oh, that. I know that." said the dean. It would have been difficult to have missed it since it was the only house on that side of town for twenty miles. An old grey house and a bright red barn. Not even a tree in that vast flat prairie for fifty miles.

"You like the barn? I painted it myself." Dean Brown sniffed as though she smelled the turpentine.

"We'll get you a job. What can you do?"

"I can drive a tractor, run a combine, bind feed, bale hay. I can hoe. I don't like to run a combine because I caught my foot in the canvas last year and I almost lost my foot. My own fault. I can repair any kind of farm machinery. I'm real good at reading directions. I can read anything."

"Can you wait tables?"

"What's that?"

"I don't know what we'll do with you, but we'll do something. We don't have too many valedictorians entering this little college. God, when God passed out father-images, you must have been behind the door. I wonder what's going to happen to you. What a time you are going to have when you get out in the world."

"It can't be any worse than what I've already seen," said Emma, somewhat angrily.

"That's what you think." said the dean.

"Dean Brown, are you married?"

"No, of course not."

"Did you have a father-image?"

"Certainly."

"So did I, and if my pa wasn't as civilized as yours, still I know right from wrong and I think you are saying something nasty to me. I don't know just how or what it is, but when I get married, I'll be as good a wife as anybody and if I decide to be a dean, I'll be just as good a dean as you. I can learn. I got the whole world to learn on."

Emma walked out of the building and thought about forty dollars and room and board. She had no place to sleep, no money, and nothing to eat.

The one college building bordered an alfalfa field where an irrigation ditch filled with running water looked cool and inviting. Emma knelt and dipped her face into the cool water. She thought about the three hams, ready to eat, hanging in the adobe smokehouse on the north side of the barn.

She pulled off her tennis shoes and was ashamed, "What did the dean think of me! Dirt all over my toes." She slipped her sand-caked toes into the water and shivered with delight as the coolness caressed her.

The lack of food and a place to sleep did not bother her unduly. She had always known this town and of this town and none of it had ever harmed her. And beyond the alfalfa field, a half dozen cows had turned their heavy dripping udders toward home for the night milking.

She would wait until darkness, then skirt the alfalfa field and strip the cows' milk into her mouth like a cat. A cow always began making new milk as soon as she was relieved of the old.

Around her Emma could see irrigated fields overburdened with fat tomatoes, fat peppers, radishes, onions, and sweet potatoes, unripe peanuts.

But the problem was a place to sleep. All her life she had slept on the same corn shuck mattress in the same little room, except in the summer when the bedbugs got too bad, then she slept out under the stars on a quilt and listened to coyotes call each other. But now she did not have a quilt, nothing for cover against the cold New Mexico nights.

And too, Pa Lotter would be looking for her. There was no friend to take her in and no hotel to accept a nonpaying — or paying — guest.

She took the cardboard slats out of the poke bonnet and used it as a washcloth, dunking it into the irrigation ditch, washing her face and hands. But the impulse to dip her head into the water overcame her. She immersed her head and brought it up quickly with a breath of shock at the coldness of the water. She dunked her head again and again, feeling the sand loosen itself and float away, like red dye.

She wiped her hair dry with the damp bonnet, combed her hair with her fingers. Dean Brown came out of the college and saw Emma sitting on the irrigation bank, but Emma pretended not to see.

When twilight fell she went from field to field, pulling up a few radishes, onions, picking a pepper here and some tomatoes not quite ripe. With them held in the front of her dress, sack-like, she returned to the college with a plan in her mind.

She went from window to window, looking for an open one, remembered the window in the dean's office. With a sliver of stick, she forced the screen latch and climbed in, first wiping the stolen food of dirt and dropping it through the window. From room to room she walked, enjoying the darkness, seeing the dim outlines of desks and chairs and visualizing herself in these classrooms. In the home economics room she found a cot, a gas stove, and faucets, one of them still dripping, and a pitcher.

She left the building in the same manner she had entered, threw the pitcher to the ground, crawled out after it then went to the barn where the cows had been milked. She stripped them, acquiring a quart of milk. It did not occur to her that she could do without milk, that it was unnecessary to her in her predicament. She had always drunk milk at supper time. Always. She had not always eaten fresh vegetables though. Fresh vegetables were a luxury to her.

She boiled her vegetables in a pot because it did not occur to her to eat them fresh. She washed her black dress and the tennis shoes and hung them on cabinet knobs and passed the night sleeping naked and soundly on the cot.

The next morning she cleaned after herself carefully, left the college, taking only a fork with which to comb her hair until she had money for a comb.

Paula Gunn Allen

IYANI: It Goes This Way

We are the land. To the best of my understanding, that is the fundamental idea embedded in Native American life and culture in the Southwest. More than remembered, the Earth is the mind of the people as we are the mind of the earth. The land is not really the place (separate from ourselves) where we act out the drama of our isolate destinies. It is not a means of survival, a setting for our affairs, a resource on which we draw in order to keep our own act functioning. It is not the ever-present "Other" which supplies us with a sense of "I". It is rather a part of our being, dynamic, significant, real. It is ourself, in as real a sense as such notions as "ego," "libido" or social network, in a sense more real than any conceptualization or abstraction about the nature of human being can ever be. The land is not an image in our eyes but rather it is as truly an integral aspect of our being as we are of its being. And the integral nature of this fact continues beyond mortal dissolution of bodies — human, beast or plant. The old ones come from Sipap to participate in the eternal living being of the land/people as rain. The gods come from the skies and mountain peaks to participate in the welfare of this immutable gestalt. In this return, the corn and squash, the deer and game, the men and women are renewed. The Shiwana show us what the truth about being, our collective/entire being is. And so, Indian poets of the Southwest return again and again to this relationship, as the singers, the priests, the dancers, the animals and the gods return. It is within this larger being that we are given life, and in the acknowledgement of the singleness of that being that we eat, that we plant, that we harvest, that we build and clean, that we dance, hunt, run, heal, sing, chant and write.

Nor is this relationship one of mere "affinity" for the Earth. It is not a matter of being "close to nature." The relationship is more one of identity, in the mathematical sense, than of affinity. The Earth is, in a very real sense, the same as ourself (or selves), and it is this primary point that is made in the fiction and poetry of the Native American writers of the Southwest.

On occasion, the point is made by its absence; writers mourn the loss of that unity, or its absence among those who are strangers to the circle, or the person's own distance from that knowledge is chronicled in anger or pain. Yet even despair is a result of known belonging with and to the land: "you can't lose something you never had," as the saying goes, and having known that perfect peace of being together with all that surrounds one, other attempts at gaining satisfaction or joy are too pale to be worth considering. That knowledge, though perfect, does not have associated with it the exalted romance of sentimental "nature lovers," nor does it have, at base, any self-conscious "appreciation" of the land, or even of the primary event of unification. It is a matter of fact, one known equably from infancy, remembered and honored at

191

levels of awareness that go beyond consciousness, and that extend long roots deep into primary levels of mind, language, perception and all the basic aspects of being that have as one of their expressions our writing.

Carol Lee Sanchez talks about how deep this awareness goes in a poem for Wendy Rose:

> it seems proper that language should also
> reflect harmony — a giving way;
> a moving in; a coming out.
>
> these things we speak about
> (from our respective memories-
> these traditions we keep
> not knowing why we do so
> or even (sometimes-
> how we 'know' the right ways.
> maybe, that 'racial memory' (he mentioned.
> a genetic imprint
> handed down from many grandmothers
> those grandmothers who watch — over us
> whisper in the wind-
> remind us of our duties. . . .

Goweitduweetza (Veronica Riley) writes about this loss, and the knowledge of how it has been/should/will be in "Untitled Journey," saying that after a sojourn in a "peaceful land/Of untouched beauty" a child will return to this place of "lances that pierce/ . . . And/Hands that hold/Falsely" who will bring again that beauty and peace to human hearts:

> Child of beauty
>   Are you ready?
> Then
> Return my healed heart to earth
> Bring with you seeds
>   Of a new generation
>
> Begin
> Only when it is safe
> And plant wisely
> I will guard these seeds
>   with my life

Her poem speaks to very ancient metaphysical truths of her people, and so simply, so clearly, that she evokes for us both the reality of the pain of this strange distance from the Earth and Earth's beauty, and the perfect knowledge of the kind of unification with the source of our being that is naturally ours.

The theme of the difference between the remembered unity and the present-experienced alienation is movingly chronicled in Larry Emerson's "Gallup." The protagonist, lost on Saturday in Gallup, alienated from himself, his people and his family, still can remember what was good about being, and can wonder at its disappearance. He is trapped with the case of beer and surrounded by hostile people — the bartender, the cop, the "punks," the drunks and his drunken and demoralized self when he begins to think of his home:

> For the first time, really, in a long time, I thought of my old home when I was young. My mother a long time ago. She had strong features. My father and his tough-looking hands. Old Man's turquoise earring. They were all gone now. The home was gone. The place where we little ones used to return each evening was gone. The corral empty . . . And all those sheep who had all sorts of different personalities. All the sheep, each with their own relatives, their own family trees, their own histories, were gone, stopped. It was like putting an end to a whole human race or a culture—whatever that is.

The importance, the centrality of the earth, its existence as our own being, is delicately articulated in Simon Ortiz's "Woman Singing". In this tale of distance from home, the song is home. The people are migrant farmworkers, subject to the brutalities of that life. The woman who sings is raped, like the land has been raped. But there is her song, which is her strength, her tie to her people, which is, finally The People, and which tells us about the meaning and eternal being that is this Earth. It is this knowledge of what it means to endure that is, I think, the essential contribution of Native American writers and Native American peoples to literature. And it is this knowledge that is woven through the works which appear in this volume that embodies each of them with their most vital significance. In a poem entitled "Dry Root in a Wash," Simon Ortiz writes of endurance, unity and the eternal being of all things:

> The sand is fine grit
> and warm to the touch.
> An old juniper root
> lies by the cutbank of sand
> it lingers, waiting
> for the next month of rain.
>
> I feel like saying,
> It will rain, but you know
> better than I these centuries
> don't mean much
> for anyone to be waiting.
>
> Upstream, towards the mountains,
> the Shiwana work for rain.
>
> They know we're waiting.
>
> Underneath the fine sand
> it is cool
> with crystalline moisture,
> the forming rain.

Goweitduweetza (Veronica Riley)

UNTITLED JOURNEY

Winged Bird
   Steal my pierced heart
Fly with it high   and higher
Till man and his earth
   Are blurred and lost
Blind my eyes and deafen my ears
To lances that pierce
Voices that soothe
And
Hands that hold
Falsely

Carry my heart to a peaceful land
   Of untouched beauty
Where Soul and Mind
   Together
   Disturbing no other
Lie in blissful Love

Let their child
The mother of a new creation
Be
Untainted by memories
   Of a world past
   Or flaws of destruction
Let the child live
In the fruits
In the wisdom
   Of a peaceful land
Growing
Maturing

Child of beauty
   Are you ready?
Then
Return my healed heart to earth
Bring with you seeds
   Of a new generation

Begin
Only when it is safe
And plant wisely
I will guard these seeds
   With my life

Leslie Marmon Silko

STORYTELLER

Every day the sun came up a little lower on the horizon, moving more slowly until one day she got excited and started calling the jailer. She realized she had been sitting there for many hours, yet the sun had not moved from the center of the sky. The color of the sky had not been good lately; it had been pale blue, almost white, even when there were no clouds. She told herself it wasn't a good sign for the sky to be indistinguishable from the river ice, frozen solid and white against the earth. The tundra rose up behind the river but all the boundaries between the river and hills and sky were lost in the density of the pale ice.

She yelled again, this time some English words which came randomly into her mouth, probably swear words she'd heard from the oil drilling crews last winter. The jailer was an Eskimo, but he would not speak Yupik to her. She had watched people in the other cells; when they spoke to him in Yupik he ignored them until they spoke English.

He came and stared at her. She didn't know if he understood what she was telling him until he glanced behind her at the small high window. He looked at the sun, and turned and walked away. She could hear the buckles on his heavy snowmobile boots jingle as he walked to the front of the building.

It was like the other buildings that white people, the Gussucks, brought with them: BIA and school buildings, portable buildings that arrived sliced in halves, on barges coming up the river. Squares of metal panelling bulged out with the layers of insulation stuffed inside. She had asked once what it was and someone told her it was to keep out the cold. She had not laughed then, but she did now. She walked over to the small double-pane window and she laughed out loud. They thought they could keep out the cold with stringy yellow wadding. Look at the sun. It wasn't moving; it was frozen, caught in the middle of the sky. Look at the sky, solid as the river with ice which had trapped the sun. It had not moved for a long time; in a few more hours it would be weak, and heavy frost would begin to appear on the edges and spread across the face of the sun like a mask. Its light was pale yellow, worn thin by the winter.

She could see people walking down the snow-packed roads, their breath steaming out from their parka hoods, faces hidden and protected by deep ruffs of fur. There were no cars or snowmobiles that day so she calculated it was fifty below zero, the temperature which silenced their machines. The metal froze; it split and shattered. Oil hardened and moving parts jammed solidly. She had seen it happen to their big yellow machines and the giant drill last winter when they came to drill their test holes. The cold stopped them, and they were helpless against it.

Her village was many miles upriver from this town, but in her mind she could see it clearly. Their house was not near the village houses. It stood alone on the bank upriver from the village. Snow had drifted to the eaves of the roof on the north side, but on the west side, by the door, the path was almost clear. She had nailed scraps of red tin over the logs last summer. She had done it for the bright red color, not for added warmth the way the village people had done. This final winter had been coming down even then; there had been signs of its approach for many years.

II

She went because she was curious about the big school where the Government sent all the other girls and boys. She had not played much with the village children while she was growing up because they were afraid of the old man, and they ran when her grandmother came. She went because she was tired of being alone with the old woman whose body had been stiffening for as long as the girl could remember. Her knees and knuckles were swollen grotesquely, and the pain had squeezed the brown skin of her face tight against the bones; it left her eyes hard like river stone. The girl asked once, what it was that did this to her body, and the old woman had raised up from sewing a sealskin boot, and stared at her.

"The joints," the old woman said in a low voice, whispering like wind across the roof, "the joints are swollen with anger."

Sometimes she did not answer and only stared at the girl. Each year she spoke less and less, but the old man talked more—all night sometimes, not to anyone but himself; in a soft deliberate voice, he told stories, moving his smooth brown hands above the blankets. He had not fished or hunted with the other men for many years although he was not crippled or sick. He stayed in his bed, smelling like dry fish and urine, telling stories all winter; and when warm weather came, he went to his place on the river bank. He sat with a long willow stick, poking at the smoldering moss he burned against the insects while he continued with the stories.

The trouble was that she had not recognized the warnings in time. She did not see what the Gussuck school would do to her until she walked into the dormitory and realized that the old man had not been lying about the place. She thought he had been trying to scare her as he used to when she was very small and her grandmother was outside cutting up fish. She hadn't believed what he told her about the school because she knew he wanted to keep her there in the log house with him. She knew what he wanted.

The dormitory matron pulled down her underpants and whipped her with a leather belt because she refused to speak English.

"Those backwards village people," the matron said, because she was an Eskimo who had worked for the BIA a long time, "they kept this one until she was too big to learn." The other girls whispered in English. They knew how to work the showers, and they washed and curled their hair at night. They ate Gussuck food. She laid on her bed and imagined what her grandmother might be sewing, and what the old man was eating in his bed. When summer came, they sent her home.

The way her grandmother had hugged her before she left for school had been a warning too, because the old woman had not hugged or touched her for many years. Not like the old man, whose hands were always hunting, like ravens circling lazily in the sky, ready to touch her. She was not surprised when the priest and the old man met her at the landing strip, to say that the old lady was gone. The priest asked her where she would like to stay. He referred to the old man as her grandfather, but she did not bother to correct him. She had already been thinking about it; if she went with the priest, he would send her away to a school. But the old man was different. She knew he wouldn't send her back to school. She knew he wanted to keep her.

III

He told her one time, that she would get too old for him faster than he got too old for her; but again she had not believed him because sometimes he lied. He had lied about what he would do with her if she came into his bed. But as the years passed, she realized what he said was true. She was restless and strong. She had no patience with the old man who had never changed his slow smooth motions under the blankets.

The old man was in his bed for the winter; he did not leave it except to use the slop bucket in the corner. He was dozing with his mouth open slightly; his lips quivered and sometimes they moved like he was telling a story even while he dreamed. She pulled on the sealskin boots, the mukluks with the bright red flannel linings her grandmother had sewn for her, and she tied the braided red yarn tassels around her ankles over the gray wool pants. She zipped the wolfskin parka. Her grandmother had worn it for many years, but the old man said that before she died, she instructed him to bury her in an old black sweater, and to give the parka to the girl. The wolf pelts were creamy colored and silver, almost white in some places, and when the old lady had walked across the tundra in the winter, she disappeared into the snow.

She walked toward the village, breaking her own path through the deep snow. A team of sled dogs tied outside a house at the edge of the village leaped against their chains to bark at her. She kept walking, watching the dusky sky for the first evening stars. It was warm and the dogs were alert. When it got cold again, the dogs would lie curled and still, too drowsy from the cold to bark or pull at the chains. She laughed loudly because it made them howl and snarl. Once the old man had seen her tease the dogs and he shook his head. "So that's the kind of woman you are," he said, "in the wintertime the two of us are no different from those dogs. We wait in the cold for someone to bring us a few dry fish."

She laughed out loud again, and kept walking. She was thinking about the Gussuck oil drillers. They were strange; they watched her when she walked near their machines. She wondered what they looked like underneath their quilted goosedown trousers; she wanted to know how they moved. They would be something different from the old man.

The old man screamed at her. He shook her shoulders so violently that her head bumped against the log wall. "I smelled it!" he yelled, "as soon as I woke up! I am sure of it now. You can't fool me!" His thin legs were shaking inside the baggy wool trousers; he stumbled over her boots in his bare feet. His toe nails were long and yellow like bird claws; she had seen a gray crane last summer fighting another in the shallow water on the edge of the river. She laughed out loud and pulled her shoulder out of his grip. He stood in front of her. He was breathing hard and shaking; he looked weak. He would probably die next winter.

"I'm warning you," he said, "I'm warning you." He crawled back into his bunk then, and reached under the old soiled feather pillow for a piece of dry fish. He lay back on the pillow, staring at the ceiling and chewed dry strips of salmon. "I don't know what the old woman told you," he said, "but there will be trouble." He looked over to see if she was listening. His face suddenly relaxed into a smile, his dark slanty eyes were lost in wrinkles of brown skin. "I could tell you, but you are too good for warnings now. I can smell what you did all night with the Gussucks."

She did not understand why they came there, because the village was small and so far upriver that even some Eskimos who had been away to school would not come back. They stayed downriver in the town. They said the village was too quiet. They were used to the town where the boarding school was located, with electric lights and running water. After all those years away at school, they had forgotten how to set nets in the river and where to hunt seals in the fall. Those who left did not say it, but their confidence had been destroyed. When she asked the old man why the Gussucks bothered to come to the village, his narrow eyes got bright with excitement.

"They only come when there is something to steal. The fur animals are too difficult for them to get now, and the seals and fish are hard to find. Now they come for oil deep in the earth. But this is the last time for them." His breathing was wheezy and fast; his hands gestured at the sky. "It is approaching. As it comes, ice will push across the sky." His eyes were open wide and he stared at the low ceiling rafters for hours without blinking. She remembered all this clearly because he began the story that day, the story he told from that time on. It began with a giant bear which he described muscle by muscle, from the curve of the ivory claws to the whorls of hair at the top of the massive skull. And for eight days he did not sleep, but talked continuously of the giant bear whose color was pale blue glacier ice.

IV

The snow was dirty and worn down in a path to the door. On either side of the path, the snow was higher than her head. In front of the door there were jagged yellow stains melted into the snow where men had urinated. She stopped in the entry way and kicked the snow off her boots. The room was dim; a kerosene lantern by the cash register was burning low. The long wooden shelves were jammed with cans of beans and potted meats. On the bottom shelf a jar of mayonnaise was broken open, leaking oily white clots on the floor. There was no one in the room except the yellowish dog sleeping in front of the long glass display case. A reflection made it appear to be lying on the knives and ammunition inside the case. Gussucks kept dogs inside their houses with them; they did not seem to mind the odors which seeped out of the dogs. "They tell us we are dirty for the food we eat—raw fish and fermented meat. But we do not live with dogs," the old man once said. She heard voices in the back room, and the sound of bottles set down hard on tables.

They were always confident. The first year they waited for the ice to break up on the river, and then they brought their big yellow machines up river on barges. They planned to drill their test holes during the summer to avoid the freezing. But the imprints and graves of their machines were still there, on the edge of the tundra above the river, where the summer mud had swallowed them before they ever left sight of the river. The village people had gathered to watch the white men, and to laugh as they drove the giant machines, one by one, off the steel ramp into the bogs; as if sheer numbers of vehicles would somehow make the tundra solid. But the old man said they behaved like desperate people, and they would come back again. When the tundra was frozen solid, they returned.

Village women did not even look through the door to the back room. The priest had warned them. The storeman was watching her because he didn't let Eskimos or Indians sit down at the tables in the back room. But she knew he couldn't throw her out if one of his Gussuck customers invited her to sit with him. She walked across the room. They stared at her, but she had the feeling she was walking for someone else, not herself, so their eyes did not matter. The red-haired man pulled out a chair and motioned for her to sit down. She looked back at the storeman while the red-haired man poured her a glass of red sweet wine. She wanted to laugh at the storeman the way she laughed at the dogs, straining against their chains, howling at her.

The red-haired man kept talking to the other Gussucks sitting around the table, but he slid one hand off the top of the table to her thigh. She looked over at the storeman to see if he was still watching her. She laughed out loud at him and the red-haired man stopped talking and turned to her. He asked if she wanted to go. She nodded and stood up.

Someone in the village had been telling him things about her, he said as they walked down the road to his trailer. She understood that much of what he was saying, but the rest she did not hear. The whine of the big generators at the construction camp sucked away the sound of his words. But English was of no concern to her anymore, and neither was anything the Christians in the village might say about her or the old man. She smiled at the effect of the subzero air on the electric lights around the trailers; they did not shine. They left only flat yellow holes in the darkness.

It took him a long time to get ready, even after she had undressed for him. She waited in the bed with the blankets pulled close, watching him. He adjusted the thermostat and lit candles in the room, turning out the electric lights. He searched through a stack of record albums until he found the right one. She was not sure about the last thing he did: he taped something on the wall behind the bed where he could see it while he laid on top of her. He was shrivelled and white from the cold; he pushed against her body for warmth. He guided her hands to his thighs; he was shivering.

She had returned a last time because she wanted to know what it was he stuck on the wall above the bed. After he finished each time, he reached up and pulled it loose, folding it carefully so that she could not see it. But this time she was ready; she waited for his fast breathing and sudden collapse on top of her. She slid out from under him and stood up beside the bed. She looked at the picture while she got dressed. He did not raise his face from the pillow, and she thought she heard teeth rattling together as she left the room.

She heard the old man move when she came in. After the Gussuck's trailer, the log house felt cool. It smelled like dry fish and cured meat. The room was dark except for the blinking yellow flame in the mica window of the oil stove. She squatted in front of the stove and watched the flames for a long time before she walked to the bed where her grandmother had slept. The bed was covered with a mound of rags and fur scraps the old woman had saved. She reached into the mound until she felt something cold and solid wrapped in a wool blanket. She pushed her fingers around it until she felt smooth stone. Long ago, before the Gussucks came, they had burned whale oil in the big stone lamp which made light and heat as well. The old woman had saved everything they would need when the time came.

In the morning, the old man pulled a piece of dry caribou meat from under the blankets and offered it to her. While she was gone, men from the village had brought a bundle of dry meat. She chewed it slowly, thinking about the way they still came from the village to take care of the old man and his stories. But she had a story now, about the red-haired Gussuck. The old man knew what she was thinking, and his smile made his face seem more round than it was.

"Well," he said, "what was it?"

"A woman with a big dog on top of her."

He laughed softly to himself and walked over to the water barrel. He dipped the tin cup into the water.

"It doesn't surprise me," he said.

V

"Grandma," she said, "there was something red in the grass that morning. I remember." She had not asked about her parents before. The old woman stopped splitting the fish bellies open for the willow drying racks. Her jaw muscles pulled so tightly against her skull, the girl thought the old woman would not be able to speak.

"They bought a tin can full of it from the storeman. Late at night. He told them it was alcohol safe to drink. They traded a rifle for it." The old woman's voice sounded like each word stole strength from her. "It made no difference about the rifle. That year the Gussuck boats had come, firing big guns at the walrus and seals. There was nothing left to hunt after that anyway. So," the old lady said, in a low soft voice the girl had not heard for a long time, "I didn't say anything to them when they left that night."

"Right over there," she said, pointing at the fallen poles, half buried in the river sand and tall grass, "in the summer shelter. The sun was high half the night then. Early in the morning when it was still low, the policeman came around. I told the interpreter to tell him that the storeman had poisoned them." She made outlines in the air in front of her, showing how their bodies laid twisted on the sand; telling the story was like laboring to walk through deep snow; sweat shone in the white hair around her forehead. "I told the priest too, after he came. I told him the storeman lied." She turned away from the girl. She held her mouth even tighter, set solidly, not in sorrow or anger, but against the pain, which was all that remained. "I never believed," she said, "not much anyway. I wasn't surprised when the priest did nothing."

The wind came off the river and folded the tall grass into itself like river waves. She could feel the silence the story left, and she wanted to have the old woman go on.

"I heard the sounds that night, grandma. Sounds like someone was singing. It was light outside. I could see something red on the ground." The old woman did not answer her; she moved to the tub full of fish on the ground beside the work bench. She stabbed her knife into the belly of a whitefish and lifted it onto the bench. "The Gussuck storeman left the village right after that," the old woman said as she pulled the entrails from the fish, "otherwise, I could tell you more." The old woman's voice flowed with the wind blowing off the river; they never spoke of it again.

When the willows got their leaves and the grass grew tall along the river banks and around the sloughs, she walked early in the morning. While the sun was still low on the horizon, she listened to the wind off the river; its sound was like the voice that day long ago. In the distance, she could hear the engines of the machinery the oil drillers had left the winter before, but she did not go near the village or the store. The sun never left the sky and the summer became the same long day, with only the winds to fan the sun into brightness or allow it to slip into twilight.

She sat beside the old man at his place on the river bank. She poked the smoky fire for him, and felt herself growing wide and thin in the sun as if she had been split from belly to throat and strung on the willow pole in preparation for the winter to come. The old man did not speak anymore. When men from the village brought him fresh fish he hid them deep in the river grass where it was cool. After he went inside, she split the fish open and spread them to dry on the willow frame the way the old woman had done. Inside, he dozed and talked to himself. He had talked all winter, softly and incessantly about the giant polar bear stalking a lone man across Bering Sea ice. After all the months the old man had been telling the story, the bear was within a hundred feet of the man; but the ice fog had closed in on them now and the man could only smell the sharp ammonia odor of the bear, and hear the edge of the snow crust crack under the giant paws.

One night she listened to the old man tell the story all night in his sleep, describing each crystal of ice and the slightly different sounds they made under each paw; first the left and then the right paw, then the hind feet. Her grandmother was there suddenly, a shadow around the stove. She spoke in her low wind voice and the girl was afraid to sit up to hear more clearly. Maybe what she said had been to the old man because he stopped telling the story and began to snore softly the way he had long ago when the old woman had scolded him for telling his stories while others in the house were trying to sleep. But the last words she heard clearly: "It will take a long time, but the story must be told. There must not be any lies." She pulled the blankets up around her chin, slowly, so that her movements would not be seen. She thought her grandmother was talking about the old man's bear story; she did not know about the other story then.

She left the old man wheezing and snoring in his bed. She walked through river grass glistening with frost; the bright green summer color was already fading. She watched the sun move across the sky, already lower on the horizon, already moving away from the village. She stopped by the fallen poles of the summer shelter where her parents had died. Frost glittered on the river sand too; in a few more weeks there would be snow. The predawn light would be the color of an old woman. An old woman sky full of snow. There had been something red lying on the ground the morning they died. She looked for it again, pushing aside the grass with her foot. She knelt in the sand and looked under the fallen structure for some trace of it. When she found it, she would know what the old woman had never told her. She squatted down close to the gray poles and leaned her back against them. The wind made her shiver.

The summer rain had washed the mud from between the logs; the sod blocks stacked as high as her belly next to the log walls had lost their square-cut shape and had grown into soft mounds of tundra moss and stiff-bladed grass bending with clusters of seed bristles. She looked at the northwest, in the direction of the Bering Sea. The cold would come down from there to find narrow slits in the mud, rainwater holes in the outer layer of sod which protected the log house. The dark green tundra stretched away flat and continuous. Somewhere the sea and the land met; she knew by their dark green colors there were no boundaries between them. That was how the cold would come: when the boundaries were gone the polar ice would range across the land into the sky. She watched the horizon for a long time. She would stand in that place on the north side of the house and she would keep watch on the northwest horizon, and eventually she would see it come. She would watch for its approach in the stars, and hear it come with the wind. These preparations were unfamiliar, but gradually she recognized them as she did her own footprints in the snow.

She emptied the slop jar beside his bed twice a day and kept the barrel full of water melted from river ice. He did not recognize her anymore, and when he spoke to her, he called her by her grandmother's name and talked about people and events from long ago, before he went back to telling the story. The giant bear was creeping across the new snow on its belly, close enough now that the man could hear the rasp of its breathing. On and on in a soft singing voice, the old man caressed the story, repeating the words again and again like gentle strokes.

The sky was gray like a river crane's egg; its density curved into the thin crust of frost already covering the land. She looked at the bright red color of the tin against the ground and the sky and she told the village men to bring the pieces for the old man and her. To drill the test holes in the tundra, the Gussucks had used hundreds of barrels of fuel. The village people split open the empty barrels that were abandoned on the river bank, and pounded the red tin into flat sheets. The village people were using the strips of tin to mend walls and roofs for winter. But she nailed it on the log walls for its color. When she finished, she walked away with the hammer in her hand, not turning around until she was far away, on the ridge above the river banks, and then she looked back. She felt a chill when she saw how the sky and the land were already losing their boundaries, already becoming lost in each other. But the red tin penetrated the thick white color of earth and sky; it defined the boundaries like a wound revealing the ribs and heart of a great caribou about to bolt and be lost to the hunter forever. That night the wind howled and when she scratched a hole through the heavy frost on the inside of the window, she could see nothing but the impenetrable white; whether it was blowing snow or snow that had drifted as high as the house, she did not know.

It had come down suddenly, and she stood with her back to the wind looking at the river, its smoky water clotted with ice. The wind had blown the snow over the frozen river, hiding thin blue streaks where fast water ran under ice translucent and fragile as memory. But she could see shadows of boundaries, outlines of paths which were slender branches of solidity reaching out from the earth. She spent days walking on the river, watching the colors of ice that would safely hold her, kicking the heel of her boot into the snow crust, listening for a solid sound. When she could feel the paths through the soles of her feet, she went to the middle of the river where the fast gray water churned under a thin pane of ice. She looked back. On the river bank in the distance she could see the red tin nailed to the log house, something not swallowed up by the heavy white belly of the sky or caught in the folds of the frozen earth. It was time.

The wolverine fur around the hood of her parka was white with the frost from her breathing. The warmth inside the store melted it, and she felt tiny drops of water on her face. The storeman came in from the back room. She unzipped the parka and stood by the oil stove. She didn't look at him, but stared instead at the yellowish dog, covered with scabs of matted hair, sleeping in front of the stove. She thought of the Gussuck's picture, taped on the wall above the bed and she laughed out loud. The sound of her laughter was piercing; the yellow dog jumped to its feet and the hair bristled down its back. The storeman was watching her. She wanted to laugh again because he didn't know about the ice. He did not know that it was prowling the earth, or that it had already pushed its way into the sky to seize the sun. She sat down in the chair by the stove and shook her long hair loose. He was like a dog tied up all winter, watching while the others got fed. He remembered how she had gone with the oil drillers, and his blue eyes moved like flies crawling over her body. He held his thin pale lips like he wanted to spit on her. He hated the people because they had something of value, the old man said, something which the Gussucks could never have. They thought they could take it, suck it out of the earth or cut it from the mountains; but they were fools.

There was a matted hunk of dog hair on the floor by her foot. She thought of a yellow insulation coming unstuffed: their defense against the freezing going to pieces as it advanced on them. The ice was crouching on the northwest horizon like the old man's bear. She laughed out loud again. The sun would be down now; it was time.

The first time he spoke to her, she did not hear what he said, so she did not answer or even look up at him. He spoke to her again but his words were only noises coming from his pale mouth, trembling now as his anger began to unravel. He jerked her up and the chair fell over behind her. His arms were shaking and she could feel his hands tense up, pulling the edges of the parka tighter. He raised his fist to hit her, his thin body quivering with rage; but the fist collapsed with the desire he had for the valuable things, which, the old man had rightly said, was the only reason they came. She could hear his heart pounding as he held her close and arched his hip against her, groaning and breathing in spasms. She twisted away from him and ducked under his arms.

She ran with a mitten over her mouth, breathing through the fur to protect her lungs from the freezing air. She could hear him running behind her, his heavy breathing, the occasional sound of metal jingling against metal. But he ran without his parka or mittens, breathing the frozen air; its fire squeezed the lungs against the ribs and it was enough that he could not catch her near his store. On the river bank he realized how far he was from his stove, and the wads of yellow stuffing that held off the cold. But the girl was not able to run very fast through the deep drifts at the edge of the river. The twilight was luminous and he could still see clearly for a long distance; he knew he could catch her so he kept running.

When she neared the middle of the river she looked over her shoulder. He was not following her tracks; he went straight across the ice, running the shortest distance to reach her. He was close then; his face was twisted and scarlet from the exertion and the cold. There was satisfaction in his eyes; he was sure he could outrun her.

She was familiar with the river, down to the instant the ice flexed into hairline fractures, and the cracking bone-sliver sounds gathered momentum with the opening ice until the sound of the churning gray water was set free. She stopped and turned to the sound of the river and the rattle of swirling ice fragments where he fell through. She pulled off a mitten and zipped the parka to her throat. She was conscious then of her own rapid breathing.

She moved slowly, kicking the ice ahead with the heel of her boot, feeling for sinews of ice to hold her. She looked ahead and all around herself; in the twilight, the dense white sky had merged into the flat snow-covered tundra. In the frantic running she had lost her place on the river. She stood still. The east bank of the river was lost in the sky; the boundaries had been swallowed by the freezing white. And then, in the distance, she saw something red, and suddenly it was as she had remembered it all those years.

VI

She sat on her bed and while she waited, she listened to the old man. The man had found a small jagged knoll on the ice. He pulled his beaver fur cap off his head; the fur inside it steamed with his body heat and sweat. He left it upside down on the ice for the great bear to stalk, and he waited downwind on top of the ice knoll; he was holding the jade knife.

She thought she could see the end of his story in the way he wheezed out the words; but still he reached into his cache of dry fish and dribbled water into his mouth from the tin cup. All night she listened to him describe each breath the man took, each motion of the bear's head as it tried to catch the sound of the man's breathing, and tested the wind for his scent.

The state trooper asked her questions, and the woman who cleaned house for the priest translated them into Yupik. They wanted to know what happened to the storeman, the Gussuck who had been seen running after her down the road onto the river late last evening. He had not come back, and the Gussuck boss in Anchorage was concerned about him. She did not answer for a long time because the old man suddenly sat up in his bed and began to talk excitedly, looking at all of them—the trooper in his dark glasses and the housekeeper in her corduroy parka. He kept saying, "The story! The story! Eh-ya! The great bear! The hunter!"

They asked her again, what happened to the man from the Northern Commercial store. "He lied to them. He told them it was safe to drink. But I will not lie." She stood up and put on the gray wolfskin parka. "I killed him," she said, "but I don't lie."

The attorney came back again, and the jailer slid open the steel doors and opened the cell to let him in. He motioned for the jailer to stay to translate for him. She laughed when she saw how the jailer would be forced by this Gussuck to speak Yupik to her. She liked the Gussuck attorney for that, and for the thinning hair on his head. He was very tall, and she liked to think about the exposure of his head to the freezing; she wondered if he would feel the ice descending from the sky before the others did. He wanted to know why she told the state trooper she had killed the storeman. Some village children had seen it happen, he said, and it was an accident. "That's all you have to say to the judge: it was an accident." He kept repeating it over and over again to her, slowly in a loud but gentle voice: "It was an accident. He was running after you and he fell through the ice. That's all you have to say in court.

That's all. And they will let you go home. Back to your village." The jailer translated the words sullenly, staring down at the floor. She shook her head. "I will not change the story, not even to escape this place and go home. I intended that he die. The story must be told as it is." The attorney exhaled loudly; his eyes looked tired. "Tell her that she could not have killed him that way. He was a white man. He ran after her without a parka or mittens. She could not have planned that." He paused and turned toward the cell door. "Tell her I will do all I can for her. I will explain to the judge that her mind is confused." She laughed out loud when the jailer translated what the attorney said. The Gussucks did not understand the story; they could not see the way it must be told, year after year as the old man had done, without lapse or silence.

She looked out the window at the frozen white sky. The sun had finally broken loose from the ice but it moved like a wounded caribou running on strength which only dying animals find, leaping and running on bullet-shattered lungs. Its light was weak and pale; it pushed dimly through the clouds. She turned and faced the Gussuck attorney.

"It began a long time ago," she intoned steadily, "in the summertime. Early in the morning, I remember, something red in the tall river grass . . ."

The day after the old man died, men from the village came. She was sitting on the edge of her bed, across from the woman the trooper hired to watch her. They came into the room slowly and listened to her. At the foot of her bed they left a king salmon that had been split open wide and dried last summer. But she did not pause or hesitate; she went on with the story, and she never stopped, not even when the woman got up to close the door behind the village men.

The old man would not change the story even when he knew the end was approaching. Lies could not stop what was coming. He thrashed around on the bed, pulling the blankets loose, knocking bundles of dried fish and meat on the floor. The man had been on the ice for many hours. The freezing winds on the ice knoll had numbed his hands in the mittens, and the cold had exhausted him. He felt a single muscle tremor in his hand that he could not suppress, and the jade knife fell; it shattered on the ice, and the blue glacier bear turned slowly to face him.

WHEN SUN CAME TO RIVERWOMAN

June 10, 1973

that time
    in the sun
    beside the Rio Grande.

voice of the mourning dove
    calls
        long ago   long ago
    remembering the lost one
    remembering the love.

Out of the dense green
       eternity of springtime
   willows rustle in the blue wind
      timeless
   the year unknown
      unnamed.

The muddy fast water
    warm around my feet
    you move into the current slowly

    brown skin   thighs
    deep intensity
    flowing water.

Your warmth penetrates
              yellow sand and sky.
Endless eyes shining always
      for green river moss
      for tiny water spiders.
Crying out   the dove
         will not let me forget
    it is ordained
    in swirling brown water

            and it carries you away,
            my lost one
            my love,
               the mountain.
man of Sun
      came to riverwoman
      and in the sundown wind
   he left her
      to sing
        for rainclouds swelling in the northwest sky
        for rainsmell on pale blue winds
                 from China

HORSES AT VALLEY STORE

Everyday I meet the horses
    with dust and heat they come
        step by step
Pulling the day
    behind them.

At Valley Store
    there is water.
    Gray steel tank
    Narrow concrete trough.

Eyes that smell water,
In a line   one by one
    moving with the weight of the sun
    moving through the deep earth heat
They come.

People with
    water barrels
    in pick-ups in wagons
So they pause and from their distance
    outside of time
They wait.

SLIM MAN CANYON

early summer Navajo Nation, 1972 for John

700 years ago
    people were living here
    water was running gently
    and the sun was warm
  on pumpkin flowers.
It was 700 years ago
    deep in this canyon
    with sandstone rising high above
The rock the silence tall sky and flowing water
    sunshine through cottonwood leaves
    the willow smell in the wind
        700 years.
The rhythm
    the horses feet moving strong through
        white deep sand.
Where I come from is like this
    the warmth, the fragrance, the silence.
Blue sky and rainclouds in the distance
    we ride together
        past cliffs with stories and songs
        painted on rock.
        700 years ago.

Story from Bear Country

You will know
when you walk
in bear country
By the silence
flowing swiftly between the juniper trees
by the sundown colors of sandrock
all around you.

You may smell damp earth
scratched away
from yucca roots
You may hear snorts and growls
slow and massive sounds
from caves
in the cliffs high above you.

It is difficult to explain
how they call you
All but a few who went to them
left behind families
        grandparents
        and sons
        a good life.

The problem is
you will never want to return
Their beauty will overcome your memory
like winter sun
melting ice shadows from snow
And you will remain with them
locked forever inside yourself
        your eyes will see you
        dark shaggy and thick.

We can send bear priests
loping after you
their medicine bags
bouncing against their chests
Naked legs painted black
bear claw necklaces
rattling against
their capes of blue spruce.

They will follow your trail
into the narrow canyon
through the blue-gray mountain sage
to the clearing
where you stopped to look back
and saw only bear tracks
behind you.

When they call
faint memories
will writhe around your heart
and startle you with their distance.
But the others will listen
because bear priests
sing beautiful songs
They must
if they are ever to call you back.

They will try to bring you
step by step
back to the place you stopped
and found only bear prints in the sand
where your feet had been.

Whose voice is this?
You may wonder
hearing this story when
after all
you are alone
hiking in these canyons and hills
while your wife and sons are waiting
back at the car for you.

But you have been listening to me
for some time now
from the very beginning in fact
and you are alone in this canyon of stillness
not even cedar birds flutter.
See, the sun is going down now
the sandrock is washed in its colors
Don't be afraid
                we love you
                we've been calling you
                all this time
Go ahead
turn around
see the shape
of your footprints
in the sand.

                                        24 July '75
                                        Ketchikan

210

AN OLD-TIME INDIAN ATTACK
CONDUCTED IN TWO PARTS:
Part One: Imitation "Indian" Poems
Part Two: Gary Snyder's Turtle Island

IMITATION "INDIAN" POEMS

Since white ethnologists like Boas and Swanton first intruded into Native American communities to "collect" prayers, songs and stories, a number of implicit racist assumptions about Native American culture and literature have flourished. The first is the assumption that the white man, through some innate cultural or racial superiority, has the ability to perceive and master the essential beliefs, values and emotions of persons from Native American communities. (This assumption has been applied to non-white communities world-wide.) It is this assumption which, in 1927, allowed Oliver La Farge, New England born, Harvard educated, to write his novel, *Laughing Boy,* which won the Pulitzer Prize in 1929. The novel was written after La Farge spent a number of summer vacations doing ethnological field work on the Navajo Reservation.

I do not disagree with the fact that La Farge cared deeply for the Navajos as well as for other Indian people; he not only had sincere intentions, he actively worked to "better the lot" of Indian people. But as an artist and a writer, La Farge fell victim to the assumption that he could write a novel centered in the consciousness of a Navajo man; a Navajo who by La Farge's own design, had grown up with almost no contact with white people.

In the summer of 1971, the Navajo students in a Southwestern Literature class at Navajo Community College concluded that *Laughing Boy* was entertaining; but, as an expression of anything Navajo, especially with relation to Navajo emotions and behavior, the novel was a failure.[1] And, for the non-Navajo or the non-Indian, it is worse than a failure: it is a lie because La Farge passes off the consciousness and feelings of Laughing Boy as those of Navajo sensibility.

Fifty years later, this racist assumption is thriving; it flourishes among white poets and writers who romanticize their "power" as writers to inhabit souls and consciousness far beyond the realms of their own knowledge or experience. Not long ago, in an Albuquerque bookstore, I found William Eastlake's latest novel, hot off Viking press which also happens to be my publisher. The blurb on the bookcover said that Eastlake was "the only white man who knows enough about Indians" to say the "irreverent" things he says about Indians. Eastlake's "Indian" characters have as much relation to Navajos, as Topsy and Uncle Tom have to Blacks; what disturbs me more, is his presumption to speak for Navajos. In 1973, during a panel discussion in Tempe, Arizona, Eastlake rhapsodized about the good will and generosity of white traders operating trading posts on the Navajo Reservation. His ignorance was remarkable. Within a few months of Eastlake's "knowledgeable" remarks, the Federal Trade Commission filed a report indicating gross illegal conduct by white traders against Navajo people. So much for Bill Eastlake, knowledgeable white spokesman for the Navajos. . . .[2]

If you examine this notion that the writer has the "power" to inhabit any soul, any consciousness, you will find this idea restricted to the white man: the concept of a "universal consciousness" did not occur until sometime in the early Eighteenth century. Ask an older tribal person to attempt to recreate the thoughts and feelings of a white person, and they will tell you that they can't: they will tell you that they can describe *their* observations of whites, even probable responses in whites, but they will tell you they certainly will not pretend to know or understand what is going on *inside* those white people.

The second implicit racist assumption still abounding is that the prayers, chants, and stories weaseled out by the early white ethnographers, which are now collected in ethnological journals, are public property. Presently, a number of Native American communities are attempting to recover religious objects and other property taken from them in the early 1900's that are now placed in museums. Certainly, the songs and stories which were taken by ethnographers are no different. But, among white poets — Rothenberg and Snyder, to mention the most prominent, the idea that these materials should be left to those tribes and their descendants is unthinkable. White poets cash in on the generosity which many tribes have and still practice; white poets delight in saying "Indians believe in sharing," and so they go on "sharing," collecting book royalties on plagiarized materials.

What is an "imitation" Indian poem? Almost certainly, it is a poem labeled by the white poet, a "translation." White poets use the term "translation" very loosely when applied to Asian or Native American material; few, if any of them, are conversant in the Asian or Native American languages they pretend to "translate." What they do is sit down and rearrange English transcriptions done by ethnologists and then call this a "translation."

In an interview in the Summer, 1975 issue of *the Chicago Review,* Louis Simpson said:

> *I think that there are many kinds of Indian poems. There would be the poem which you wrote like an Indian, where you understood how he thought, his magic, his life, his values. Then there's the white man's Indian poem, in which, after all, the Indian is not just the Indian, he is a concept like the "noble savage" which the white man has had in his head for a long time. (page 105)*[3]

Simpson's views are interesting for a number of reasons. First, because they evidence that implicit racist assumption that a white man *can* think and feel whatever a Native American thinks and feels. Secondly, Simpson gives an insight into the white "Indian poems" which, along with Li Po "oriental" poems, began to emerge in the early sixties:

> *. . . the new poems we were writing in the sixties were a literary construction. We were trying to use the Indian as a means of expressing our feeling about the repressed side of America that should be released. However, if I or anyone were to continue to write Indian poems, we should know more about Indians than we did. I was writing with sympathy and a historical sense of feeling, but to write about Indians you should in a sense become an Indian. (page 105)*[4]

Again, the unmitigated egotism of the white man, and the belief that he could "in a sense become an Indian." And finally, the reduction of Native American people to the grossest stereotype of all: the literary device.

But what about the white poets who are knowledgeable, sympathetic, who "feel deeply," who "identify" with belief and values of many Native American communities? What about the white poets with Indian friends, surely these special few have "earned" their poetic license to write white "Indian" poems? The answer is complicated.

Above all else, the old people have taught us to value the truth. I value the truth. We are taught to remember who we are: our ancestors, our origins. We must know the place we came from because it has shaped us and continues to make us who we are.

In contrast, the Anglo-American attitude for the past two hundred years has been to cast off familial and geographic ties; to "go West, young man," to change identities as easily as changing shoes. And so, in the early sixties, young white Americans travelled to Japanese monasteries, or studied books of Native American "lore" in an attempt to remake themselves, and to obliterate their white, middle-class ancestry and origins. It was with the attempt to cultivate a "new" sensibility and "new" consciousness that imitation "Indian" poems, and "orientalism" in American poetry began to appear.

Ironically, as white poets attempt to cast-off their Anglo-American values, their Anglo-American origins, they violate a fundamental belief held by the tribal people they desire to emulate: they deny the truth; they deny their history, their very origins. The writing of imitation "Indian" poems then, is pathetic evidence that in more than two hundred years, Anglo-Americans have failed to create a satisfactory identity for themselves.

PART TWO: GARY SNYDER'S *TURTLE ISLAND*

Without question, Gary Snyder is one of the white poets Louis Simpson was referring to in his remarks about the white "Indian poems" and the "orientalism" of the early sixties. The title *Turtle Island* is itself "borrowed," we are told in the introduction; the concept of the turtle being that the continent was shared by more than one Native American tribe. Still, there is only one poem, "Prayer for the Great Family" which is clearly a "translation"; it appears with the notation "from a Mohawk prayer" (p. 25).[5] What about the other poems in *Turtle Island?*

Although Snyder talks about "harking back again to those roots" in his introductory note, there are actually only two instances in *Turtle Island* where this happens: one is his dedication of the book to his mother and mention of "my Mother's old soft arm" as he helps her up the trail to visit his place ("The Egg," p. 37)."[6]

The other instance occurs in the poem "Dusty Braces" where Snyder for the first time acknowledges his own ancestors:

O you ancestors
lumber schooners
    big moustache
long-handled underwear
sticks out under the cuffs
tan stripes on each shoulder
dusty braces
nine bows
nine bows
you bastards

my fathers
    and grandfathers, stiff-necked
punchers, miners, dirt farmers, railroad men
killed off the cougar and grizzly (p. 75)[7]

Of course, he has often written about his people, his ancestors; it is just that he seldom acknowledges them as fathers and grandfathers. They are the drivers of logging trucks who hit deer on highway forty-nine; they are cowboys in the Maverick Bar in Farmington where the band played "Okie from Muskokie;" but Snyder has seldom revealed his roots and relationship with this part of his identity although Snyder himself was born in a Texas town, and the last I heard, his mother was living in a housetrailer in Florida.[8] Until *Turtle Island,* we had heard nothing of mothers or fathers and grandfathers; his hide-away in the Sierras underscored this detachment. But now, as he "harkens us back to those roots," maybe we can expect to see the connection made with his own roots and origins. Until this connection is made, Snyder will not be able to complete the philosophical and artistic synthesis he is attempting to make for Anglo-Americans in his *Turtle Island* Manifestos. Since the manifestos are addressed primarily to Anglo-American technocrats, I prefer to deal with things in *Turtle Island* which involve me or the people.

Although Snyder goes on at length about the land, the earth, and the Native Americans' relationship to it, he does not deal with the facts surrounding his ownership or "use," if you prefer, of the acreage in the Sierras. He clearly acknowledges that the land he is occupying is

the land that was deer and acorn
grounds of the Nisenan
branch of Maidu (p. 79)[9]

But he intellectualizes his complicity in the land theft by enthusiastically quoting the pre-Columbian notion that "the land belongs to itself" (p. 80). Snyder reasons that since he doesn't believe in land ownership either, he doesn't really "own" the land (although he apparently purchased it and pays taxes on it), and therefore, he is without guilt. Snyder is, of course, missing the important point: for whatever the different Native American communities have thought or continued to think about their relationship to the earth, Native Americans are very much aware of the occupancy and use rights to the land. We continue to fight bitterly to regain control of the occupancy and use of land that was taken.

In "Control Burn" he writes:

What the Indians
here
used to do, was
to burn out the brush every year . . .

I would like,
with a sense of helpful order,
with respect for laws
of nature,
to help my land
with a burn, a hot clean
burn . . .

And then
it would be more
like,
when it belonged to the Indians

Before. (p. 19)[10]

Again though, Snyder somehow fails to realize that although he is careful, even reverent with this land he is occupying, it is *not* "his" land, as he erroneously claims; he is occupying stolen property. And even when Anglo-Saxon common law is applied, the fact remains: stolen property, no matter how many times it is sold or changes hands, no matter the "good faith" of the innocent subsequent purchaser, remains stolen property; and at common law, all property rights remained vested in the original legal owner. In this case, legal title still remains with the Maidu people.

It is admirable that Snyder is attempting to make

the rediscovery of this land and the ways by which we might become
natives of the place, ceasing to think and act [after all these centuries]
as newcomers and invaders.[11]

as the blurb on the jacket of the book indicates. It is admirable and perhaps even worthy of a Pulitzer Prize. But unless Snyder is careful, he is headed in the same unfortunate direction as other white pioneers have gone, a direction which avoids historical facts which are hard to swallow: namely, that at best, the Anglo-American is a guest on this continent; and at the worst, the United States of America is founded upon stolen land. Unless Snyder comes to terms with these facts, and his own personal, ancestral relation to them, the "rediscovery" which so many Americans are waiting for, will be just another dead-end in more than two hundred years of searching for a genuine American identity.

Gary Snyder once said to me "you must create your own new myths." That is good advice to follow.

BIBLIOGRAPHY AND NOTES

1. I was an instructor at Navajo Community College during two summer sessions (1971 and 1972) and during one full year from Fall of 1972 through May of 1973.
2. The panel discusion took place during a meeting of the Coordinating Council of Literary Magazine's November, 1973 meeting held in Tempe, Arizona. Also sitting on the panel was Frank Waters. I was there, and there were other persons who heard Eastlake expound these "facts." My husband worked for the Navajo legal services organization which alerted the Federal Trade Commission to the widespread and grossly illegal practices of white traders in their dealings with Navajos.
3. *The Chicago Review,* Volume 27 No. 1, Summer, 1975 "A Conversation With Louis Simpson" interviewed by Lawrence R. Smith (pp. 99-109)
4. *Ibid.*
5. *Turtle Island* by Gary Snyder. New Directions paperback
6. *Ibid.*
7. *Ibid.*
8. Snyder himself told me this.
9. *Turtle Island*
10. *Ibid.*
11. Blurb on the back of *Turtle Island.*

Paula Gunn Allen

SNOWGOOSE

North of here where
water marries ice,
meaning is other than what
I understand.

I have seen in picture how
white the bulge of the glacier
overshadows the sea,
frozen pentecostal presence,
brilliant in the sun —
way I have never been.

I heard the snowgoose cry today
long-wheeled wings overhead,
sky calling untroubled blue
song to her and morning.
(North wind blowing.)

RAIN FOR KE-WAIK BU-NE-YA

Out the back window the sky is dead. Rain
promises the garden its grave relief, its
promise buried in furrowed hearts:

      Shiwanna

            Shiwanna

old footsteps echo on the southern hills.
To the west, the sky is bright:

Paitamo, set us at rest.

Last night under the yellow light
we told of bright things, spoke of sleep
tried to renew old firelight dreams
like the old ones we sat
gathering fragments of long since broken hearts:

bring tomorrow.

HOOP DANCER

It's hard to enter
circling clockwise and counter
clockwise moving no
regard for time, metrics
irrelevant to this dance where pain
is the prime counter and soft
stepping feet praise water from the skies:

I have seen the face of triumph
the winding line stare down all moves to desecration
guts not cut from arms, fingers joined to minds,
together Sky and Water one dancing one
circle of a thousand turning lines beyond the march of years—
out of time, out of
time, out
of time.

IKCE WICHASHA

Elusive, sense of you after years; noise
around you I remember, no eagle on your god-side
shoulder, no peace, a stunted
vision.
Today, message: hope gotten
into you somehow, ceremony,
time. I wonder at your face, the
silence around your chair. What
ever is said, you said
"Black Elk,"
"the ghosts of old Wounded Knee stand
in the moonlight,"
"Inipi" you said: close and smoke-dark,
sweet sage I guess is what contains you,
fragrant wakan smoke now: and
moonlight spirits walking under five eagles,
Black Elk still praying, still
making things happen out there.

MADONNA OF THE HILLS

She kept finding arrowheads
when she walked to Flower Mountain
and shards of ancient pottery
drawn with brown and black designs —
cloud ladders, lightning stairs and rainbirds.

One day
she took a shovel when she walked that way
and unburied fist-axes, manos, scrapers,
stone knives and some human bones,
which she kept in her collection
on display in her garden.

She said that it gave her
a sense of peace to dig and remember
the women who had cooked and scrubbed
and yelled at their husbands
just like her. She liked, she said,
to go to the spot where she'd found
those things and remember the women
buried there.

It was restful, she said,
and she needed rest . . .
from her husband's quiet alcohol
and her son who walked around dead.

TUCSON: FIRST NIGHT

for Larry Evers

the stars.
softness on the brutal land.
the song.
rest here. the reflective
pause (reflection)
what things we do, being
(hands like butterflies in July evening sun) I recall
water calling down the grass
moment hovers.
Do I say clouds? See how they piled
over the mesa,
the rocks that made one boundary of my home
found there alongside the blue-framed door
that meant entering
(the land is central to this)
focused or unfocused
the eyes form shapes to be dissolved

where time is finally illusion
carved out of rock, motion, a word to put upon the stones,
The road was the other boundary.
The highway went around us before I was born:
motion elliptical as the thought I took,
moving away until found, it holds: "the Road," we said,
implying that time had no changing. (Like Plato in our innocence)
clouds that were there
are here. Now. My mind and the sky,
one thing on the edge of surmise (sunrise).

I travel a lot these days:
Albuquerque
San Francisco,
Phoenix,
Tucson,
Nova Scotia,
San Diego.
Sometimes I don't know which place this one is,
or what year, like in this desert
cactus lines the walks
the pool is still
expensive people walk by
soft air almost touches my shoulders
benediction
sign of home
voices of friends scattered all over the world
the moon hanging low in the sky
bottom curve lit, looking pregnant. The last week before
the descent, and this night: dry and candles in the bar,
voices around us, swirling, ignored.
We look out on the patio, Tucson lights bright below.
You show me my childhood, etching memories —
making things emerge
strange to sit in a strange city
beside a man I met years ago somewhere else and haven't seen since,
a passing acquaintance passing me over to my past
unreal in all its dimensions, familiar, loved —

There is the history:
in the papers, 2 Acoma youths accused of killing a State cop,
in the courts, tried, convicted, appealed (Indians believe in witchcraft,
the expert ethnologist says)
in the fiction, they exorcised a brujo, they killed a son of a bitch,
on the people's tongues — especially on the tongues — Willie was
never any good anyway   he broke his parent's hearts —
how many stories, which makes which history true?
Hero become villain,
villain fool — and
what about Willie Fillipe?
Mind gone, they say, as was predicated in the Albuquerque Journal story
24 years ago says.
The judge is dead. The governor a foolish old man.
Nash Garcia's blood long ago turned to sand and blown away —

all of that I left, and the earth has turned a lot since
(ate its past like some fish and tom cats eat their young)
until now it turns up again, like replowed earth, and
the familiar is retold, becomes what is strange.
I shiver in the recognition of that place that is finally myself.
What is familiar is their own way of thinking — the papers
the trial, the stories told and written down —
and no drinking on the reservation, no Indian can buy booze,
the corruption of office,
the two men who left no trace after a few days in journalistic
history. (The bootleggers, unnamed and uncaught, untried,
were to blame, the paper said.)
No redemption this time. The sacrifice goes on.

The night sits soft on my shoulders.
Weight seems gone.
Where I can pause (hover) on the edge of midnight
(so that time no longer counts)
and words like *balance, together, reverence, being*
are understood.
The assumption is implied,
like hands almost touching, drawn away,
the self-consciousness of time and place
describing in withdrawal that private ache
moving outward on the dark, stop, hold —
arching the air like cathedrals, left to mark their time
(the repetition) to make dreams into spoken into pre
cipitation, not the other way around, (crystallized)

As we talk, I come silent all the way around again to home.
All the mixing (like the rainbow ones)
all the confusion (noise of transience)
all the colors (that certain kind of space)
on the way after it all
boundless in the pausing, motion, rest, accumulation
and concretion: thoughts leap toward the unseen ranges
east
north
south
your finger points at the unseen light
(the pass) showing sun on saddleback before its rise:

/there is change
and the will to change.
And there is a softness about the stars
like a smile about the lips or
wind blowing in anticipation of dawn.
There is water, fresh and recognized on the tongue.
There is time.
And motion.
There is space.
The pause.

THE SACRED HOOP: A CONTEMPORARY INDIAN PERSPECTIVE ON AMERICAN INDIAN LITERATURE

Literature is a facet of a culture. Its significance can be best understood in terms of its culture, and its purpose is meaningful only when the assumptions it is based on are understood and accepted. It is not much of a problem for the person raised in the culture to see the relevance, the level of complexity, or the symbolic significance of his culture's literature. He is from birth familiar with the assumptions that underlie both his culture and its literature and art. Intelligent analysis in this circumstance becomes a matter of defining smaller assumptions peculiar to the locale, idiom, and psyche of the writer.

The study of nonwestern literature poses a problem for the western reader. He naturally tends to see alien literature in terms that are familiar to him, however irrelevant they may be to the literature he is considering. Because of this, students of American Indian literature have applied the terms "primitive," "savage," "childlike," or "heathen" to Indian literature. They have labeled its literature folklore, even though the term specifically applies only to that part of it that is the province of the general populace.

The great mythic[1] and ceremonial cycles of the American Indian peoples are neither primitive in any meaningful sense of the term, nor are they necessarily the province of the folk; much of the material on the literature is known only to educated, specialized persons who are privy to the philosophical, mystical, and literary wealth of their own tribe.

Much of the literature that was in their keeping, engraved perfectly and completely in their memories, was not known to the general run of men and women. Because of this, much of that literature has been lost as the last initiates of particular tribes and societies within the tribes died, leaving no successor.

Most important, American Indian literature is not similar to western literature because the basic assumptions about the universe and, therefore, the basic reality experienced by tribal peoples and westerners are not the same, even at the level of "folk-lore." This difference has confused non-Indian students for centuries, because they have been unable or unwilling to grant this difference and to proceed in terms of it.

For example, the two cultures differ greatly in terms of the assumed purpose for the existence of literature. The purpose of Native American literature is never one of pure self-expression. The "private soul at any public wall" is a concept that is so alien to native thought as to constitute an absurdity. The tribes do not celebrate the individual's ability to feel emotion, for it is assumed that all people are able to do so, making expression of this basic ability arrogant, presumptuous, and gratuitous. Besides, one's emotions are one's own: to suggest that another should imitate them is an imposition on the personal integrity

---

1 Mythic: 1. Narratives that deal with metaphysical, spiritual, and cosmic occurrences which recount the spiritual past and the "mysteries" of the tribe; 2. Sacred story. The *Word* in its cosmic, creative sense. This usage follows the literary usage rather than the common or vernacular sense of fictive or not-real narrative dealing with primitive, irrational explanations of the world. 3. Trans-rational.

of others. The tribes seek, through song, ceremony, legend, sacred stories (myths), and tales to embody, articulate, and share reality, to bring the isolated private self into harmony and balance with this reality, to verbalize the sense of the majesty and reverent mystery of all things, and to actualize, in language, those truths of being and experience that give to humanity its greatest significance and dignity. The artistry of the tribes is married to the essence of language itself, for in language we seek to share our being with that of the community, and thus to share in the communal awareness of the tribe. In this art the greater self and all-that-is are blended into a harmonious whole, and in this way the concept of being that is the fundamental and sacred spring of life is given voice and being for all. The Indian does not content himself with simple preachments of this truth, but through the sacred power of utterance he seeks to shape and mold, to direct and determine the forces that surround and govern our lives and that of all things.

There is an old Keres song that says:

> I add my breath to your breath
> That our days may be long on the Earth
> That the days of our people may be long
> That we may be one person
> That we may finish our roads together
> May my father bless you with life
> May our Life Paths be fulfilled.

In this way we learn how we can view ourselves and our songs so that we may approach both rightly. Breath is life, and the intermingling of breaths is the purpose of good living. It is in essence the great principle on which all productive living must rest, for relationships between all the beings of the Universe must be fulfilled so that our life paths may also be fulfilled.

This idea is apparent in the Plains tribes' idea of a medicine wheel[2] or sacred hoop[3] The concept is one of singular unity that is dynamic and encompassing, including, as it does, all that is in its most essential aspect, that of life. In his introduction to Geronimo's autobiography, Fredrick Turner III characterizes the American Indian cultures as static[4] a concept that is not characteristic of our own view of things; for as any American Indian knows, all of life is living—that is, dynamic and aware, partaking, as it does, in the life of the All-Spirit, and contributing, as it does, to the ongoing life of that same Great Mystery. The tribal systems are static in the sense that all movement is related to all other movement, that is, harmonious and balanced or unified; they are not static in the sense that they do not allow or accept change. Even a cursory examination of tribal systems will show that we have undergone massive changes and still retained those characteristics of outlook and experience that are the bedrock of tribal life[5] So the primary assumptions we make can be seen as static only in that they acknowledge the essential harmony of all things, and in that we see all things as of equal value in the scheme of things, denying the qualities of

2 Hymeyohsts Storm, *Seven Arrows* (New York: Harper and Row, 1972), p. 4 [p. 139 herein].
3 John G. Neihardt, *Black Elk Speaks* (Lincoln: University of Nebraska, 1961), p. 35.
4 Geronimo, *Geronimo: His Own Story*, edited by S.M. Barrett, introduction by Frederick Turner III (New York: Ballantine Books, 1968), p. 7.
5 D'Arcy McNickle, *Native American Tribalism: Indian Survivals and Renewals* (London: Oxford University Press, 1973), pp. 12-13.

opposition, dualism, and isolationism (separatism) that characterize non-Indian thought in the world. Civilized Christians believe that God is separate from man and does as He wishes without the creative participation of any of His creatures, while the non-Christian tribesman assumes a place in creation that is dynamic, creative, and responsive, and he allows his brothers, the rocks, the trees, the corn, and the nonhuman animals (the entire biota, in short) the same and even greater privilege. The Indian participates in destiny on all levels, including that of creation. Thus this passage from a Cheyenne tale: Maheo, the All-Spirit, created four things out of the void—the water, the light, the sky-air, and the peoples of the water.

"How beautiful their wings are in the light," Maheo said to his Power, as the birds wheeled and turned, and became living patterns against the sky.

The loon was the first to drop back to the surface of the lake, "Maheo," he said, looking around, for he knew that Maheo was all about him, "You have made us sky and light to fly in, and you have made us water to swim in. It sounds ungrateful to want something else, yet still we do. When we are tired of swimming and tired of flying, we should like a dry solid place where we could walk and rest. Give us a place to build our nests, please, Maheo."

"So be it," answered Maheo, "but to make such a place I must have your help, all of you. By myself, I have made four things . . . Now I must have help if I am to create more, for my Power will only let me make four things by myself."[6]

In this passage we see that even the All-Spirit, whose "being was a Universe,"[7] possesses limitations on his Power as well as a sense of proportion and respect for the Powers of his creatures. Contrast this with the Judeo-Christian God who makes everything and tells everything how it may and may not function if it is to gain his respect and blessing, and his commandments don't allow for change or circumstance. The Indian universe is one based on dynamic self-esteem, while the Christian universe is based on a sense of sinfulness and futility. To the Indian, the ability of all creatures to share in the process of life (creation) makes us all sacred.

The Judeo-Christian God created a perfect environment for his creatures, leaving them only one means of exercising their creative capacity and their ability to make choices and thus exercise their intelligence, and that was in disobeying him and destroying the perfection he had bestowed on them. The Cheyennes' creator is somewhat wiser, for he allows them to have unmet needs which they can, working in harmony with him, meet. They can exercise their intelligence and their will in a creative, positive manner and so fulfill themselves without destroying others. Together Maheo and the water-beings create the earth, and with the aid of these beings, Maheo creates first man and first woman and the creatures and environment they will need to live good and satisfying lives on earth.

Of interest, too, is the way the loon prays: he looks around him as he addresses Maheo, for "he knew that Maheo was all about him,"[8] just as earlier, when the snow-goose asked if the water fowl could sometimes

6 Alice Marriott and Carol K. Rachlin, *American Indian Mythology* (New York: Mentor Books, 1968), p. 39.
7 *Ibid.*
8 *Ibid.*, p. 6.

get out of the water, she addressed him in these words: ". . . I do not know where you are, but I know you must be everywhere . . ." [9] In these words we see two things: that the creatures are respectful but not servile, and that the idea that Maheo is all around them is an active reality. As he is not thought of as superior in a hierarchical sense, he is not seen as living "up there." Here again, the Indian sense of space relationships is different from that of the West. The one sees space as essentially circular or spherical in nature, while the other views space (and thus all relationships within that space) as laddered. The circular concept requires that all "points" which make up the sphere of being be significant in their identity and function, while the linear model assumes that some "points" are more significant than others. In the one, significance is significant, and is a necessary factor of being in itself, while in the other, significance is a function of placement on an absolute scale which is fixed in time and space. In essence, what we have is a direct contradiction of Turner's notion about the Native American universe versus that of the western: it is the Indian universe that moves and breathes continuously, and the western universe that is fixed and static. The Christian attitude toward salvation is a reflection of this basic stance, for one can only be "saved" by belief in a savior who came and will never come again, and the idea that "once a saint always a saint" is an indication of the same thing.

In the Native American system, there is no idea that nature is somewhere over there while man is over here, nor that there is a great hierarchical ladder of being on which ground and trees occupy a very low rung, animals a slightly higher one, and man a very high one indeed—especially "civilized" man. All are seen to be brothers or relatives (and in tribal systems relationship is central), all are offspring of the Great Mystery, children of our mother, and necessary parts of an ordered, balanced, and living whole. This concept applies to what non-Natives think of as the supernatural as well as to the more tangible (phenomenal) aspects of the universe. Native American thought makes no such dualistic division, nor does it draw a hard-and-fast line between what is material and what is spiritual, for the two are seen to be two expressions of the same reality—as though life has twin manifestations that are mutually interchangeable and, in many instances, virtually identical aspects of a reality that is, essentially, more spirit than matter, or that more correctly, manifests its very spiritness in a tangible way. The closest analogy in western thought is the Einsteinian understanding of matter as a special state or condition of energy. Yet even this concept falls short of the Native American understanding, for Einsteinian energy is essentially stupid, while energy in the Indian view is intelligence manifesting yet another way.

To the non-Indian, man is the only intelligence in phenomenal existence (often in any form of existence). To the more abstractionist and less intellectually vain Indian, man's intelligence arises out of the very nature of being, which is, of necessity, intelligent in and of itself, as an attribute of being. Again, this idea probably stems from the Indian conception of a circular, dynamic universe: where all things are related, are of one family, then what attributes man possesses are naturally going to be attributes of all beings. Awareness of being is not seen as an abnormality peculiar to one species, but, because of the sense of relatedness (instead of isolation) the Indian feels to what exists, it is assumed to be a natural by-product of existence itself.

9 *Ibid.*, p. 7.

225

In English, one can divide the universe into two parts — one which is natural and one which is "supernatural." Man has no real part in either, being neither animal nor spirit. That is, the supernatural is discussed as though it were apart from people, and the natural as though people were apart from it. This necessarily forces English-speaking people into a position of alienation from the world that they live in. This isolation is entirely foreign to Native American thought. At base, every story, every song, every ceremony, tells the Indian that he is part of a living whole, and that all parts of that whole are related to one another by virtue of their participation in the whole of being. Incidentally, the American practice of forbidding Indian children to speak their own language forces them into isolation from their sense of belonging, or at best, creates a split in their perception of wholeness. This practice was specifically undertaken in the last century as a means of destroying the person's adherence to "heathenish" attitudes, values and beliefs. It was felt that a person who spoke only English would necessarily forget his own way, and that one who spoke a Native language could not be assimilated into white culture. Those who decided on this policy spoke of "civilizing" Indian people, through the agency of alienation, isolation, and "individuation." Other aspects of this centuries-long process have included de-tribalization of land holdings and living arrangements, and prohibition of religious ceremonies and observances, forcing on American Indians the very sense of isolation that plagues and destroys other Americans.

In Native American thought, God is known as the All-Spirit, and others are also spirit—more spirit than body, more spirit than intellect, more spirit than mind. The natural state of existence is whole. Thus healing chants and ceremonies emphasize restoration of wholeness, for disease is a condition of division and separation from the harmony of the whole. Beauty is wholeness. Health is wholeness. Goodness is wholeness. A witch — a person who uses the powers of the universe in a perverse or inharmonious way — is called a two-hearts: one who is not whole but split in two at the center of being. The circle of being is not physical; it is dynamic and alive. It is what lives and moves and knows, and all the life-forms we recognize — animals, plants, rocks, winds — partake of this greater life. It is acknowledgement of this that allows healing chants such as this from the Night Chant to heal (make the person whole again).

> Happily I recover.
> Happily my interior becomes cool.
> Happily I go forth.
> My interior feeling cool, may I walk.
> No longer sore, may I walk.
> As it used to be long ago, may I walk.
> Happily, with abundant dark clouds, may I walk.
> Happily, with abundant showers, may I walk.
> Happily, with abundant plants, may I walk.
> Happily, on a trail of pollen, may I walk.
> Happily, may I walk.[10]

10 From a prayer of the *Night Chant* of the Navajo people.

Because of the basic assumption of the wholeness or unity of the universe, our natural and necessary relationship to all life is evident; all phenomena we witness, within or "outside" ourselves are, like us, intelligent manifestations of the intelligent Universe from which they arise as do all things of earth and the cosmos beyond. Thunder and rain are specialized aspects of this universe, as is the human race. And consequently the unity of the whole is preserved and reflected in language, literature, and thought, and arbitrary divisions of the universe of being into "divine" and "worldly," "natural" and "unnatural" do not occur.

Literature takes on more meaning when considered in terms of some relevant whole (like life itself), so let us consider some of the relationships between definite Native American literary forms and the symbols usually found within them. The two forms basic to Native American literature are the Ceremony and the Myth. The Ceremony is the ritual enactment of a specialized perception of cosmic relationships, while the Myth is a prose record of that relationship. Thus, the *wiwanyag wachipi* (Sun Dance) is the ritual enactment of the relationship the Plains people see between consecration of the human spirit to *Wakan Tanka* in his manifestation as Sun or/Light and Life-Bestower. Through purification, participation, sacrifice, and supplication, the participants act as instruments or transmitters of increased power and wholeness (which works itself out in terms of health and prosperity) from *Wakan Tanka*.

The formal structure of a ceremony is as holistic as the universe it purports to reflect and respond to, for the ceremony contains other forms such as incantation, song (dance), and prayer, and it is itself the central mode of literary expression, from which all allied songs and stories derive. For the Oglala, all the ceremonies are related to one another in various explicit and implicit ways, as though each was one face of a multifaceted prism. This interlocking of the basic forms has led to much confusion among non-Indian collectors and commentators, and this complexity makes all simplistic treatments of Native American literature more confusing than helpful. Indeed, it is the non-Indian tendency to separate things from one another—be they literary forms, species or persons, that causes a great deal of unnecessary difficulty and misinterpretation of Native American life and culture. It is reasonable, from an Indian point of view, that all literary forms should be interrelated, given the basic idea of the unity and relatedness of all the phenomena of life. Separation of parts into this or that is not agreeable to Native American systems, and the attempt to separate what are essentially unitary phenomena distorts them.

For example, to say that a ceremony contains songs and prayers is misleading, for prayers are one form of address and songs are another. It is more appropriate to say that songs, prayers, dances, drums, ritual movements, and dramatic address are compositional elements of a ceremony. It is equally misleading to single out the *wiwanyag wachipi* and treat it as an isolated ceremony, for it must of neccessity include the *inipi* (rite of purification) and did, at its point of origin, contain the *hanblecyeyapi* (vision quest)—which was how it was learned of in the first place.[11] Actually, it might best be seen as a communal vision quest.

11 This is an inference I am making from the account of the appearance of White Buffalo Cow Woman to Kablaya as recounted by Black Elk in *The Sacred Pipe,* recorded and edited by Joseph Epes Brown (New York: Penguin Books, 1971), pp. 67-100.

The purpose of a ceremony is integration: the individual is integrated, fused, with his fellows, the community of people is fused with that of the other kingdoms, and this larger communal group with the worlds beyond this one. A "raising" or expansion of individual consciousness naturally accompanies this process. The isolate, individualistic personality is shed, and the person is restored to conscious harmony with the universe. Alongside this general purpose of realization of ceremonies, each specific ceremony has its own specific purpose. This specific purpose usually varies from tribe to tribe, and may be culture-specific—for example, the rain dances of the Southwest are peculiar to certain groups such as the Pueblos, and are not found among some other tribes, or war ceremonies which make up a large part of certain plains tribes' ceremonial life are unknown among many tribes of California.[12] But all ceremonies—whether for war or healing create and support the sense of community which is the bedrock of tribal life. This community is not merely that of members of the tribe, but necessarily includes all orders of beings that people the tribe's universe.

It is within this context that the formal considerations of Native American literature can best be understood. The structures which embody expressed and implied relationships between men and other beings as well as the symbols which signify and articulate them are designed to accomplish this integration of the various orders of beings. It is assumed that beings other than the human participants are present at ceremonial enactments, and the ceremony is composed for their understanding participation as well as that of the human beings who are there. It is also understood that the human participants include those members of the tribe who are not physically present, for it is the community as community which enacts the ceremony, and not simply the separate persons attending it.

Thus devices such as repetition and lengthy passages of "meaningless syllables" take on meaning within the context of the dance. Repetition has an entrancing effect. Its regular recurrence creates a state of consciousness best described as "oceanic." It is hypnotic, and this exact state of consciousness is what is aimed for. The individual's attention must become diffused. The distractions of ordinary life must be put to rest, so that the larger awareness can come into full consciousness and functioning. In this way, the person becomes literally "one with the Universe," for the individual loses consciousness of mere individuality and shares the quality of consciousness that characterizes most orders of being.

The most significant and noticeable structural device is repetition, which serves to entrance and to unify—both the participants and the ceremony. In some sense, it operates analogously to a chorus in western forms, serving to reinforce the theme and refocus the attention on central concerns, while intensifying the participants' involvement with the enactment. One suits one's words and movements (if one of the dancers) to the repetitive pattern. Soon breath, heartbeat, thought, and word are one. The structure of repetition lends itself best to the purpose of integration or fusion, allowing thought and word to coalesce into one rhythmic whole that is not as jarring to the ear as rhyme but which unifies in larger units which are more consistent with the normal attention span of an adult.

12 Theodora Kroeber and Robert F. Heizer, *Almost Ancestors: The First Californians,* edited by F. David Hales (San Francisco: Sierra Club, 1968), pp. 28-30.

Margot Astrov suggests that this characteristic device stems from two causes: one which is psychic and one which is magical.

> ... this drive that forces man to express himself in rhythmic patterns has its ultimate source in psychic needs, for example the need of spiritual ingestion and proper organization of all the multiform perceptions and impressions rushing forever upon the individual from without and within. ... Furthermore, repetition, verbal and otherwise, means accumulation of power.[13]

She finds evidence of the first, or the need to organize perception to predominate some tribes' ceremonies such as the Apaches, and the second, a "magically creative quality"[14] more characteristic of others, such as the Navajo. In other words, some tribes appear to stress form while others stress content, but in either case, the tribe will make its selection in terms of which emphasis is best likely to serve the purpose of fusion with the cosmic whole, which is dependent on the emphasis which is most congenial to the literary and psychic sense of the tribe.

It is important to remember when considering rhythmic aspects of native poetic forms that all ceremony is chanted, drummed, and danced. Indians will frequently refer to a piece of music as a "dance" instead of a song, because song without dance is very rare, as is song without drum or other percussive instrument. It is also important to note that the drum does not "accompany" the song, for that implies separation between instrument and voice where no separation in the performing sense is recognized. These aspects combine to form an integral whole, and accompaniment is as foreign to the ceremony, as is performance before an audience. Where the ceremony is enacted before people who are neither singing nor dancing, their participation is nevertheless assumed. For participation is a matter of attention and attunement and not of activity versus passivity.

Repetition is of two kinds, incremental and simple. In the first various modes will occur. Perhaps a stanza will be repeated in its entirety four times—once for each of the directions, or six, once for each lateral direction with above and below added, or seven, which will be related to those mentioned with the addition of the center of these. Alternatively, the repetition may be of a phrase only, as in the *Yei be chi* quoted above, or of a phrase, repeated four times with one word, the ceremonial name for each of four mountains, say, or significant colors, animals, or powers, inserted in the appropriate place at each repetition, as in this Navajo mountain chant:

> Seated at home behold me,
> Seated amid the rainbow;
> Seated at home behold me,
> Lo, here, the Holy Place!
>> Yea, seated at home behold me.
> At Sisnajinni, and beyond it
>> Yea, seated at home behold me;
> The Chief of Mountains, and beyond it,
>> Yea, seated at home behold me;

---

13 Margot Astrov, editor, *American Indian Prose and Poetry* (New York: Capricorn Books, 1962), p. 12.
14 *Ibid.*

In Life Unending, and beyond it,
        Yea, seated at home behold me;
In Joy Unchanging, and beyond it,
        Yea, seated at home behold me.

Seated at home behold me,
Seated amid the rainbow;
Seated at home behold me,
Lo, here, the Holy Place!
        Yea, seated at home behold me.
At Tsods*chl*, and beyond it,
        Yea, seated at home behold me;
The Chief of Mountains, and beyond it,
        Yea, seated at home behold me;
In Life Unending, and beyond it,
        Yea, seated at home behold me;
In Joy Unchanging, and beyond it,
        Yea, seated at home behold me.

Seated at home behold me,
Seated amid the rainbow;
Seated at home behold me,
Lo, here, the Holy Place!
        Yea, seated at home behold me.
At Doko-oslid, and beyond it
        Yea, seated at home behold me;
The Chief of Mountains, and beyond it,
        Yea, seated at home behold me;
In Life Unending, and beyond it,
        Yea, seated at home behold me;
In Joy Unchanging, and beyond it,
        Yea, seated at home behold me.

Seated at home behold me,
Seated amid the rainbow;
Seated at home behold me,
Lo, here, the Holy Place!
        Yea, seated at home behold me.
At Depenitsa, and beyond it,
        Yea, seated at home behold me;
The Chief of Mountains, and beyond it,
        Yea, seated at home behold me;
In Life Unending, and beyond it,
        Yea, seated at home behold me;
In Joy Unchanging, and beyond it,
        Yea, seated at home behold me.[15]

It has been said that this device is caused by the nature of oral literature; that repetition ensures attention and remembrance, but if this is a factor at all, it is a peripheral one, for nonliterate people have memories that are more finely developed than those of literate people.

15 Natalie Curtis, editor and recorder, *The Indians' Book: Songs and Legends of the American Indians* (New York: Dover Books, 1968), p. 356. I have reproduced this part of the chant in its entirety though the Curtis version has only one verse with a note regarding the proper form.

The child learns early to remember complicated instructions, long stories verbatim, multitudes of details about plants, animals, kinship, and other social relationships, privileges and responsibilities, all "by heart." Since a person can't run to a bookshelf or a notebook to look up either vital or trivial information, reliance on memory becomes very important in everyday life. The highly developed memory of everyday is not likely to turn into a poorly developed one on ceremonial occasions, so the use of repetition for adequate memorization is not important.

Another reason that is given by folklorists for the widespread use of repetition in oral ceremonial literature is touched on by Ms. Astrov in her discussion of the "psychic" basis of the device:

> A child repeats a statement over and over for two reasons. First, in order to make himself familiar with something that appears to him to be threateningly unknown and thus to organize it into his system of familiar phenomena; and, second, to get something he wants badly.[16]

It is assumed that repetition is childish on two counts: that it (rather than rational thought) familiarizes and defuses threat, and that the person, irrationally, believes that repetition of a desire verbally will ensure its gratification. Let us ignore the obvious fact that shamen, dancers, and other adult participants of the ceremony are not children, and instead concentrate on actual ceremonies to see if they contain factors which are or might appear "threatening" to the tribe or if they simply repeat wishes over and over. There is nothing in the passages quoted so far that could be construed as threatening, unless beauty, harmony, health, strength, rain, breath, life unending, or sacred mountains can be so seen. Nor is there any threatening unknown mentioned in the songs and chants she includes in her collection; there are threatening situations, such as death or great powers, but while these constitute true unknowns to many civilized people, they are familiar to the tribes. And, by her own admission, death or severe illness are approached in positive ways, as in this death song:

> From the middle
> Of the great water
> I am called by the spirits.[17]

"Light as the last breath of the dying," she comments, "these words flutter out and seem to mingle with the soft fumes and mists that rise from the river in the morning," which hardly seems a threatening description. She continues:

> It is as though the song, with the lightness of a bird's feather, will carry the departing soul up to where the stars are glittering and yonder where the rainbow touches the dome of the sky.[18]

Throughout her discussion of Indian songs, she does not indicate a sense that the singers feel threatened by the chants, but rather that they express a serenity and even joy in the face of what might seem frightening to a child. Nor do there appear any passages in an extensive collection that are the equivalent of "God Won't You Buy Me a Color TV," which weaken the childhood-magic theory of repetition.

16 Astrov, *op. cit.*, p. 12.
17 Astrov, *op. cit.*, p. 50.
18 *Ibid.*, p. 50.

The failure of folklorists to comprehend the true psychic nature of structural devices such as ceremonial repetition stems from the projection of one set of cultural assumptions onto another culture. People of western cultures, particularly those in professions noted for their "objectivity," are not going to interpret "psychic" in its extramundane sense, but rather in its more familiar psychological sense. The twin assumptions that repetition serves to quiet childish "psychic" needs and to give the participants in a ceremony the assurance that they are exerting control over external phenomena—"getting something they want badly"—are projections. The ceremonial participants do indeed believe that they can exert control over natural phenomena, but not because they have childishly repeated some syllables. Rather, they assume that all of reality is "internal" in some sense, that the dichotomy of the isolated individual versus the "out there" does not exist more than apparently, and that ceremonial observance can serve to transcend this delusion, unite people with the All-Spirit, and from a position of unity within this larger self, effect certain results such as healing one who is ill, ensuring that natural events move in their accustomed way, or bringing prosperity to the tribe.

The westerner's bias against nonordinary states of consciousness is as unthinking as the Indian's belief *in* them is said to be. The bias is created by an intellectual climate which has been carefully fostered in the west for centuries, and which is only beginning to yield to masses of data which contradict it. It is a cultural bias which has had many unfortunate side-effects, only one of which is the deep misunderstanding of tribal literatures which has for so long found an untouchable nest in the learned and popular periodicals which deal with tribal culture.

In his four-volume treatise on nonordinary reality, Carlos Casteneda has described what living in the universe as a shaman is like. Unfortunately, he does not indicate that this experience is rather commoner to ordinary people than extraordinary, that the state of consciousness created through ceremony and ritual and that detailed in mythic cycles is exactly that of the "man of knowledge." He makes the whole thing sound exotic, strange, beyond the reach of most persons; yet the great body of American Indian literature suggests a quite different conclusion. It is in the context of psychic journey that this literature can best be approached. It is only in the context of the consciousness of the universe that it can be understood.

Native American thought is essentially mystical and psychic in nature. Its distinguishing characteristic is a kind of magicalness—not the childish sort espoused by Ms. Astrov, but on the order of an enduring sense of the fluidity and malleability (or creative flux) of things. This is a reasonable attitude in its own context, derived quite logically from the central assumptions that characterize tribal thought. Things are not perceived as inert but as viable, as alive; and living things are subject to processes of growth and change as a necessary component of their aliveness. Since all that is in existence is alive, and all that is alive must grow and change, all existence can be manipulated under certain conditions and according to certain laws. These conditions and laws, called ritual or magic in the west, are known to Native Americans as "walking in a sacred manner" (Sioux), "standing in the center of the world" (Navajo), or "having a tradition" (Pomo).

Given this attitude, the symbolism incorporated in Native American ceremonial literature is not symbolic in the sense usually understood: that is, the four mountains in the "Mountain Chant" do not stand for four other mountains. They are those exact mountains perceived psychically, as it were, or mystically. Red, used by the Oglala, doesn't stand for sacred or earth, but is the quality of a being, the color of it, when perceived "in a sacred manner" or from the point of view of earth herself. That is, red is a psychic quality, not a material one, though it has a material dimension, of course. But its material aspect is not its essential one; or as Madame Blavatsky put it, the physical is not a principle, or as Lame Deer suggests, the physical aspect of existence is representative of what is real.

> ... The meat stands for the four-legged creatures, our animal brothers, who gave of themselves so that we should live. The steam (from the stew-pot) is living breath. It was water; now it goes up to the sky, becomes a cloud again.
> ... We Sioux spend a lot of time thinking about everyday things, which in our mind are mixed up with the spiritual. We see in the world around us many symbols that teach us the meaning of life. We have a saying that the white man sees so little, he must see with only one eye. We see a lot that you no longer notice. You could notice if you wanted to, but you are usually too busy. We Indians live in a world of symbols and images where the spiritual and the commonplace are one. To you symbols are just words, spoken or written in a book. To us they are part of nature, part of ourselves, even little insects like ants and grasshoppers. We try to understand them not with the head but with the heart, and we need no more than a hint to give us the meaning.[19]

Not only are the "symbols" statements of perceived reality rather than metaphorical or "poetic" statements, but the formulations which are characterized by brevity and repetition are also expressions of that perception. Life is seen as part of oneself; a hint to convey which particular part is all that is needed to convey meaning. This accounts for the "purity" and "simplicity" which apparently characterized Native American literature, but it is simple in the sense of what is known and familiar, not in the sense of childish or primitive.

In a sense, all that exists is perceived as symbolic to the Indian; it is this that has given currency to the concept of the Indian as one who is close to the earth; he is close to the earth, but not as a savage (primitive form of civilized man), or as a child (another version of the same idea), but as a person who assumes that the earth is alive in the same sense that he is alive. He sees this aliveness in nonphysical terms, in terms that are familiar to the mystic or the psychic, and this gives rise to a mystical sense of reality that is an ineradicable part of his being. In brief, we can say that "the sun" or "the earth" or "a tree" is a symbol of an extraordinary truth rather than the other way around, as western critics understand it.

This attitude is not anthropomorphism. No Indian would take his perception as the basic unit of universal consciousness (or as the only one). We believe instead that the basic unit of consciousness is the All-Spirit, the living fact of intelligence from which all other perceptions arise and derive their power.

> I live, but I will not live forever.
> Mysterious moon, you only remain,
> Powerful sun, you alone remain,

19 John Fire/Lame Deer and Richard Erdoes, Lame Deer Seeker of Visions (New York: Simon and Schuster, 1972). pp. 108-09.

Wonderful earth, you remain forever.
All of us soldiers must die.[20]

Nor is this attitude superstitious. It is based very solidly on experience, and it is experience which is shared to whatever degree by most of the members of the tribal group. It is experience which is verified by hundreds and thousands of years of experience, and it is a result of actual perception—sight, taste, hearing, smell—as well as more indirect social and natural phenomena. In the west, if a person points to a building and says "there is a building" and other people, looking in the direction indicated agree, then we say that the building is there. If that building can be entered, walked through, touched, and this is done by many people, we say the building is really there.

In the same way, metaphysical reality is encountered and verified by Indians. No one's experience is idiosyncratic. When the singer tells of journeying to the west and climbing under the sky, the journey is one that many have gone on in the past and will go on in the future. And every traveler will describe the same sights and sounds, and will enter and return in like fashion.

This peculiarity of psychic travel has been noticed by many westerners, who attempt to explain it in psychological terms, such as the "collective unconscious" predicated by Jung. But they are saying that our imaginations are very similar; that the unconscious life of man is the same. The experiences, sights, sounds, and so forth encountered on psychic journeys are presumed to be imaginary and hallucinatory, just as thoughts are believed to be idiosyncratic events of no real consequence. Nowhere in the literature on ceremonialism have I encountered a western writer willing to suggest that the "spiritual and the commonplace are one."[21] Many argue that these hallucinations are good, others that they are the product of a diseased mind[22] but none suggests that one may *actually* be "seated amid the rainbow."

So symbols in Native American systems are not symbolic in the usual sense of the term. The words articulate reality—not "psychological" or imagined reality, not emotive reality captured metaphorically in an attempt to fuse thought and feeling, but that reality where thought and feeling are one, where objective and subjective are one, where speaker and listener are one, where sound and sense are one.

There are many kinds of Native American literature, and they can be categorized in various ways, but given the assumptions behind the creation and performance of the literature, a useful division might be along functional lines rather than along more mechanistic ones.

It might be said that the basic purpose of any culture is to maintain the ideal status quo. What creates differences among cultures, and literatures, is how that system goes about this task, and this in turn depends on (as much as maintains) basic assumptions about the nature of life and man's place in it. The ideal status quo is generally expressible in terms of "peace, prosperity, good health, and stability." Western cultures lean more and more heavily on technological and scientific

---

20 Crazy Dog Society song of the Kiowa People. This version appears in *Kiowa Years: A Study in Culture Impact* by Alice Marriott (New York: Macmillan, 1968), p. 118.
21 Lame Deer, *op. cit.*, p. 115.
22 Sigmund Freud, *Totem and Taboo: Some Points of Agreement Between the Mental Lives of Savages and Neurotics*, James Strache, translator (New York: W.W. Norton, 1950), p. 14.

methods of maintenance, while traditional cultures such as those of American Indian tribes tend toward mystical and philosophic methods. Because of this tendency, literature plays a central role in the traditional cultures which it is unable to play in technological ones. Thus, the purpose of a given "work" is of central importance to understanding its deeper significance.

The most basic division is ceremonial literature and popular literature, rather than the western "prose and poetry" distinction. Ceremonial literature includes all literature that is accompanied by ritual actions and music and which produces mythic (metaphysical) states of consciousness and/or conditions. This literature may appear to the westerner as either prose or poetry, but its distinguishing characteristic is that it is sacred, whether to greater or lesser degree. "Sacred," like "power" and "medicine," has a very different significance to tribespeople than to members of the "civilized" world. It does not mean something that is of religious significance and therefore believed in with deep emotional fervor, "venerable, consecrated or sacrosanct," as *Random House Unabridged* has it, but rather that it is filled with an intangible but very real power or force, for good or bad, as Lame Deer says in his discussion of symbolism:

> *Four* is the number that is most *wakan*, most sacred. Four stands for Tatuye Tope—the four quarters of the earth. One of its chief symbols is Umane, which looks like this:

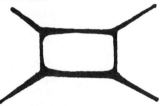

> It represents the unused earth force. By this I mean that the Great Spirit pours a great, unimaginable amount of force into all things—pebbles, ants, leaves, whirlwinds—whatever you will . . .
> This force is symbolized by the Umane. In the old days men used to have an Umane altar made of raised earth in their tipis on certain special occasions. It was so *wakan* you couldn't touch it or even hold your hand over it.[23]

In this statement, Lame Deer isn't saying that one was forbidden to touch the altar. He is saying that one *couldn't* touch it. The Umane doesn't represent the power, it is the power. "Sacred," "power," and "medicine" are related terms. Having power means being able to use this extra force without being harmed by it—it is a particular talent possessed to greater or lesser degree, and "medicine" is a term used for the personally owned force which one has power through; medicine is powerful in itself, but its power can usually only be used by certain persons.

So ceremonial literature is sacred; it has power. It frequently uses language of its own, archaisms, "meaningless" words, or special words that are not used in everyday conversation. It can be divided into several subcategories, some of which will appear in some tribes but not in others, and other types which will be found throughout Native

23 Lame Deer, *op. cit.*, p. 115.

America. Ceremonial literature includes healing songs; initiation songs; planting, harvesting, other agricultural songs; hunting songs; blessing songs of various kinds, such as for new houses, journeys — new undertakings; dream-related songs; war songs; personal power songs; food-preparation songs; purification songs; vision-seeking songs; and the major ceremonial cycles which include origin and creation cycles, migration and celebration of new laws, and legendary or "mythic" occurrences. Each of these serves the purpose of holding the society together; of creating harmony, restoring balance, ensuring prosperity and unity; and establishing right relationships within the social and natural world. At base they all restore the psychic unity of the people, the terms of their existence, and their sense of reality, order, and propriety. The most central of these perform this function at levels which are far more intense than others, and these are the great Ceremonies which, more than any single phenomena, distinguish one tribe from another.

Every people has a responsibility with regard to the workings of the universe; today as yesterday, human beings play an intrinsic role in the ongoing creation. This role is largely determined by the place where the tribe lives, and will change when that people changes its location. In the Southwest, the Zuni dance Shalako every winter at the solstice so that the sun will turn in his course and move once again toward summer. Cosmic cycles such as Shalako or Wúwuchim are related to life-processes on earth and, by virtue of natural relationship, within the universe. They are aimed toward forces far bigger than the community or the individual, though each is inescapably dependent on the other, "circles within circles" as Lame Deer says, "with no beginning and no end."[24]

The greater and lesser symbols incorporated into the ceremonies take their meaning from the context of the ceremony—its purpose and its meaning. Without knowledge of this purpose, attempts to understand ceremonial literature often have ludicrous results. The symbols cannot be understood in terms of another culture, whether it be of Maya or England, because those other cultures have different imperatives and have grown on different soil, under a different sky, and within a different traditional context. "Owl" in one situation will have a very different significance from owl in another, and a given color—white or blue—will vary from place to place and from ceremony to ceremony in its significance, intensity, and power. In other words, the rules that govern Native American literature are very different from those that govern western literature, though the enormity of the difference is, I think, a fairly late occurrence.

Literature must, of necessity, express and articulate the deepest perceptions, relationships, and attitudes of a culture, whether it does so deliberately or accidentally. Tribal literature does this with a luminosity and clarity that is largely free of pretension, stylized "elegance," or show. What are held to be the most meaningful experiences of human life, from levels which completely transcend ordinary experience to those which are commonplace, are those experiences celebrated in the songs and cycles of the people.

The more commonplace experiences are in the area of popular tales and songs; these may be humorous, soothing, pedagogical, or entertaining in purpose. Among those kinds of literature found in this

24 *Ibid.*, p. 112.

category are lullabies, corn-grinding and ditch-digging songs, jokes, "pour-quoi" tales, "little" stories, and stories which are contemporary in setting. Included here too are those delightful dances called "49s."[25]All but the latter appear in every collection of Indian lore, sometimes masquerading as true myths or simple songs. This masquerade, of course, does little to clear up misunderstandings regarding Native American literature, for frequently "myths" that seem childish are forms expressly for children, and bear only a slight resemblance to the true mythic forms.

Between the trivial, popular forms and the ceremonial are songs and stories such as various "games," incantations and other simple forms of magic, prose cycles such as the "trickster" tales recorded by Paul Radin, and some kinds of journey and food-related songs and legends.

It should be apparent that individual songs may be difficult to classify, though the level of symbology incorporated and the amount of prescribed ritual and associated ceremony, the number and special qualifications of the celebrants and the kind of physical setting and costume used can help distinguish one kind from another. In order to do this for any given song, though, it is necessary to have more than a nodding acquaintanceship with the tribe whose song or story is under consideration and with the locality. Another unfailing clue is the relative secrecy of parts or all of the ceremony, especially in terms of the presence of "tourists" and cameras. This will vary to some extent from tribe to tribe, some being more open than others, but the rule is still a good basic one. Another such clue, particularly valuable for classroom work, is the source the song or story was found in. Only very erudite tomes are likely to have much that is really sacred, and even that has usually been altered in some way. Popular books are likely to carry mainly popular literature, with a little from the next more powerful category. It would be well to mention, in this connection, that the use of really sacred materials is pretty well forbidden to ordinary mortals and publishers, and they do not make good classroom materials for a variety of reasons: they are arcane; they are usually taboo; they lead to confusion on the part of the students (if non-Indian) and resentment (if Indian); they create questions and digressions that are usually beyond the competence of the teacher—or the academic situation—to cope with. Frequently they lead to ridicule, disrespect, and belittlement; non-Indian students are not inclined by training or culture to view the sacred as that which has power beyond that of economics, history, or politics.

For all its complexity, Native American literature possesses a unity and harmony of symbol, structure, and articulation which is peculiar to itself. This harmony is based on the essential harmony of the universe and on thousands of years of refinement—the essential sense of unity

25 49 Songs were sung (danced) just before a war party went out. They are widely enjoyed today after a powwow has "officially" ended after twelve midnight. One 49 goes like this:

When the dance is ended sweetheart
I will take you home
He-ya he-he-ya
He-ya he-he-ya.

among all things that flows like a clear stream through the songs and stories of the peoples of the Western Hemisphere. This sense is embodied in these words of an old man, long ago:

> There are birds of many colors - red, blue, green, yellow - yet it is all one bird. There are horses of many colors - brown, black, yellow, white - yet it is all one horse. So cattle, so all living things - animals, flowers, trees. So men; in this land where once were only Indians are now men of every color - white, black, yellow, red - yet all one people. That this should come to pass was in the heart of the Great Mystery. It is right thus. And everywhere there shall be peace.[26]

So Hiamove said, more than fifty years ago. It remains for scholars of Native American literature to look at this literature from the point of view of its people. From this vantage only can the richness, complexity, and true meaning of a people's lives be fully understood; only in this way can we all learn the lessons of the past on this continent: the essential lesson of respect for all that is.

Bibliography

Alexander, Hartley Burr. *The World's Rim: Great Mysteries of the North American Indians.* Lincoln: University of Nebraska Press, 1953.

Astrov, Margot, ed. *American Indian Prose and Poetry.* New York: Capricorn Books, 1962.

Black Elk. *The Sacred Pipe: Black Elk's Account of the Seven Rites of the Oglala Sioux.* Recorded and edited by Joseph Epes Brown. Baltimore: Penguin Books, 1971.

Casteneda, Carlos. *The Teachings of Don Juan: A Yaqui Way of Knowledge.* New York: Ballantine Books, 1968.

———*A Separate Reality: Further Conversations with Don Juan.* New York: Pocket Books, 1972.

———*Journey to Ixtlan: The Lessons of Don Juan.* New York: Simon and Schuster, 1972.

———*Tales of Power.* New York: Simon and Schuster, 1974. Curtis, Natalie, editor. *The Indian's Book: Songs and Legends of the American Indians.* New York: Dover Publications, 1968.

Deloria, Vine, Jr. *God is Red.* New York: Grosset & Dunlap, 1973.

Freud, Sigmund. *Totem and Taboo: Some Points of Agreement Between the Mental Lives of Savages and Neurotics.* James Strache, translator. New York: W.W. Norton & Company Inc., 1950.

Geronimo, *Geronimo: His Own Story.* S.M. Barrett, editor. Introduction by Fredrick Turner III. New York: Dutton, 1970, and Ballantine paperback.

Goetz, Delia and Sylvanus G. Morley. From the translation of Adrian Recinos. *Popul Vuh: The Sacred Book of the Ancient Quiche Maya.* Norman: University of Oklahoma Press, 1950.

Gunn, John M. *Schat-Chen: History, Traditions and Narratives of the Queres Indians of Laguna and Acoma.* Albuquerque: Albright and Anderson, 1917.

26 Curtis, *op. cit.*, p. x.

Kilpatrick, Jack Frederick and Anna Gritts. *Walk in Your Soul: Love Incantations of the Oklahoma Cherokees*. Dallas: Southern Methodist University Press, 1965.

Kroeber, Theodora and Robert F. Heizer. *Almost Ancestors: The First Californians*. F. David Hales, editor. San Francisco: Sierra Club, 1968.

Lame Deer, John Fire/and Richard Erdoes. *Lame Deer Seeker of Visions*. New York: Simon and Schuster, 1972.

Marriott, Alice. *Kiowa Years: A Study in Culture Impact*. New York: The Macmillan Company, 1968.

——— and Carol K. Rachlin. *American Indian Mythology*. New York: Crowell Books, 1968, and Mentor paperback.

McNickle, D'Arcy. *Native American Tribalism: Indian Survivals and Renewals*. London: Oxford University Press, 1973.

Momaday, N. Scott. *House Made of Dawn*. New York: Harper & Row: 1968, and Signet paperback.

Neihardt, John G. *Black Elk Speaks*. Lincoln: University of Nebraska Press, 1961, and Pocket Books paperback.

Parker, Chief Everett and Oledoska. *The Secret of No Face: An Ireokwa Epic*. Healdsburg: Native American Publishing Company, 1972.

Radin, Paul. *The Trickster: A Study in American Indian Mythology*. New York: Philosophical Library, 1956, and Schocken Books, paperback.

Roy, Cal. *The Serpent and the Sun: Myths of the Mexican World*. New York: Farrar, Straus and Giroux, 1972.

Rushmore, Helen and Wolf Robe Hunt. *The Dancing Horses of Acoma and Other Acoma Indian Stories*. New York: The World Publishing Company, 1963.

Sanders, Thomas and Walter W. Peek. *Literature of the American Indians*. New York: Glencoe Press, 1973.

Storm, Hyemeyohsts. *Seven Arrows*. New York: Harper & Row, 1972.

Tyler, Hamilton A. *Pueblo Gods and Myths*. Norman: University of Oklahoma Press, 1964.

Underhill, Ruth M. *Red Man's Religion: Beliefs and Practices of the Indians North of Mexico*. Chicago: University of Chicago Press, 1965.

Waters, Frank and Oswald White Bear Fredericks, with spokespeople from the Hopi people. *Book of the Hopi*. New York: Viking Press, 1963 and Ballantine paperback, 1964.

Carol Lee Sanchez

(CONVERSATIONS #1)

The poster invites me to take
a trip to the Museum—
Native Americans on display:
Pueblo — Paiute — Apache
in authentic Native Costumes:
Lecture by Museum Guide.

those potteries rest
in glass cases
to haunt museums.
                    they concentrate
                    a formal essence,
a geometry of understanding,
from another place.

that Navajo Rug on the wall—
those Costumes described to you:
not as clothing still worn
for a particular occasion
But—
        as theatrical accoutrements
for these isolated dramas—
                    re-enacted,
"They'll sell anything these days,"
she sd.   she was right
not intending to be, but reminded
of those gaudy signs
riding West on 66
when we were young
                    NEXT STOP *****
                    Water, Cactus Candy

SEE REAL INDIANS MAKE AUTHENTIC
INDIAN JEWELRY *****

those gaudy signs
that lead to every junk Curio Store
filled with degrading imitations of
everything dear and sacred to us:

                    cardboard TomToms
                    felt headbands with
                    chicken feathers for
                    LITTLE BIG CHIEFS,
                    rubber Tomahawks
GENUINE plastic turquoise & tin
jewelry——and I shiver looks
at the Posters WE create
as another Grey Line Bus
pulls away from Taos La Fonda to:

SEE THE INDIANS AT THE PUEBLO.

(CONVERSATIONS #2)

They have disappeared me
as they have done to all
my ancestors before me.
Are you watching?

I wear a modified version
of the traditional dress
of my tribe — Pueblo Laguna.
It is not familiar to
those outside the southwest
but it IS real!

Look close
I may vanish before
your very eyes.

This is Not a Pocahontas dress.
I do Not wear feathers
or a headband
or beaded moccasins
because my tribe
does not wear those things.

Each tribe adapted various
forms of European beads and
ruffles and braids that
became traditional
ceremonial dress by
the late 1700's—
but — they are Indian!
because: WE wear them!
because: WE put them together
in a certain way.

Are you watching?
I may be disappearing
right now
it keeps happening
when I remind you who I am
and pretty soon
you don't see me anymore—
because: I'm a left over Primitive
and you're supposed to feel sorry
for me because:
> I am poor and
> diseased and
> ignorant and
> alcoholic and
> suicidal.

You see how it happens?
What goes on in your mind
when you see any of us
wearing our ceremonial dress?

We have Not been terminated
or exterminated.
We are here, all around you—
but — YOU disappear US
every day!

Are YOU watching?

(CONVERSATIONS #4)

Father Europe:
I divorce you
from this tierra indigena
to me
this land filled with
tradition
long before your
displaced dropouts
began the rape and plunder
of what was already ordered.

your genocidal tendencies
have stripped 'la gente indigena'
of costumbre and ritual;
that crucifixion complex
woven through this social fabric
sent that proper ritual underground
or dispersed it into
fragments of cross breeds
to leave only splinters
to fester
in wonder of what
can't be remembered
that was forgotten or
lost forever.

Father Europe:
I repel your future stake
in breaking my last connection
to my tierra—
this sacred altar
still holds the bones
of who I was.
those roots of me that
ache for knowledge of
who I might have been
before your Manifest Destiny
robbed my flesh
and diluted my blood.

I carry your cunning
in my veins—
your skill for mind-warp
and manipulation
along with my remembrance
of the old ones
who still vibrate
in me.
I am prepared to reclaim
my land.

I stand before you:
fully equipped.
I am a New Age
electronic Indian!
carefully bred and
tutored by you.

Father Europe:
I dispossess you!
take back my birthright
with the force of
my being.

This America
belongs to:

my people.

LA TIENDA

Hand chiseled sandstone
terraced false front
born 1867
tribute to the craft
of an unremembered mason
          'there used to be an
                    old pot bellied stove . .'

I never saw it
but the large economy sized
Coleman oil heater that
replaced it wasn't very new
and it had to be filled
twice a day to keep it going.

1.
8 o'clock opening time . .
the 'store crew' stands
around the stove just long
enough to ease early
morning chill.
The old men of Cubero
find their places around
it from mid-morning on.

In twos or threes they
shuffle in . . . stopping at the
counter to make a token
purchase before the daily
'junta' begins.
Backsides up against the stove . .
gloved hands protect them
from the intense heat.
Old man Durand was always
first to arrive and last to leave.
His hearing aid didn't help
his hearing much, nor did the
cupped hand . . . and if he wasn't
asking someone to repeat
something he missed . .
he was asking them to talk louder.
The other men would finally ignore
him . . . shaking their heads with
pained impatience.

> 'He doesn't ever pay attention . .'
> 'Wants to know every word . .'
> '*Dejalo* . . . leave him be . .'

> 'Rafael is in the Paratroopers now . .'
> 'Augustine's brother is making good
> money in San Diego. Defense Plant.
> Too old to fight.'
> 'The Postmaster's boy was in that
> Division on Bataan . . no word . . no
> one knows . .'
> 'So was Begote's *hijo* . . . *Julián* . .
> '*Que lástima* . .'
> '*Manuelito* is politicking again . .'
> '*Si* . . County Convention coming
> pretty soon . .'
> 'And another *gringo* running for
> County Commissioner . . .'
> '*Por Diós* . . we have to listen to
> those awful speeches unless we
> insist on an interpreter . .'
> '*No lloras hombre* . . we eat more meat
> during campaigns . .'
> '*Si* . . *bailes y juntas* . . the *músicos*
> will get paid . .'
> '*Ah si* . . *poco mas carne, pero siempre
> frijoles* . . .'

Lunch hour conversations done
Clemente stops to get a new
sack of *Dúkes* on the way out.
They trudge back up the road
past Lauro's *Cantina* to arrive
one by one in their *adobe* homes
in time for mid-day *comida*.

2.

Afternoon sun bounces off tall panes . . . shimmers around
a lone gas pump outside
warming the slab of mirror
finished concrete that always
had to be salted in the winter.
Two Indian ladies sit up against
the green board store front
wrapped in their shawls, waiting
for a ride down the road to one
of the Pueblo Villages off the
main highway.

Three or four younger townsmen
hired for the day, sit, feet
dangling from the warehouse
platform . . . hand rolled smokes
hanging lazy on their lips . .
waiting for a carload of flour
to arrive.

An old battered pick-up truck
pulls up to the pump, driven
by an older white haired
Acoma Indian man.

> 'How's your cattle . . my friend . . .
> Ready for delivery?'
> 'Not so good . . my friend . . . some
> got pink-eye . .'
> 'That's not so good . . you doctor
> them?'
> 'I been doing that . . but no help
> these days . . . only old men like us
> left to do all the work . .'
> 'You bring your gas coupons?'
> 'I got them . . but not so many left
> for this month . . . good thing we still
> got horses.'

3.

June . . sheep camp time.
Red chili stew and salt
pork beans bubbling in
cast iron kettles on the fire.
Thick black coffee steaming
in a blue speckled enamel pot.
Tin plates and cups clatter as
dark brown sheep herders lunch
in the shade of scrub cedar trees.
Five sacks filled with the morning's
shearing. Six, maybe seven to go.
(good yield this year). Back to
the corrals to bleating sheep that
wait to lose their winter coats.

245

Up on a platform . . a man climbs
into a burlap sack suspended
between two cedar poles to pack
loose wool into place. (should
weigh out 350 lbs. if it doesn't
shrink too much). Late afternoon
and a dust cloud announces the
arrival of The Store truck to
collect the fat bags of wool.
Tired men amble to the fire,
fill their coffee cups, roll
smokes and wait . . hunched on
their heels.

The truck rolls to a stop
beside the wool stack.
Two Cubero men climb down
and begin swinging 300 lb.
bags onto the truck bed.
A couple of Indian men
climb on the back to help.
> 'Bueno . . amigo . . the *Patrón* says
> to tell you we weigh it *mañana* . . .
> about 10 o'clock.'
> 'Sta Bien . . . amigo . . . we be there.
> 10 o'clock.'

A year's work . . . measured in
several thousand lbs. of
wool . . rolls slowly back down
a rutted dirt road to be
stored in a barn til there's
a carload full.
Then . . it will be shipped by
rail to Woolen Mills on the
East Coast. A year's worth
of food and clothing for
one family . . .
on account . . .
at the 'Old Cubero Store."

4.
> 'Ga-wa-tsi . . ,
> 'Dow-wah-eh . .'
> 'Is that you? . . my goodness . .
> you're such a big girl now . .
> how's your mama? . . . we haven't
> seen her in a long time . .'

Deep red . . flowered shawl. Silk fringed . .
the special one . . for outings. Hugged close
in winter and draped behind the shoulders
in summer . . always hiding rich black hair.

'We used to keep you with us . .
    do you remember? . . you were so
small and always running away
from your mama.'

And there was always some cellophane wrapped
rock candy in the pocket of your checked
gingham apron. The checks were cross stitched
in bright colored thread and the smell of
fresh baked bread and wood smoke clung to
the edges of it.

'How much . . . *Ha-tsu-nah-tsah?*
don't you understand Laguna?'
'No . . Aunt Marie . . only a few words . .'
'Shame on you . . you should get
your grandma to teach you . .'
'I will Aunt Marie . . it's good
to see you . . .'
'*Shro-oh* . .'
'*Ha-ah* . .'
'Well . . we must go now . . . tell your
folks hello for us . . . you come to
Paguate sometimes and visit us . . .'

PROPHECY

1.
Overhead, the stars are moving in the heavens—
Overhead, Play Moon is cold and still,
Below, in the kiva the dancers are fasting—
Below, in the kiva the singers are chanting.

On the earth, I stand in silence.
On the earth, I stand in waiting.
On the earth, I stand in preparation—
The time of resting has come.

Drum beats sigh across the mesas
Muffled in the rising wind,
Quickened with the thunder roll
Softened in the plaza shadows.
Winter spreads his white eagle feathers,
The time of resting has come.

The Song of the Deer Dance ascends from the plaza—
Antlers bobbing and dried gourd rattles
Keep time with belled moccasin steps,
In morning's frozen light.

In the houses, no venison strips are drying—
Food for the feast comes from a store.
In the houses, unused metates are dusty—
No corn is stacked and waiting as before.
No altars with fresh spruce and cornmeal
For the Dancers to bless when they come.

Overhead, Pa-muya begins to wane
On the earth, I kneel in silence.
Overhead, Cloud People begin to mourn
On the earth, I kneel in waiting.

Below, near the mountains, the rocks are moving—
On the earth, I kneel in preparation.
Below, beneath the lakes, Shipapu is rising—
The time of returning has come.

2.
In the plaza, I bow my head in sadness
trying to remember my grandmother's songs.
In the plaza, I hear my ancestors mourning
The old ways that are lost and forgotten.
In sorrow, I walk through my pueblo village;
The time of returning has come.

Aaiieee my brothers, remember the Ways—
The unmasking is at hand.

The grandmother's spirit whispers soft on the wind—
A young Corn Maiden appears in the mist—
Butterfly Maidens and Basket Dancers
Come smiling — out of the clouds.
Rainbow God has given his blessing
Unfolding his many colored robe.

Aaiieee my sisters, remember the Songs—
the unmasking is at hand.

Tsi-tche-na-a-ko draws in her life giving breath—
The old Spider Woman no longer sings.
Oraibe and Acoma grow silent and empty,
The Corn Mother will wither too soon.
Thus, it was sung at Wu-wuchimtu—
The time of returning has come.

Aaiieee my sisters, our children are lost—
the unmasking is at hand.

The Katsinas will gather in all the plazas—
Those spirits of the old ones gone before;
To dance for the people, one last dance.
They will come together in all the kivas
To sing one last forgotten song—
The last Wu-wuchimtu song.

Aaiieee my brothers, the moon falls close—
The unmasking is at hand.

Thus, it was sung at Wu-wuchimtu—
Thus, it was spoken in the Councils:
'We did not make peace with our brothers—
We did not teach him our songs—
The migrations have not been completed;
The fourth ending has begun.'

Aaiieee my sisters, Morning Star grows dim—
the unmasking is at hand.

Already, the new seeds are planted—
Already, the new stars appear.
Sa-qua-so-huh begins his journey
To dance in the plaza at sunset.
When the Blue Star Katsina dances unmasked—
Oraibe—will be no more.

Aaiieee my brothers, Earth Mother trembles—
Sa-qua-so-huh, Blue Star, approaches:
The time of unmasking has come.

MORE CONVERSATIONS FROM THE NIGHTMARE

illuminaron mis sentimientos
as they sat
hugged in coors and memory—
:when you were little
                they sd.
he ya ah ah he ya ah ha
he ya he ya.
válgame diós, hija
here we all are—
Urban Indians
feasting out of context
multilayered collages
of who we used to be.
                    [it's a shame
                    these people have to be
                    in the city—all those
                    colorful reservations and
                    picturesque houses they
                    were torn away from]
the Creek Baptist Minister
began the Indian marriage:
            'Dearly Beloved,
            we are gathered here . . .

the bride: Chicasaw—Oklahoma—
dressed in white bucksin
beaded frontpiece, exquisite
mink headpiece.
we try so hard to
live up to those exotic
images of: *'Rural Primitives'*

the drum begins and we fake the songs
mix them up—more coors down the hatch—
forget the steps to the Corn Dance
but we all know the Circle Dance and we
work to be authentic—because those
white folks who watch us know a 'fake'
when they see one.
                                 [*don't you miss your*
                                 reservation, dear?]
the extremes are always cruel—but
the intention is kindly meant.
                                 [*are those REAL moccasins?*
                                 I mean, handmade?]

how sacrilegious to like the city
and be an Indian—of whatever degree.
somebody forget that MY *'primitive'* ancestors
of the Southwest built Pueblo Bonito and
Mesa Verde! —Quaint apartment complexes
that can hardly be called anything else
but Urban! We Pueblos always were 'citified.'
                                 [*what's it really like on the*
                                 reservation? dear?]
now I watch us duplicate some textbook
stereotype of who we never were.
                    he ya he ah ha ah
                    he ya he he ya he

Harold Littlebird

DECEMBER 22, 1977
(For Barbara)

"she's asleep, but I'll tell her you were here, and thank you!"
12:30, ready to go to town to do laundry
then on to Albuquerque to pick up Maya's Grandma from Denver
for Christmas
looked outside from south kitchen window
a flock of sixty or seventy bluebirds, 'Shu-lu-ya'
stopping to drink from our ditch and asking to see
our little girl, their sister

that soft fluttery flight like whispers and the whistle sounds
deep from each one a subtle reminding of who she is
not wanting to disturb their drinking and low singing
but in a hurry and know its getting late
open the screen door
a burst of excited wings fills the whole grey winter sky and
our yard is alive with tiny blue praying
and maybe you're right, I was thinking the same thing
they came to wish her long life and happiness for the coming year

OLD MAN FOR HIS PEOPLE

[*In memory of Alex Sherwood*]

I remember still the meal we shared and
that time with you and your 'partner'
and the stories you told of how it was back then
bringing our lives, separated by many years, that much closer
and you holding my children on your lap and laughing
and I remember the greeting for your sister and
her man in Chewelah when entering their house
and how calm your handshake was when we first met
and your eyes that looked through me and cradled me
gently in wisdom and love

Old man for his people
watching us eternally
moving quietly among us
lending strength

and it was with heart heavy in our home
that we heard of your passing
quietly reminiscing and grieving
we spoke of you and Margaret
and the days your stories recalled

of the berry picking feasts and camas gathering
of going many miles in the wagon to celebration
and playing stick game
of bringing home deer and making meat for the winter

Old man for his people
I hear you singing
not of the sorrow that finally took you
but of the happy days with your wife
and the things you shared

up there, in the mountains that echo your voice
up there, blowing high above human ears
your medicine sings strong and good
for "Children of the Sun"

I will pray, up there
in the mountains
that my own children
will not forget the song you sing

all of us who knew you
now know how much you are truly missed and loved
but ours here is to go on and
respect you daily
through the things that meant and mean
so much to you, Old man
it is not forgotten

in the clear mountain air
in the Spokane River rising
in the pine-filled forests
in the salmon swimming
in the white-tail bounding
and ruffed-grouse calling
in the old men singing
and women dancing
will you be heard and
be forever with us, Grandfather

there is singing
song in motion
in simple melody
high through the heavens and in the space between
sky and earth are you
growing and vibrant and unique
and in your growing there is your brother, Elk Rider
your sisters, Hay-a-shee, Dya-tza-ah
all from the mountains and sky
and from this you stem

you whose name I can't remember but know your singing
there in the grey house surrounding you that knew your beginning
in your cradle of oak swaying
and outward to the brown-grey land and alfalfa fields
to the river swollen in Spring, flowing and rolling swiftly
and beyond
in that current of life all around

from the smallest flower your existence began
a seedling alive and growing
in its rightful place
blessed by spirits of wind and water
taking hold to its mother
sucking from the womb of the earth
whispering unseen
giving thanks for its being

from this you came happily
one crisp morning in the dark of the new moon
bonding and adding strength to your mother and father
both of which I know and love as you
it is from this and more that you are now a year and growing
it is from legends and stories and songs listened to and lived by
that messengers in the night will tell you in your dreaming
you will carry, learn and share
and it is this and more that you are growing
more than I can say with words
it is in the likeness of breaths on corn pollen
and silent prayer to holy things on the fourth morning
and all of this I know you singing, eyes shining
and simply caring in your mountain home!

mountains snow covered and glowing in the afternoon's brilliance
air thick of pine and pitch
springs erupting from cracks in the sides of rough granite land flow
gushing and pumping the life-blood of the earth mother far to the valleys below
and the peaks towering like sentries high into the clouds and further
and the fullness and wonder and serene beauty
this pass called Independence
surrounded in awe, wide-eyed and reverent
like the time in Utah at sweat, with Bruce and Adrianna
the all-mother came and washed me
blessing with air and cold and I sang in solemn laughter
and my thoughts were of home
and my dad's father and his father before him and his father's father before him
the language to describe this wholeness and being a part of it
one part in many
my heart was pounding mountain summer and asking to breathe, taste, and share
and like dancing and the cottonwood drum every muscle and vein was taut
    and swollen
intent on moving without strain, ready to burst forth for the people in harmony
    and song
the wind gusting, trees swaying
springs running, grasses growing
snow covering, the earth living . . .
these and more I know my father and his father and his father's father danced
and my father has let it be known to me
up there is prayer without words
surrounded by spirits of caring
and the tears in my eyes were for knowing that's from where I come
and that's where song and motion and language is born and re-born
and the sound from any one person is power re-called and
should be held in deepest respect and mystery
for it is sacred like breath itself

Joe S. Sando

ECHO FROM BEYOND

We are the First Inhabitants
    Of Jemez Pueblo
We are the ones
Who traveled South
From the mountains,
With bows in hand,
In the prime
of our youth.

    It was we who
    broke the trails
    To your hunting grounds,
    Cleared the land
    Which is your lifeline,
    Harnessed the river
    Which waters your fields,
    We, who with wet—
    streaked faces,
    Saw in
    Setting sun the
    Promise of Tomorrow.

        Here we lived
        And loved
        Fought and drove the Spaniards,
        The Apaches, The Navajos,
        And the Comanches,
        From our fields
        And homes.
        Built the kivas
        For your recreation
        And education.

            We served our turn.
            We laid the
            Strong foundations.
            We are content.
            Look not back
            Too long
            Too often
            But build, like us,
            Carry on,
            For your sons,
            For a better day
            Tomorrow.

Joseph L. Concha

Grandmother
before i learned to crawl
you turned golden
like an aspen leaf
and flew away
from my open arms . . .

CHOKECHERRY HUNTERS

a new morning
among the drifting cotton
the chokecherry hunters sing . . .

spoon mountains
                    in a rainstorm

thunderflash
                    end of rainstorm

under the stars
                    a sweet smell
                                        leaves out thoughts.

AUGUST

Drifting across the Taos mountains
early morning fog blankets

the crying horses
a call to memories

a drum beats by the creek
stirring anxious hearts in rhythm . . .

LEAF

a leaf floats downstream
upon its last dream
not able to fly . . .

Alone
on a hill
the wind blows
and you came like a dream . . .

holy sun, full of light
the moon is with you
blessed art thou among nature
and blessed is our way of life
holy earth, mother of gods
hear our songs
now and at the four corners . . .

Simon J. Ortiz

WOMAN SINGING

"Yessir, pretty good stuff," Willie said. He handed the bottle of Thunderbird wine to Clyde.

Clyde took a drink and then another before he said anything. He looked out the window of their wooden shack. Gray and brown land outside. Snow soon, but hope not, Clyde thought.

"Yes," Clyde said. But he didn't like it. He didn't drink wine very much, maybe some sometimes, but none very much.

Willie reached for the bottle, and Clyde thought that Willie didn't mind drinking anything. Any wine was just another drink. But he knew, too, that Willie liked whiskey, and he liked beer too. It didn't make any difference to Willie. Clyde wished he had some beer.

They had come from the potato fields a few minutes before. It was cold outside and Willie threw some wood into the kitchen stove as soon as they came in. He poured in kerosene from a mason jar and threw in a match. After a moment, the kerosene caught the small fire and exploded with a muffled sound. Willie jumped back and laughed. Clyde hung up his coat and then put it back on when he saw there were only a few pieces of wood in the woodbox. He looked over at Willie, but Willie was taking his coat off and so Clyde went on out to get the wood. Willie didn't do anything he didn't have to.

There was singing from the shack across from theirs. Singing, The People singing, Clyde said to himself in his native Indian tongue. It was a woman. Sad kind of, but not lonely, just something which bothered him, made him think of Arizona, his homeland. Brown and red land.

Pinon, yucca, and his father's sheep, the dogs too around the door of the hogan at evening. Smoke and smell of stew and bread, and the older smell of the juniper mingled with the sheep. His heart and thoughts were lonely. Woman singing, The People singing, here and now, Clyde thought to himself. He stood for a while and listened and then looked over at the shack. The door was tightly shut, but the walls were thin, just scrap lumber and roofing paper, and the woman's voice was almost clear. Clyde was tempted to approach the shack and listen closer, his loneliness now pressed him, but he would not because it was broad daylight and it was not the way to do things. The woman was Joe Shorty's wife, and she was the mother of two children. Clyde picked up an armful of wood and returned to his own shack.

"Have some more, son," Willie said. Willie was only a few years older than Clyde, but he called him son sometimes. Just for fun, and Clyde would call him father in return. Willie was married and the father of two children. They lived in New Mexico while he worked in the Idaho potato fields.

"I think I'll fix us something to eat," Clyde said after he had taken a drink. He began to peel some potatoes. Willie's going to get drunk again, he thought. Yessir. They had gotten paid, and Willie had been fidgety since morning when they had received their money from Wheeler, their boss. He had told the Indians who worked for him, "Now I know that some of you are leaving as soon as you get paid, well that's okay with me because they ain't much to do around here until next year. But some of you are staying for a while longer, and I'm telling those guys who are staying that they better stay sober. Besides, it's getting colder out, and we don't want no froze Indians around." Wheeler laughed, and Willie laughed with him. Clyde didn't like the boss, and he didn't look at him or say anything when he received his pay. He was going to stay for at least another month, but he didn't want to. But he figured he had to since he wasn't sure whether he could get a job around home right off or even at all. Willie was staying too, because he didn't feel like going home just yet, besides the fact that his family needed money.

"I think I'm gonna go to town tonight," Willie said. He was casual in saying it, but he was excited and he had been planning for it since morning. "Joe Shorty and his wife are coming along. You want to come?"

"I'm not sure," Clyde said. He didn't know Joe Shorty too well, and he had only said Hello to his wife and children.

"Come on," Willie insisted. "We'll go to a show and then to the Elkhorn Bar. Dancing there. And all the drunks have left, so it'll be okay now. Come with us."

"Yeah, I might," Clyde said. He listened for the woman's singing while they ate, but the fire crackling in the stove was loud and Willie kept talking about going to town. "Isn't Joe Shorty and his family going back home?" Clyde asked.

"I don't know," Willie answered. He pushed back his chair and carried the dishes to the sink. Clyde began to wash the dishes but Willie stopped him. "Come on, let's go."

When they knocked on Joe Shorty's door, a boy answered. He

looked at the two men and then ran back inside. Joe came to the door.

"Okay, just a little while," Joe said.

Willie and Clyde sat down on the front step. They could hear movement and mumbled talk inside. Clyde thought about the singing woman again. He felt uncomfortable because he was thinking of another man's woman. It was a healing song, strong mountains in it, strong and sharp and clear, and far up. Women always make songs strong, he thought. He almost told Willie about the song.

Joe and his wife and children, two boys, came out and they all began to walk on the road towards town. It was five miles away, and usually someone was driving into town and would give them a ride. If not, they would walk all the way. The children ran and walked ahead. They talked quietly with each other, but the grownups didn't say anything.

When they had walked a mile, a pickup truck stopped for them. It was Wheeler. "Hey, Willie. Everybody going to town, huh? Come," Wheeler called.

Willie and Clyde got in front with Wheeler, and Joe and his family got in the back.

"Well, gonna go have a good time, huh? Drink and raise hell," Wheeler said loudly and laughed. He punched Willie in the side playfully. He drove pretty fast along the gravel road.

Willie smiled. The wine he had finished off was warm in him. He wished he had another bottle. Out of the corners of his eyes, he searched the cab, and wondered if Wheeler might have a drink to offer.

"You Indians are the best damn workers," Wheeler said. "And I don't mind giving you a ride in my truck. Place down the road's got a bunch of Mexicans, had them up at my place several years back, but they ain't no good. Lazier than any Indian anytime, them Mexicans are. Couldn't nothing move them once they sit down. But you people — and for this reason I don't mind giving you a lift to town — Willie and your friend there do your work when I tell you, and that means you're okay for my farm."

Clyde felt the wine move in his belly. It made him swallow and he turned his head a little and saw that the woman's scarf had fallen away from her head. She was trying to put it back on.

"That Joe's got a pretty woman," Wheeler said to Willie. He looked at Clyde for comment, but Clyde would not look at him. Willie smiled and nodded.

"Yeah, don't get to see too many pretty Indian women around the camps, but she's a pretty one. You think so, Willie?" Wheeler nudged Willie with his elbow.

"Yes," Willie said and he shrunk down in his seat. He wished that Wheeler would offer him a drink if he had any. But he knew that he probably wouldn't.

"Hey, Clyde, you married? A woman at home?" Wheeler asked, but he didn't look at Clyde. They were approaching the town and Clyde stared straight ahead at it but he decided to answer.

"No," Clyde said. "Not yet, maybe when I get enough money." He smiled faintly to show that he was making a minor joke.

"Someday you'll get a woman, maybe a pretty one like Joe's, with or without money," Wheeler said. And he laughed loudly. He pulled the pickup truck over to a curb in the center of the small town. "Well, take it easy. Don't overdo it. Or else you'll land in jail or freeze out in the cold or something," Wheeler said with no special concern.

"We're going to the show," Willie said, and he smiled at Wheeler.

"Okay," Wheeler said, gave a quick laugh, and turned to watch Joe's wife climb out of the truck. He wanted to catch her eye, maybe to wink at her, but she didn't look at him. He watched the Indians walk up the street towards the town theater. The woman and her children followed behind the men. Wheeler thought about all the drunk Indians he'd seen in his life. He shrugged his shoulders and turned down the street in the opposite direction.

The movie was about a singer. Hank Williams was the singer's name. Clyde knew who he was, used to be on the Grand Ole Opry on radio, he remembered, sang songs he remembered too. Clyde thought about the singers back home. The singers of the land, the people, the rain, the good things of his home. His uncle on his mother's side was a medicine man, and he used to listen to him sing. In the quiet and cold winter evenings, lying on his sheepskin beside the fire, he would listen and sing under his breath with his uncle. Sing with me, his uncle would say, and Clyde would sing. But he had a long ways to go in truly learning the songs; he could not sing many of them and could only remember the feeling of them.

Willie laughed at the funny incidents in the movie, and he laughed about the drunk Hank Williams. That made him wish he had a drink again, and he tried to persuade Joe to go with him, but Joe didn't want to leave. Joe's wife and children watched the movie and the people around them, and they watched Willie fidget around in his seat. They figured he wanted to go drink.

At the end of the movie, they walked to a small cafe. On the way Willie ran into a liquor store and bought a pint of whiskey.

"Come on, son," he said to Clyde. "Help your father drink this medicine." Joe followed along into an alley where they quickly gulped some of the liquor.

"Call your woman and ask if she wants some," Willie said to Joe. He was in good spirit now. The whiskey ran through him quickly and lightly.

"Emma, come here," Joe called to his wife. She hesitated, looked up the street, and stepped into the alley. Her husband handed her the bottle and she drank quickly. She coughed and gasped for a moment, and Willie and Joe laughed.

Clyde saw the two children watching them. They stood in the weak overhead glare of a streetlight. Traffic barely moved, and a few people from the movies were walking on the streets. The children waited patiently for their parents.

They ate a quick dinner of hamburgers and cokes. And when they finished, they paid up and walked to the Elkhorn Bar a couple of blocks away.

"Do se doe," Willie said when he heard the music coming from the bar. Saturday night was always a busy night, but most of the Indian potato pickers were gone now. There were only a few cars and trucks;

some men and women stood by the door. A small fire blazed several yards from the bar, and around it were a few Indians quietly talking.

Willie walked over to the fire, and Clyde followed him because he didn't want to be left alone. Joe and his family stood beside the door of the bar and peered in.

"Here comes a drunk," someone in the circle of Indians said as Willie and Clyde walked up. They laughed, but it was not meant in harm. For a moment, as he did upon entering a crowd away from his home, Clyde felt a small tension, but he relaxed quickly and he talked with an acquaintance. Willie passed him a bottle, and he made a small joke, and Clyde laughed. He felt better and took a long drink. Whiskey went down into the belly harder than wine but it made him fel warmer. And when he thought that it didn't make any difference to Willie what he drank he laughed to himself. The men talked.

The talk was mostly about their home and about The People at home. Clyde again felt the thought travel into his heart. It made him long for his home. He didn't belong here even though he had friends here, and he had money in his pocket and a job. He was from another place, where his people came from and belonged. Yet here some of them were around this fire, outside the Elkhorn Bar, and they worked in the Idaho potato fields cultivating, irrigating, and picking potatoes. Someone began a song. It was the season for sings back in The People's land. The song was about a moving people.

When no one passed a bottle for a while, Clyde decided to go get a drink at the bar. The liquor in him made him sleepy, but he was getting cold too. There was no wind, but it was getting colder. He remembered Wheeler's words, thought about them for a moment, but he knew it would not freeze tonight. The bar was crowded. Someone was on the floor near the doorway, and others stepped over him without taking much notice.

Clyde met Joe Shorty and his wife, and they drank some beer together. Joe was getting drunk and his wife was drinking quietly. It was too noisy for Clyde to remember the song anymore. The children were standing by the jukebox, watching the revolving discs. Clyde wondered when they were going back to the camp by the potato fields, and he went to look for Willie.

"So there you are, son," Willie said when Clyde found him. He was with the men around the fire. "Come join us." He was drunk, and he handed Clyde another bottle.

The Indians, who were very few now, were singing in the high voice of The People. Like the wind blowing through clefts in the mountains. Clyde wondered if it was only that he was getting drunk with the liquor that he could make out the wind and the mountains in the song. But it was the men getting drunk too, which didn't make it sound like the wind, he thought. He drank some more, but he was getting tired and colder, and he told Willie he wanted to go.

"No, stay," Willie said. "It is still a long night. These nights are long, and at home the sings last all night long."

This Idaho was not where The People's home was, Clyde thought. And he wanted to tell Willie that. He wanted to tell the others that, but they wouldn't pay attention to him, he knew.

The women would sit or stand quietly by the singing men at home. The fire would be big, and when it got smaller someone would bring an armload of wood and throw it in. Children would hurry through the crowd of The People until they were tired and sleepy. Here there were no children except by the jukebox, watching it play records. In the morning, there would be newly built fires before camps of families. In the mountains of The People. And the light beginning in the East would show that maybe it will snow sometime soon, but here by the Elkhorn Bar there would be no fires and no one to see the light in the East. Maybe, like Wheeler talked, there'd be some frozen Indian left lying around.

Clyde walked away. The town was quiet. A police cruiser went in the direction of the bar and the officer looked at Clyde. When he got to the edge of town, he lengthened his stride.

When he had walked for a while, he saw that someone was walking in front of him. He slowed down, and he saw that it was a woman and two children. Joe Shorty's family. Joe must have stayed, drunk I guess, Clyde thought, and his family had left without him. Clyde didn't want to talk with them because they were another man's wife and children. They heard him and one of the boys said loudly, "It's Clyde. Clyde, come walk with us."

The woman was slightly drunk. Clyde could see her smile. She staggered some. "It's cold," she said. "We left Joe Shorty. He's going to come home in the morning."

Joe Shorty's wife and sons and Clyde walked quietly and steadily. The children stepped carefully in the dark. Once, Clyde looked back, and he could barely make out a pale light over the town. He thought about Willie and thought he would be all right. It was cold and Clyde let his hand out of his pocket to test the cold. Willie would be all right. Joe Shorty and Willie would probably come back to the camp together in the morning.

The lights of a truck lit them up and Clyde said, "We better get on this side of the road." The younger boy stumbled and grabbed for Clyde's hand. The boy's hand was cold, and Clyde felt funny with Joe Shorty's son's hand in his.

The truck was Wheeler's. It passed them and then slowed to a stop fifty yards ahead. Wheeler honked his horn. Clyde and Joe Shorty's family walked toward the truck as it backed towards them.

"It's Wheeler, the potato boss," Clyde said to the woman. She did not look at him or say anything. The younger boy clung to his mother's skirt.

The pickup truck drew back alongside of them and stopped. Wheeler rolled down his window and studied them for a moment. He looked at Clyde and winked. Clyde felt a small panic begin in him. He realized that he still held the child's hand in his. What did this mean to the potato boss, Clyde asked himself.

"Well come on," Wheeler said. "Get in, but just a minute," and he got out. He stood by the side of the truck and urinated. The woman and her children and then Clyde climbed into the back of the truck.

When Wheeler saw that they had climbed in back, he said gruffly, "Come on, get in front." And then with a softer tone, "There's enough room and it's colder than hell out," and he reached out a hand to one of the boys. But the boy hung back. Wheeler grabbed the other and swung him over the side. The woman and the other boy had no choice but to follow.

Clyde felt his feelings empty for a while and then he slowly felt himself burning. He watched the woman climb out of the back into the front. It was not cold as before and it was the liquor, he thought. When he jumped down from the back and got into the front he felt light and springy. He smiled at Wheeler.

Joe Shorty's wife did not say anything. She was looking at the dashboard and her children huddled against her.

"Well, Joe Shorty must be having a good time," Wheeler said. He laughed and steered wildly to keep the truck on the road.

The woman did not say anything. She held one of her children, and the other huddled against her tightly. Clyde was on the side against the door. He could feel her movement and her warmth. But he looked straight ahead until Wheeler spoke to him.

"Weren't you having a good time, Clyde? Maybe there's good times other places, huh?"

Clyde felt a hot liquid move in him. It was warm in the truck. The heater was blowing on his ankles. It's the whiskey, he thought. What does this man think of this, he thought. And then he thought of what all the white men in the world thought about all the Indians in the world. I'm drunk, he thought, and he wanted to sing that in his own language, The People's language, but there didn't seem to be any words for it. When he thought about it in English and in song, it was silly, and he felt uncomfortable. Clyde smiled at Wheeler, but Wheeler wasn't paying attention to him now.

Wheeler drove with one hand and with the other he patted Joe Shorty's older son on the head and smiled at Joe Shorty's wife.

"Nice, nice kid," Wheeler said. The woman fidgeted, and she held her other son tightly to her.

Clyde felt her move against him and he tensed. He tried to think of the song then. The People singing, he thought, the woman singing. The mountains, the living, the women strong, the men strong. But he was tense in his mind, and there was no clear path between his mind and heart. Finally, he said to himself, Okay, potato boss, okay.

They drove into the camp and stopped in front of Clyde's and Willie's shack. Clyde thought, Okay, Potato boss, okay. He opened the door and began to climb out. The woman and her children began to follow him.

"Wait," Wheeler said. "I'll drive you home. I'm going your way." His voice was almost angry.

Wheeler grabbed her arm, but she wrenched away. Clyde stopped and looked at Wheeler.

"She lives over there," Clyde said, pointing to Joe Shorty's shack, but he knew that Wheeler knew that.

Wheeler scowled at him and then he searched for a bottle under the seat. The woman did not move away anymore. She watched Wheeler and then said something to her children. Clyde looked at her. The song, he thought, and he tried very hard to think of the woman singing. The children ran to the shack, and Joe Shorty's woman and Wheeler followed.

For a long time, Clyde stood behind the door of his and Willie's shack. Listening and thinking quiet angry thoughts. He thought of Willie, Joe Shorty, the Elkhorn Bar, Hank Williams, potatoes, the woman and her sons. And he thought of Wheeler and himself, and he asked himself what he was listening for. He knew that he was not listening for the song, because he had decided that the woman singing was something a long time ago and would not happen anymore. If it did, he would not believe it. He would not listen. Finally, he moved away from the door and began to search through Willie's things for a bottle. But there was no bottle of anything except the kerosene and for a moment he thought of drinking kerosene. It was a silly thought, and so he laughed.

When the bus pulled out of the town in the morning, Clyde thought of Willie again. Willie had come in when the sun was coming up. He was red-eyed and sick.

"We had a time, son," Willie said. He sat at the table woodenly. He did not notice that Clyde was putting clothes into a grip bag.

"That Wheeler, he sure gets up early. Joe Shorty and I met him outside his house. 'The early bird gets the worms,' he said. Sure funny guy. And he gave us some drinks," Willie mumbled. He was about to fall asleep with his head on the table.

"I'm going home," Clyde said. He had finished putting his clothes in the bag.

"You never have a good time," Willie said. Clyde thought about that and asked in his mind whether that was true or not.

When Clyde thought about the woman's singing he knew that it had been real. Later on he would hear it someplace again and he would believe it. There was a large hurt in his throat and he began to make a song, like those of The People, in his mind.

HEYAASHI GUUTAH

The diaphanous morning cloud
                              comes
                                   down

from the southwest mesa
from Acu
and into Tsiahma,
passes,
and heads up the wet black road
to Budville.

            Poor wrecking yard,
            Baptist Indian Mission,
            tilted sign dangling
            over the door to Kings Bar.

That man stumbles
against the lurch in his belly.
The night's terrored sleep
is a reflection in the dark window.
Mud from the ravine
clings to his pants.

It's not open yet.

Across the road, a woman waits.

The ghost moves slowly northwards
towards Kaweshtima.
It looks back
and waits for them, patiently.

TIME TO KILL IN GALLUP

City streets
are barren
fronts for pain
hobbles toward
Rio Puerco wallow hole
            up under the bridge.
My eyes are pain,
"Yaahteh."
Yesterday
they were visions.
Sometimes my story
has worked
but this time
            the falling scabs
reveal only a toothless
woman.

Gumming back sorrow,
she gags on wine.
One more countless time
            won't matter.

Says,
"One more,
my friend."
I know him, standing,
by the roadside.
He got lost,
"didn't wanna go home,"
            and we left him
a ghost to remember.
Only sorrow has no goodbyes.

These Gallup streets
aren't much
for excuses
            to start on at least
one last goodtime.

"So forgetful,"
it's easy, "you are,"
she said.
            Sweeping her hand,
knocking on cold railroad tie.
She shudders
too often a load
of children bound
to be bound
in rags.

The children
have cried too many times,
would only dig more graves,
lean on church walls.
For warmth,
"Sure why not."
Look for nickels, dimes,
pennies, favors,
            quick cold kisses.
The child whimpers
pain
into gutters.
These streets never
were useful
for anything
except tears.

She rubs her one last eye.
The other is a socket
for a memory
she got ripped,
ripped off
at Liberty Bar,
saving a pint of wine,
thinking she was saving
grace
and would be granted
redemption
if she fought
or turned over
            one more time.

Sister. Sister. These streets
are empty.
They have only told sighs
which are mean
and clutch with cold evil.

There are no pennies
or favors left, no change.
But might be if we ask for keeps.
There is change.
We must ask for keeps.

> I will come back
> to you for keeps
> after all.
> I will, for your sake,
> for ours.
> The children will rise.

She walks on.
The streets are no longer
desperation.
The reeking vapors
become the quiet wind.
It rains at last.

You can see
how the Chuska Mountains favor
her dreams
when she walks toward them.
Her arms and legs unlimber.
All her love is returning.
The man she finds
is a roadside plant.

She sings then,
the water in her eyes
is clear as a child.
> of rain.
> It shall.
> It shall.
> It shall.
> It shall
> be
> these gifts
> to return
> again.

It will happen again, cleansing.

The People will rise.

A SAN DIEGO POEM: JANUARY-FEBRUARY 1973

The Journey Begins

My son tells his aunt,
"You take a feather,
and you have white stuff in your hand,
and you go outside,
and you let the white stuff fall to the ground
That's praising."

In the morning, take cornfood outside,
say words within and without.
Being careful, breathe in and out,
praying for sustenance,for strength,
and to continue safely and humbly,
you pray.

Shuddering

The plane lifts off the ground.
The shudder of breaking from earth
gives me a splitsecond of emptiness.
From the air, I can only give substance
and form to places I am familiar with.
I only see shadows and darkness
of mountains and the colored earth.

The jet engines drone heavily.
Stewardesses move along the aisles.
Passengers' faces are normally bland,
and oftentimes I have yearned, achingly,
for a sharp, distinctive face, someone
who has a stark history, even a killer
or a tortured saint, but most times
there is only the blandness.

I seek association with the earth.
I feel trapped, fearful of enclosures.
I wait for the Fasten Seat Belt sign
to go off, but when it does
I don't unfasten my belt.

The earth is red in eastern Arizona,
mesa cliffs, the Chinle formation
is an ancient undersea ridge lasting
for millions of years.
I find the shape of whale still lingers.
I see it flick gracefully by Sonsela Butte
heading for the Grand Canyon.

I recite the cardinal points of my Acoma life,
the mountains, the radiance coming
from those sacred points, gathering
into the center.
I wonder: what is the movement
of this journey in this jet above the earth?

Coming into L.A. International Airport,
I look below at the countless houses,
row after row, veiled by tinted smog.
I feel the beginnings of apprehension.
Where am I? I recall the institutional prayers
of my Catholic youth but don't dare recite them.
The prayers of my native selfhood
have been strangled in my throat.

The Fasten Seat Belt sign has come back on
and the jet drone is more apparent in my ears.
I picture the moments in my life
when I have been close enough to danger
to feel the vacuum prior to death
when everything stalls.
The shudder of returning to earth
is much like breaking away from it.

Under L.A. International Airport

Numbed by the anesthesia of jet flight,
I stumble into the innards of L.A. International.
Knowing that they could not comprehend,
I dare not ask questions of anyone.
I sneak furtive glances at TV schedule consoles
and feel their complete ignorance of my presence.
I allow an escalator to carry me downward;
it deposits me before a choice of tunnels.
Even with a clear head, I've never been good
at finding my way out of American labyrinths.
They all look alike to me. I search
for a distinct place, a familiar plateau,
but in the tunnel, on the narrow alley's wall,
I can only find bleak small-lettered signs.
At the end of that tunnel, I turn a corner
into another and get the unwanted feeling
that I am lost. My apprehension is unjustified
because I know where I am I think.
I am under L.A. International Airport,
on the West Coast, someplace called America.
I am somewhat educated, I can read and use a compass;
yet the knowledge of where I am is useless.
Instead, it is a sad, disheartening burden.
I am a poor, tired wretch in this maze.
With its tunnels, its jet drones, its bland faces,
TV consoles, and its emotionless answers,
America has obliterated my sense of comprehension.

Without this comprehension, I am emptied
of any substance. America has finally caught me.
I meld into the walls of that tunnel
and become the silent burial. There are no echoes.

Survival This Way

Survival, I know how this way.
This way, I know.
It rains.
Mountains and canyons and plants
grow.
We travelled this way,
gauged our distance by stories
and loved our children.
We taught them
to love their births.
We told ourselves over and over
again,
"We shall survive this way."

DRY ROOT IN A WASH

The sand is fine grit
and warm to the touch.
An old juniper root
lies by the cutbank of sand;
it lingers, waiting
for the next month of rain.

I feel like saying,
It will rain, but you know
better than I these centuries
don't mean much
for anyone to be waiting.

Upstream, towards the mountains,
the Shiwana work for rain.

They know we're waiting.

Underneath the fine sand
it is cool
with crystalline moisture,
the forming rain.

TO INSURE SURVIVAL

for Rainy Dawn
born July 5, 1973

You come forth
the color of a stone cliff
at dawn,
changing colors,
blue to red
to all the colors of the earth.

Grandmother Spider speaks
laughter and growing
and weaving things
and threading them
together to make life
to wear;
all these, all these.

You come out, child,
naked as that cliff at sunrise,
shorn of anything
except spots of your mother's blood.
You just kept blinking your eyes
and trying to catch your breath.

In five more days,
they will come,
singing, dancing,
bringing gifts,
the stones with voices,
the plants with bells.
They will come.

Child, they will come.

TRAVELS IN THE SOUTH

1. EAST TEXAS

When I left the Alabama-Coushatta people,
it was early morning.
They had treated me kindly, given me food,
spoken me words of welcome, and thanked me.
I touched them, their hands, and promised
I would be back.

When I passed by the Huntsville State Pen
I told the Indian prisoners what the people said
and thanked them and felt very humble.
The sun was rising then.

When I got to Dallas I did not want to be there.
I went to see the BIA Relocation man.
He told me, "I don't know how many Indians
there are in Dallas; they come every week."
I talked with Ray, a Navajo; he didn't have a job,
was looking, and he was a welder.
I saw an Apache woman crying for her lost life.

When it was evening of the next day,
I stopped at a lake called Caddo.
I asked a park ranger, "Who was Caddo?"
And he said it used to be some Indian tribe.

I met two Black women fishing at the lake.
I sat by them; they were good to be with.
They were about seventy years old and laughed,
and for the first and only time in my life
I cut a terrapin's head off because,
as the women said, "They won't let go until sundown."

When it was after sundown in East Texas, I prayed
for strength and the Caddo and the Black women
and my young son at home and Dallas and when
it would be the morning, the sun.

2. THE CREEK NATION EAST OF THE MISSISSIPPI

Once, in a story, I wrote that Indians are everywhere.
Goddamn right.

In Pensacola, Florida, some hotdog stand
operator told me about Chief McGee.

"I'm looking for Indians," I said.
"I know Chief Alvin McGee," he said.
I bought a hotdog and a beer.
"He lives near Atmore, Alabama,
cross the tracks, drive by the school,
over the freeway to Atlanta, about a mile.
He lives at the second house on the right."

I called from a payphone in Atmore.
Mr. McGee told me to come on over.
I found his home right away,
and he came out when I stopped in his yard.
He had a big smile on his face.
I'd seen his face before in the history books
when they bothered to put Creeks in them.

He told me about Osceola.
"He was born in this county," Chief McGee said.
He showed me his garden and fields.
"I have seventy acres," he said.
"We used to have our own school,
but they took that away from us.
There ain't much they don't try to take."

We watched the news on TV.
It was election time in Alabama,
George Wallace against something.
People kept coming over to his house,
wanting the Chief's support. "Wallace is the one."
"Brewer is our man." They kept that up all night.
The next morning the election was on,
but I left right after breakfast.

Chief Alvin McGee put his arms around me
and blessed me. I remembered my grandfather,
the mountains, the land from where I came,
and I thanked him for his home, "Keep together,
please don't worry about Wallace, don't worry."

I was on that freeway to Atlanta
when I heard about the killings at Kent State.
I pulled off the road just past a sign which read
NO STOPPING EXCEPT IN CASE OF
    EMERGENCY
and hugged a tree.

3. CROSSING THE GEORGIA BORDER INTO FLORIDA

I worried about my hair, kept my car locked.
They'd look at me, lean, white, nervous,
their lips moving, making wordless gestures.

My hair is past my ears.
My Grandfather wore it like that.
He used to wear a hat, a gray one,
with grease stains on it.
The people called him Tall One
because he was tall for an Acoma.

I had a hard time in Atlanta;
I thought it was because
I did not have a suit and tie.
I had to stay at the Dinkler Plaza,
a classy joint, for an Indian meeting.
The desk clerk didn't believe it
when I walked up, requested a room,
towel rolled up under my arm,
a couple books, and my black bag of poems.
I had to tell him who I really wasn't.
He charged me twenty dollars for a room,
and I figured I'm sure glad
that I'm not a Black man,
and I was sure happy to leave Atlanta.

A few miles from the Florida line,
I picked some flowers beside the highway
and put them with the sage I got in Arizona.
After the Florida line, I went to a State Park,
paid two-fifty, and the park ranger told me,
"This place is noted for the Indians

that don't live here anymore."
He didn't know who they used to be.

When I got to my camping site
and lay on the ground,
a squirrel came by and looked at me.
I moved my eyes. He moved his head.
"Brother," I said.
A red bird came, hopped.
"Brother, how are you?" I asked.
I took some bread, white, and kind of stale,
and scattered some crumbs before them.
They didn't take the crumbs,
and I didn't blame them.

YUUSTHIWA

"Whenever people are driving along and stop
to offer Yuusthiwa a ride, he refuses
and says, 'I still have my legs, "
my father says, saying it like the old man,
a slow careful drawl. And my mother corrects him,
" 'While I'm still able to walk.' "
Yuusthiwa has been sick lately;
either something fell on him
or else he got bit by something, she heard.
Apparently, he still gets around though
pretty much because like my father says
one fellow had said, " 'That old man,
he's still tom-catting around, visiting.'
You see him in Acomita along the road
or in McCartys." I chuckle at the expression
picturing the old guy in mind; after all,
Yuusthiwa is only 114 years old at last count.

"One time, David and I were coming
from Acomita," my father says, "and we stopped
for him. Recognizing me, he got in and said
'Ahku Tsai-rrhlai kudha." And as we drove
westwards up this way, he told us things.
I had asked him, 'Naishtiya, how do you come
to live as many years as you have, to be so fortunate
as to mature as healthy and firm as you are?'
And he said, 'If you live enjoying and appreciating
your life, taking care of yourself, caring for
and being friendly with others; if you use the plants
that grow around here, seeing and knowing
that they are of use, boiling them into medicine
to use in the right way in caring for yourself,
cleansing and helping your body with them;
that's the way I have lived.' That's the way
he said it," my father says.

THE BOY AND COYOTE

for a friend, Ed Theis,
met at VAH, Ft. Lyons, Colorado,
November and December 1974

You can see the rippled sand rifts
shallow inches below the surface.
I walk on the alkalied sand.
Willows crowd the edges of sand banks
sloping to the Arkansas River.

I get lonesome for the young afternoons
of a boy growing at Acoma.
He listens to the river,
the slightest nuance of sound.

Breaking thin ice from a small still pool,
I find Coyote's footprints.
Coyote, he's always somewhere before you;
he knows you'll come along soon.
I smile at his tracks which are not fresh
except in memory and say a brief prayer
for goodluck for him and for me and thanks.

All of a sudden, and not far away,
there are the reports of a shotgun,
muffled flat by saltcedar thickets.
Everything halts for several moments,
no sound; even the wind holds to itself.
The animal in me crouches, poised immobile,
eyes trained on the distance, waiting
for motion again. The sky is wide;
blue is depthless; and the animal
and I wait for breaks in the horizon.

Coyote's preference is for silence
broken only by the subtle wind,
uncanny bird sounds, saltcedar scraping,
and the desire to let that man free,
to listen for the motion of sound.

JUANITA, WIFE OF MANUELITO

*after seeing a photograph
of her in Dine Baa-Hani*

I can see by your eyes
the gray in them like by Sonsela Butte,
the long ache
that comes about when I think
about where the road climbs
up onto the Roof Butte.

I can see
the whole sky
when it is ready to rain
over Whiskey Creek,
and a small girl
driving her sheep
and she looks so pretty
her hair tied up
with a length of yarn.

I can see
by the way you stare
out of a photograph
that you are a stern woman
informed by the history
of a long walk
and how it must have felt
to leave the canyons
and the mountains of your own land.

I can see, Navajo woman,
that it is possible for dreams
to occur, the prayers full of the mystery
of children, laughter, the dances,
my own humanity, so it can last unto forever.

That is what I want to teach my son.

THE SIGNIFICANCE OF A VETERAN'S DAY

I happen to be a veteran
but you can't tell in how many ways
unless I tell you.

A cold morning waking up on concrete;
I never knew that feeling before,
calling for significance,
and no one answered.

Let me explain it this way
so that you may not go away
without knowing a part of me:

that I am a veteran of at least 30,000 years
when I travelled with the monumental yearning
of glaciers, relieving myself by them,
growing, my children seeking shelter
by the roots of pines and mountains.

When it was that time to build,
my grandfather said, "We cut stone and mixed mud
and ate beans and squash and sang
while we moved ourselves. That's what we did."
And I believe him.

And then later on in the ancient and deep story
of all our nights, we contemplated,
contemplated not the completion of our age,
but the continuance of the universe,
the travelling, not the progress,
but the humility of our being there.

Caught now, in the midst of wars
against foreign disease, missionaries,
canned food, Dick & Jane textbooks, IBM cards,
Western philosophies, General Electric,
I am talking about how we have been able
to survive insignificance.

MY FATHER'S SONG

Wanting to say things,
I miss my father tonight.
His voice, the slight catch,
the depth from his thin chest,
the tremble of emotion
in something he has just said
to his son, his song:

> We planted corn one Spring at Acu —
> we planted several times
> but this one particular time
> I remember the soft damp sand
> in my hand.

> My father had stopped at one point
> to show me an overturned furrow;
> the plowshare had unearthed
> the burrow nest of a mouse
> in the soft moist sand.

> Very gently, he scooped tiny pink animals
> into the palm of his hand
> and told me to touch them.
> We took them to the edge
> of the field and put them in the shade
> of a sand moist clod.

> I remember the very softness
> of cool and warm sand and tiny alive mice
> and my father saying things.

"WE SHALL ENDURE"

March 31, Indian 1973

It was snowing in the Southwest and the wind was harsh the past few days. A major late winter storm had hit through the Dakotas. Anyone familiar with winter Midwest weather knows the hard and bitter cold that it is. Helicopters were dropping supplies to Navajo People stranded in isolated areas of the reservation in Arizona and New Mexico. The FBI, U.S. Marshals, and BIA police in full battle gear still surrounded the Indian People at Wounded Knee. Inside the war zone, the Indian People held fast and determined.

The march on Gallup was announced on that Saturday's previous march in Albuquerque. "There will be buses leaving from Johnson Gym on UNM campus next Saturday. Bring your own lunches and beans because we don't want to contribute to the economy of Gallup traders." That brought cheers, laughter, a good feeling.

The march on Saturday from the university campus down Central Avenue to Eighth Street was good, strong; it drew many People into a vibrant and hopeful crowd. The theme was: In Support of Wounded Knee. And Larry Casuse had been killed by the Gallup police three weeks before. There were Indian People of all ages in the crowd; there were some whites, Chicanos, numbers of Blacks. Cardboard signs made statements. EMMETT GARCIA: INDIAN KILLER. Garcia was a Gallup businessman and a former mayor. He had recently been appointed to the UNM Board of Regents despite the protests of Indian People. He was an administrator of the Gallup area alcohol rehabilitation program. And he was the owner of a liquor store and bar, the Navajo Inn, near Window Rock, right off the reservation; it was the largest such business anywhere in the country. He was a hypocrite and the enemy.

There were other signs. CHEROKEE NATION. NAVAJO NATION. OGLALA NATION. INDIANS ARE AMERICA'S P.O.W.'s. A large banner: PEOPLE'S MARCH FOR HUMANITY. And WE SHALL ENDURE.

There was a drum and singers, of course. The crowd sang all the way down Central Avenue. The sun's warmth was good and the walking People laughed and joked and hollered. When the marchers got downtown, by Fourth and Central, someone remarked it was like in the movie, "Flap." Flap had just come into town, a crowd of movie extras around him; he was supposed to be taking over the town. Someone said, "Just like Flap coming to town." The crowd was feeling good. "Flap" was a ridiculous movie. Nobody needed Flap. "That's what she said."

The day before the march on Gallup, Ruben spoke at the University of Albuquerque. He talked about the eagle which had come to Mount Rushmore. Led by AIM, there was a big rally there that day, a lot of tourists too, he said. At some point, and suddenly, "People began to look up and high in the sky there was an eagle circling." All heads turned and that was really something, the circling eagle. "For a long,

long time, the eagle hasn't come around like that because there have been too many people around there," Ruben said about Mount Rushmore in the Black Hills. There have been too many of the people who could care less but the power of the circling eagle is still there.

Tying In

I packed a lunch for the trip to Gallup. Baloney — "Indian steak" — and lettuce and a couple pieces of peanut brittle which Joy had made. Joy decided not to go because of the cold weather. She was pregnant with our coming child. A friend of ours came by and we walked over to Johnson Gym.

There was a small crowd waiting. The march announcement had said nine o'clock. It was after nine already. But what the hell, we knew we would have to wait anyway. Wait at the PHS clinic, wait at the Area Office, tribal office, wait in line at the Employment Office, waiting all this time, it feels like. "We don't know if he's going to be able to see you this afternoon. Why don't you come back tomorrow." Wait for word or letter from the BIA, from the welfare. Tired of waiting, you know, because it drains you, pisses you off, and it's depressing. And you never wanted to be in the position of having to wait in the first place. But we were patient this time, waiting.

"Tie yourself in." I thought about a poem idea, thought about the connections between and among everything.

Indian People had been at Wounded Knee for over a month. For the past week, helicopters had been flying over parts of the Navajo reservation. Wounded Knee was totally surrounded by the United States of America. All that anybody outside of that small village on the Pine Ridge reservation knew for sure was that the Indians had not given up and were not going to. The Sioux People wanted the Sioux Treaty of 1868 honored and they wanted the USA forces to get the hell out of Indian land. The People wanted the BIA to stop screwing over their lives. America was deaf to any of this, and its armed police continued to insist that Indian People surrender.

It was past mid-morning when we began to load on the first bus. We had to get our names checked off on a list. You had to have reservations. We got slips of paper, our "reservations," and waited. We sat on the bus for half an hour or so. At the front of the bus was a No Smoking Allowed sign. A long time friend arrived as I was smoking outside.

"Haven't seen you for a long time."

We smiled and shook hands; it had been a long time. She said she had quit the BIA. I asked about her children.

"Fine," she said. "They're okay, growing. My baby is in the first grade. And my biggest is this tall," she said, lifting her hand to almost her own height. "They take care of me now." She looked strong, enduring. Mary and I talked about things.

"I quit drinking," I said. I had too, trying and trying. "Couldn't do any work worth a damn, couldn't revive quickly anymore mornings after. It would take me three, four days to get over a drunk. Too heavy, paranoia and shit, fighting cops for no good reason." Jailtime.

"Yeah?" she said, glowing. "Me too, been sober for a year. Well maybe once during that time I got an urge for a beer and got drunk." Trying and trying so damn hard, you know. "Did you take antabuse?"

"No, huh-uh, just did it. Just tired of the same old stuff, you know, making an ass outta myself, waking next morning and wondering what I had said to everybody. Buncha crap. I'm saving money too."

"Yeah, shoot, when you're on, you don't give a damn."

Two Indians talking about those days and times. We laughed about our confessions, feeling kind of foolish I suppose, but okay and strong about it. I thought about the poem idea again.

She said, "Hey, what you got in your lunch? I'll trade you one of mine for one of yours."

"I have baloney, lettuce, and mayonnaise."

"I have potted meat." Mary laughed just like a little kid and I was so happy to see her.

Finally, one of the UNM Kiva Club leaders announced we would be going pretty soon. He spoke about the purpose of the trip and the march. It was to be non-violent, for humanity's sake, and we should all be peaceful and calm. He mentioned the possibility of danger. Nobody seemed to be too worried though. We had been waiting for a long time and we were anxious to get going.

"Up The Line"

I was used to walking a lot, having given up on driving cars as too dangerous. I regarded it as a small protest on my own. On Saturdays, in town, you usually see a lot of Indian People walking around. A couple of weekends before, we'd seen a couple guys on their way from Kansas to Gallup, bedrolls and packs strapped on. "Trucking to Gallup," they said and wanted to know the best way to get there. "Get down to the freeway. You should be able to get a ride." "Okay, thanks," they said. "Goodbye, see you."

You used to see the People using wagons also on the rez. You would see them going somewhere, children in the back, maybe a fifty-gallon barrel for water, bales of hay, wood, sacks. You hardly see them anymore. You see trucks and cars now, some battered and held together by rusty wire and the work of ingenious and luckrich shade tree mechanics.

Years back, Navajo People would come to the Laguna Fiesta in covered wagons and on horseback. They passed through the Acoma villages of McCartys and Acomita. The People there would be waiting for them around that time; the corn, melons, chili, peaches would be ripened and ready to eat then, and the women would bake bread and make tamales. The Navajo People brought mutton, rugs, and jewelry. The People would trade with each other and exchange gifts and talk and laugh a lot.

Sometime after that time, we would see Navajo People going to Laguna Fiesta in cattle and produce trucks. That was probably during the time of the carrot fields when Grants, near McCartys, used to hail itself as the "Carrot Capitol of the World." No lie. There were a lot of Mormon-owned produce fields in the Bluewater Valley and the owners used a lot of Indians for slave labor and wages in the fields and "sheds" where carrots were packed and loaded unto railroad freight cars.

That was during the fifties before the "Uranium boom." Grants now hails itself as the "Uranium Capitol of the World," and the uranium and mill companies use a lot of Indian labor. Even with improved working conditions and wages, much of it is still slave labor. Anyway, there were those stakebed trucks passing through on the highway to Laguna Fiesta loaded with Navajo People. After some years the Acoma People no longer readied their crops expecting their friends to come by at that time. The cattle and produce trucks were provided by the owners of the fields. I guess to keep the Indians happy.

All that land along the highway which is Interstate 40 now, forty miles west of Albuquerque, is Laguna and Acoma land. To the north of their villages is a great signal of a mountain; Kaweshtima, the People call it. *All* that land, excepting of course what has been stolen — or if preferred, "legally acquired" by one trick or another — by the USA, the state, and American capitalism which means traders, settlers, missionaries, highways, real estate dealers, the corporate utility companies, the railroad. And the Mexican and Spanish colonialists before them, some of whose land grant heirs have been screwed by the USA also.

The corporate monster, Anaconda, is still digging a hole in the hills and mesas of the Laguna reservation. You can see the grayed earth piled so high, miles and miles of it, just as so much debris. The footslopes of the great signal of the mountain, Kaweshtima, are being turned inside out. The massive irregular hole right to the east and south of Paguate village is getting ever bigger and bigger. The People are afraid that the old village will one day soon collapse into the open-pit Jackpile Mine. A lot of Laguna men work there; some even have pretty good, higher-up jobs, been working for the past twenty years or so. And even though they see one part of their Laguna life and community and People being destroyed, what the hell can they do? Ask that question and expect no adequate answer. It's good pay and all, minework, overtime and bonuses, if you forget the sacrifice. The Anaconda monster's engineers and geologists keep on digging and looking for more uranium and the corporation's directors and stockholders keep on stockpiling money.

Passing on the Interstate by Seama, there is no way you cannot fail to understand why the Indian People fought the USA at Wounded Knee. They hit you in the face, the reasons why.

The state of New Mexico, like other states in the nation, has always required only token approval from Indian People for right of way through their land. The same with the AT&SF railroad to the south of the highway. And transcontinental gas, electric, and telephone lines go right smack through Acoma and Laguna land and further west through Navajo land. When the People have protested or refused to give immediate right of way permission, they've been quickly dismissed with, "Hell, we'll just condemn the land, and you won't get a single cent. We'll do it by law."

There are the trading posts at Paraje, Cubero, and San Fidel, the gas stations, bars, and chicken fry place which are all non-Indian owned, though most of the customers are Indian. There was a man who owned a trading post-garage-wrecking yard at Budville. He had also been a justice of the peace before whom you got hauled if you were ever picked up by the state police in the area. Someone knocked him off some years ago during a robbery. When people learned about him being knocked off, you should have heard them laugh and joke though they'd stop short and say half-heartedly, "Oh I guess I shouldn't joke about it." But the clearest truth was that nobody liked that white man much. He'd screwed over the Indian People too many times.

The Cubero Land Grant is along there. Descendants of the original grantees have a small settlement. The heirs have had most of the Grant land taken by the Americans who came into the Southwest in the mid-1800s. The Bibos were among them. They came all the way from Westphalia, Germany to get Acoma and Cubero Grant land. The American government sent surveyors in the 1800s and they worked with the Bibos, one of whom had married an Acoma woman. The government came to survey and verify what land the Indian People owned. They did. Consequently, the Acoma People have less land now than before all that happened.

Around there, everyone knows what you mean when you say, "Up the line." You go up the line to the Dixie Tavern, Pete's Bar, Chief Rancho. There used to be the Main Bar and the Black Bull but they burned down. There's a lot of stories about them.

I remember one about one time at the Black Bull. It was pretty crowded all the time even though parents and tribal officials warned against its evils all the time. Somebody asked this one guy, Sweet Corn, who was in a lot of funny stories — and he was a good storyteller too — "Brother, where have you been the past several weeks, we haven't seen you around?" And he answered, "I've just come back from Los Lunas. The facilities there are still standing strong and the brothers are doing okay but restless." He said it this way, "Well, there was a good fight at the Black Bull. The state police came and searched me and threw me in the county for possessing a dangerous weapon and narcotics." "Haiee dyumuu, what kind of weapon and stuff did you have on you?" And Sweet Corn got a kick out of explaining, "I was on my way home from deer hunting on Oso Ridge and I stopped in for a couple of cold ones when it happened. I had an arrowhead and some pollen for my hunting prayers in a little bag in my pocket. That's what they found." Incredulous, the guys hearing the story would laugh. Yeah, there are stories alright, and some of them aren't very funny at all.

All that land is good land and it used to be mainly farmed. The Rio de San Jose, which is really just a small creek now, runs through there and is used for irrigation. There isn't that much farming done anymore, less in Laguna than in Acoma, just small garden crops, some corn, alfalfa, beans, chili, and a few orchards. The water isn't much good either since Grants has grown because of the uranium mining and milling. The Grants city sewage system is directly upstream of Acoma land. The uranium industry has affected the water table and quality irreparably on Indian People's land. Not too long ago, the People used the creek for drinking water but now even fish refuse to survive in it. Even the Public Health Service has reported that the Acoma domestic water from underground sources is unfit for human consumption.

This is all on the route to Gallup and Larry Casuse must have known this journey very well.

Make It Breath

"I am full of wonderment, how do we remain a People forever?

"I see a direction from our elders, a trail to be used by all Indians and based upon our ancestry. . . . I believe strongly that Indian Spirit will be the last hope of mankind.

"I wish to remain savagery forever, savagery to fight for our people, and our people to be forever, just as our enemies once saw us and will see us again.

"They say much of the truth comes through the ancient. Maybe this is the answer, make it breath by walking in the old ways."

Lorrena Deel in *Navajo Times*

At the side of the highway, west of Rehobeth Mission school, is a Christian rest stop. The sign says, "Rest and Reflect," and it is a tiny framework shelter of two-by-fours with a steeple and a bench for the weary.

It would be a quiet place, close enough to Gallup to pause for reflection, except that it is right off one of the busiest transcontinental Interstates. The motor din of semis hauling freight cross country, vacation mobile campers bearing names of Indian tribes, and cars is constant.

On the east side of town is a huge gaudy sign. WELCOME TO GALLUP THE INDIAN CAPITAL. No kidding, that's the way it's spelled.

It was a Saturday and we could tell right away there were a lot of Indian People in town. We could tell by the numbers of mudsplattered pickup trucks and by the crowds of the People on the streets. There didn't seem to be many white people around. In fact, there didn't seem to be any at all.

Gallup Is A Fever

Being in Gallup is always pretty much the same feeling. It is a feeling of something not balanced well in the belly. It has to do with not wanting to be there and only being there because you have to be. There is a feeling of grit under the skin and a need to keep moving all the time. No matter how much you want to be cool or breathe easier there is the tension all bunched up in your shoulders, at the back of your neck. It's like all of a sudden someone is going to accuse you of something or to accost you, and you wouldn't know how to react because of the imbalance.

Once I wrote in a poem, "You better not get in trouble in Gallup, and you better not be Indian." It's true. You can tell it, the way we walk down the streets, trying not to look like we're hiding into the walls, our movements broken with hesitation, always on the lookout. Especially in our children's eyes, wary. I don't know who it was that said that Indians come to Gallup to relax. I read it in the newspaper. He must not have been Indian.

There didn't seem to be any police visible. The city must have ordered them to keep out of sight, to make them less obvious. Usually, there are a lot, almost at every corner downtown, riot helmets strapped down tight, arrogant and very visible. I've never seen one spoken with in a friendly manner and Indian People give them wide leeway on the sidewalks. I've seen things too often to pass the feeling off as mere paranoia. I surmise that at some time some Indian has absurdly wished he were John Wayne if he had to be in Gallup.

Just before our bus turned north across the railroad tracks someone pointed at the sporting goods store where the shooting took place. The Gallup police reported that Larry Casuse died from a self-inflicted gunshot. It was backed up by an official independent investigation. The police had nothing to do with it. In fact it seemed they were merely bystanders that afternoon; maybe they weren't even there. The *Gallup Independent* (The Truth Well Told) said so. The police were completely guiltless.

Some of the People who were witness to it that Thursday said Larry was coming out of the store. They said his hands were above his head. And the police had shot. And shot. And shot. A Navajo Vietnam veteran said he was down the street; he heard the firing. He cried, "I was at Khe Sahn. I was at Khe Sahn."

The police and the city officials didn't believe the People. They dismissed their testimony for the most part and they didn't even bother to hear some. After the shooting had died down, the Gallup police dragged Larry Casuse's body out on the sidewalk in front of the store. It was all on the ten o'clock evening tv news. Later on, the television showed Garcia, who was still mayor then, who had been abducted by Larry at City Hall. The mayor had jumped through the store window. He was lying in a hospital bed, bandaged; he had been cut by flying glass or something. He didn't look like much of anything, not even the ambitious politician that he was nor much of a media hero of the hour. It is doubtful that he would have learned much if Larry had marched him around the state to educate him. Emmett Garcia just looked empty and tired, but he was alive. And Larry Casuse was dead.

Finally, I saw a carload of white people. Their license plate was out-of-state, just passing through. They were probably curious about the busloads of Indian People. They might have thought we were an Indian Tour, or a church group, or a detachment of Uplift America, Inc. Yeah. Someone in the bus raised his clenched fist in greeting and smiled. Immediately the smiles vanished off the faces pressed tightly against the car windows. I saw the first cop, parked at the curb near Milan's Bar.

"It's Good To See You."

We arrived at the Ceremonial grounds where the march would start and end. There was a huge circus tent set up in the parking lot to the south. We wondered what it was for and then someone said it was a Christian revival tent. That wasn't part of our march, we were sure. Nobody seemed to be at the revival for the moment. It was too early in the afternoon to be saved.

There was a large crowd already, and it was growing, gathered at the steps of the National Guard Armory where there were microphones, loudspeakers, and speakers. The wind blew once in a while but gently and voices of the speakers drifted away and then back.

Around the microphone were Indian People, some Black People in business suits, some Chicano People and a couple of lawyers. A TV newsman wielded a microphone like a club in front of the Indian man presently speaking.

The Indian man said, "We must act with dignity," several times. He said other things but that was his message. The People must act with dignity. There is strength in that. You show your courage by having dignity. The People cheered and shouted for his words. The Indian man who was from Jemez was an elder with graying hair and a broad face. The Black men spoke about brotherhood and support from their People. There was warm applause. There were messages from the others. They were all important, statements of courage, commitment for the struggle that we were involved in. We would all grow stronger in unity.

"We must act as who we are, Indian People, human persons. Don't let anyone provoke you to violence. We are strong People." A telegraph message was read from Wounded Knee, from the Indian brothers and sisters there. "We are remembering our brother, Casuse, and we are fighting for the same things he fought for and gave his life for." There were cheers and shouts and applause for the messages of support. "We are here for all humanity, for that purpose. We are here to let Gallup know, to let New Mexico know," one of our leaders said. We were the People who had journeyed here, to remember our brother, to not let his effort and passing be in vain, and it was a good, strong and vibrant feeling.

There were more and more People arriving all the time. White People, Black People, Chicano People, but the Indian People outnumbered all others, and the Navajo People outnumbered the others. Larry Casuse was a Navajo son. All of us, all of us, we were the People, and not for such a long, long time had we gathered in such numbers and force to show who we are, to say who we must be, to be strong together.

We met friends from all over the Southwest, from Denver, from Salt Lake City, even from Los Angeles. From all the Indian People's reservations, we gathered. "Hey man, where you been?" "We just got here from Colorado, drove eight hours." "It's good to see you." "So good to see so many People." "Yeah, geesus, I've never seen this many Indian People here except for the crummy Ceremonial." We carried signs and banners which reaffirmed our concern and our struggle. They were signals like that mountain, Kaweshtima, we had passed by in the morning, strong like that. There were older People and little kids. Teenagers, so many young Indian People. The elder People were mostly quiet but you could tell in their faces, the strength and pride in it, the courage and the humility of acknowledging the collective surge of our expression. It felt like being at home, Acqu, when there is dancing, the gathering of the People, and there are voices all around talking and laughing and welcoming, woven together into a unified purpose. It felt whole, being a People; that's what it felt like.

The leaders announced the start of the march. We were all bunched up at first, moving off the Ceremonial grounds through a maze of parked cars. The drum was at the head. The men and boys with the drum sang and the women with them sang. It was good to hear that, the high shrill clear voices of the women threading through the men's. Singing and walking, we were the People. Joking and laughing, commenting about anything. "Are you joining in the boycott?" "What boycott?" "Meat boycott." "Oh hell, I've been for a while, can't afford it, even hamburger." "Beans, we eat a lot of beans." "Even that costs a lot now too." "That damn Nixon."

The People strung out in a long sturdy line as we went over the hill west of the Ceremonial grounds. From the middle I could see the head of the march, way ahead, already turning the first corner towards town, and the tailend was just leaving the grounds. There must have been two thousand People at the beginning and more were still arriving. The People who lined the march route, who were hesitant at first, kept joining in until there were thousands marching. Other People sat in their cars and trucks along the way, and they shouted and honked their horns. Kids in the backs of trucks waved to us.

A helicopter roared overhead. It was a huge one with blue stripes on a white background. Someone said, "It's the Red Cross." "It's the BIA." "It's Super Navajo," we laughed. Something metallic glinted in its window. No, it wasn't Super Navajo; it was probably the state police or the FBI, maybe both. The helicopter was too much noise, the air being broken by rotorblades, momentarily dying away as it banked in a wide circle and turned back toward us. It kept doing that, circling overhead. We tried to ignore it, but it was hard to get used to. At the front of the marching People, half a block ahead, was a police patrol car. We passed by a patrolman at a barrier blocking off a street. He looked deadly serious.

Stay Away Joe

We crossed the Rio Puerco over the bridge. The river is mostly a dry wash and is called the Perky River by the townspeople. This time it was partially filled with red, muddy water. When it's dry you see Indian People sitting on its clay banks. Sometimes they're passed out, sometimes just sitting, dazed, forlorn, lonesome, shaking. Some have drowned in this measly excuse of a river.

There were more and more People lining the streets as we drew nearer to downtown. They watched us and they waved and hollered to us. We smiled and waved for them to join us. Some did and others hung back, packed on the sidewalks. The crowd was standing three and four deep on the walks by the Indian Center. It was a bright and sunny day and only once in a while was there a bit of wind. It was strange that there were no trains holding up traffic at the crossing. Almost anybody who knows Gallup knows that to drive from the north and south sides of town, you have to cross the AT&SF railroad tracks and there is usually a slow freight train at the crossing. The railroad crossing which, until lately, was the only one in town, has been one of the most cursed problems in Gallup. For the townspeople, the problem has been proverbial.

The other problem, also proverbial in Gallup, is the "drunk problem." Or what is known as the drunk problem because it is convenient terminology and probably easier for them to define that way. If there is one thing which is most visible to a newcomer or someone passing through Gallup, it is the drunk. The fact is, there are many drunks. And they are Indian People. They stagger down the streets, pausing once in a while to lean on storefront walls, a daze in their eyes, oblivious to everything. The drunks crowd the Gallup bars; they come up to you asking for wine or change to buy wine. The drunks gather in small unsteady groups at street corners, and they are Indian People. Like those who have drowned in the Rio Puerco, they are the victims. They are the victims of American colonialism.

On their faces you can see the pain. It has to do with victimized histories; all those things have surfaced on their faces and hands; the scars are there. You ache so deeply and the frustration comes about because it seems there is no immediate and lasting escape from that pain. You see beneath the daze, and your anger seethes. You want to approach someone, even a strange tourist, the bartender, or the missionary, the police; you want to take them by the shirtfront and shake them furiously and tell them deep, deep things. But sometimes there are no words, no words to describe the pain and the ache; instead you go into one of those crummy, winestinking Gallup bars and resign yourself to another drink. The hurt is pushed deeper back into you and while you drink it sulks and looks out from inside of you. It looks out at what has victimized the People. The clearest truth it wants you to see is the destruction wrought by American colonialism, and it wants you to express your sober anger loudly and decisively.

As we crossed the main street, no one mentioned or looked at the sporting goods store which was half a block down. There was no need to. Out of a corner drugstore window, a couple of white faces stared out from behind a display. The refraction through the glass and the sheen made their faces shiny and misshapen as they tried to look bored by the passing Indian People and extremely composed. One of them moved his lips in a silent utter. A marcher pointed and smiled and the faces behind the glass were startled; they shifted anxiously and concentrated hard at looking at no one in particular. There must have been other townspeople around but for the moment those were the only two I saw. They should have been marching with us.

A couple of Indian guys joined in from the sidewalk. They were slightly wobbly and they made jokes. "Right on, right on." They smiled a lot at the People on the sidewalk, waved at pretty girls, urging them to join in. An older Navajo man spoke as we marched down the center of town. His voice was firm, admonishing, urging, encouraging. His bearing was dignity itself, and he didn't mind the couple wobbly guys horsing around. "Right on, right on," they kept saying, raising their fists in signals to friends on the sidewalks.

Near the Chief Theater, we turned east. The head of the march was already several blocks away and the tail end had yet to cross the railroad tracks. The First State Bank's revolving sign read 2:43 and flashed the temperature: 62. The Chief Theater marquee displayed: STAY AWAY JOE. Right above the marquee was a head sticking out of a tiny second-story window. It was a Chicano guy but just his head was showing, and it looked ludicrous somehow. Once, when I was a boy, in the late 1940's, I saw this carnival game where people threw baseballs at a "Little Black Sambo" inside of a target ring. When the Sambo was hit, he fell down into a tub of water and the baseball thrower was a prizewinner. I remember wincing every time the man was hit.

Outside the American Bar was a crowd of men. They leaned against a wall and a couple of pickup trucks. Several jeered and catcalled, pointing at the wobbly Indian guys. They were white and Indian rednecks with even a Chicano thrown in. It became a bit tense when one of them yelled, "Fuck you." Another hollered, "Why don't you join the Army." He was answered with, "Man, I've been and it is fucked." We kept on moving with the feeling of a river. Nothing was going to stop its flow. The Indian People signaled to us from the sidewalks. They knew us and we knew them.

We turned again at the next corner and passed by one of Gallup's most notorious bars. Smitty's Bar. It is sickeningly filthy inside, smelly, and evil-looking. State and city health officials don't give a damn though; it's an "Indian bar." During the Ceremonial I've seen that bar packed completely. I mean packed, People passed out on the floor, vomit on their clothes, no shoes, others walking over them. There are bouncers at the doors then, mean-looking offduty cops and nightwatchmen, vigilantes with phony-looking badges pinned to them. They wear white hats and Indian-made bolo ties and are white. I've seen them swing suddenly and deadly, their clubs bouncing off heads with dull cracks, red blood splattering to the cement.

"You Are False Persons."

The walking People headed back for the Ceremonial grounds. There were so many People now. Later estimates spoke of fifteen to twenty thousand including the People who participated with their support from the sidewalks. Gallup had never seen anything like this. The size of the march went beyond the expectations of even the most optimistic leaders. Gathering together so many People is difficult. You can talk all you want, meet with People, print and pass out posters, leaflets, release press statements, organize, pray, but it's damn hard to get People to come even when events affect them directly. But here the People were. The march had grown to thousands of People. It had been a long time coming, a long time.

This kind of support and involvement, marching and the gathering of large numbers of Indian People is no longer as unusual as it used to be. Individual self-consciousness has eased away and the People are willing to get out on the road, on the streets, to the courthouse, walking and demonstrating, making themselves be heard. It comes from a rebirth of self-esteem and pride and hard work by the organizers. It used to be that Indian People were not heard in any way except through formal complaints and procedures, bureaucratic channels devised by the American ruling system. This device of colonialism has effectively prevented the People from involving themselves in efforts to raise and focus on issues of vital concern. Now — in Gallup that day — you see the People. It was so good to see this and know. And the way it was carried through, that was something to witness and participate in. No one seemed so somber or overburdened with grief or irrationally enraged. The People's mood was determined and joyous, surging with the lifeblood that flowed through us tying us all together. The mood was flowing like the river of People with the continuous history and life and purpose that we have. That is the way it should be. "Gallup has never seen anything like this."

In the late sixties, several young Indian People began to focus on the Gallup Indian Ceremonial. It was an annual affair organized by the Chamber of Commerce which exploited Indian People and their culture purely for the economic gain of Gallup merchants. It attracted nationwide audiences and was a "tradition" for people to come to, to see "real" Indians. Indian People were paid fees to perform their dances and a few were allowed to sell their craft work and art. The Gallup Ceremonial Association described the Ceremonial as a "tribute" to the Indian.

The young Indian People talked with city and Ceremonial and tribal officials, protesting the exploitation. They passed out informational leaflets at the Ceremonial grounds and were arrested for violating a city ordinance. The next year they organized a larger protest for the several days during the Ceremonial held in August. Indian organizations throughout the state and Indian People from reservations marched in the protest. The issue was clearly defined: We don't want your kind of tribute to the Indian People. The traders and Gallup businessmen were making bundles of money because of Indian People. They didn't care about the People except for maybe a surface paternalism which is always self-serving. That's what the young Indian People were leading the fight against. They were letting their People know the fight was worth it and essential because it meant being able to hold their heads up and being known for who they truly were, Indian People. And that was the one thing that was worth anything. Although it wasn't yet articulated in such terms, it was a fight against colonialism. And like Alcatraz in 1969, the Trail of Broken Treaties in 1972, Wounded Knee presently being liberated, it was a new phase of the continual resistance that Indian People have waged for almost five hundred years.

Some Indian People didnt take it seriously at first and along with many white citizens of Gallup and New Mexico, they decried the activities of the young People. Some even called them "punks," refraining a description a Gallup city leader had used. But the Indian

People were determined and the young People went to court where they lost inevitably. They didn't quit nevertheless and they continued to teach the People. The young leaders were back in Gallup again along with leaders of other organizations. The People had learned and here they were by the thousands. Some of them had chided the previous efforts but here they were now en masse, and that was the important thing.

There is a lot going on. Indian People are growing daily more aware. They are concerned for the unified welfare of the People. They realize it is a shared responsibility that we must have. It used to be only Indian People who worked directly with organizations which dealt with Indian-related issues, Indian People who had TVs to watch or radios to listen to, or read newspapers, or who were "conference Indians," who knew what was happening in Indian America. That was the case for a long time; most of our effective communication had been disrupted since the Federal establishment of reservations in the 1800s. Now, almost everyone had some idea that things were happening. You met an Indian brother or sister somewhere and some Indian-related event or issue cropped up in your conversation. Talk was about points of familiarity, whether they be a dance in your community or the nearby reservation, problems with the PHS clinic, or Wounded Knee or the Indian People in Gallup.

Something was going on, and it was political. Indian People grew more aware of issues which affected them, no matter how remote they seemed. We were now able to identify ourselves in relationship to other People — Indian and non-Indian — and view problems as social rather than personal. By that identification, we were able to pinpoint what was the cause of those problems. We were able to see our resources, even find ones we had thought were lost or no longer useful. The People looked at previous failures and developed new strategies towards the solution of problems oppressing us. The People began to come clearly to the decision that indeed, like the banner at the head of our march stated, we were in a struggle on behalf of all humanity. And it was very political. Even in the smallest villages on reservations, this was happening. Television, that American one-eye ogre, strangely proved to be one agent which helped to make Indian People aware because usually you found a beat-up black and white redeemed from a hockshop or a big color set with thirty payments to go in even the poorest home.

The Indian siege of the Bureau of Indian Affairs was televised nationwide. Everybody was aware of the November 1972 events. Indian People converged upon Washington D.C. and shook the very foundations of bureaucracy and the reverberations were felt in even the most remote village in Indian country. The television accounts were of course dramatic and focused mainly upon the "militant Indians" and the damaged BIA. The media called the seizure infamous. There wasn't much news coverage of the actual Broken Treaties Caravan which had led the People to Washington or the purpose for it. Not many people were aware that the Caravan, starting from the West Coast, had been crossing the nation throughout October, holding rallies in towns and cities and on reservations, talking with People. There wasn't even much notice given by anybody, including the established press, when the Caravan first arrived in the Nation's capitol. But the instant the seizure of the BIA began to happen, BAM, there was instant media presence and coverage. It was an infamous act alright and the newspeople had a field day. America had not ever had anything like that, Indian People's power physically confronting the U.S. Government at its very seat.

The deeper purposes of the Broken Treaties Caravan began to obscure immediately. A large reaction arose from all public quarters of the nation. An amount of it was very supportive while some of it was very negative. This was manipulated and exploited to the hilt by the Federal government. Its own reaction was predictable: repression and the planting of agents among the People. The news media for the most part editorially disapproved and called by implication or direct statement for the quick arrest and punishment of Caravan leaders who were mostly American Indian Movement members.

Indian People across the country had mixed reactions generally. They waited as usual, although there were some tribal leaders who immediately denounced the action, calling it irresponsible and criminal on the part of the "urban oriented Indians who were not representative of all Indians." These remarks were quickly manipulated and exploited also by the Federal government. A few courageous Indian tribal leaders held fast and determined to their conviction: Indian People had just reason to battle the BIA. And immediately also, there were Indian People who praised the People's action and proudly said, "It has been a long time coming." Nevertheless, there was a lot of appehension mixed with opinions and emotions. The question of how the events would affect Indian policy and money from Congress obviously became a major issue. If it was not raised by Indian People in their councils and homes, it was bluntly raised by the Bureau of Indian Affairs via memo and telephone.

The Indian People in the Broken Treaties Caravan had travelled across the country. They had sought out and listened to People on their reservations and in their villages. The People told them what their problems were. The Caravan became familiar with problems in education, legislation adverse to the People, Federal and state conflict and interference with the People's councils, and a major one: the treaties broken by American colonialism. There were many issues and many problems, and they brought these to Washington, D.C., not only to be attended to by the Bureau of Indian Affairs but to the President and the Congress on the eve of the national elections.

They brought demands to the doorstep of the American government. They demanded that the American government and its agencies look at Indian Treaty rights. These meant considering real questions of land, water, and People. In a Twenty Point demand, the Indian People demanded what their ancestors had assured for them when the Treaties were first signed. The demands were the same demands as the original signers': a land base, respect for Indian People's culture, and self government. This, they told the USA, is what your representatives agreed to in those Treaty negotiations; this is what our elders guaranteed for us, and their words are sacred. We have come to collect.

292

But no matter how pressing the deep purpose, how clear it was, of the Caravan of Broken Treaties, most of it was obscured because of the national news controlled by private industry and the U.S. government. The Bureau of Indian Affairs was under Indian siege, furniture and files were being destroyed, and somebody was bound to get hurt. You can't have anybody doing that, much less Indians.

Despite manipulated news coverage, the events in November generated discussion everywhere. The nation as a whole became grudgingly more aware of Indian People and what we were saying. Indian People have always been at the back of the public's mind, or hidden somewhere in there, but this time we surfaced plainly into sight and very painfully to its national mind. Along with the Presidential elections, politicians' rhetoric and promises, the Vietnam peace being negotiated, Indian People commanded national attention. Indian news became prominent and it gained stature. We could talk about what was going on in our home community, what kind of shit the BIA was up to, what we could do in getting the local public school board to wake up. That became important. It was significant. And this significance generated not only interest but probably had bearing on other actions initiated by Indian People.

In Gallup, six Indian men occupied the PHS hospital; they were arrested and charged variously with such things as carrying deadly weapons, assault, and such. It was a move designed to bring attention to the treatment of Indian People in the hospitals that serve them. The Indian men wanted the American public to see the health care problems of Indian People. This action was attacked by the press and public officials as harassment by irresponsible Indians, but the problems with regard to Indian health care could not be denied. Indian People knew them at first hand as very real and pressing. Reactions of the Indian People and the public was similar to the Caravan descending upon Washington, D.C. There was a lot of calling down and denunciations but there was also a lot of soul searching. And many People said, ''It's about time.''

The problem, needless to describe for the Indian People who have experienced bad treatment, waiting in overcrowded waiting rooms, lack of clinics, is horrendous. Although PHS staffs and hospitals have made changes to alleviate the problem, it is still there. And it is still there because the same system is still there. The PHS cites the lack of personnel, money, Congressional insensitivity, and some, of course, just do not give a damn. But the main cause of the problem is that Indian People do not have any control over their own health and medical care. Colonialism does not allow it. Shortly before the six Indian People were arrested in Gallup, a group of PHS doctors at the Ft. Defiance hospital publicly stated that the health service provided Indian People in that area was extremely inadequate. In many cases, the lack of Indian health services constitutes criminal negligence. But this is not a crime in America because in the kind of system still existent, the colonized People are merely recipients of what health care they get. They too are the victimized.

The Indians went to the Gallup PHS hospital on a Sunday night and sat down in the administrative office. The hospital operations continued without a hitch. They left on Monday morning after some discussion with the FBI and the local police. They were charged and indicted by a grand jury. Later on, they were tried; some charges were dropped but some stuck and the Indian men were sentenced.

In Washington, D.C. the BIA Commissioner, a Mohawk man, who had appointed some younger progressive styled Indian leaders to his immediate working staff, was fired. The structure of the Bureau was reshuffled. What hopes and power that Indian People had precariously enjoyed for at least a year vanished. The power of the Department of Interior wielded its fist, clamped down on community programs and its authority became brutally apparent once again. A career BIA man replaced the dismissed Commissioner; the Indian leaders were diverted to other Government programs, their effectiveness curtailed, or they were banished from Washington. Federal power pulled its strings up short on Indian People; the progress towards self-determination that Indian communities had made was stifled.

The daily news was replete with peace talks in Paris, negotiations, and POW's returning from captivity in Hanoi. U.S. troops were leaving Vietnam. Nobody wholeheartedly believed that the war was really ending even though the government said it was and the media backed it up. I think that somewhere in the national mind, there was a feeling even then that what the Vietnamese People were showing with their growing eventual victory was that there were other People's struggles elsewhere which would also prove victorious.

Suddenly, there was Custer, South Dakota. People outside of South Dakota generally didn't even know there was a town named after the infamous "Indian fighter," George Armstrong Custer. He was the Army officer who was the inglorious loser in the Battle of the Little Big Horn. In 1876, he and his troop of cavalry were wiped out by Sioux and Cheyenne resistance warriors. At Custer, a white man killed an Indian youth, Bad Heart Bull. He was charged with manslaughter. Indian People, led by AIM, gathered in Custer and demanded that the man be charged with murder instead of the lesser charge. The People justly claimed it was the same old system that had been killing their People: when an Indian is killed, it's no big thing. When a white man is killed, especially by an Indian, everything hits. That, too many times in the Indian People's experience, has been the case.

The tense feeling from Gordon, Nebraska, right off the Pine Ridge reservation and not far from Custer, was still tight in the wind. Three men had caused the death of Yellow Thunder, a Sioux man, from the nearby reservation. AIM led hundreds of Indian People into Gordon; they were from all parts of the country. Yellow Thunder had been mutilated. Racism had been doing that in one way or another to Indian People all along in American history, and the People came to Gordon to put it against the wall. Their protests were broadcast nationwide. And those Indian voices were real and hard.

The Custer courthouse burned. The Chamber of Commerce building went with it. Indian leaders were on national television again; the events were reported in national newspapers. The Indian spokesmen did not mince their words: Indian People within a white-dominated society were shafted by the American judicial process. And that quickly proved itself to be true again as the man who killed Bad Heart Bull was quickly released on bail. It was the same old story. Indian people continued to be killed and treated unequally.

Media reports released from South Dakota said that Indians were rioting in Pine Ridge. There were some arrests. A few places were reportedly wrecked in town. Dick Wilson, chairman of the Oglala Sioux on the Pine Ridge reservation, re-avowed his disapproval of the American Indian Movement. He stated that he wanted them to leave the reservation, and he was determined that it be accomplished. He recruited a group of men who came to be called "goons." Under his initiative and direction, they began to harass Oglala Sioux People who spoke against his administration.

Because of his vociferous opposition to AIM and the Indian People it led, the tribal chairman was characterized as an Indian honkie. A Sioux redneck. Information about Wilson's and BIA's ties was cited. That could not be denied. The modern-day government and council at Pine Ridge was empowered by the Bureau of Indian Affairs under the Indian Reorganization Act of 1934. The Bureau and the tribal council were one and the same. And the chairman was a BIA puppet. The Federal government had broken the terms of the Treaty of 1868 which guaranteed the Sioux People a land base and Wilson was not actively doing anything about that even though he was a Sioux man. Wilson was working more for the Federal government than for the Sioux People. Indian People, led by AIM, decided to answer the call for help asked for by traditional elder Oglala Sioux People, and they moved into the small rural village of Wounded Knee.

During March, U.S. Marshals, the FBI, and BIA police as well as goons armed by the government, completely surrounded the Indian People at Wounded Knee. The couple hundred Indians and their supporters were a tiny group compared to the amassed military might of the United States forces. All power was assumed by the Federal government, though that was nothing new on reservations, and the Sioux People including the chairman were powerless. That was brutally clear. The Indian People inside the perimeters of Wounded Knee could see the armed personnel carriers and they saw automatic weapons fire spitting up sand around them. The physical assertion of the USA was displayed incredibly, massively, and seemed to be limitless. Nevertheless, the Independent Oglala Sioux Nation declared itself as sovereign. It was a tremendously courageous act. On the last day of March, thousands of us were marching in Gallup in support of that act of liberation.

On March 1st, on a Thursday afternoon, Larry Casuse, a young Navajo man, was shot and killed by the Gallup city police. Their officials reported different of course. What else could they have said? Except to protect themselves and their system, they had no other purpose to say anything except deny their guilt and justify their act. They were protecting their city, their institutions, their vested interest. Colonialism attempts to stamp out any threat to it. Casuse called these people "false people." They didn't deny it. They couldn't and they didn't have to. In fact, one of their successful sons, Emmett Garcia, was a recently appointed Regent of the University of New Mexico. He was a prominent politician, an able administrator, and the owner of that bar selling almost exclusively to Indian People.

Until the Navajo Inn closed a month later, in April, one saw Indian People lying scattered in the mud around that bar. Groups of Indian People sat against the walls of that bar passing bottles of wine. There had been an apalling number of Indian People killed and maimed by the traffic passing only yards away. One does not have to be Indian to imagine the broken lives of People, broken like the bottles around Navajo Inn. And Emmett Garcia, the proud son of colonialism, was the head of the Gallup alcohol rehabilitation program. Larry Casuse had called him a false person. Garcia probably never did understand what that young Navajo man meant.

The Moving People's Story

The moving People headed back for the beginning. We passed by the Indian Center where there were a number of People selling crafts and food. People were gathered around the backs of trucks and items spread on small tables and the ground. People chatted and bought things. There were still People standing along the march route. The huge helicopter was no longer circling in the air. We crossed the Rio Puerco again. I waved to a friend from Chinle who was leaning upon the bridge railing.

The march route had been several miles long and we were tired. But it was the kind of tiredness that is the aftermath of elation. We were relaxed and quietly joyous. We could tell it in everyone. It was a collective calm jubilance. On the way down the hill west of the ceremonial grounds, we passed by a house; a Chicano family sat and stood on the front porch. They talked cheerily with some People they knew in the march. Several teenage boys passed us by, headed for the front of the march. One of them had a sparrow hawk on an arm held high in the air. The sparrow hawk screeched. It was a sound that pierced through all the other sounds the People made; it sounded like a signal of victory. At the head of the march, the drummers and singers were strong, leading us back.

We arrived to the beginning. The large crowd formed into several circles of People, one within another, and began to round dance and sing. There were yells and shouts and vibrant laughter. To sing and dance together on that afternoon was a sure sign. Friends greeted each other again. "Man, I've never seen anything like this." "I know, I know." The circle of People kept going around and around. There was no way the moving circle of People was going to stop anymore.

The Jemez man spoke again. "I am very proud of the way you acted with pride and dignity." He was beaming; his brown face was shining. The TV news man was still taking it all down. His damn microphone and camera were still obstrusive. "That is the Indian People. You showed it today," the Jemez elder said. "Now," he spoke, turning to the young, "you must go back to your homes and tell the older People who were not here."

The leaders of the march spoke again also. "Gallup is listening now. We want to tell you Gallup people that we are tired of being pushed around. We want respect. We are not going to let you push us around anymore." A list of demands was read aloud. They were directed at Gallup, the state of New Mexico, and the Federal government. They were not unreasonable; they were clear-cut concerns of the People. They were declarations of the People's fight for survival and their resistance which would continue. Emmett Garcia must resign as a Regent of the University of New Mexico. Navajo Inn must be closed down. "We want official investigations into police brutality and harassment. We want investigations into the shooting of Casuse. We want to know and we want action," they said. Indeed, the People's struggle against colonialism would continue. The People at Wounded Knee would not surrender. The moving People were not going to stop anymore.

The cheers from the crowd were tremendous. A couple of local politicians who were very nervous before the crowd made a brief appearance. They spoke briefly, congratulating the marchers for their behavior. We had not broken any windows or harassed the city police or caused undue tension. The politicians quickly snuck away with relief.

The march leaders wished us all safe journeys to our homes then. They thanked us, and we said goodbye with good words and love.

Before we got back on the buses for Albuquerque, a friend and I walked over to the circus tent. The Christian revival had begun. A man was singing-talking to a small crowd of People sitting on wooden folding chairs. The revival had a sound system of two huge stereo speakers. A man dressed in a shiny suit sat at an electric organ. He was pretty good, hitting notes blues style every once in a while, playing religious soul as best he could.

The revivalist spoke in stereo. "Raise your hands, my friends. Raise your hands for Jesus. Oh raise your hands and feel Him. Raise your hands." He wasn't asking for money yet. A wobbly thin Indian man stood up from the front row of folding chairs and approached the preacher. He leaned his ear down to the Indian man but he kept his microphone well away from him. We could hear him say impatiently, "Wait a minute. I'll talk to you in just a minute." And then the revival preacher went back on stereo, "Raise your hands, brothers and sisters. Raise your hands." We left before he asked for money.

The story of a People is the history of what they are doing. It is the story of their struggle to continue. It is the story of their resistance against that which will take their humanity away. It is their will to win victory for all the People. It is not a brief story and it is not pushed into a dark corner or a book or a newspaper and forgotten. It lives and endures and continues.

Manuel Pino

Reminiscing with Pa-Pa (Grandmother) About Ka-tse-ma [1]

"Try to remember, *pá-pa,*[2] as I will also try to remember, when the old ones of *Acomatra* (people of Acoma) were very well off spiritually and in harmony with everything around them." *Pá-pa* reminds me of the peaceful times when *Acomatra* lived on *Ka-tse-ma.*

"The mountains around *Acó*[3] were also in harmony with all that was around them — the four-leggeds, the trees and the rocks. Our fields were plentiful with crops.

"Our people were strong at this peaceful time." *Pá-pa* reminds me of the time before our people had ever seen *Ma-tash-cana.*[4] I give *Pa-Pa* my undivided attention, amazed at the seriousness in her beautiful squinting little black eyes. "If your *Na-Na* (Grandfather) were alive, he would have told you this story, for it teaches many things.

"It is good to know this story of the old ones. They have taught us to try and correct our mistakes at times when we are most fortunate. Greed is one thing the old ones told us to be careful of. We, as *Acomatra,* should never have that greed enter our lives.

"There was a most sorrowful incident that happened at this time when our people were most happy. It has been said greed made us lose two generations of our loved ones on *Ka-tse-ma.*

"At this time it was decided that the *Pá-Pas* would stay on *Ka-tse-ma* with the babies while the healthy ones were working in the fields on the valley floor. You see, as I am getting old in my years, I am unable to do the work in the fields as I used to when I was young. The *Pá-Pas* were like me, unable to work in the fields. The babies were too young.

"The young healthy ones who were busily working in the fields below *Ka-tse-ma* overworked the land. The rains had been good that spring and had provided good moisture for a good growing season. The old ones said we had enough crops to feed everyone on *Ka-tse-ma* for the coming winter. However, our people continued to overwork Mother Earth.

"One day, while our young ones worked in the fields, a rainstorm approached Acoma Valley. But the young ones ignored the approaching storm and continued working. Soon rain was pouring from the sky like *Acomatra* had never seen before. The fields began to erode. As our people ran back to the stairway which went to the top of *Ka-tse-ma,* they found it was washed out by the tremendous rain. Thunder roared in the sky. Jagged formations of lightning lit up the sky.

---

1. *Ka-tse-ma* is the ancient home of the Acoma people. The Spanish called it Enchanted Mesa when they first saw it.
2. *pá-pa,* though pronounced the same as *Pá-Pa* (Grandmother), is grandson. Many Keres words look and sound the same but have different meanings.
3. *Acó* is Acoma Pueblo, oldest inhabited village in the U.S.
4. *Ma-tash-cana* is the name first given to non-Indians.

"The concern turned to the old ones and young ones on top of *Ka-tse-ma*. Everyone panicked and began to weep, and as the people wept, the storm became worse, destroying our crops, and the stairway was completely washing out. The rain continued for many days, causing great sorrow among our people. Some became very sick and died.

"You see, *pá-pa*, our people felt the sorrow after it was too late. The greed shown by our people in overworking Mother Earth caused a separating of our people. By making the judgment that some of us were too weak to help out is something Great Spirit had to teach us out of that experience.

"We lost two generations and it caused great sorrow, but Great Spirit had a reason for this. Without our old ones, we are weak, just like the young ones who were left with the old ones. And without our young, we lost strength in a generation we had already created to carry on the teachings the old ones would have handed down to them.

"This is why we tell you today to respect your elders, respect the unborn, respect the young, respect Mother Earth and all that is around her. At that time when our bellies were full, we wanted still more. So you see, grandson, Great Spirit watches over us, but when we abuse Mother Earth by overworking her, it is wrong.

"The old ones learned many ways of respect after this sorrowful time of our people. This is why I tell you this today. The hardest part of our people to overcome was to hear our ancestors crying on top of *Ka-tse-ma*. There was nothing they could do but cry too and ask Great Spirit to help us overcome our ignorance.

"This is why we listened very intently to one of the four birds of wisdom who told us to move to *Acó* — where we now sit — and we should give our thanksgiving every day to Great Spirit for allowing us to become a strong people after this sorrowful incident. We also give thanks to the ones who were left on *Ka-tse-ma* so that we could correct our mistake of greed.

"If you listen sometimes, *pá-pa*, you will hear these old ones on *Ka-tse-ma* calling us and advising us. Listen to them, *pá-pa*, for you will learn from them. Their advice is said to always be good for they were the last of our people to live on our most beloved *Ka-tse-ma*.

"You will be a man soon, *pá-pa*, remember all these things. They are for your own good. In your lifetime you will encounter these situations. I always look back at this story of the great suffering of our people. I am old, but this story makes me grateful for my lifetime. I hope it will make you grateful for yours. And always remember to respect all that is around you, for this is the greatest lesson *Acomatra* were taught by Great Spirit. Remember our lost generations."

Laura Watchempino

Pottery Maker

I watch over her shoulder as she paints her designs
   Lines so smooth and flowing
So close I can feel the rhythm of her breathing
   As she calmly fills the spaces with color
Even the flies do not disturb her.

Aaron Carr

Solar systems
Pace their lonely orbit
Around the galaxy. The universe
Can end or go on for
Eternity.

Unknown objects,
From worlds light years away,
Over our heads — watching us

Larry Emerson

GALLUP
("Gallup" is a chapter from a novel in progress)

It was almost completely dark in Gallup now. Saturday night. The neon lights were beginning to blink, but it was still kind of light yet. Where would I go tonight? Would I just live through another night? Of course, I would. Where would I go anyway?

My stomach still hurt from last night when I got drunk again. I remember all the watery bowels, the yellow of my eyes, when I'd looked into the mirror over at the Indian center. I remember all the times I've just slept in the center on the old worn-out couches. Or other times just sitting outside on the brick fence, just looking around at the other people. Or wondering about the Navajo kids, dressed real nice, working, trying to keep the Indian center clean—for us?

The Indian center was closing now. They closed early on Saturday nights. They did this because of us, always fighting and shouting, making a lot of noise. We attract cops.

It was completely dark now and chilly. I walked past a couple of men fighting in an empty supermarket parking lot across the street from the Indian center. Who was tougher? They fought. They were both drunk and couldn't fight anyway. Three younger youths—cowboys probably from Tohatchi—looked on and poked jokes at the men who paid no attention to the youths. They fought on, missing each other with great punches which whizzed by each other's head, causing one of them to fall down.

The youths laughed at this one. Their voices were still teenager voices. They wore huge cowboy hats, pointing at the two fighters.

I wondered what day it was and remembered it was Saturday. Tonight, Gallup would be up in lights with the sound of cars and pickup trucks racing up and down Route 66. If there was going to be a western dance in town tonight, then all the young kids would come to town.

Most of them would be coming in from the reservation to live it up. The best place to go tonight would be to the bars where all the Navajos hung out. I was walking around looking for someone to talk with. Maybe someone who had some wine. I saw a whole group of young guys standing around in a circle, laughing, tipping the old bottle. I made my way around the group, because they would make jokes at me. If only I could find some friends, I would be set for the night.

I passed a pickup with loud Waylon Jennings music on. Its windows were open as I passed it, trying to make my way towards the back of the Indian center. I didn't look in, but someone inside made a "s-h-h-h-h-d" noise, and I looked towards the pickup.

There were some young punks, about four of them, sitting inside the pickup. These guys were probably from Window Rock area or somewhere like that. They were dressed nicely, because I could see their fancy western shirts and their large black hats. They wanted to buy some booze. Would I get them some? I guess I appeared to them to be a desperate drunk in search of an extra bottle of wine.

I remembered the long night ahead and me without any money. I told them yes and got inside their pickup. And we drove down to a nearby bar just north of the Indian center, about two blocks. I got out of the pickup and looked around. It was now completely dark. Cars passed by. I could get myself some booze, too, they laughed.

They gave me some money and said if I didn't come out with their booze, they'd beat the shit out of me.

What could I say? "You guys buy me a pint of wine?" I asked. They were just punks, maybe in high school yet.

"Okay," they said, "with the left over change." Now I turned away from them to go inside.

"Buy us a case of Ripple," one of them said in his teenager voice. All his friends laughed at this one.

"Bring me a chick, too," laughed another. More laughs.

"Bring yourself one, too," said another. More laughs.

"Gimme one dozen eggs," laughed another, as I opened the door to the bar and went in. The doorway was on the corner of the bar, and the large window with a blinking Coors sign faced the busy street. Cars were pouring into Gallup now, and there were a couple of young guys inside the bar buying their night's supply.

The bar keeper, a white man, looked me over real mean-like. He recognized me. As it is with most bar keepers, they did not like to talk to us drunkards. We talk too much and try to be too friendly, they think. Yet they keep us drunk, and we keep them alive with our few pennies.

"Give me a case of Buds, please," I said, looking around, looking outside to see if the boys were still there. No one outside. I guess they went around the block, I thought. "And a pint of Twister," I added.

The bar keeper was slim and short. He had dark hair that he kept slicked to the side of his head—like the old Waylon Jennings. He had long sideburns and a cigarette hanging out of his red lips like a gangster. His cigarette was hanging out of the left corner of his mouth, making his left eye squint as he looked at me. I looked away from him.

I knew he was suspicious of me—a ragged Indian, standing there, trying to buy a case of beer and a pint of cheap wine. If I got caught buying booze from his place and then giving the booze to young punks, he wouldn't like it, especially if the police were in on it. But he didn't say anything about the order I made. It happens all the time. Just so they get their money.

He pushed the booze down the counter and put the Twister on top of the case. No paper sack for me. Never. I gave him the money, and he took it, and he slammed it into his cash register. "Don't get your ass blown by your squaw," he snickered. The bar keeper then looked at his next customer. "What cha need, Chief,?"

I laughed at his weird joke, glancing at him, but he was already walking to his refrigerator. So I walked out into the cold street, hoping the warm pickup full of the punks was still waiting for me.

The pickup was gone. Maybe the police scared them off. I felt real strange standing there with that whole case of beer—just standing there. I put the case down and took the wine and put it between my belt and stomach. Where were the punks? Now the whole street where I was standing was empty. I was scared at the way the dim street lights made the street empty. I wished the boys would come back and take their beer. Finally, in the distance a whole line of cars were coming. The city wasn't empty.

The line of cars passed by one by one. In the middle of the whole line was a long fancy car full of white people. The father driving and the mother sitting in the front seat, looking the other way. All the kids in the back seat were sitting up, still sleepy. The kids were looking at me, all wide-eyed! The rest of the line was all made up of Indian cars, and the tourists were right in the middle.

The Indian cars were full of guys and girls, laughing, probably drinking booze, too. A lonely girl with her hair really done up drove by. What a hairstyle!

Where were the punks? Where were they?

Suddenly, two drunks came around the corner of the back side of the bar, talking to each other, hands in their pockets. I hope they don't see me, I thought. So I picked up the case and started walking towards them. If I could walk pass them they would think I was going someplace definite, and maybe they wouldn't bother me about the booze I was carrying.

Now they stopped and looked at me and my case. This meant some fast explaining or even a fight. Would I fight them for the booze? The booze belonged to the punks and if they came back, they would want it. If I didn't have it, I might as well call it quits. Could I win a fight with these two?

"Where you going?" said one.

"I bought some beer for my nephew and his friends," I said, looking straight ahead. If they knew I was with a bunch of guys they would leave me alone.

"Where are they?"

"I think they're parked around the corner here," I told them, pointing with my lips to the rear of the bar where there was a parking lot.

"You got some wine?"

"Maybe later, if my nephew give me some money."

"We'll wait."

I walked past them and got to the corner. Damn hell, they better be there, I thought. If they were, I would be almost doomed because I took so long. If they weren't then those two drunks behind me would start asking me for drinks, and I would surely be doomed, especially if the punks found me later that night. I could hide out for a couple of hours. I'd still be done for if those guys ever saw me again.

Now I came to the corner where it was darker than on the front street. I kind of looked in back of me and saw the two men waiting—just like they said they would. I looked around the corner. No pickup.

So I went around the corner into the dark. Maybe the pickup was parked on the other side around the next corner. I looked back and saw the two men following me now. Goddam these beers.

A case of beer in this town can be so much trouble, especially if you don't have a car. It can mean your life, your family, your money—all those things we were warned about in school. We laughed then. We laughed about the Gallup drunks, the uneducated ones who did nothing but loaf around and drink away their money. We would never do that, we said.

My bare stomach was pressing hard against the wine bottle. I was breathing like a scared rabbit or something. When I came to the next corner, I held my breath. I was hoping that that damn pickup was going to be there.

I looked around the corner at all the cars which were empty. Near the street that faced the traffic was a police car, and the policeman just sitting quietly in the car. A honky-tonk music from inside the bar came right through the brick wall. Was I trapped? It was sort of funny to be in this situation.

"A policeman," I said, turning around, hoping to scare the two men who were following me. They were standing right behind me.

Just then the policeman flashed his spotlight on me and the case of beer. I froze, somewhat relieved, but also scared of the police. The men behind me, I imagined, ran away. So it was just me, standing there with that crazy case.

"Come over here," the policeman called out.

I walked over. I wondered where the damn punks were now. For an instance, I looked around the parking lot to see if I had missed them somewhere, but the instance was too short to really see anything. I wished I wasn't dressed so dirty. I wished I was at least wearing a good hat so I wouldn't look like I had been rolled or something. I wished I didn't look so poor. But I was young, I thought, younger looking than the rest of the Gallup drunks. I would look like I was just here for the Saturday night.

"Where you going, Hoss?" the policeman in the dark car asked. I couldn't see his face. I didn't know if he was a white or a Mexican. He had a high voice—not deep or anything like that.

"My brother is waiting for me."

"Where?"

"He said he'll be back when I come out," I told him. The warm air from his police car was stuffy and smelly—like cigar smoke.

The case was really getting heavy now. How am I to carry this crazy thing around, I thought, especially with that cop here, looking at me. I wasn't doing anything wrong, and maybe he had arrested me before. Maybe he knew my face and knew I was telling him a bunch of lies.

"I hope you find him," the cop said, reaching for his radio. The cop didn't say nothing else. He just talked into his microphone.

I stood there by his car. I just stood there all dumb and everything. What's a guy supposed to do in this situation? I walked towards the front of the liquor store where I had bought the booze. The lights from inside were yellow on the sidewalk. I stood right on the yellow. I could still see the cop out of the corner of my eye. Was he looking at me?

Now his headlights turned on. I hope he leaves now, I thought. If he does my troubles are far from over, I told myself. I would still have to battle it out with the two men who were after my booze—not me, but the booze. The damn case was more trouble to me than anything else in the world. Yet, it was my key to some fun and adventure for the evening—this Saturday evening. It would mean sharing the wine with the other leeches. Anyway, I hadn't paid for it.

Cars and cars passed by, looking at me. Most of them probably knew my situation. If I were looking out from their car windows, I would see a Navajo guy, drunk, still young-looking, standing outside a liquor store with a case of beer. I would look nervous, and would be standing in the light in order to be seen, looking like I was waiting for someone—or trying to at least. I would smile to myself, as I saw that Navajo man standing there, remembering the same situation I was in at one time.

More cars and pick-ups. Some full of girls on the night out. Others nothing but hats. Girls' hairstyles—up in the air like beehives. Western music or an Oklahoma radio station with the latest rock and roll.

Where in the hell were the goddamn punks, I thought? I wondered how much time had passed by since I was just on my way to get into some wine-action at the Indian center. Or earlier that morning when I woke up in the hills north of Gallup.

I needed to get to the men's room or something. Just to find a tree or an empty-looking spot in an arroyo—just anything. Three more people were coming my way, but they were still across the street, walking slowly.

For the first time, really, in a long time, I thought of my old home when I was young. My mother a long time ago. She had strong features. My father and his tough-looking hands. Old Man's turquoise earring. They were all gone now. The home was gone. The place where we little ones used to return each evening was gone. The corral empty. The whole place that used to buzz with all kinds of laughter, anger, shouting, and calm talk was all gone.

And all those sheep who had all sorts of different personalities. All the sheep, each with their own relatives, their own family trees, their own histories, were gone, stopped. It was like putting an end to a whole human race or a culture—whatever that is. All of them, the sheep, I could remember each of their faces. They were gone into the thin air. My own mother and father. I should have stayed home and worked for them while they lived. My wife? Hell.

More pickups. A sporty car full of young Indian guys passed by, and they were laughing, looking at me. I wondered if they were laughing at me, really. Maybe not, because they were me, too. But they laughed anyway. We Indians have a funny thing about us. We can forget things that bother us in a split second. Like me, I just live on by the second and forget the previous second. I don't do anything, don't learn anything. I just live.

Anyway, life was the last thing I was thinking about, much less "seconds" or remembering life. The whole town of Gallup sounded like a forest when the wind blows. Only it was cars and people making the noise. Gallup's lights were really lit up now. The rattles of the cars and pickups passing by could be heard real well.

I turned away and looked into the window of the bar. I saw the bar keeper looking at the cash register keys, then punching them, holding a money bill in his other hand. He had a cigarette in his mouth, and as he made a joke to the Indian customer, the cigarette moved up and down, dropping ashes to the floor. This was a scene seen many times by everyone who knows any bar, anywhere in the U.S.A.

The customer was a old Navajo man, buying only Twister wine.

Maybe he would divert the other two men from me, and I could get a chance to walk to some dark place when this was all over and gulp down my wine. Instead, I just stood there, looking so foolish and feeling so dumb in the yellow light.

The bar keeper had already seen me, glancing twice at me. He was not too serious about checking on me, but he had noticed me standing there, dumb-looking, I suppose. I thought that if I stayed there too long, he would chase me away from his bar. That's the way they are when they see drunk Indians messing up their place, I guess.

I had to move away from that spot. The case was heavy. I moved over a few feet into the dark out of the view of the bar keeper. I put the case down, it was so heavy. I put it right against the corner where the wall met the sidewalk.

Should I stand there, I thought? Should I put my foot on the case and act like nothing's going on? Am I supposed to lean against the wall? How should I stand while these cars pass by? How does one look when waiting for something?

A light flashed on me. It was the policeman again. I thought he had left by now. He had only gone around the corner, maybe, but here he was again.

"Hey, Hoss, come here," he called.

Shall I leave the case and walk right over to him? Or shall I take it? How do I act? This was such a crazy situation.

"Come here I said," he yelled, louder.

I picked up the case and walked to the car, not wasting too much time.

"Your brother ain't back yet?" he said in a Mexican accent.

"No, he's not back yet. Maybe he got a flat tire somewhere, you know?"

"Well, you gonna stand there all night?"

I remember I laughed nervously at his joke—if it was a joke. My face started getting up tight. I could feel it. I looked down the street, hoping the punks would not show up now.

"I don't know where my brother is. He's a damn brother, you know?" Again, I laughed nervously, looking at the Mexican, then at his billy club that police always carry around. Then at him. He was looking at me.

"He better come soon or I'll have to take you and your beer."

Now I forced a laugh to come out, trying to make the cop feel that his joke was funny, if it was a joke.

"I ain't shittin' you, Hoss," he said, not smiling.

"Okay, okay, officer," I said, forcing my laugh to die out, looking at his car seat and feeling the warm air from his car coming out.

I realized how cold it was outside. My sweaty feet were cold. Maybe with cold feet, they won't be so smelly, I thought. Did this mean I could go?

I had to force myself away from that car and the cop. It was like pulling myself away from a bad magnet. And I walked back towards the place in front of the bar—into the yellow light again. I had turned my back on the policeman. He had never told me I could go. Did this mean that I was defying the cop?

306

I knew he was watching my back to see how I walked. To see how I carried the case, how strong I was, how drunk I was. What the hell was I doing? Walking away from him. Had I made a mistake with the Mexican?

Sure enough I heard his car door open. I was caught, again. It did not matter if I did wrong or not. I was caught and that was it. I had to give up to him. There was no other way. My Saturday night was shot to hell. That was that.

Just then the pickup full of punks passed by, slowly, trying to look at the situation and trying not to at the same time. Their signal lights flashed left. They went around the corner and stopped. I saw their brake lights.

"My brother just came," I said to the cop who was standing by his car. I was hoping he hadn't seen the young punks.

"Where?"

"Right here, sir, around the corner."

"Listen, Hoss," the officer said, turning back to his car," no nonsense, hear?"

"Yes, officer, we just going home now, after we pick up my sister from the cafe."

"Git!" the Mexican said.

Man, I really did git that time.

I climbed into the warm pickup and told the punks that the cop was on our tail and that we should drive around a while so the cop wouldn't get us. I told the young driver in a deep voice that he was supposed to be my brother. The cop knows I might be lying, I told him. I also knew, as we drove off towards downtown, how scared these shitheads were, now that the cops entered the scene. I could now act tough with them. To confuse the cop, we went straight east, keeping away from the downtown section.

"Shit, man, I been in trouble with the law all the time," I said. "They ain't shit, but they sure can beat your ass."

The punks were looking around now, quiet and scared.

We drove a few more blocks, turning around corners, working our way back downtown, trying to get lost in the cars.

No way, though. The cop had either followed us or something. Red lights flashed behind us. Was it for us? Yes, because now the cop's spotlights were right on us. "Goddamn you," the young driver said to me.

When the cop came over to the pickup and looked at all of us with his crazy flashlight, he said "Goddamn you, Hoss" to me.

Luci Tapahonso

THE SNAKEMAN

The child slid down silently and caught herself at the end of the fire escape. She eased herself down until she felt the cold, hard sidewalk through her slippers — then she let go.

The night was clear and quiet. The only noise that could be heard was the echo of the child's footsteps in the moonlit alley behind the old, brick buildings.

The little girls, watching her from the top floor of the dorm, swung the window screen in and out, catching it before it struck the window frame. They always talked about what would happen if the top hinges suddenly gave way but they hadn't yet.

"Good thing—it's spring." one of them said.

"She would freeze her toes off for sure," another hissed.

"SHHH-H" the biggest one hissed.

They whispered in lispy voices and someone on the other side of the room would only hear "s. . .sss," hissing and an occasional "shut-up!" The room was large with windows on three sides. The fire escape the child slid down was in the center of the north windows, which faced a big, dark hill, its slope covered with huge, round rocks and dry tumbleweeds. Opposite the fire escape was the door to the hall.

Sometimes the dorm mother, who lived at the other end of the hall, heard them giggling or running around. She would walk down the dark, shiny hall so fast her housecoat would fly behind her in billows. The girls would scurry to their beds, tripping over their long nightgowns, finally faking snores as she turned on the harsh, bright lights in each room. After she went back to her room, the children jumped up and laughed silently with wide, open mouths and pounded their fists into their beds.

One of the girls whispered loudly, "She's coming back." They all ran noiselessly to the window and watched the small figure coming. The little girl walked briskly with her hands in her housecoat pockets. She wore the soft, wool slippers all the little girls made for their sister or mother at Christmastime. But she had neither, so she wore them herself.

"Seems like she floats," one girl commented.

"How could she? Can't you hear her walking?" the biggest retorted.

The girls went back to their beds and the ones that were closest to the fire escape window opened the window and held it up until she was in. Then they all gathered at one bed and sat in the moonlight telling ghost stories or about how the end of the world was REALLY going to be. Except for the girl who left, she always went to sleep and wasn't noisy like the rest.

Sometimes late in the night or towards morning when the sun hadn't come up completely and everything was quiet and the room filled with the soft, even breathing of the children — one of them might stand at the window facing east and think of home far away and tears would stream down her face. Late in the night someone always cried and if the others heard her — they would pretend not to notice. They understood how it was with all of them . . . if only they could go to public school and eat at home everyday.

When they got up in the morning before they went downstairs to dress, two of them emptied their pockets of small, torn pieces of paper and scattered them under the beds. The beds had white ruffled bottoms that reached the floor and the bits of paper weren't visible unless one lifted the ruffles. This was the way they tested the girl that cleaned their room. When they returned to their bedroom in the evenings, they checked under their beds to see if the paper was gone. If it wasn't, they immediately reported it to the dorm mother, who never asked why they were so sure their room hadn't been cleaned.

The building was divided into three floors and an attic. The little girls who were in grade school occupied the bottom and top floors and the junior high girls had the middle floor. The top floor was used only for bedrooms and all daytime activity was on the bottom level. The building was old, like all the other buildings on campus, and the students were sure it was haunted. Besides, there was a graveyard a little ways away. How could it not be? they asked among themselves.

This was especially true for those little girls in the east end of the dorm, since they were so close to the attic door. There was a man in there, they always said in hushed voices, he always kept the attic door open just a little, enough to throw evil powder on anyone that walked by. For this reason, they all stayed out of the hallway at night. Once they had even heard him coming down the attic stairs to the door and the smaller girls started crying. They all slept two-to-a-bed, and the big girls made sure all the little girls had someone bigger with them. They stayed up later than usual, crying and praying, so that no one woke early enough to get everyone back into their right beds. The dorm mother spanked each of them but at least, they said, that night nothing happened to any of them.

Once when the little girl went on one of her walks at night, the other children were waiting for her as they usually did. Two of them were by the hall door trying to figure how to get to the bathroom two doors down the hall when they heard a scratching noise outside on the sidewalk.

"You guys!! come here! he's over here!!" they whispered loudly.

They ran to the east window and saw a dark figure go around the corner and the biggest girl took control.

"You two get over by that window. You on that side. Someone get on the fire escape in case he tries to get up here."

They watched the man below and tried to get a description of him, in case someone asked them. They couldn't see him very well because he was on the shady side of the building. Some of the girls started crying, and some crawled quietly back into bed. Two of them, the bigger ones, waited to open the window for the other girl when she got back. When she came back, they all huddled around her and told her and started crying again. She said it was probably someone's father trying to see his daughter. Probably the mother won't let him see her, she said. So the girls calmed down and tried to figure out whose parents were divorced or fought a lot. They finally decided that he was the boyfriend of a junior high girl downstairs.

When a new girl came, she asked why the girl always walked at night, and the biggest one had said:

"Wouldn't you if you could see your mother every night, dummy?"

"Well, where's her mom? Can't she see her on weekends like us? That's not fair."

"Fair? FAIR??" they had all yelled in disbelief.

Then the girl who walked explained that her parents had died years before, when she was six, and they were buried at the school cemetery. So that's why she went to see them. Just her mother, mostly, though.

"How is she? Does she talk?"

"Can you REALLY see her?" the new girl asked.

"Yeah," she answered patiently. "She calls me and she waits at the edge of the cemetery by those small, fat trees. She's real pretty. When she died, they put a blue outfit on her. A Navajo skirt that's real long and a shiny, soft, light blue blouse. She waves at me like this: "Come here, shi yashil, my little baby.' She always calls me that. She's soft and smells so good."

The little girls all nodded, each remembering their own mothers.

"When it's cold or snowing, she lets me stand inside the blanket with her. We talk about when I was a baby, and what I'll do when I get big. She always worries if I'm being good or not."

"Mine, too." someone murmured.

"Why do mothers always want their girls to be goody-good?"

"So you won't die at the end of the world, dummy."

"Dying isn't that bad. You can still visit people like her mother does."

"But at the end of the world, all the dinosaurs and monsters that are sleeping in the mountains will bust out and eat the bad people. No one can escape, either," said the biggest girl with confidence.

Then the little girl who talked to her mother every night said quietly:

"No one can be that bad." She went to her bed and lay there looking at the ceiling until she fell asleep.

The other girls gathered on two beds and sat in a little circle and talked in tight, little voices about the snakeman who stole jewelry from some of the girls.

"You can't really see him," one said, "cause he's sort of like a blur, moves real fast and all you can see is a black thing go by."

"He has a silver bracelet that shines and if he shines it on you, you're a goner cause it paralyzes."

They talked about him until they began looking around to make sure he wasn't in the room.

The bigger girls slept with the littler ones, and they prayed that God wouldn't let that man in the attic or the snake-man come to them, and that the world wouldn't end until after their moms came to visit.

As the room got quiet and the breathing became even and soft, the little girl got up, put on her housecoat and slid soundlessly down the fire escape.

CONVERSATIONS

we stopped wondering
why things happen
like they do.
Saturday, at a party,
I saw you passed out
on top of a
red car.

when we were at Esquire,
drinking and laughing,
I saw that lady
I babysat her kids once
they cried all night for her.
I wonder if my baby cries.
maybe she's used to it by now.

towards evening,
I get restless,
being alone.
to have a man
appreciate a good meal.
to sleep beside a
warm, strong body.
to whisper and laugh
over a 2 o'clock snack.
after everything . . .
I could easily
welcome him back.

sometimes
in the dark quietness
of the night.
when i worry of rent,
groceries and diapers.
I even curse him and
hope his eyes
are dead and
stare at nothing.

FOR LORI TAZBAH

tonight it rained hard
the thunder cracked
my blood froze.
I caught my breath
and thought of you
you slept peacefully
your breathing gentle, soft
unaware of my sudden panic.

last year you memorized
the pledge of allegiance perfectly
your teacher proud of your perfect salute.
when she asked everyone
to sit "Indian style" and
you asked why sitting
cross-legged was Indian
when everyone could do it.

now you're six,
you've waited so long
to be in "regular school."
no more naps, snacks or color games.
you're impatient and want to
learn to read and do times.
the first day you went
I cried for hours.

MISTY DAWN

this fierceness of love
i feel for you
recreated within me
by gentle kicks,
twitches of rhythm
in the warm darkness
of my being.

312

Nia Francisco

men tell   and talk

men tell   and talk about their pride
   being so proud of being a father
of so many children born to them
and the joy ride

men do not know   birth and its pain
but i assume those who know the drum tightness
                    do know

they sing reverently
            holding the drum gently
            and the liquid in the drum
            vibrates with good ancient songs

              a woman moans
           the tightness of her drum
             contains unborn life
           and it moves ticklishly touching
         the touching of the baby inside her drum

         at the coming of early morning
          the baby moves
         at the coming of early morning
          hunger teases
         the unborn life

           and the mother laughs

               today many young men deny their birth
               they cast their children upon each other
               and it is they who do not know
               the tightness of the drum, the liquid,
               and the woman's pregnancy

i have sat through sunlight

i have sat through sunlight   with patience
   it takes a while for a brook mint to bloom
i have sat through sunlight and   run my fingers over
   good memories of the time   i sat by you
   whispering to you   i love you and i miss you dale

you did not believe me then
now you know it takes time to tell
   sort out what is true   and what is true
    at the spur of the moment

i have sat through moonlight too
   it takes a while to yearn for the sweet taste
   of corn pollen   wait for my touch
okay luv?

314

BLOWING WIND

The wind was blowing cold and if given enough time would numb everything in its path. The clumps of sagebrush and pinon trees seemed to enjoy the wind's game, pushing and pulling every which way. The clouds were in streaks of gray and it gradually became dark. They were the darkest near the top of the mountain. The sun was ready to take its heat and light back. I stood and looked up the slope of the hill at the tin water tank.

It has been less than a week since I had seen him, alive and ready for any basketball game. The sun had not yet come up and it was still and dark in the house. Words of discipline and caution came from within the darkness as he leaned over and spoke to his nephew. My son, too young yet to know the meanings of these words, moved his fisted hands and continued to sleep.

He went off to work at the Army Depot before even the grayness of the morning stirred the sun.

Massive confusion. Sunday I had finally found an apartment for the school year. Early Monday morning a friend located me and told me about my mother's phone call. I returned the call and found that they were flying him down to Albuquerque. He needed intensive care.

There were low muttering voices in the wind. Faces of long unvisited relatives, old past acquaintances — unfamiliar, yet familiar, friends just made — and us.

The security guard at the hospital misjudged our inner thoughts and feelings—he was the first to accidentally inform us of my brother's death. The receptionists tried to make excuses for him, saying it probably wasn't him but someone else. Hearing bits and pieces of the doctor's explanation—TIME—an hour earlier, chances, done everything possible, neck injury. The hopeless feeling. Being unable to breathe, the uselessness at seeing your mother cry while wiping your own tears. The anger at time, Gallup P.H.S., the train, the doctors, the ambulance driver, everything, but mostly TIME.

The sound of breaking sagebrush branches broke the silence of mind. Frank went chasing his cowboy hat. The wind made his hat race and hurdle even faster than he could. On the opposite side Alice had her skirt caught on a dry bush, and was trying to free herself while cleaning off mud from her shawl.

He was willing to help out anyone who needed or asked for help. He paid Mom's bills, bought her things she really didn't need. But she was the one who had to buy his clothes.

He teased his two nephews until we finally had to laugh. Those evenings at home, stretched across the floor trying to read the newspaper while they crawled over him, making the small print impossible for him to read.

The Monday morning newspaper had said the car stalled on the railroad tracks. The train pushed the car for a half-mile.

The wind blew the dry brown grass over until it lay almost flat. A few daring ones would stand up straight again only to be forced down again. Along the fence pieces of old paper and trash were desperately trying to escape with the help of the wind. Between the wire to continue on until they reached another detour. Faded plastic flowers and wire wreath stands poke up from under the patches of snow.

I had touched his hand, it was colder and harder than the wind. There were chunks of frozen ground piled on each side. The flapping of the brown robe almost drowned out the words of the priest. In a short while all was done. The hard thumping of the frozen dirt on the box was replaced by the scraping of the shovel. My aunt, with the tight secure knot at the back of her head—not even the wind could loosen it up and blow a strand of her grey hair out of place. She lifted herself into the back of the blue pick-up truck.

Grey Cohoe

TOCITO VISIONS

Child of infinite
Navajo dreams,
changer of sacred visions,

little magician
browses far
on visionary hills
amidst imbuing
tints of habitats
under untamed
summer sun.

Over Chuska
skyline
illusioning eyes
peer cussing cicada
that maneuvers
its trailing
thread between

Tocito's open
sky of twining
junipers and
over diversing
dunes of marks
of wandering,
curving trails of

Sanostee
sidewinders
through twining,
turquoise,
salty sages.

i remember
a face so
clear of dreads,
straining to
gesture accents
of every thought
from his
callow soul

all to flowers
too mute for
riddling words.

As wonders
beyond roads
of temptations
he dissects
fast lizards
as answers
to why
little people
outrun him.

Beast of sacrifice
he is.
His preys are
curiosities
beyond joys
of cracker jack toys.

It's musing,
his callow prodigies
as in miracle of
a nighthawk
dropping a
blinded sparrow.

Secrets in his
prowling dreams
made no difference to
playing neighbors
who still die.

Relics of scars
had long softened
from aging hills
since now
that mellow
moonlight casts
silvery visions of

healing illusions
of those magics
of infinite memories
of the child
in the poet,
changer of moon spirits.

Jean Natoni

Catoni

Where are you, Catoni
with your sparkling brown eyes
which gaze
over the flat lands
where are you
you who are in love with life
a face creased
with knowledge
a walk
so determined

Bernadette Chato

Mickey

that little john
or was she a florida indian
making crooked tortillas
the 8-hour bread
truckin' on her broken-down bike
believing 7x8=49

To Nilinigii

Rivers
Changed his course
       But can't dry up
His winding life
Has left a trickle
       In Joanie's mind
But now he has a wife.

Shighan — the Navajo Way

home away from home   just homely
    adventure   set forth my journey
      away   day to day
       yearn to return   but still
          here i are
              home not too far . . .

Geraldine Keams

Cry of Nature

Child of nature
Child of the sun,
Believe in the whispers of wind
   swelling from trees.
Life is young;
Nature dances beneath our feet.
The dry wilted weed
   blows freely in the wind
   crying out loud:
I am a child of nature!

THE FLIGHT OF THE ARMY WORM

Characters:

General Carleton A man in his early fifties. The General is dressed in a late 1800's cavalry outfit. He is on the verge of senility.

Young Person May be played by male or female. He/She dresses in a contemporary style. This person is the collegiate type, very intelligent and witty. This person is also a young Navajo from Canyon de Chelly.

Grandmother A very old Navajo. Poetic, wise, she has lived a long life.

Announcer An old-fashioned Southern lady, she wears glasses and has a degree in Library Science.

Guitar Player Young, long-haired Indian, going to college. Trying to "make it."

Place:

The action takes place at a small, secluded hogan, in the deep canyon of de Chelly.

320

Time:

Mid-morning of June 7th, 1976

NOTE:

This play is meant to bring out some very real things about the history of the Navajo people.

It is also meant to be humorous, at least in places where it should be. The dialogue between the General and the Young Person should have a quick pace. The play should move right along without any long delays. It's funny when the lines are delivered in the fast comedic style. Of course, when the grandmother appears, the play takes on a different twist. It should catch the sincerity of emotion; the reality of looking at suffering. If the play works for you, then it should make you laugh, angry, sad and lonely.

The characters are all Indians, except for General Carleton and the Announcer. Good Indian actors can play them well with make-up and a slight southern drawl.

Enjoy . . .

ACT ONE

(Lights come in very dimly, giving a silhouette effect.

An Army military march begins at a loud volume. The General marches out to stage right. He salutes as he marches in place; he gives the impression of a robot.

Grandmother takes her place at a rug loom, located at stage left.

She sits on a goat skin, pours a cup of coffee, and begins to weave.

The grandmother has her own space on stage. Besides the loom, there is a stool next to her, on which sits a pot of coffee and a pail of water. An old tub leans against the stool. On her right is a kerosene lamp and some old suitcases piled on top of one another. The top is covered with a towel, and on top of that there are a number of various things. A picture of John F. Kennedy stands out.

Up center is a wooden rocking horse, the General's "wheels." It is painted red, white, and blue, with stars painted on the bottom.

So, the robot marches, grandmother weaves, and the audience only sees outlines of these characters.

A spotlight shines on downstage center as the

guitar player enters, strumming away.)

GUITAR PLAYER

I'd like to welcome everyone here. Hope you enjoy the play. Here's a song to get you into the show.

Send a word, share a dream,
cried the young warrior.
I'm going down to the valley,
to send a word, share a dream.
Visions of black skies,
— dancing in daylight.
Many smoke rising,
from aluminum lies.
Take the children and beware.
Talk to mother earth and take care.
To all the earth people,
Send a word, share a dream.
Send a word, share a dream.

(Guitar player walks off stage right, strumming his guitar; it slowly fades out.)

(Announcer enters, very briskly, notices the audience. She straightens out her dress, puts on her spectacles and begins to read from a piece of paper she has brought in with her.)

ANNOUNCER

The name of this ferocious animal is *vermix carletonianus*. His habits have been understood by the people of New Mexico for some time, and one of his peculiar characteristics is his fondness for sheep. (Pause) Heretofore he has been considered a wanderer, but recently under the auspices of General Carleton, U.S. Volunteers, his ravages have been confined to the Bosque Redondo, where it is well known his destruction upon commissary stores alone have cost Uncle Sam over two million dollars. He is not only a carnivorous animal, destroying millions of sheep, and thousands of horses, mules, and cattle — as the destruction of hundreds of the fortunes of our people in the history of the past will prove — but at this time his graniverous qualities are being exhibited to such an extent as to threaten a total destruction of the corn, wheat and beans, (emphasize ''beans'') of the country. Watch out! the *vermi carletoniani* are multiplying to an alarming degree. Who knows when you might be attacked by this terrible enemy. The prices are beyond your reach and are becoming higher and General Carleton's policy says this destroying worm must live if you should starve.

(Announcer exits stage right. Lights come up on General Carleton. He is chanting a military ballad.)

GENERAL CARLETON

Come dress your ranks, my gallant souls, a standin' in a row.
Kit Carson he is waiting, to march against the foe.
At night we march to Moqui, O'er lofty hills of snow.
To meet and crush the savage foe,
Bold Johnny Navajo,
Bold Johnny Navajo.

> (Lights come up on the old woman spinning wool. She is singing a Navajo lullaby. Young Person enters from stage right. She is slowly moving across the stage, looking at her grandma. She respectfully gazes at the loom. She finally gives a loving look at the old woman and to the audience.
>
> NOTE: (I use the gender ''she'' in the play to avoid syntactic verbosity. The original character was also played by a female, so . . .)

YOUNG PERSON

She's my grandmother. She has worked hard all her life. Never asked for more than she needed. She knows the balance of harmony in nature. I guess you can say that she understands change.
They don't come as enduring anymore. You know, my grandmother went on the Long Walk, when she was about seven. The Navajo call it Hweelte. She doesn't really like to talk about it, because it's a sad part of her life.
Can you imagine? Anywhere from 7,000 to 9,000 captives, walked 300 miles in the middle of winter with no food, no clothes. They were kept in a place that was little better than a concentration camp for four years.

> (The General comes to life and moves into the light.)

GENERAL CARLETON

Now wait a minute . . . Wait just a hot dang minute!

YOUNG PERSON

Who are you? Where did you come from? What's going on here anyway?

GENERAL CARLETON

Now, would you let me get a word in edgewise. Those Navajos deserved what they got. I'm here to give you my side o' the story. Now, I'm a hard working man — okay? Okay. I'm not a violent man. I'm patient and I like to think I'm kind, okay. BUT them Indians weren't willing to live up to their promises to the government. They promised not to steal, rape and kill. Well, they went right on pillaging and committing depredations of every degree. When I became military commander of New Mexico in 1862, I knew it was my mission to get the Indians under control.

YOUNG PERSON

I want to know who you are. What is your name?

GENERAL CARLETON

Well, I'm Carson . . . no, wait a minute. He was one of my boys? I'm uh . . . uh, Canby, yes, that's it, Canby. You know, I must admit that being in the military as long as I have, sometimes makes you forget who the hell you are.

YOUNG PERSON

Well, so you're Canby, Edward R.S. Mildmannered, plain appearing, prudent Canby? Brother-in-law of the Confederate president Jefferson Davis?

GENERAL CARLETON

NO! that's not me. I mean I'm not him. Uh, he's not me. (Pause) OH! I almost forgot, I'm Carleton. General James H. Carleton, long time veteran of the Plains Service in Oklahoma trying to civilize the Kiowas and Comanches.

YOUNG PERSON

I heard it was a campaign to reduce Indian land. To give them the worst land so you could get rich from the mineral resources. Well, Colonel, as you can see, America is rich. (singing)

> See the USA, in your Chevrolet
> Get your kicks Today
> But don't let the smog get in the Way!

In those days you and Honest Abe got together and decided it was in the interest of the American people, democracy, freedom, justice for all, to get the Indians off their land. Thus, the confinement of the Navajo people at Hweelte, or Bosque Redondo.

GENERAL CARLETON

Don't forget it was also called Ft. Sumner. Ft. Carleton, Hmmmm.

YOUNG PERSON

At BOSQUE REDONDO, located in the center of New Mexico. Forty square miles of arid wasteland was established as the reservation.

GENERAL CARLETON

That was not the main issue in the beginning. We picked this particular area because, number one, it was a fortress against further raids by Southern Plains Indians, and number two, the Apaches were already there and we thought it would be good if we combined the two groups. You know, killing two birds with one stone. This would end all atrocities against the New Mexicans and they would begin acting like those nice Pueblo Indians. Never had much trouble with *them*.

YOUNG PERSON

Atrocities! What nerve! Let me tell you something. From 1855 to 1868, the Navajos signed four meaningless treaties. I mean, Navajos wanted peace AND they thought you would protect them. First, you told them you would do both these things, but your words were as meaningless as the paper it was written on. The Mexicans stole livestock, took our people for slaves, but one crazy Indian goes and steals one skinny cow, and you guys declared war! The treaties were always asking for two main things: the reduction of land and livestock, and the surrender of all thieves from all tribes. We should have known then that the U.S. was Halloweening us with Trick or Treaties!

YOUNG PERSON

Your people were new here. Navajos didn't like strangers telling them to butt out, how many sheep they should have, and who they should have war with.
Another thing: each clan was like a tribe; independent. But when one clan did a no-no, you blamed everyone and you justified breaking every treaty.

GENERAL CARLETON

I can't believe it! How in the hell do you know so much? Where did you . . . How did you . . . I mean . . .

YOUNG PERSON

Don't you think I'm right. Telling it like it was. (to the audience) And that's the way it was — one hundred years ago.

GENERAL CARLETON

Well, uh, there might be some truth to what you're . . .

YOUNG PERSON

Am I right! Do you think I'm right or NOT!

GENERAL CARLETON

I don't know. Maybe, just maybe . . .

YOUNG PERSON

Look out there. (to audience) See all those people. If they find out that you're lying, you better watch out!

GENERAL CARLETON

Alright, alright . . .

YOUNG PERSON

I'm right. Right?

GENERAL CARLETON

Right . . .

YOUNG PERSON

RIGHT.

GENERAL CARLETON

RIGHT.

YOUNG PERSON

That will be enough!

GENERAL CARLETON

I still can't believe . . . how in damnation do you know all this? You're not supposed to know. Indians are not supposed to know. They must not learn. I mean, it's confidential information.

YOUNG PERSON

Well, to go on; by the time you broke three treaties with the Navajos, you decided to imprison them. By that time, there were 400 Apaches confined at Bosque. In the meantime, Navajoland was an open field for slave trading. Everyone got in on the act. With your blessings, of course. To top it all off, the Civil War was raging in the South to free the Black people. You had a Major Brooks, remember him? Remember when he called a war on the Navajo when one Black SLAVE was killed. Nothing makes sense when it comes to money, power and war!

326

GENERAL CARLETON

(In panic) Oh Jesus, uh . . . uh . . . Oh, my God. (Abruptly) Listen, they didn't tell you the ending, did they?

YOUNG PERSON

Ending of what???

GENERAL CARLETON

You know. This story . . . I . . . uh . . . I think I should . . . uh . . . leave. It's getting late, I really should be getting back.

(He jumps on his horse.)

YOUNG PERSON

Wait a minute, get back here. I didn't ask you to come here, but you barged in defending yourself, so defend yourself. Besides, I was just getting to the main part.

GENERAL CARLETON

I really shouldn't take up any more of your time. I'm sure you have better things to do than talk to me. Well, it was a pleasure . . . (inner monologue) like hell it was! (Cheerfully) Adios!

YOUNG PERSON

(walks over to horse)
I kinda like talking to you. Aren't you having fun?
(The General nods in approval)
Relaaaax, Colonel. Come down off your horse. Yes, that's it . . .

YOUNG PERSON

There . . . now, let's see, where was I?

GENERAL CARLETON

Oh, brother . . . here we go again.

YOUNG PERSON

Oh yeah! 'Ol Rope Thrower, Kit Carson, got his Ute scouts together and began rounding up the Navajo. He never won any medals for patriotic duties, but I heard you sent out slave raiders disguised as "volunteer troops." Did you get any medals for that, Carleton? Hmmmm? Did you?

(Carleton is shaking in his boots)

GENERAL CARLETON

Noooo! They . . . uh . . . didn't tell you. They couldn't have. Not the WHOLE truth.

YOUNG PERSON

(nodding her head) The WHOLE truth. It's not so bad, Carleton, EVERYONE is getting inspected these days. You won't get rejected or defected. People like you are still getting selected and re-elected!

BLACK OUT

> (The lights come up. The actors are relaxed, out of character. Young Person notices the audience.)

YOUNG PERSON

OH! we're back, well I guess we're ready for the ending.

GENERAL CARLETON

(disinterested) Ending?

YOUNG PERSON

It's not nice to keep an audience waiting. File your nails later.

> (Carleton notices the audience. He jumps up, straightens himself out.)

GENERAL CARLETON

Yes, of course.

YOUNG PERSON

> (Trying to remember her lines. She nervously searches for her cue cards. Finds them, glances at them and gets back into character.)

I see, Carleton, that the outcome of your utopian reservation took a bad turn. Actually never had a good turn to begin with. It looks as though you defeated your purpose, because the raiding actually increased on the outside.
In March of '65 things began falling apart. Consecutive crop failures because of Army worms, bad soil with too much alkalai, and the water with too much minerals. What you guys were trying to do with a stunt like that, I'll never know . . . strange . . .

Well, at this point the government decided it was getting too expensive civilizing the Indians, so they blamed you. They had to blame SOMEbody. All the Apaches and some 2,000 Navajos, couldn't handle the whole stupid scene and left. You say they escaped . . . You must have been a nervous wreck . . . poor thing.

(Young Person grows sympathetic. The General imaginatively relives the whole stupid scene. He breaks down, kicking, screaming and crying. Carrying on like a bat out of hell.)

GENERAL CARLETON

Oh, Jesus, I tried. I really did . . . honest I did . . .

(He grabs her leg by surprise)

GENERAL CARLETON

Oh please, I can't take this. I'm sorry . . . I'm sorry. OH! my heart, the old ticker can't take this! (Gasping for air)

YOUNG PERSON

Are you alright? It's okay . . . It's okay.

(Exhausted, the General, collapses.)

YOUNG PERSON

It's one of those things. You blew it. Look at it this way, we would have never had this play, if you didn't do all those things. I mean, wouldn't things get boring IF everything went right ALL the time.
ANYWAY, we're still hanging in there. It's 1976 and we still have sheep, still doing our thing! . . . well, one thing that bothers me . . . is the land dispute area.

GENERAL CARLETON

The *what* area?

YOUNG PERSON

(introspectively) More atrocity.

GENERAL CARLETON

What did you say?

YOUNG PERSON

Never mind . . . You see, they're doing it again. You just wait and see,

some 8,000 Navajos will accept a few measly bucks, and give up acres and acres of precious land. I tell you sometimes I wonder if Navajos don't act just like the sheep they herd! (frustrated) OOH!
In any case, the Hopis will get the land . . .

GENERAL CARLETON

So . . . you still can't get along, huh? The Hopis never did like you all's company, probably because of your dirty, rotten, stinkin' mutton!

(The General rises slowly)

YOUNG PERSON

Sometimes, I just don't know what to think. You just can't trust ANYBODY these days . . .
Hell, well . . . we have to be positive, hopeful, that it can change for the better. I mean, we still have traditionals, sheepherders, a few medicine men.

(The General pauses, listening closely.)

YOUNG PERSON

SOME of us still don't have electricity. On the other hand, we have bonafied politicians, lawyers who are members of the BAR association, yes, and we have rodeo stars, doctors, conference Indians, college queens, and janitors.
Yep, we get around, doing big numbers with Exxon, Peabody, Barry Goldwater and The Colonel.

GENERAL CARLETON

OH?

YOUNG PERSON

Only this one is into chicken. They just opened one in Chinle. (Brightly) I'm hungry . . .

GENERAL CARLETON

I learned my lesson . . . not to trust politicians. I worked for them for years . . . busted my ass. What did I get in the end? Nothing . . . a big fat zero. (Regretfully) Oh god, I did want to at least make good civilized Christians out of those Indians.

YOUNG PERSON

Civilize! Goes to show how much you know, Civilize, according to Webster, means to advance in an orderly manner, to refine.
As you can see, none of that kind of civilization took place.

You know too much! If you're the only one that knows all this, be careful who you talk to. You know what they do to people, especially minority types, who talk too much.

> (pantomimes cutting throat. The General acts as though he hears noises, angry voices. He looks around him, growing more afraid. He looks out into the audience and "freaks" out.)

THE INDIANS ARE COMING
THE INDIANS ARE COMING

BLACK OUT

> (The General jumps on his horse, the young person steps back. Both are now in the shadow. The old woman begins to get up for the first time during the play.
> She is unaware of the other two characters.)

GRANDMOTHER

Oh, my aching bones. They get in the way everytime I have something to do. I have to finish this rug.

> (She gets a drink of water and turns back to her weaving.)

GENERAL CARLETON

Umm, quite old, ain't she?

YOUNG PERSON

Over a hundred. She went on the Long Walk.
Grandma, shi ma sani. Please tell us of the Long Walk.

GRANDMOTHER

> (She continues her line of action, still unaware of the other characters.)

I wish not to speak of such times, but I will begin. I am old, and soon will leave this earth. The old ones would have wanted me to speak to the young people, to tell them that they should never forget. All the days we were away from our beloved land we shedded tears. The Long Knives' dogs were living better. For us it was the moaning of death everywhere. Sacred spirits seem to be dead themselves. We had done

no wrong, but our very lives were cut, just as the root beings and four legged beings were cut from life. Many tears dropped on the earth, as many walked naked in the wake of winter. Hunger ate bitterly at our stomachs. (Pause) We were taken for no reason.
Some say we stole and killed, but we only lived with our clan brothers and sisters in peace.
There is evil . . . many of the young men from different clans were impatient, in the warrior spirit. Many say they were never caught . . . that they went right on killing . . . and we suffered.
I was very young . . . then . . . all I remember is Death all around. There was talk that our tribe would be wiped out.
The years were long there. The people, once a strong nation, now had nothing to eat. The earth was hard to plant. I remember the Long Knives on their horses, sitting way up high, telling us to dig faster. I used to pick potatoes. I used to want to take one to eat, but I saw what happened to those that did . . . they were whipped. The potatoes were only for the Long Knives and their dogs. (she pours a cup of coffee)

GRANDMOTHER

My grandmother died on the way there. She was a good woman, very strong. We lived . . .
Now, today, we still are not safe. They, the Hopis, want our land. I don't understand why the Hopis would be like this. The way I think, we are all Indians. We all used to live together, long ago . . .
I don't know where my children will go?
Will my children survive?
Will they remember me?
Only Mother Earth knows.
Only Mother Earth knows.

> (The guitar player enters, singing a song. As he plays, all lights come up. The General rides his horse, waving his sword. The Young Person, drinks a cup of water and gazes off wondering . . . and the Grandmother continues to weave.)

GUITAR PLAYER

And that's the way it is in 1976. BiCentennial year for most. For some of us, it's sharing a dream 300 years old.

> Amerika, Amerika,
> Can't be your wooden Indians anymore,
> Won't be your Tonto Indian anymore.
>   (change of tune)
> Mother Earth glances, sweet look
> In her eyes.
> Warrior earth spirit, the strength
> to survive

Come all the tired children who
hear the Earth song.
Let's band together,
For a humble victory.
Hear the Earth song.
And It won't take long
Sing the Earth Song.
And It won't take long.

BLACK OUT

Roman C. Adrian

Happening

Black clouds spark
    the thunderous rain
        and with the mixing
            winds carry lightning's
            crooked finger to
                touch my mother
                Earth.

Bel Woman

Woman, I may be a stone from
    which you step up to better
    things,
        I don't mind.

But during the time you linger
    here with me, the joy of you
        will be a comfort to my spirit.

Then, the day may come when
    you look and the stone
        will be gone.

It will have been broken
    and sunk beneath the
        river you crossed.

Refugio Savala

The Bee Hunt

In our country, people live largely on wild honey, and the bee hunter traces the bees from wherever they get their water. The small bees that manufacture honey in a hive are very smart. When they depart from the water to their hive, they leave in different directions. In this case, only a very good bee hunter will get onto their track. The bees also ascend to an altitude which makes them imperceptible to the human eye, so the good hunter, who has very good eyesight, will find the bees crossing the sunbeams. This is the only way the hunter can get on the track of this small bee, because in the sunlight, the bee is visible even at a considerable height. Once this track is found, certainly the next will be found. The nearer the hive is, the lower the bees travel. The bee hunter usually knows if the honey is good to harvest, but if it is not ready, he does not attempt to destroy it.

Another kind of bee is larger and is less wise about its enemy. The only way it hides its track is by carrying the water very low under the cover of the trees. It is also hard to track at first, but a close observation reveals that the water carrier travels fast in one direction and those working in the honey suckle are slow and fly in a different direction. Following the fast ones will take the hunter to the nest of bees. This kind of bee manufactures its honeycomb in the hollow of a tree. To make the bees leave it, a fire is built at the foot of the tree. The smoke is cast into the hollow and the bees begin to leave, though sometimes this kind of bee battles a great deal before giving up the honeycomb. Here is where the bee hunter gets a good licking. If he gets stung, he cures it with the honey-wax and a bee so that all the pain and swelling end soon.

The hive bee is taken in the same manner, but these do no battle against the intruder. Quite to the contrary, they abandon the hive when the smoke is made, taking their queen in order to avoid the death of a single bee.

This kind of bee is also domesticated by the bee hunter, not only for honey, but for the pleasure of watching them work. The worker bees carry the gum of the mesquite tree and the ground-up cottonwood and other soft wood. The gum is layed, then the wood. If the work is done all day, the size of the ball is about like a grapefruit. Every night it is closed so it looks like a ball, but in the morning it is opened and the work continues until the size of the hive is big enough. This work they start in the spring.

Sionima

Among the Yaqui Indians there was a young man of Potam Pueblo. He had the native Yaqui name Sionima, or Geronimo. This young man had a terrible vice, gambling, and was what Yaquis call an "Onnauha." This would sound to you very much like "on now" and is a title for one who never wins but always gambles. One day, as it happened, he had lost all his money and some good clothes and a beautiful serape. He was trimmed of all his clothing, this being the reason for his bad appearance.

He was in a wild part of the country, and he saw a woman descending from a nearby hill. He was surprised to see her in the wilderness, and he shivered when the woman advanced toward him. He almost rose to run away, but he thought to do it would be too much. Now, the woman was by his side in a moment, and she asked what his grief was all about. He told her his bad habits had brought him to such a condition. The woman then told him that she would make him a gambler of great esteem. Since the woman was so lovely, Sionima soon was listening to everything she had to tell him. The woman gave him a coin. This he was always to use in his first bet when starting a game, and he would never lose but win always. After all this, she told him to be very careful, that if he would make love to another woman, she would kill him, and if she did not, her brother would do it surely. The woman was lovely, as I said before, and Sionima thought he would never give her up for another woman. He told her this and she was very much pleased.

Now that Sionima had the silver coin, he went into the pueblo and was going to try his new art. He did just as he was advised, and in a moment, he readily realized that everything was true. He was ready to go on to big things, and from then on Sionima was a great gambler. People were astonished to see him as a good gambler and no longer was he called the "Onnauha."

At the end of a year, he had money enough to be among the rich people, and he dressed like them. When he desired to see his lover, all he had to do was saddle his horse and go. He was always doing it, so one day, he told her to come to the pueblo with him. She refused plainly and told him that nothing in the world would make her go. At that time, Sionima, being very young, thought it wise to listen to her rather than to raise an argument. He continued to visit regularly and was very happy, and what's more, he had realized his great ambition.

Now, since he had money, he had many friends and was invited to many parties of the Indians and Mexicans where he was ever in acquaintance with pretty girls. But because he was loyal to his woman in the wilderness, he refused to go into any love affair with another woman.

One day a young Mexican girl asked Sionima why he was so timid among women, and he told her that he thought to deal with women would be to look for trouble. At this the girl laughed and said that he was not man enough to face the trouble. Sionima was greatly disappointed over this and thought that somehow he would prove himself capable of it.

He began to go almost everywhere with the young woman, and she plainly told him of her love. Sionima thought that he was already in trouble, but he also reflected that a little bit wouldn't hurt, so he broke his promise and told the girl that he loved her exceedingly. They continued a few days in their idyll of love. Then he departed again to see his woman. When he arrived, she was angry but received him and told him to quit his lovemaking with the girl and that if he would continue, she would die. She left before the boy did, and he stared after her to see where she would go. Presently she said, "If you want to see me, come tomorrow. I shall be dead, for thy cruelty hast been too much for me." Sionima was frightened — he was staring at a big rattlesnake. He then left and went to see the girl.

The next morning, he went to the place as the woman had told him to, because she told him she would be dead. Upon his arrival, he thought to see the lovely woman, but instead, he found the big rattlesnake right on the spot, and he realized that this snake was the woman. He was frightened and tried to go home, but he was not many steps away when suddenly another big snake bit him, and it was so poisonous that he could not go another step. He died there, right next to the dead snake.

nila northSun

some thoughts

the northwest waits. lush. green. moist, alive. diverse. mountains, valleys, raging rivers, prehistoric ferns, vines entwining, mingling with voices from the past and present. our voices. salmon, carp, skink, eels. grandmother loon. deer, beaver, grandfather raven. coyote, rabbit. us.

our voice. praising, singing, gossiping, telling stories. passing our tradition from one generation to the next. they call it oral tradition. teaching by word of mouth. a good way to share. at one time our brother and sister animals talked. to each other. to us. now we pass on their legends and adventures in our stories. we are part of the land. it is in our songs and prayers. it is part of everyday life. giving and talking with the land. loving. rich dark forests. enjoying.

regions do not have lines drawn by men. then, as now, it is travel and trade. sharing. exchanging.

as our surroundings changed, so did our voice. there are still trees. but there is also logging trucks coming down the road. eagle is almost no more. not many live in willow lodges. TV brightens dark nights. and some of us write.

some still have a very tight hold on the more traditional ways. translations and transcriptions take the old ways. put them on paper. songs & prayers. the old stories passed down so as not to be lost or twisted. stories grandmother told them. we write these while sitting at a table. on a typewriter. trying to remember what they said. others write about what we see now. today. semi-urbanized indians. driving around in a pickup. drinking. looking for the way back.

if one were to attempt to find, among the diversity of contemporary indian writing, a major 'thrust' or 'concern,' perhaps it is to reestablish, within a larger society that all but precludes it, a society linked in harmony with the earth.

perhaps, it is what James Welch is looking for as he leaves town in *Winter in the Blood:*

> I had had enough of Havre, enough of town, of walking home, hung over, beaten up, or both. I had had enough of the people, the bartenders, the bars, the cars, the hotels, but mostly, I had had enough of myself. I wanted to lose myself, to ditch these clothes, to outrun this burning sun, to stand beneath the clouds and have my shadow erased, myself along with it . . .
>
> I walked down the street, out past the car lots, the slaughterhouse, away from Havre. There were no mirrors anywhere.

or perhaps it is what Phil George sees overhead in ''Eagle Feather, IV'' (in SCREE 4):

> Look Up!
> The Spirit is alive:
>> Ermine spots are clouds;
>> Sun streamers are horse hair strands
>> And the red and yellow is for new days
>
> Look Up!
> Eagle is of freedom:
>> Gliding among clouds . . .
>> Catching light of sun . . .
>> Beginning our tomorrows . . .
>
> LOOK UP!

or, perhaps it is both.

(with editorial assistance from Kirk Robertson)

Ray A. Young Bear

THE LAST DREAM

the old man was already well ahead
of the spring, singing the songs
of his clan as well as others,
trying to memorize each segment
and each ritual, the differences
of the first-born, who would drink
the water from the drum, why it was
hard teaching the two-legged
figurine to connect itself
to the daylight, wondering
which syllable connected his body
to that of a hummingbird's,
to have its eyes and speed,
why it was essential to be able
to see and avoid the aura
of bleeding women.

the women's tin huts along
the hill drained the snow of its
water, but the old man knew he
had no regrets. the winter's
visit was much shorter.
the way the bird sat, the way
it cleaned its wings, the way
it breathed, told him he had kept
his distance. the winter had been
friendly. with only one dream
to think about, he collected
the cold bodies of muskrats
given to him by well-wishers
and he carved their bodies
into boats, positioned their
stomachs to the sky, hoping
for snow and subtlety.

it was easy every time his
food ran out to hobble over
to the road knowing he'd get
a ride into town for groceries
and back, making little use
of his cane. the people knew
there were no more like him.
it wasn't unusual for him
to look out his window and see
families bringing whiskey,
bright-colored blankets,
assorted towels, canned
triangles of ham.

his trunks and suitcases were
full with the people's gratitude.
through the summer and fall,
he named babies, led ghost
feasts, and he never refused
whenever families asked him
to speak to the charred mouths
of young bodies that had died
drunk. he was always puzzled
to see their blood seeping
through the bandages, the fresh
oil of their long hair, the distorted
shadows finally catching up to their
deaths. he spoke to suicides just
as he would anyone who had led a peaceful
life. he knew it was wrong
to ask them to go on, but he
couldn't refuse lives that were already lost. everybody
counted on him. each knew that
if they died within his time,
he would be the one to give away
the last dream,
the grandfather of all
dream.

War Walking Near

death designs swirl high above faces that are
    of disbelief.
a captured people dressed in red hold hands and hum
to themselves a strange song.
brown rain slips fast into the old man
who visioned the coming revolution.

he tells to his reflection a small word
not to reveal that in the night
he controls the night enemy
night-enemy-who-takes-us-with-magic-medicine.
he heard the eagle with eyes of war walking near.
they say the spring air comes without much intention.

FOR THE RAIN IN MARCH:
THE BLACKENED HEARTS OF HERONS

i see myself sleeping
and i see other ignorant people
locked securely in their houses
sleeping
unaware of the soft dawn-lit
furbearing animals
wrapping themselves with the bark
and cone from pinetrees
within each of their thoughts
there is the vision
of the small muskrat's
clasped hands
the struggling
black and yellow
spotted body of a salamander
freeing itself from a young
girl's womb

in my dark blue pickup
i came upon a cigar smoking
badger
who invited himself and
later came to my home
gathering chips and splinters
of my firewood and starting
a fire
for an hour we sat
and then he suddenly stood
on his hindlegs and walked
over to the stove
and opened it
he took out two narrow pieces
of burning wood and rammed them
into his eyes
he fell on all fours
and then made rumbling sounds
mocking my pickup with its two
dull headlights
disappearing into
the forest

i dream of a painter
in the desert who tells me
his twisted and contorted
paintings of indians
amuse him because its
the type of stuff whites buy
and enjoy
how i guess they still see us
because his family once helped

the spaniards build missions
in california
at least he knew his parents
were indians
thats what the old man
in the field kept telling us
flower petals crumbled through
his fingers
but we already know how the cycle
goes
the trees and the weeds
quickly grow and decay
in the reflection
of his sunglasses
his lips and teeth are still
stained with coffee and tobacco
the cross-eyed boy
smirked at his remarks
he was impressed
with the mountains anyway
not the seeds that went into
the earth
not with the man-sized fish
who waited each spring
for the river ice
to break up
to feed on the offerings
of miscarriages
he was told and experienced
all in one night
somewhere in canada
the cactus and the medicine
they called peyote
deep inside that night
he thought he knew and he probably
sat through the whole two day ride
back to chicago thinking he was
truly indian
he probably thought it
right up until the moment
he pissed and examined
his shriveled body
in the showers
seeing and feeling for the last time
the bitter green liquid

within each of our lives
as we are growing we are given
and we experience these choices
but it is until later after we have
filled ourselves with bowls and bowls
of another food that we realize we have
chosen the wrong side
i know it will be the same for me

for there was a time last week
when i forgot to bring alive
into someone's mind
a hand reaching into hot boiling
water
a ball of fire bouncing
in front of the yard
in my childhood i can remember
what it felt like to feel the power
and mass of a ship i later recognized
as a spanish galleon
everytime i vomited into
the light-green lard can
i saw the underside of this
ship
sailing past the man who
called to me
he sat back against the black
cardboard wall and whenever he smiled
i could see his coarse white hair
his yellow fingernails

the next time i saw him
a bald-headed hooked-nosed man
in overalls stood in the brilliance
of the summer daylight
the bright green grass reflected
on the linen and the dishes shined
and the aroma of chicken and corn
filled into the nostrils of people
and the mangy dogs who were my pets
watched from under the porch
he will stand in the place
of your grandfather
your grandfather will watch
this day pass through
his eyes
years later he sometimes waved
to me on the road as he drove back
from his soybean fields
he would stand on his tractor
i never knew what he said to me
that one day under the appletree
when he stood in replacement
of my grandfather
i was too busy thinking
about the middle aged man
who lifted up the sleeping girl's
dress that morning:
he was laughing but it sounded
more like grunting
i had just woke and it seemed
like he had been standing over the girl
waiting for me to open my eyes

because the blankets had been moved
to one side of her
he pointed under the dress
he touched and then he clowned and mimicked
and then hobbled out of the house
with a barrel of dishes

from then on whenever i saw him
he did his clown act which always
left me humored
but i will never forget one fall night
ten years ago when the sound of a pheasant
brought us together
through his song i watched
the day and night split in half
inside the electric lightbulb
and through each motion
of my mind and body
i saw a birchtree give birth
to snowflakes
there was a horse
and then a man
they each divided portions
of themselves and then they walked
away as one
the next day without any night's rest
i chopped wood for my grandmother
all afternoon
i imagined the wood as being things
i wanted to rapidly go behind me
there was no room for the mother
who shot her son in the neck
no room for the man who said
he'd pull the trigger on the lives
of six people
all lined up in a row
unless it was completely understood
why he came back

through the screen over the opened
window i felt the small hands
of a toad examining my round
face
the hammock moved within
the toad's breath and when he
walked away boils grew over the places
where it had touched me
it was later explained to me
that i was born the same moment
a baby strangled on its own cord
several miles away
so now whenever i stand in front
of a mirror
i go over the small star-shaped

scars
and tell myself that i will
always be afraid of all those born
before me
i listen for the whippoorwill
directing dwarves to the place
where they will find cigarette butts
the rubber tires of the automobiles
crunch against the rocks
on the road
through the rubble of the fire
of the old blind man's house
all they found was his pink
wooden leg

my mother spilled a box of bullets
on the table
she placed one into an empty coffee can
and poured several capfuls
of grey ash into it
from the window
sparks and the retort of the rifle
spiraled into the blackened hearts
of herons
we looked into the forest
and we saw the silhouette of a pickup
the occasional dim red glow
of someone smoking
it was us in our life ahead
i will never know who i actually am
nor will the woman who lives with me
know me or herself or the children
we want
i am always surprised at how many
different minds drift across
each other
some resenting everyone
some imitating what they will
never be
others make room for others
and then there are us
afraid of everyone because they
are afraid of us
unable to fit anywhere
although we live in apartments
we take weekend drives and visits
to our land with the idea
of getting away from our frustrations
we find ourselves confronted
because of our unity
sisters and aunts blab
within their drinks
when we enter the skidrow taverns
as if they had sat in complete boredom

with nothing to discuss
until they saw us
ordering a couple of beers
from the corner in the dark
restoring everyone's indignation
towards us
we shrug our shoulders
thinking it isn't as bad as trying
to outstare the whites all weekend
but it is
rednecks press their fat longhaired
faces against the window counting us
and i reach into my coat
setting my pistol's safety catch
into fire
it is their daily fantasy
while pouring cement into foundations
or else while scattering cowshit over
the fields of their fathers
to think of themselves finally
secluding me and beating me with their fists
and it is my fantasy to find myself
cornered by four of them
to see the sparks
of my automatic
flashing under their hairy bellies
sirens of police cars and ambulances
whine through the brick alley
they question me
and i tell them it was self-defense
a story they never believe or get tired
of hearing
but the big redhead thinks different
i knew these boys
they wouldn't jump anyone
he turns around and i place
the cold barrel of his .38
behind his pink ear
i squeeze the trigger
and the blood explodes
and splatters everywhere
on the white panel of the ambulance
i create the design and the painting
of his life
i walk away from the wet black streets
of the country town
thinking of my painting
the salamander spearfishing
in the coldest day of winter
for dead fish

coming back i read the poem pow-wow
written by w.d. snodgrass after
visiting my people's annual tribal

celebration
you can't get away from people
who think what they see
is in actuality all they will
ever see
as if all in one moment they can sense
automatically what makes a people
what capabilities they have of
knowledge and intellect
he was only shown what was allowed
to be shown
what the hell did he expect
out of his admission fee?
and as far as he thinking that he knew
more about indians than they themselves did
he should have thought twice
its the same way with the poem
i am a sioux brave, he said in minneapolis
by james wright and countless others
he will never know the meanings
of the songs he heard
nor will he ever know that these
songs were being sung long before
his grandfathers had notions
of riding across the ocean
long before translators
and imitators came
some claiming to be at least a good 64th
grabbing and printing anything
in scrapbook form
dedicating poems to the indian's loss
writing words and placing themselves
within various animals they know nothing of
snodgrass will never know what spirit
was contained in that day he sat above
the feathered indians
eating his hot dog
he saw my people in one afternoon
performing and enjoying themselves
i have lived there 26 years and although
i realize within my life i am incomplete
i know for a fact that my people's ways
aren't based on grade-b movies
and i also know that the only thing
he will ever experience in life
as being phenomenal
will be his lust
stirring and feebly coming alive
at the thought of women
crumbs from the bread
of his hot dog
being carried away
by images of crushed
insects

my father speaks to us
as we sit in the living room
he is in the other room
sketching in detail the face of his father
he'll be there for several days
and we won't see him
we have gone back for the weekend
again
nothing changes
there's not much i can say
to the indian who beats other indians
he lives in his long trailer thinking
he has finally settled into
the land he hardly knows
thinking he will forever
be a man even if my brother and i
make his face bruised and swollen
nothing seeps into people like him
sitting here i can see
his teethmarks on my knuckles
and he has vowed to me
the only thing which will separate us
is death
between coming here to this desk
and going outside this apartment
for fresh air
i spend my time throwing my fists
in rapid succession toward the mirror
i have always been confident with myself
ever since i entered the boxing ring
in des moines years ago
i used to think i was an asshole
stepping into the canvas and now its
no different
i am training for a fistfight
which will be fought in an alley
or out on some country road
against a drunk whose honor
i offended
i didn't make it easy for my father
as my grandmother had told me to
friday night
leave your ill feelings outside
the house
or else you will disturb
or push against him
what he is looking for
while my sisters take turns
combing my mother's hair
we hear him talking within
his room shelling kidney beans
we are with him on his walk
through the fog with wilbur
his cousin

checking the traps along
the river
on the way back they see a young
dismembered body of a girl
scattered for a quarter of a mile
they do not talk to each other
through the whole stretch
of the railroad tracks

a man comes to us
and he greets us and we exchange
kind words with him but we are puzzled
when we find after he has left
that we are still thinking about him
i place a hand in my pocket
and i touch and feel one single bean
for an evening we sit
trying to figure out how
the man placed it there
for each block and section
of color or a shade which
comes close to it
he divides them into several
of the more luminescent ones
the black paint of the tempera
outlines our features
shadows are layers of color
going from darkest to lightest
dead fish pile on top
of one another and the snow
continues towards spring
before the frogs sing
furry-shaped men light their fires
as they wake in their caves
a handsome man paddles by in his boat
and the three women on the shore
of the river frantically wave their arms
to him but he ignores them and he goes
downriver
he is bothered by the thought
of flashing minerals
dates and calendars
how the times remind
him of the russian
messenger

Coming Back Home

somewhere inside me,
there is a memory
of my grandfathers
catching robins
in the night
of early spring.
the snow continues
to gather children
outside, and i think,
as long as they are moving.
the frost sets itself
on the window before
the old man's eye.
we sit together
and imagine designs
which will eventually
vanish when the room
and talk become warm.
he goes over the people,
one by one, and stops
at one, because he can't
find any answers as to why
she took the sacred rattle
and used it, as if she were
one. they do not like her
much, he says. the same old
crowd will be out of
jail soon, and then,
back again. the trees
will be running with
sweet water and hard work
is to be expected.
so we covered everything
with quick conclusions
and sometimes there were
none, better to be left alone.
i pressed my fingers
against the window, leaving
five clear answers of the day
before it left, barking down the road.

4 SONGS OF LIFE

1. a young man

the blue rain
quiet in feelings
losing
nothing—showing no one
that i am cold
in this
earth
singing different songs
i never heard
from the same people
unable
to
create or remember
their own
songs to keep.

2. an old man alone

i remember well
my people's
songs,
i will not reveal
to anyone
that i
know these songs.
it was
intended for me
to keep
them
in
secrecy
for they are now
mine to die with me.

3. one who realized

i sang
to the warm sun
and cold moon
this morning
and offered
myself
to the land
and gods
for them
to
teach
me
the old

hard ways
of living
all over again.

4. he was approached

a time
in sadness
within
the night
holding me
and comforting me.
here i am
being
taught
to be
a man
with life
and old sacred
songs to guide
me
and love me forever

Elizabeth Cook-Lynn

IV

Not everything in the world had to have a beginning because some things
just always were. Some of the Sioux say that Inyan, the rock, is the
ancestor of all beings and all things. Inyan was said to be soft and without
shape and all-powerful until he opened himself and bled and then he
became hard, giving some of his power away. From that time on, the
People could talk of Creation.

V

There was once a Sisseton woman who could converse with rocks, and she
was known among her people for this remarkable ability. Once when a
young white boy drowned in Lake Kampeska his family called upon this
woman in a last resort to locate the body of the unfortunate swimmer. She
came from her home in Browns Valley and walked around the edge of the
lake all night, at dawn indicating where she said they would find the body.
They dragged the lake at that spot and, *ma tuki*, the body was found
exactly where the woman said it would be. When they asked her how she
was able to perform this incredible act she would say only that the rocks
had helped her.

XV

When the Dakotapi really lived as they wished, they thought it important to possess a significant tattoo mark. This enabled them to identify themselves for the grandmothers who stood on the ghost road entering the spirit world asking, "Grandchild, where is your tattoo?" If the Dakotah could not show them his mark, they pushed that one down an abyss and he never reached the spirit land.

XVI

"Wichinchila waste wa luha," he said to her father, lifting his chin at the little girl. You have a good girl there. He said this every time they came, yet the father smiled and was pleased.

They didn't know this man well but, then, nobody did. His name was Jack LaDeaux and his face looked like "twenty miles of bad road," her brother used to say. He spoke French as well as he spoke the dialect of the Tetonais, maybe better and also some English. Her father used to go to LaDeaux's place along the river because he had good sweet corn in July and they could take a wagonload of it home for the women to dry and parch for the winter store.

LaDeaux was a distant man, as unknowable as the land and the past, and few of the Indians around socialized with him. He wore the leather beaded moccasins and leggings old Sioux women made, but there was no other evidence that he had a woman. Otherwise, he seemed to live alone with two bird dogs who yelped and moaned and cried whenever someone came into the yard.

He was a strange figure, walking everywhere he went, apparently not coveting the horses in which Sioux men took pride and he was never without a hunting rifle at his side. It had the longest barrel the little girl had ever seen.

Her father would sit on the ground and smoke with LaDeaux while she and her brother took their time loading the wagon full of corn. He would tell her father rumors of the bone keeper's feast out near the Black Hills, and when the corn was nearly loaded they would all share the strong coffee he always made.

If they didn't see LaDeaux for many weeks it seemed as natural as when they saw him frequently. But one October morning, she awoke early and heard her father talking quietly to her grandmother about something which had frightened him during the night. She followed him outdoors and watched as he looked up at the feather-plumed clouds in the sky and the motion of them seemed somehow ominous. Without understanding, she knew that something terrible had happened. Under her breath she spoke LaDeaux's name and her father said, *"Cheya sni yo,"* but she hid her face and cried anyway, ashamed that she couldn't help herself.

There was no sound except that of the wagon wheels as they rolled over the hard earth into the barren yard, the dogs strangely silent, crouching in the dark places under the porch, the flies unseasonably thick around the door. She stayed in the wagon, fearful of death, and watched her father go inside the cabin. He was still there when men from the agency came and stood outside the door and they all waited for her father's song to end. When they brought LaDeaux out her father was carrying the old breed's long-barreled rifle and, oddly, his tobacco pouch. LaDeaux was wrapped in many blankets and his face had been painted, "so they will know who he is," her father told her. She never saw the bullet hole nor did she know until much later that he had been dead and alone for nearly two weeks.

XVII

WHEN YOU TALK OF THIS

Wine-puffed
lesions
below the eyes
won't tell what dreams are

> *Christ, I'm*
> *sick!*
> *Oh, Christ,*
> *I'm sick!*

Roused from
acquiescent
torpor
his gestures seem bizarre
raking garbage
from shiny tins

Don't say
he didn't remember
he'd shot his brother
and why
Say:
his children loved him
and his wife
was a good and faithful woman.

I

THE BARE FACTS

The spirit lives
when it moves and sings your name
when grandfather and coyote keep warm
together, and lizard gets damp
from the earth, stays fast and hard to kill,
when lark flies straight and high to clouds
and you hear the buzzard weeping under blankets,
when butterfly still talks to women,
when ants will fight and die to carry stones,
seedlike and shiny, from mound to rattle,
when we hang by fingernails, remote and hidden,
at the ridge of words.

The end comes quick
when cricket tells us everything
he knows.

XXII

THE LAST REMARKABLE MAN

Old Hunka* of the people
your scarred breast
grows soft and translucent
in blue-gray photos on the wall
in oval frames, hidden under dust
A man to be remembered
your ancient tongue warms men
of fewer years and lesser view
You tell of those who came, too busy fingering lives
with paper to know what they can't know,
    They liked the oratory but thought the case was
      hopeless:
    go home, old Benno, it loses something in
      translation
    drink the wind and darken scraps of meat and bone
    stars won't rise in dreams again
Heads bent to clay-packed earth,
we smoke Bull Durham for bark of cedar
but know: in council, talk's not cheap
nor careless in its passing. The feast
begins with your aftervision, ahead of its time.
    We speak of you in pre-poetic rite.

*An Ancestor; *hunka lowanpi* is a rite of the Dakotapi called The Making
of Relatives.

XXIII

JESUS SAVES or DON'T ASK ME TO JOIN AA
AND BE A FOOL

I told you once, there is a trend
toward sounding senseless, as it were,
I think I'll sing a forty-nine* instead.

The second, third and fourth descend,
I should be sober, to be sure,
I told you once there is a trend

toward seeking vision, faceless end
but fools are fools, we all concur,
I think I'll sing a forty-nine instead.

The question is: Do you defend,
bear witness to a false quick-cure?
I told you once there is a trend

and you're as sick as I, my friend,
though songs of Passion, hearts bestir
I think I'll sing a forty-nine instead.

You want for me what's in your head
but what's in mine I must prefer,
I told you once there is a trend
I think I'll sing a forty-nine instead.

*The forty-nine song is a contemporary art form popular among young
people, sung mostly at intertribal powwows to the accompaniment of
drums. They are drinking songs, social songs, casual and extempor-
aneous, and they often express humorous or absurd themes not meant to
be serious though sometimes they are.

Robert L. Perea

DRAGON MOUNTAIN

Dragon Mountain did look like a reclining monster from a distance. I
gazed toward it as our jeep made its way through the winding road from
Pleiku. The mountain's eastern end looked like some sort of huge tail,
while the western end resembled a giant head. The head of the big
monster faced the Cambodian border. A Cambodian mountain range
could be seen probably sixty or so kilometers away. I was wondering if
there were any local legends about the mountain, it seemed so
awesome. I could imagine the big mountain reaching out and striking
down anything coming from the West. I was getting an eerie feeling
looking at it, so I turned to catch a glance of the LEPER COLONY sign
off to our right as we went by. None of us had ever made the turn off up
the dirt road that led to the leper colony.

"Bet ol' Charlie never bothers them," said the lieutenant as we hit a
bump in the road. He was seated in front.

"What, sir?" said the first sergeant who was driving.

"Those lepers. That leper colony. Bet no Viet Cong have ever
attacked that place."

"They'd be crazy to, sir," said the first sergeant.

Now the big mountain loomed directly over us. We were in its
shadow. I got the same strange feeling looking up at it.

But the mountain was important to us from a military standpoint. Our
engineer battalion was extending the road south from Pleiku, and the
road building camp was out of radio contact with our base camp at
Engineer Hill. The big mountain was the highest point for miles around
and perfect for a radio-relay station. Although the base camp could not
make radio contact with the road-building camp directly, both could
make contact with Dragon Mountain which was located almost dead

center from each site. That would be my job, relaying radio messages from each site.

As we approached the winding dirt road that led up the mountain's side, a group of Vietnamese, mostly old men and women, rushed our jeep, trying to sell us what they had. Their main customers were usually convoys that passed by.

"You like? Very nice souvenir," said an old mama-san holding up a handful of cheap peace medallions.

"You got M.P.C.?" said another, referring to the military script we used in Vietnam. "Maybe you got chop-chop? We trade?"

"Here G.I., I give you good buy," said a third old lady as she shoved a pair of Ho Chi Minh sandals into the first sergeant's face.

"Say, these ain't bad. Made from old tires, how much you want?" said the first sergeant.

"Five hunret piastre, or three dollah M.P.C.," answered the old lady, smiling, her teeth blackened from chewing betel nut. "You buy? Very nice."

"Let's get outta here," said the lieutenant, half-yelling. The small, noisy crowd was starting to irritate him. "We haven't got time for this kind of stuff!"

"Sorry, mama-san, but we gotta dee-dee now," said the first sergeant.

"You cheap, you no good, you numba' ten," the old lady answered, looking rather dejected.

"You numba' fuckin' ten," added an old papa-san who had been watching everything.

"Step on it!" yelled the lieutenant, and we left the crowd in a small cloud of dust as we headed up the side of the mountain.

It took us about three or four minutes to drive up the winding road. Near the top was a small hut where a Vietnamese sentry stood. He waved us by. On one side of the mountain top lived three squads of Vietnamese infantry whose job it was to keep control of the mountain and protect our radio-relay station. Every night about twenty of them would stand guard and patrol the base of the mountain.

We drove past some wooden barracks and then headed to the other side of the mountain, pulling up in front of the radio-relay hootch. I'd been up here before to help bring the same type of supplies we now had in the jeep: C-rations, water, and gas for the generator.

"Hey Busby! Get your ass out here and give us a hand," yelled the first sergeant. Out of the hootch stepped a tall, well-built, boyish-looking private.

"Good to see ya. We're getting low on gas," was Busby's reply as he came over to help us.

It took us about ten minutes to unload everything. Afterwards we stood near the doorway drinking water and catching our breath. I noticed how really simple the whole set-up was inside. There were two bunks and on a table, two radios. The hootch was rather small, twenty by twenty feet, I imagined. One of the radios was set on the frequency of the base camp and the other set on the frequency of the road-building camp. There was a switch device that connected the two frequencies, but because it often didn't work, most of the actual relaying was done by voice. With a hand microphone in each hand, the job consisted of receiving a message in one radio and repeating it into the other radio. So while the base camp and the road-building camp could exchange messages, the only voice each ever heard was that of the relay-operator on Dragon Mountain.

I walked out back. There was an even smaller hootch where a small store of hand grenades, smoke grenades, flares and M-16 rounds was kept. The generator that supplied power for lights and for the radios was also out back.

The view was fantastic. The Central Highlands of Vietnam could match scenery with any place I'd ever seen. It was a soft, beautiful green as far as the eye could see. It reminded me of the Black Hills in the summertime, what had once been the land of my mother's people. My father's people of Northern New Mexico would have also appreciated the beauty. Off to the north, I could make out the outlines of Pleiku, a distance of five clicks or so. A few kilometers to the east was a Montagnard village. The beauty of the view held me spellbound as I stood there gazing. It made me think that my two months up here might not be so bad. Besides, there would be even less stateside-type bullshit up here. At base camp, we rarely saluted, rarely shined our boots and never had inspections. Up here, it would be even better. As long as there was somebody at the radios twenty-four hours a day, we would be pretty much on our own. It would be Busby and myself—Specialist Fourth Class Ernest Rodriguez—with three squads of soldiers from the Army of the Republic of South Vietnam—ARVN's for short—protecting us.

*   *   *   *

After a few weeks we had a routine going. One of us would watch the radios and generator in the daytime, while the other would do whatever he wanted. I liked to hitch-hike from the bottom of the mountain into our base camp on Engineer Hill, about five clicks north of Pleiku. It was my only chance to get a cold beer and take an equally cold shower. I would get rides with whatever came by: trucks, jeeps, track vehicles, anything that moved and had room. The only thing I had to worry about was being back before dark. The Central Highlands was ours by day, but ol' Charlie owned it at night.

I was working the radios when I heard an explosion outside, but I wasn't too startled.

"Damn it, Busby, quit wasting grenades!" I yelled, sticking my head out the doorway of the hootch.

"We got plenty," Busby yelled back.

"Well, just make sure nobody's comin' up the mountain when you throw them."

Busby had been in the Army almost three years, counting the year he'd spent in Leavenworth for punching out a major, and he was still trying to make it past private. He did happen to be the acknowledged company expert on fixing generators. He also had a knack for getting extra supplies from base camp, especially cans of pork and beans, which was about the only tasty thing in the C-ration boxes. So I tried to ignore his war games.

His height, about six foot two, was also an asset because it kept away the ARVN soldiers. He was twice as tall as most of them, or so it seemed, and the ARVN soldiers were somewhat in awe of him. They used to pester us for C-rations, cigarettes, coffee, and whatever else they saw that we had. Busby put an end to that.

The only Vietnamese we allowed into the hootch without first knocking was Sergeant Le Trung Minh. Sergeant Lee, as we called him, was sort of our liaison with the other ARVN soldiers because he spoke English. He was our friend and he had helped us when we needed it. Once, when lightning struck our hootch and burned out the wiring, Sergeant Lee showed us how to rewire everything.

Just then, Sergeant Lee walked in with Busby.

"Hey, Sergeant Lee, how are you doing? Have a seat."

"Got cigarette? I all out," he said.

"Sure, we got bou-coup. Busby just brought up a couple boxes of C-rations, so help yourself."

"Winston taste good, like cigarette should," he said, taking a big puff and smiling.

"Hells-bells, where'd the fuck you learn that?" said Busby.

"Oh, I read in American magazine when I in Cam Ranh Bay hospital," he answered. Sergeant Lee had told us about his month stay in the American Army hospital at Cam Ranh Bay. He used to be a paratrooper, and during one jump, he landed in a patch of pungie sticks. One pungie stick ripped a big hole in his foot and he had to be medevacked to Cam Ranh Bay. He had a few other battle scars, but the huge ugly scar on his right foot was his real pride.

"Won' see big scar again?" said Sergeant Lee, pointing to his foot.

"That's alright," said Busby, "we've seen it enough times already."

"Sergeant Lee, it sure seems like it's been quiet at night lately. Have the patrols been goin' out?" I said, changing the subject.

"Yes, but no see nothing. O.K. by me," Sergeant Lee answered.

"Me, too."

"It's kinda boring, if you ask me," added Busby.

"Well, nobody's asking your sorry ass. You want to be a gung-ho hero and end up like those ARVN soldiers we see begging on the streets of Pleiku? Their arms and legs gone?"

"I ain't no gung-ho motherfucker, but I ain't afraid a' no fuckin' gooks either," said Busby. "Gooks don't scare me none."

"What him say? I no bick," said Sergeant Lee.

"You shouldn't use that word around Sergeant Lee."

"You heard him. He just said he don't understand what it means," answered Busby.

There wasn't much traffic on the radios, just commo checks, so we sat around and kept talking. Sergeant Lee was always asking about the States. We couldn't convince him that there were poor people in America. He said they couldn't be as poor as those in Vietnam. The Indians on reservations were probably as poor, but Sergeant Lee still didn't believe me.

"It late, I go now," said Sergeant Lee, getting up.

"Take some more cigarettes from the C-ration box. I never smoke those things."

"Many thank. You numba' one," said the sergeant as he headed for the door. "Night."

"Night, Sarge," we replied.

As we got ready to sack out, I walked over to the radios and turned the volume knob up. If somebody called during the night, we'd wake up.

"You know, Rodriquez, it's kinda strange," Busby said to me as he pulled a blanket over himself, "but I tried to get Wendy to bring up some gals from Pleiku tonight, and she said all the Madam K's she knows were busy." Wendy was a Vietnamese girl, probably no more than seventeen. She lived in Pleiku, but spent most of her time with the vendors at the bottom of the mountain. We never knew her real name and probably couldn't have pronounced it anyway. She was friendly and talkative and rather cute. Wendy never went to bed with G.I.'s, but on occasion brought up some Madam K's to spend the night.

"Did you tell her we've got bou-coup C-rations?"

"Yup, sure did," answered Busby.

"Maybe they were busy."

"It still seems a little goddamn weird, if you ask me," continued Busby.

"Well, nobody's askin' for your doofus opinion."

"Aw, go fuck yourself," replied Busby.

I leaned over and turned off the light. I'd just closed my eyes when I heard footsteps outside the hootch. Sergeant Lee quickly entered. He was shaking slightly and he was out of breath. He had his pistol in his hand.

"What the fuck's going on?" said Busby, as we both started putting on our boots and pants.

"Someone out there, someone out there! I hear someone, I hear someone!" Sergeant Lee said.

"O.K., O.K., sit down and take it easy." I grabbed his arm and made him sit down. He sat on the edge of the bunk and took a deep breath. Busby put a lit Winston in his hand. He took a few puffs and looked somewhat calmer.

"O.K., now who is out there, and where are they?"

Sergeant Lee told us he'd been walking to his hootch on the other side of the mountain when he'd stopped to piss. While pissing he'd heard a noise coming from a nearby abandoned shed. He said he was sure someone was in the shed, possibly a sapper. He'd hurried back as fast as he could without making any noise.

"I'll be right back," I said as I went out the back. I grabbed a few M-16 ammunition clips from the storage hootch and returned.

"Sergeant Lee, where'd Busby go?" I said looking around.

"Him go out front door fast," replied the sergeant.

"That stupid . . ."

I grabbed my M-16 and flipped off the safety. We went out the door and crouched down by the side of the hootch. Sergeant Lee had his pistol ready. We got behind a pile of sandbags. The shed was a couple hundred yards in front of us, but it was too dark to see anything. Just then, we heard rounds go off from the direction of the shed. Someone was running toward us.

"Is that you, Busby?" I yelled.

"Yeah, don't shoot! It's me!" he answered.

He jumped over the sandbags and crouched next to us.

"You stupid . . ."

"I got him! I got the sapper! I got me a gook!" Busby said excitedly. "I yelled for him to come out and then I opened fire on his sorry ass."

"Hold it, what's that?"

"Somebody shoot," said Sergeant Lee, pointing in the direction of the shed. We heard more rounds from that direction. Then, we heard a couple of thuds hit the sandbags.

"They're, they're shootin' at us," said Busby, almost standing up.

"Get down!" yelled Sergeant Lee to Busby. "You dinky-dow or something?" and he hit Busby on the side of the head with his hand.

"I . . . I . . . I . . . I'm sure I got him," stuttered Busby. But before we could say anything to him, Busby got up and started running down the back side of the mountain, leaving his M-16 behind. We heard a crashing sound in the tall grass and knew he'd made it to the woods. They'd never find us there, I thought, as I felt the panicky urge to run, too. But Sergeant Lee grabbed my arm.

"That no good, Busby not smart," he said.

"You're right," I answered as the urge to run left me. More rounds started coming. We ducked down. Sergeant Lee asked me where our grenades were and I told him out back.

More rounds started whizzing overhead. More thuds could be heard hitting the sandbags. The feeling of panic started coming back.

"I'll go get some grenades," I told Sergeant Lee. But I couldn't move. My right leg was shaking. I couldn't control it. I didn't know what to do. The leg just kept shaking. Sergeant Lee looked at my helpless condition.

"You shoot, I go get grenade," he said. I saw him low-crawl back to the small hootch. He came back a few seconds later with some grenades. I'd managed to get off a few rounds even though my leg was still shaking uncontrollably.

Then we heard some voices. Somebody was yelling in Vietnamese from the shed. I asked Sergeant Lee what they were saying.

"Them our ARVN soldiers," he said. "Them say G.I. shoot two ARVN soldiers in shed."

"Ask them how they know it was a G.I.," I said, my leg finally stopping. Sergeant Lee yelled back and got a reply.

"Them say one ARVN soldier dead, other wounded, but still live. Him hear American words before bullets come."

"Goddamn that stupid Busby!" I said.

"What we do now?" said Sergeant Lee.

"Sergeant Lee, they're not after you . . ."

"No sweat. I stay and help G.I.," he replied. If I make it out of this, I thought, nobody will believe me when I tell them an ARVN soldier didn't run.

"Ask them to hold their fire. Ask them to give us a few minutes." Sergeant Lee yelled again and the ARVN's answered.

"Them say O.K., but in tee-tee time them come and get us," Sergeant Lee explained.

I went inside the hootch and grabbed the hand-mike to one of the radios. I could barely hold on to it, my hands were so sweaty. I noticed the sweat was dripping from my forehead and my jungle fatigues felt clammy. I was completely soaked in sweat.

"Whiskey-Mike Two, this is Relay-One, do you read me? over."

"Read you loud and clear, over," was the answer from the base camp.

"Where's Four-Niner? over."

"He's right here, over."

"Put him on, right now. It's urgent, over."

"Roger, over."

"Go ahead, Relay-One. This is Four-Niner, over," said a voice I recognized to be the lieutenant's.

"My partner shot some friendlies. One's dead and the rest are after us. What do I do? over."

There was a silence. Outside I could hear Sergeant Lee yelling something to the ARVN's. I repeated the message to the lieutenant.

"Hold it a sec', I'm thinking, over," was the lieutenant's answer. A few seconds passed.

"Did you tell them they can't do this. We're on their side. We're here to help them, over," the lieutenant finally said.

"Roger, out."

I threw down the hand-mike in disgust, grabbed my M-16 and went back outside to where Sergeant Lee was crouched to face the worst. He'd stopped yelling.

"You got twenty-five dollah M.P.C.?" said Sergeant Lee.

"What?" I answered in surprise.

"You got twenty-five dollah M.P.C.?" he repeated.

"Yeah. Why?"

"ARVN's say for twenty-five dollah M.P.C. and two case C-rations everything be O.K.," the sergeant said.

"You're kidding?"

"Twenty-five dollah and two case chop-chop," Sergeant Lee said for the third time.

"Tell 'em yes. Tell 'em hell yes! Tell 'em fuck yes! Tell 'em they can have the radios if they want 'em. Tell 'em they can have the whole goddamn hootch if they want it!"

Sergeant Lee yelled back.

"Them say call for medevac chopper," the sergeant said to me.

"Fine, fine, we'll do it. They can bring the wounded ARVN to the hootch if they want. We've got some first aid stuff inside that might be of some help."

I ran inside to radio for a medevac while Sergeant Lee yelled to the ARVN's again.

I came back out. In a few minutes we heard footsteps. My M-16 was ready, just in case. Two unarmed ARVN's appeared out of the darkness, carrying a wounded man. We helped carry him into the hootch and put him on a bunk. His leg looked badly shattered and was covered with blood. He was in great pain. Sergeant Lee tried cleaning the wound, while I handed one of the ARVN's twenty-five dollars in military script. I pulled out a half-empty bottle of whiskey from beneath my bunk and poured some of it down the wounded ARVN's throat.

The radio started blaring. The medevac was radioing in to say that they were approaching the mountain. I went outside and let off a couple of flares. The blinding light made day out of night. The whole sky seemed to light up. A couple of minutes later the whooshing sound of the chopper could be heard overhead. It landed and two medics came running from the chopper.

"You guys awright."

"Yeah," I answered, "but there's two who aren't. One's inside."

The medics put the wounded ARVN on a stretcher and carried him to the chopper. I had to keep a hand on my bush hat, because it seemed like we were in the middle of a small wind funnel. I sent up another flare as the medics returned.

"What about the other one?" one of them said.

"I think he's over there by that shed," I said, pointing.

"Be right back," said one of the medics as he took off in a slow jog toward the shed. In less than a minute he was back.

"Top of his head's missing," he said nonchalantly. "You wanna check it out?" he added, smiling.

"No thanks," I answered. My stomach was starting to feel uneasy.

Sergeant Lee and I watched the medics get back into the chopper. The wind funnel subsided. We walked back into the hootch and got two cases of C-rations and all the cigarettes we could find and handed them over to the ARVN's. They left and I made a quick call to the base camp to tell them everything was O.K. and to send someone up in the morning to take Busby off the mountain.

"Sergeant Lee, you can use Busby's bunk if you're too tired to head back." He did look awfully tired. I felt completely exhausted myself.

"We no go look for Busby?" he said.

"He'll come back in the morning, if he's not in Saigon by now."

I reached out my hand and offered a handshake to Sergeant Lee. "Thanks," I said. "Thanks a lot."

"No sweat, G.I.," he said, smiling. "You numba' one anyway."

"Yeah, but you're number fuckin' one!"

Marnie Walsh

Angelina Runs-Against
Pine Ridge, So. Dak.

I got wine
a whole bottle
and i just set here
in the weeds
by the depot
and drink my wine
its too early
for them soldiers
and their fuckin
dollars
so i drink my wine
and wave at the trains
but nobody ever waves back

i never got money enough
for a ticket home
only for wine

Vickie Loans-Arrow
1971

1
when my aunt nettie was a kid
she stole real good
from out the stores
beads rings   easy things
stole more hard stuff later
the police catch her sometimes
but she so little
with soft eyes
they dont do nothing to her

2
but her papa beat her bad
to teach her good
and put her in catholic school
her mama cried at that
but nettie learnt everything
so easy that they say
she must come to college
and she did for a while

3

my aunt nettie was real pretty
when little and when she come home
she got a baby after a time
but give it away
then it seem she dont feel
like doing nothing
dont feel like stealing
just fools around
gets drunk
and screwed

4

sometimes she like to tell me
what all she done in college
she dont tell though
why she come home
nathan say she stole money
and got throwed out
i remember one time special
she told me some poetry
she liked   told it soft
about love and some lady in a tower
by a lake

5

when aunt nettie got too drunk
she told poetry
and oh she knowed it good
but all the people laughed
and she took to crying a lot
wouldnt eat
just drank whisky all the time
dont wear nice clothes
dont go to dances
got skinny and littler
till wasnt much left of her
no mama to care an no papa to beat her
they dead and her alone

6

yesterday they find her
all crazy
screaming and naked
she say she lost
and cant find her tower
by the lake
some people take her away
but not her poetry
i stole it
and she wont miss it   where she went

John Knew-The-Crow
1880

I saw a blue-winged bird
sitting silent in the marsh,
his brothers flown away.
Ice grew among his feathers.

I saw a snake
in the forest rock.
She gave me warning, I gave her none;
I wear hers against my breast.

I saw the buffalo in rut.
They could not see me
for the earth ran away into the sky,
and the sound carried off the sun.

I saw the turtle on the grass,
too big, too blind to move.
His neck died beneath my ax,
but the claws walked on toward the water.

I saw my mother and my father die,
and the soldiers took me away.

Bessie Dreaming Bear
Rosebud, So. Dak., 1960

we all went to town one day
went to a store
bought you new shoes
red   high heels

aint seen you since

June the Twenty-Second

Down in the thickets
the locusts are sewing
their shrouds as the spiders
spin snares of lace;
and deep in the shadows,
lunching on lizards,
lies the goldenskinned buttontailed snake.

And in and beyond them,
under and over the grass and the dirt,
sober and somber, blundering blindly,
ants dig their tunnels
diverse in the earth;
hasty and rude, desperate for food
to nourish their seasonal race.

While out in the meadow
atop the blue clover
a dragonfly chooses her lover.

The Red Fox

A winter day on the prairie
finds me in a bus
going nowhere
though a nowhere
of grey snow
the bus grey also
only the road ahead
real enough
to lead somewhere

It is cold
prairie cold
and the prairie runs grey
up hills not there
runs over the bus and down
crossing the dark windrow
following us

My breath is a wet
circle of existence
against the window
through which I glimpse
the fox
sitting in his singular sunset
the wind sleeking his fur

King Kuka

DREAM SEEKER

Only darkness existed,
A mingling of burnt umber with prussian blue
in their purest form.
All this in a noonday sun.
Heat glorified to an intense burning,
Hotter! HOTTER!
Hot turned cool
like the late evening chill.
I shivered.
My eyes held on the lower rim of the Sun.
Explosions flashed before me and
brown and blue turned black!
Soon a vision.

Silence!

Peace!

Serenity . . .

Quietly from the distance I saw . . . appearing . . .
A bleached buffalo skull painted with ochre dots.
Three red spots danced on the forehead and
red stripes radiated from the eyes.
A sun symbol. A Diety.
Then I heard his voice.
A bass voice that echoed through
the canyons from where he appeared.
He said to me,
"You have nothing to fear."
Then he faded away.

MOUNTAIN SPIRITS

We are rocks
prairie rocks
scattered far and wide, wandering, searching
We are rocks
all sizes, shapes
many faces, people
always were, always will be . . .
Hunting in the mountains, sleeping on the prairies

loving beneath the stars
We hear the grass grow around us
smell the perfume of sage, see into our own eyes
We are the river rocks
washed clean, pure
Holy in a Sweat Lodge
the only time ever and forever . . .
We are the Buffalo Rocks
carriers of the spirit, messenger to Natosi
always was
always will be . . .

Minerva Allen

Returning from
scouting for meat.

Smoke hangs
low around the camp poles.
There will be fasting
and offering. The sweat lodge
will be ready.

The smell of sweetgrass
comes from the
opening of the lodge.
The pipe is offered upward
then to the ground, next
to the four winds.

Sweetgrass smoke plays
over the weapons for the hunt.
Buffalo horses are brought in
and picketed close for the run.

If the Great Spirit pities us
the hunt will be successful.
Getting ready for the hunt is
man's chief task. The buffalo
is used. It is the meaning
of life.

A warm sunny day,
We traveled for suns
through rain & storm.

now we reach the big water.
Horses are tired, so we rest.

My friend, our food is gone.
Who will try to find food?
I have looked up and down big water;
no sign of food anywhere. I am weary
I sleep. My friend, my stomach
talks. At last a snake.

No! My friend, do not eat the snake!
The snake is bad medicine. Sleep, my
friend, and your stomach will stop talking.

Dawn comes cold and gray. My friend,
my friend, where are you?

Here. Look down here.

Why? Why did you eat it?

This was my misfortune.
Go, my friend, I will help you across
the big water. Every time you come,
leave me something to eat and I will
lay across the big water for you to
cross on my back. Don't feel bad;
this is fate. Go and tell my people;
I have joined the Snake People.

In the lodge where no one lives,
the spirit of what had been
roams with the whispering wind.
The tipi flaps whip
with each gust and rain pours down the
hearth—where once a tripod stood and
a fire of buffalo chips burned.
The wind plays tag through each hole
where each stone has rolled away.
As it goes whistling, moaning, it's a
lonesome song, flapping and cracking
on decayed bodies
like spirits of the past trying to break out and
walk to the west.

Dog Soldier renounced life
to the One who causes things.

Dog Soldier was wounded
and left handicapped.
He felt envious,
and remained unfulfilled.

He can do the utmost damage.
He races toward the enemy.

The entire camp cries.
They lay him on his scaffold
tying his sashes,
drums, rattles
and medicine bundles
to a pole.

He is left alone
to blow in the breeze
to the One above.

Gladys Cardiff

THE SHOELESS MAN

In the alley, even now,
sheer blackberry vines curl their toes,
poised like divers
curving down to the blue harbor
where a grey freighter and white ferry
pass port to port.
Dreamlike, a pile of cardboard and broken bottles
rises and falls, taking shape,
as if the man lay there yet, twisting and turning
in his shoeless stupor.
Up the hill his friend is just now rounding the corner
to come upon him with kicks and yells
telling him to move on.
As it is with store windows and mirrors,
the quick glance catching your face
apart from you,
for one long heartbeat
my face was his.
I shook in my stockingfeet
despair twisting and turning inside me.

SHOELESS MAN II

She plucks his black irises,
adds them to her eyes;
flared nose, sloped cheek, wedge lip,
a triangular mask,
she slips over her face;
her hair is now black, black hair
with a fine patina of dust;
green glass sparkles like cat eyes
around her bare feet;
she dreams of shoes to wear,
shoes, that with each step,
would give her land.

LONG PERSON

Dark as wells, his eyes
Tell nothing. They look
Out from the print with small regard
For this occasion.
Dressed in neat black, he sits
On a folded newspaper
On a sawhorse in front of his blacksmith shop.
Wearing a black suit and white, round-brimmed hat,
My father stands on one side, his boy face
Round and serious. His brother stands
Like a reflection on the other side.
They each hold a light grasp on the edge
Of their daddy's shoulder, their fingernails
Gleaming like tiny moons on the black wool.
Each points his thumb up at the sky,
As if holding him too closely, with their whole hand,
Would spur those eyes into statement.
Coming out of a depth known as dream—
Or is it memory?
I can see inside the door where the dim shapes
Of bellows and tongs, rings and ropes hang on the wall,
The place for fire, the floating anvil,
Snakes of railroad steel, wheels in heaps,
Piled like turtles in the dark corners.
Long Person, you passed a stone's throw away from his door,
Your ripples are Cherokee prayers,
You carry the hopes of this nation within your banks,
You and he are alike, you are contained histories,
You are a generation of yet unbroken channels.

COMBING

Bending, I bow my head
And lay my hands upon
Her hair, combing, and think
How women do this for
Each other. My daughter's hair
Curls against the comb,
Wet and fragrant—orange
Parings. Her face, downcast,
Is quiet for one so young.

I take her place. Beneath
My mother's hands I feel
The braids drawn up tight
As a piano wire and singing,
Vinegar-rinsed. Sitting
Before the oven I hear
The orange coils tick
The early hour before school.

She combed her grandmother
Mathilda's hair using
A comb made out of bone.
Mathilda rocked her oak wood
Chair, her face downcast,
Intent on tearing rags
In strips to braid a cotton
Rug from bits of orange
And brown. A simple act,

Preparing hair. Something
Women do for each other,
Plaiting the generations.

FISH DOCK — PORT TOWNSEND

I.

To wait at the fish dock
on an overcast day
when the elements reverse as
rain-swollen air balloons
like the sea around a deep hole,
the spiral wind rushing like quick waves
around it, is to wait as if in another time
when sentinel wives leaned out from rock ledges,
hearing the herring gulls *hiyah . . . hiyah . . . hiyah* as
the voices of children on the beach.

The crane, an iron question above us,
dangles a bucket from its one tooth,
toadies up to the Bountiful like a beggar.
In a pink surf cod overcomes baitbox,
cockpit, spills under the dripping net.
Here and there flounder glisten, shiny mud.
Solitary, a cabezon plays air;
its blue mouth a tuneless concertina.
Odors of salt and sweat, oil and iodine
stick like fish scales to our noses and mouths
as we call "Good catch, good catch."
Using their gaffs like forks the fishermen
put away their catch, sluice out
the garnishment of red weeds,
The cabezon, like a god unrecognized,
is born away still singing his silence.

nila northSun

what gramma said about how she came here

i guess i'll tell you how we came here
when i was a young girl my
family lived in duck valley
my older sister was supposed to get
married to this young man
but they waited
then he saw me &
liked me better
but she was older &
was supposed to marry first

one day he rode up to the house
i was outside hanging clothes
he scooped me up on the horse
& ran away with me
that is how we got married

we had to move away
we came here to fallon
we were the first ones here
it became the paiute-shoshoni reservation
that is how we came here

what gramma said about her grandpa

he was white grandpa
his name jim butler
he's good irish man
he was nice talk our
language
big man with moustache
boss of town
tonopah
he found silver mine
we still on reservation they
come tell us 'your grandpa
found mine' so
we move to tonopah
he say 'buy anything you want
don't buy just little things
don't buy just candy
buy something big'
that's what he used to say
4th of july he make
a great long table
put sheet over it
then put all kinds of food on it
he say 'get your plate &
help yourselves'
he fed all the indians
he was good man
but then
he marry white woman
& we go back to reservation

what gramma said about her kids

when i asked 'gramma why did you
have so many?'

oh, i don't know
maybe because i wanted my mother-in-law
to like me
i had babies
but they were all girls
1 2 3 4 5 6 7 8 9 10 11
eleven girls
after each one was born
mother-in-law would come to visit
when she'd leave she'd look at all
the dresses hanging on the clothes line
shake her head & say

'when are a pair of pants going to hang
up there?'
she said this after every visit
finally
number 12 was a boy
& i stopped having kids
but by then
mother-in-law was dead

indian dancer

the pow wow circuit has come
to an end for the summer
little brother won big prize money
in the fancy dance contests:
$250 at Fort Totten
$175 at Bismark
$750 at White Swan
in hoop dance contests:
$200 at Tulsa
$275 at Calgary
got a pendleton blanket at a
give away at Crow Agency
got traveling money at Rapid City
got drunk at every pow wow
got loaded at every other
49'd some nights
69'd others
thinks he's better than the
her-many-horses brothers
or boy ladd
or norman new rider
he can kick higher spin faster
stop on a dime & keep his balance
he has more bright blue hackles
more silver sequins more
fluorescent scarves
the biggest bustle the
longest roach the loudest bells
the best beadwork the longest hair
the widest smile
he's a rootin tootin indian
that doesn't do shit when
the pow wow circuit has come
to an end for the summer

moving camp too far

i can't speak of
  many moons
  moving camp on travois
i can't tell of
  the last great battle
  counting coup or
  taking scalps
i don't know what it
  was to hunt buffalo
  or do the ghost dance
but
i can see an eagle
  almost extinct
  on slurpee plastic cups
i can travel to pow wows
  in campers & winnebagos
i can eat buffalo meat
  at the tourist burger stand
i can dance to indian music
  rock-n-roll hey-a-hey-o
i can
  & unfortunately
  i do

how my cousin was killed

by his girlfriend
they were drinking
muscatel had to drive
his old station wagon
off reservation to score
took long deserted dirt
road back
got into fight with
his honey has
to piss gets out
she hops behind steering
wheel back over him
throw it into first
drive over him throw
it in reverse back
over him
back & forth
next day indian police
shovel his body into
gunnysack that
how my cousin was killed

Wendy Rose

To Some Few Hopi Ancestors

No longer the drifting
and falling of wind,
your songs have changed.
They have
become thin willow whispers
that take us by the ankle
and tangle
us up with the red mesa stone,
that keep us turned
toward a round sky,
that follow us down
to Winslow, to Sherman,
to Oakland — to the ends
of all the spokes
that leave earth's middle.
You have engraved yourself
with holy signs, encased
yourself in pumice,
hammered on my bones
til you could no longer hear
the howl of the missions,
the screams in your silence,
the dreams on your wings.
      Is this
      why you made me
      sing and weep
      for you?
Like a butterfly
made to grow another way
this woman is chiseled
on the face of your world.
The badger-claw of my father
shows slightly in the stone,
burrowed from my sight,
facing west from home.

For the White poets
who would be Indian

just once. Just long enough
to snap up the words, fish hooked
to our tongues. You think of us now
when you kneel on the earth,
when you turn holy
in a temporary tourism
of our souls.

With words
you paint your faces,
chew your doeskin, touch
breast and tree as if
sharing a mother were
all it takes, could bring
instant and primal
knowledge.

You think of us only
when your voice wants for roots,
when you have sat back on your heels
and become
primitive. You finish your poem
and go back.

Indian Anthropologist: Overhanging Sand Dune Story

They hope, the professors, to keep
the keyhole blocked
where my mind is pipelined
to my soul; they block it with
the shovel and pick
of the pioneer spirit, the very energy
that made western earth turn over
from her stoney coma and
throw us off her back
bucking and hollering
like stars were whipping her. Mama Earth
is wearing her mask of drought,
is rolling and moaning
to smother the red-hot infant out.
I feel it like a shiver,
like the sop of wet cloth on red skin.
Parts of my soul come again and again
to face north, moss-covered, to
tap their names on my eyes,
to give me a pinch of tobacco, to say
I can go on like this only
if I shut my ears but
keep wide awake in
the eyes.

"There is no more thrilling aspect for the anthropologist than that
of being the first white man to visit a particular native
community . . ."
— Claude Levi-Strauss in *Tristes Tropiques*, 1955

"19 American Indian skeletons valued at $3000; please pay from this invoice . . ." — *museum invoice, 1975.*

Three Thousand Dollar Death Song

Is it
in cold hard cash? the kind
that dusts the insides of mens' pockets
laying silver-polished surface
along the cloth?   Or in bills?
papering wallets of they who go about
threading the night with dark words.
Or checks? paper promises
that weigh the same as words spoken once
between the grown grass of our history and
the hidden water in the clouds.
However it goes, it goes:

through my body it goes. Assessing each nerve,
running its edges along my arteries, planning ahead
for whose hands will rip me into pieces
of dusty red paper, whose hands will
smooth and smatter me into traces of rubble.
It's invoiced now:

how our bones are valued.
Our bones that stretch out pointing
to sunrise or are flexed into one last
foetal bend; our bones — removed
piece by piece and knocked about, catalogued,
numbered with black ink on
their newly-white foreheads. We come apart
as we were formed
having gone together to laughter
of white soldiers, white students,
all the same in our fleshless prison.
From this distant point
we watch our bones   auctioned
with our careful beadwork, our
quilled medicine bundles, even the bridles
of our shot-down horses.

How
have you priced us? At what cost
removed us?
What price the pits
where our bones share a single word:
            remembering . . . still
we don't see how one century
has turned our dead
into something else, what you call
'specimens'. Our blindness
might be catching, you know . . . picture the mortars,
the arrowheads, the labrets
standing up and shaking off their labels

like animals suddenly awake to find
the world went on while they slept;
watch them touch each other, become as one,
march together out the door, walk
into the wind searching for us.
Watch our bones rise to meet them.

At what cost then
our sweet-grass-smelling having-been?
Is it to be paid
in clam shell beads or steatite,
dentalia shells or turquoise,
or blood?

Trickster: 1977

I.
The Trickster's time
is not clicked off neatly
on round dials, nor shadowed
in shifty lengths
on the earth. He counts his changes
slowly and is not accurate.
He lives for his own mess of words,
his own spilled soup. He can see
when you are spread out
and captured and numb and
speechless; when you have stretched
to your limit and can
no more bear to hear the frozen words
circle like ravens above you,
than to see worms grow into songs
from your gut.
He turns to wind, he turns to sand,
he turns walking off with your singer's tongue
left invisible. We'll say he is
the whistling coyote as he steals
all the words you ever knew.

II.
Reach in deep: then leave me
to find the words alone.
The whole world is made up
of words, mountain-thick, that wait
to cave in with edges that squeeze
hurt and reason into separate sounds.
The songs become tons
of bilingual stuff to reckon with.
Tricked: let me not touch the pen.
Let my voice be still . . . let anesthesia ride each nerve.
Let the bones melt into the rain and
disappear; let me disappear
and let those soft bones go.

Soul Tattoos

1. Pain
has its
own warmth;
no different
from that
of fever.
O yes I belong
to pain.

2. Do I paint my fury
in the bones of a beavertail?
Or dampen my soul
in seawater? Why
do my eyes close
when I scream like I was
kissing a form
hanging down from the wind?

3. How do I go around hurdles
that cleverly turn to gas
the moment my legs begin their leap
then kindle
into a brushfire
that links my fingers
with frost?

4. I feel the air thinking.
Something tiny and fragile
forms eddys against my skin
to meet the rainbow-washed bones
sent to feed on me.

William Oandasan

SILENT AFTERNOON

The heat of summer has cracked the soil

Only silt moves in the riverbed

The crops brown in the silent afternoon.

The people search an empty sky

For a symbol, a meaning--rain.

There is only the growing shadow

Of the leafless oak tree.

WHO AM I?

I say to you, my friend,
Of all places in the entire
Universe, I came to life here
On earth--and that's grrreat!
My father sailed from tropical Ilocos Sur
Beside the beautiful China Sea
On the lush, northwesternmost part
Of the Philippine Isles. My mother hails
From Round Valley, the focus
Of her pre-Athabascan culture, high
In the coastal ranges of Northern California
Among the great redwoods where rivers
Rush down mountains to the sea. And I've
Been across the Golden Gate, to Big Sur,
North to Vancouver and Kodiak, and resisted
The diabolical Vietnam War too! But
I have always been here, inside
Myself, a song of heaven and earth.
Here, tonight, at Laguna, New Mexico,
Midst the dry, harsh and hard ancestral
Land of my spouse who is sleeping within
As I sit on an old and wooden porch
Beneath a mid-August moon, marking
These words on this new leaf,
The far flung roots of my tree
Have been taking shape like
Lines of a strange Pacific salmon.

Summer night and her

scent, distilled in morning dew--

the desert jasmine!

3#

from my mouth a song

for warmth pours and becomes

a red arrow, ready

to take me all the way

in the chipped and tattered

weaving of a willow basket

the voice of an older age

sleeps dreaming of breath

NATURAL LAW

Deep in the shade
Of the forest, a hunter,
Armed for survival,
And the victim, an old bear . . . .
He chews bits of bark,
Taking a step at a time,
Upwind, twenty steps from her,
Unaware of the plot. She
Positions her piece, taking aim,
Centering on the heart.
Her finger slides
To the trigger, slowly tensing
To spring the lever.
No one will witness
This killing but trees,
Grass and insects locked
In their own struggles.
Even nature lies
As if asleep,
Powerless in making
A quick end of it
As it is in preventing one.
The light of life,
High above the drama,
Shines on.

ACOMA

For many distant travelers
The way to Acoma is merely
Interstate-40,
A fourlane ribbon
Of asphalt
Squeezed in between wire
Fences and telephone lines,
Running like a scar
Across the flesh
Of an ancient landscape;
They almost never know
The old way south by north
Where you can fly today
From the pit
Of a uranium stripmine
To the sacred Sky City
Standing on top
White Rock Mesa.
Corn and ritual predate
The cradle of history there
Like a breathing shrine,
And the way to Acoma for many
Is only curiosity,
Or a refreshment stop.
But for those who still
Travel the four directions,
The way to Acoma
Is always the way.

Phil George

EAGLE FEATHER I

When I wear a tail feather in
    enwrapped otters
The carrier of prayers and songs
    positions my being erect, alert.

EAGLE FEATHER II

Last summer her solitary center feather
    caught the eyes of every wardancer.

Now she wears twin Blackeagles;
    she cannot grace the Dance of Swans

And her virgin doeskin dress
    is preserved for her daughter.

EAGLE FEATHER III

From over the heart of Medicine Bird
    I select three breath plumes.

Even Coyote recognizes
    Breath Plumes —

    He dare not play tricks on me.

EAGLE FEATHER IV

Look Up!
The Spirit is alive:
    Ermine spots are clouds;
    Sun streamers are horse hair strands
    And the red and yellow is for New Days

Look Up!
Eagle is of Freedom:
    Gliding among clouds . . .
    Catching light of Sun . . .
    Beginning our tomorrows . . .

LOOK UP!

R.A. Swanson

SOLEMN SPIRITS

Fading shadows
of a once
great race
stand quietly
in the backs
of taverns
and huddle
in the
corners of
main street
missions
waiting for
the day
when the
buffalo
will return

we are the warrior
spirits

we fought for our
lands at Wounded Knee
we fought for our holy
lands at Little Big Horn

we ran with your generals
through the fields of France
we raised the flag on Iwo
we died on Bataan and Corregidor

must we die in the cities of
New York and L.A.
Detroit and Seattle?

LONELY WARRIORS

Distant drums call from the mountain tops.
Deep in the concrete canyons of Seattle
And Tacoma lonely ears are straining
To hear the songs of their childhood.

On the main streets and first streets
Of Los Angeles and Spokane homeless
Warriors walk the night to look and
Listen for some trace of other tribesmen.

WELFARE LINE

Patterns for beadwork
form in my mind

i see the finished item
dancing
part of a costume
turning
fast and fancy

a quick spin
a sudden stop

the contest judges
call my name
my day dreams end
when the entry worker
does the same

Ted Palmanteer

Pass it on grandson

Granpa,
    he was a warrior
    wounds and cuts
    were his way,
    he was gruff
    and did as
    he pleased.

He solemnly
    instructed me,
    "If ever anyone
    questions you
    about protection;
    this is what
    you say,
    'Some things
    are passed on
    by blood alone,
    where mine goes
    or comes from
    is no one's concern,
    but my own."
    Way back in '47
    just before
    he took his last
    ride, wrapped in death.

Years later
    in '73
I graduated
from C.W.S.C.,
Went a celebraten'
to Wapato town,
    and Indian bars.
Drinking and dancing!
    Pan's Cigar.
    (place of ill repute)

I made a toast
    on our fresh bottle,
    "Here's to my mom
    and all those
    who are not here
    with us now,
    but once they
    called this place;
    Second — Home.

We laughed
(after a brief moment of silence)
    as I spilled a cap
    of wine
    on the butt-burned
    liquor-soaked rug.

The bottle went,
    "round the horn,"
    as we drank
    from the cold springs.
    (Annie Green Springs)

I was zipping
    along at fast clip,
    dancing with
    some chik-a-dee
    who was out
    for a par-tee.

When up sidled
    this old lady.
I knew I was, (in the presence),
    about to get the lean on.
She burst into
    laughter,
acting shrewd and wise.
(like she had medicine)

(In her guffaw)
She says,
"Teddy, do you remember
that place where
the old folks stayed,
or, were you *too little*.
(Teddy, I thought? Why's she
addressing me as my grandfather?)

I said to her,
    "Of course,
    I remember.
We lived on a hill;
below,
there was a stream,
it bubbled out of the
ground,
down there
where the rattlesnakes
used to lay
by the trail,
in the shade."

(I felt a rush,
feathers rustled,
she was an owl.)

393

The old lady laughed,
"Yes, that's the place.
Remember — that big rock,
to the right
of the old house,
by the cellar?"

"Sure," I answered,
(thinking, what's an
owl, just a mouth full
of feathers, to a
timber wolf?)

She looked perplexed,
(just for an instant),
then,
(like out of the way,
not inquiringly),
mentioned,
"Oh,
that rock always
interested me;
there was brush
all around it
and little quail
would hide there,
right under *that* ledge.
I often wondered,
why, in a place
so full of snakes,
why didn't they
go near that rock?
I was up there
just last weekend,
looking around,
now, I think
I've found the answer,
Your medicine is there."

"Yes, (I said, not boasting.),
    I remember people
looking there,
I often wondered
what for?
But,
do you know
what granpa
said to me?"

(a little over anxiously),
She said,
"What, what did
he say?"
(acting like life would return
to her limbs.)

(with some malice and importance)
I answered,
"He said to me,
we moved,
to another hill!"
(couldn't help myself)

A dark cloud
covered her face,
she turned
to glare
at my smiling face,
(more like a
wolfish, mocking grin)
and she understood.

I have the blood,
something
like a hint,
from an
Old Warrior.

Why not rush
into that wind, —
tide, tide, tide,
into that, —
with birds.

Jim Tollerud

EYE OF GOD

Sway song
Chant of the old
Breaths of ancestors
Whisper the shore
Rays of memories
Pass in aurora
Grandfather speaks
of yesterday
The legend moonlight hunts
Oh, morning
My spirit draws near you
The rain clears the air
and my heart feels
the sun
Long ago the waves
were saltier
and the People strong

TWENTIETH CENTURY

Pulse of the waves
Howling wind
Turning tribal rituals
Totemic faces
Hitting crisp hail
Still I'm sad
and I don't know why
Space, inner thinking
Daybreak, sunlight
Rekindle the fire
Things are different
Signed documents of
friendships
Clothing articles
Worn moccasins

RAINIER

Last time around the forest floor
Rain beating on the ferns
Red cedar roots stream with life
Mud puddles reach my shoes
The dust is wet and wind picks up
Country swept of mother guardian earth
Still, I am involved
Searching, searching for my liberty
Sunshine once again
Breathing rays descriptive
Odors of challenge bright motives

THIRSTY ISLAND

War canoes were ready
Sleek, black
Armed with whalebone clubs
The gray heavens
Drifted through sleepy morning
Tears of *theu-kloots*
Gently blessed the secluded island
Sea and cedar smoke
Blended into musky haze
The sea now brushes the shore
And from the tiny village
Sea warriors stir from their coarse sleep
They garnish themselves in cedar robes
And depart their chilled island

Janet Campbell

From The Only Good Indian (a novel-in-progress)

When Mara was eleven years old she could see it coming. She knew that this would be her last year on the home reservation in Idaho.

She was born late in her parents' lives, in her mother's early forties and her father's late fifties. Her sisters were all grown up, married, living far away from home. Her parents' friends were dead or dying or moving away to a less harsh climate or to be near relocated citified sons and daughters. Mara's father was too old to work steady now. He drew social security and V.A. pension, got drunk a lot more often. Her mother, though more than ten years younger than her father, seemed ten years older. Her mother's hair was white, her fingers gnarled and thin. The joints of her knees were deteriorating quickly.

The winter of Mara's eleventh year her mother's arthritis was never so bad. She'd never spoke so often or so longingly of going away from Idaho.

"This is simply no place for a young woman to grow up, Mara," her mother would say, "I want something better for you than this, my darling." She wanted Mara to become educated, she said, to travel, to know many people, to learn all she could and become whatever she chose to become. She didn't want Mara to have a life like so many reservation girls, married at fifteen, six kids already by the time they're twenty, old, haggard, broken-spirited at thirty.

Mara's mother's father had been a white railroad man (her mother was quite white in appearance, although not so much that it was hard for anyone to believe she was an Indian). Her mother had traveled around this country and Canada when she was a child and her father was building railroads. She'd seen a lot of the world beyond the boundaries of the reservation.

For herself, Mara's mother wanted to be able to see her other daughters as often as she liked and her young grandchildren. She wanted not to live in isolation, to have electricity, hot running water, an oil or gas heater, a washing machine, maybe even a T.V. set. This was 1973, she said, and she was an aging, sick woman who'd earned a few years of comfort before she died. It seemed she mentioned dying a lot that year.

Mara's father had said before, over the years, how this was his land, had been his father's land before him and his father's before him and he would not ever go away and leave it. He'd lived away from this land before, as a soldier, then as a prize-fighter. He didn't like what he saw. Mara's father didn't say this at all that last year. That winter, when Mara's mother's arthritis was "acting up" particularly much, her father told Mara something one day as the two of them drove back from town. He told her how beautiful and wonderful her mother had been.

"She was so tall and graceful, stood so straight. She was my brother's wife's friend. They went to Mission School together. Her skin was so

398

pale and smooth, her eyes big and green. Her hair was coal black. And she was, is, thirteen years young than me, Mara, only twenty when we met. All the men were crazy for her. She could have had anyone, just any man she wanted for her husband. But she married me. And look what I did. I made her live way out here in the sticks. You know, I delivered all our babies myself with no help at all. She should have had a doctor. Two were stillborn. Your mom's a good woman, Mara, a good woman."

That spring, when she was twelve, Mara had grown to what would turn out to be her full adult height of five feet nine inches. She was by far the tallest person in her class at school and she worried about her future, imagining herself an eight foot tall woman. She began, too, to read a great deal, to daydream and wonder what the world was like outside the isolated little reservation where she was born and had lived all her twelve years.

One overcast day in May, Mara won a red ribbon running the 660 at the St. Mary's track meet and her relay team had won a blue ribbon. Mara went home feeling happy and tired, anxious to show her parents the red ribbon.

She could see as soon as she got off the bus that her father was not home and her heart sank. He would be out drinking again, of course, and her mother would be worried, preoccupied, watching out the window. Mara put the red ribbon in her sweater pocket. She wondered if today had been a good or a bad day for her mother. She suffered so much pain these days. She could only walk very slowly now and needed the help of a cane. This would not be a good time to tell her about the track meet, Mara thought.

Mara found her mother, as she guessed she would, sitting beside the window. She was rubbing the swollen knuckles of one hand with the fingers of the other. It was getting so late, she said. She wondered where that man could be. He was so careless sometimes. She hoped nothing had happened. Oh, how she wished they could get away from that awful Godforsaken place. She had to get away.

Mara split kindling, lit a fire in the kitchen stove, began to peel potatoes. She wouldn't cook, though, unless her father came home. Her mother never wanted to eat anymore. She would make herself a peanut butter and jelly sandwich after a while. She lit the lamps, sat down in a chair near her mother.

Mara listened to the soft voice, hearing not the words anymore but the sound of it, floating in the air. It was comforting, sometimes, to listen as her mother talked. She was almost sleeping when the tone of her mother's voice changed and she began to listen to the words again.

"Oh, I don't know what I'll do when you're gone. I am already left alone so much. I wonder if I will be able to walk at all in another year or so. It just gets worse and worse.

"Sometimes I even, well, think there is something wrong, that I'm losing my mind or something. Today a strange thing happened.

"I was sitting here, going through these things, reading old letters, old newspaper clippings, looking at photographs. I was very tired and sleepy since I had a bad night last night and was kept awake. I must have fallen asleep, I guess.

"I heard these voices coming from the other room, laughing, chattering little voices. I was startled. I didn't know what to think. I could hear them, whoever it was, running around, as if they were chasing each other. I was about to go in there and investigate when they came running in here.

"There were three little girls. I didn't know right at first who these girls were. Suddenly it dawned on me. They were my own little girls, Irene, Mary, and Mara, all so young and small again. Oh, I was happy. You can't imagine how happy I was. They came close to me and I bent down and stretched out my arms to embrace them and when I did this I woke myself up. They disappeared.

"Here I was, sitting all alone again, just like before, just like always. The house was so empty, so so quiet." Mara's mother began to cry. She cried for a long time.

Mara sat across the room and thought of what her mother had just told her, pictured how it must have been. Her mother sat in the big chair by the window, crying. The fire burned low, then went out and the room became cold.

Outside it began to rain, very lightly at first, hitting the window pane in gentle little drops. Mara's mother finished crying, wiped her nose and eyes. She lifted the curtain away from the window and looked out. She peered long into the great darkness.

Our Friend, The Virgin Mary

In my dream
A crippled old woman
Lies on someone's
Shabby back porch,
Lies amid
The trash
And cheerfully
Chatters about
Her friend
The Virgin Mary.
In my dream
The old woman lies,
Her body twisted
And misshapen.
"Mary is kind to
All of us old people."
She is tiny.
"Mary is young now
But used to
Be old."

In my dream,
She in her faded
Cotton print dress,
She with white hair,
Smiles a toothless smile.
"Mary was old
But now she's young,
Such a nice girl.
She was crippled
But now she's whole.
She won't forget
That she was one of us,
Our friend,
The Virgin Mary,"
And, smiling a
Toothless smile,
Lying amid
The trash
The old woman
Closes her eyes.

Mary Tallmountain

Two Poems for Matmiya,
my Athabascan Grandmother.

WHERE BANSHEE WIND IS

Banshee wind
mutters at locked windows.
Desert lightning
slashes the valley. Under
grizzled sky, the air
resounds like iron struck.

Gripped in pincers of light,
earth shudders
at each bellow of thunder.
A writhing wall of dust
crumples and tosses
scarlet blossoms.

Once my People
lived in the Kaiyuh Flats.
Winter dugouts
crouched under a dark polar wind.

Ghostly as memory,
moosehide curtain billows.
Fire flares and gutters
under the smoke-hole.
Squatting silent, fists clenched,
black eyes wild,
Matmiya presses down.

The great belly heaves.
Red-brown hands pull out
the slippery child.
The tending women stop keening,
intent to hear
its first small cry.

"Go-isee dinaa!"—Here's the man!
Medicine Woman holds him high.
Tiny feet lash.
Mouth shrills in surprise.
Gasping, Matmiya laughs:
"Beeyeenholit!"—He's mad!

Banshee wind
hurtles closer in the street,
bearing a smudge
of ochre dust.
Almost upon me it turns:
with heavy steps trudges west.
Silence strums my ears.

SOALT' IN TLEEYAGA*

Sitsoo,
In lamplight
Chewing hide with gleam of teeth.
Matmiya,
My mountain Grandmother.

Small aunt,
I hear you
Talk in falling leaves
Of dying summer.
Crouching by your sister's pallet,
Hands outstretched
While the women chant

For Mother suspended alone,
Harshly breathing the Yukon wind.
"Tend for me your father," you say,
Mother your words
Misty as rain on the river.

I tell you
I will walk in your shoes.
You and he will soon embrace
With Soogha, older brother,
And Kitl'aa', young brother. Ahh,
I want to sing
How Soogha would build a sled,
How Kitl'aa' would play to us
Music for a night of snow.

All I am of woman
Is what you give when you say
to me in dreams:
        "Shadowed we come,
        Whom you thought not to find.
        Once in illness,
        Again in the green heart of our land,
        Now at the rim of the great Mountain."

Gently, tall Mountain
Repeats your words.
Stirs reptilian limbs,
Moves ochre stones
To set a period to the line:
"Wait. You are not alone."

Soalt' in Tleeyaga—
You, my other selves.
Through every feathered pore
Your bright spirits
Inhabit my present shape.
Lead the way
O into the Light.

*Indian Women

INDIAN BLOOD

the blackbird teacher
white claw waving
stalked the stage
I stumbled, my mukluk caught
on a slivered board
(rustle of stealthy giggles)

my midnight mittens of velvet
crusted with crystal beads
dangled from brilliant tassels
of wool wet
with my sweat

the teacher's voice was loud:
"From the land of the Midnight Sun!"
all of them stared at me
for the first time I felt
their flowing force
did she ask me to speak
or did I crouch there like a rabbit
in the curious quiet

somehow at last
it was done
they butted and shoved to the stage
questions darted
            "Do you live in an igloo?"
fingers pointed
            "You eat blubber - Hahaha!"

I was ringed by ribbons and ringlets
hair like brass
grass-pale eyes
I shivered
the silken furs of my parka trembled

in time I got away
and toward night I crept
into a closet
and bit my hand
till it was pierced
with moons of dark

Indian blood

THE LAST WOLF

the last wolf hurried toward me
through the ruined city
and I heard his baying echoes
down the steep smashed warrens
of Montgomery Street and past
the few ruby-crowned highrises
left standing
their lighted elevators useless

passing the flicking red and green
of traffic signals
baying his way eastward
in the mystery of his wild loping gait
closer the sounds in the deadly night
through clutter and rubble of quiet blocks

I heard his voice ascending the hill
and at last his low whine as he came
floor by empty floor to the room
where I sat
in my narrow bed looking west, waiting
I heard him snuffle at the door and
I watched
he trotted across the floor

he laid his long gray muzzle
on the spare white spread
and his eyes burned yellow
his small dotted eyebrows quivered

Yes, I said.
I know what they have done.

Luci Abeita

SQUASH BLOSSOM SHIT AND HEISHI HORRORS

once quietly beautifying

brown chests and wrists as the

yucca and cactus upon a summer's desert

now made quite common and ugly

to be seen from new york's poshest

to the santa fe opera

milled out by factories   japanese

and miss sarah coventry

HONEST JOHN'S SEVEN IDOLS PAWN SHOP

Yah-Tah-Hey Honest John
Where is cherry-tree man hiding
while you sleep
   dreaming of wooden Indians unchaining

    dreaming of wooden Indians transforming
      embarrassed smiles to hate-cold grins
    dreaming of wooden Indians armed
      with your Remingtons smashing
      your showcases and your
      only ticking Timex
    dreaming of wooden Indians cracking
      your round mirror reflecting
      neon COINS and leering
      at your lovely Ivory
      Lady's portrait
    dreaming of wooden Indians chaining
      your white ankles and
      putting you in a case
      becoming a real bargain
      at $14.92
      see how quickly they put
      a sold sign on your chest
      and ship you back home to
      Europe
    dreaming of wooden Indians 49'ing
      in their new 7 Naugahide Idols
      pawn shop with GENUINE
      CITY PAWN authentic Zenith
      televisions & Guaranteed Dow
      Manufactured trash bags

Yah-Tah-Hey Honest John
Where is George Washington hiding
While you sleep dreaming of
    Wooden Indians Unchaining

Dana Naone

HAIR POEM

One morning a woman woke up,
but couldn't get out of bed.
During the night her hair
had grown through the floor.
Her husband tried cutting
the strands loose
only to find that the more he cut,
the more her hair grew.
He dug a hole beneath their house.
There was a man in an underground cave
playing a musical instrument
strung with hair.
Every song made the hair grow longer.
The husband poured water
on the man's head
three times from a chalice
engraved with a bird flying upside down.
The strings of the harp turned white.
The man closed his eyes.

THOUGHT OF GOING HOME

The horses were lying down in the field
when we drove by
and thought nothing of it
even though the birds were lying
on the branches and some were on the ground
where they had fallen
in mid flight.
Evening arrived without bird songs,
but another voice
quickened us and we hurried on
under the spreading night.
One light on in the house
as we approached.
Already on the porch
we could see in the window
the figure of a woman
lying under the white sheets.

GIRL WITH THE GREEN SKIRT

She walks down the road,
her green skirt floating around her knees.

The men she passes peel off their shirts
and jump into her wide green hem.
She keeps walking, her skirt
clear as the surface of a pond.

Now they hold their arms out from their sides
like the branches of a tree, but no one is fooled
when the birds fly past them and nest
in the green forest of her skirt.

Unaware of the hot wind swirling around
the cool skirt keeps going.
The men following behind are thirsty
for the water of crushed leaves.

Falling into the deep grass
they want to live with green forever.

UNTITLED

I make all the poetic pauses
  outside your door,
paying hurried heed to the stars,
thinking, by now, you must be
  catching my moondrift.
Not seeing you for a few days
has put teeth in my fingertips
  when I touch your legs.
The flute of my desire pipes
a tune upon the fingerholes
  of your imagination.
A great bird rises from your chest
with wings that fill the room.

CONTRIBUTORS

LUCI ABEITA — (Kutchin) — poet; born in Alaska in 1953; poems in *New America* and *La Confluencia;* lives in Fort Yukon, Alaska; has published under the names of "Luci Beach" and "Luci Cadzow."

ROMAN C. ADRIAN — (White Mountain Apache) — poet; born in Phoenix in 1950; currently a prisoner at the Arizona State Prison in Florence; published in *Sun Tracks, The New Times* and *Do Not Go Gentle* (Blue Moon Press).

MINERVA ALLEN — (Assiniboine) — poet, short story writer; author of *Like Spirits of the Past Trying to Break Out and Walk to the West* (Wowapi Productions); lives with her husband and children at Lodgepole on the Fort Belknap Reservation in Montana.

PAULA GUNN ALLEN — (Laguna Pueblo-Sioux) — poet, essayist, teacher; born in Cubero, New Mexico in 1939; books, *The Blind Lion* (Thorp Springs Press) and *Coyote's Daylight Trip* (La Confluencia Press); has published in *American Poetry Review, New America, Four Indian Poets* (Dakota Press), and *Sun Tracks;* teaches at Fort Lewis College in Durango, Colorado.

CARROLL ARNETT/GOGISGI — (Cherokee) — poet, teacher; born in Oklahoma City in 1927; seven books of poetry, including *Not Only That, Through the Woods, Come, Tsalagi, Then, Like a Wall* and *Earlier* (all through Elizabeth Press); published in numerous journals; teaches at Central Michigan University.

R.M. BANTISTA — (Kiowa) — poet, short story writer; born in Lawton, Oklahoma in 1952; anthologized in *Arrows Four* (Washington Square Press), *American Indian Prose and Poetry* (Putnam), and *Zero Makes Me Hungry: A Collection of Poems for Today* (Lothrop); currently a student at the University of New Mexico.

JIM BARNES — (Choctaw) — poet, editor, teacher; born near Poteau, Oklahoma in 1931; co-editor of *The Chariton Review;* published in *Carriers of the Dream Wheel* (Harper & Row), *Southwest: A Contemporary Anthology* (Red Earth Press), *Chicago Review, New America, Cutbank;* teaches at Northeast Missouri State University in Kirksville, Missouri.

RUSSELL BATES — (Kiowa) — short story writer, screen writer; born in Anadarko, Oklahoma; specializes in science fiction writing; author of a *Star Trek* screenplay "How Sharper Than a Serpent's Tooth" which was filmed in the later animated series; screenplay, "The Patient Parasites," published in *Star Trek: The New Voyages 2* (Bantam Books); working on an anthology of science fiction writings by and about American Indians; will be a contributing screen writer for *Battlestar Galactica,* soon to be aired on ABC-TV; lives alternately in Anadarko and Los Angeles.

DUANE BIG EAGLE — (Osage-Sioux) — poet; born in Claremore, Oklahoma in 1946; book, *Bidato - Ten Mile River Poems* (Workingman's Press); published in *Sun Tracks, The Nation, Chicago Review, Florida Quarterly, From the Belly of the Shark* (Random House) and *Cottonwood Review;* lives on a sheep ranch in Mendocino County, northern California.

PETER BLUE CLOUD/ARONIAWENRATE — (Mohawk) — poet, carpenter, wood carver, drum-maker; born at Caughnawaga Reserve in Quebec in 1927; published in *Akwesasne Notes;* books, *Coyote and Friends* (Blackberry Press), *Turtle Bear & Wolf* (Akwesasne Notes) and *White Corn Sister* (Strawberry Press); lives in Nevada City, California.

JOSEPH BRUCHAC — (Abnaki) — poet, novelist, editor, publisher; born in New York state in 1942; books, *Flow* and *Entering Onandaga* (Cold Mountain Press), *Indian Mountain* (Ithaca House), and *Turkey Brother* (Crossing Press); widely published in magazines and anthologies; publisher of *Greenfield Review;* lives in Greenfield Center, New York.

BARNEY BUSH — (Shawnee-Cayuga) — poet, teacher; born in Saline Co., Illinois in 1946; published in *Sun Tracks, Scree, Arizona Highways,* and *Dacotah Territory;*

anthologized in *The First Skin Around Me* (Territorial Press); currently teaching at Milwaukee Area Technical College; has a book of poems forthcoming from UCLA.

JANET CAMPBELL — (Coeur d'Alene) — poet, novelist, painter; born on the Coeur d'Alene Reservation in Idaho in 1947; has lived on the Colville and Yakima Reservations of Washington; taught in Native American Studies at Berkeley; novel, *The Owl's Song* (Doubleday); poems, *Custer Lives in Humboldt County* (Greenfield Review Press); anthologized in *The Whispering Wind* (Doubleday) and *The American Indian Speaks* (Dakota Press); now a third-year law student living in Spokane.

GLADYS CARDIFF — (Cherokee) — poet; born in Browning, Montana in 1942; book, *To Frighten a Storm* (Copper Canyon Press); published in *Carriers of the Dream Wheel* (Harper & Row), *From the Belly of the Shark* (Random House), *Northwest Review* and *Puget Soundings*; lives in Edmonds, Washington.

AARON CARR — (Navajo-Laguna Pueblo) — poet, short story writer; born in New Mexico in 1963; high school student at Truman High School in Albuquerque; in addition to writing, he is studying acting, film making, and music; published in *Sun Tracks* and *Planet Quarterly*.

BERNADETTE CHATO — (Navajo) — poet, born in New Mexico; published in *New America*; attended the University of New Mexico; author of *'49 Poems*, an unpublished book-length manuscript; lives in Austin, Texas with her husband and child.

GREY COHOE — (Navajo) — poet, painter, graphic artist; born at Shiprock, New Mexico; attended the Institute of American Indian Arts in Santa Fe, 1965-67; presently an instructor at IAIA; anthologized in *The Whispering Wind* (Doubleday) and *The American Indian Speaks* (Dakota Press); has had several exhibitions of paintings and other art work in Oklahoma City, New York, Washington, D.C., and countries in South America and Africa.

JOSEPH L. CONCHA — (Taos Pueblo) — poet; born at Taos Pueblo in 1954; attended the Institute of American Indian Arts and the University of New Mexico; author of *Lonely Deer* (Red Willow Society) and *Chokecherry Hunters* (The Sunstone Press); published in *Puerto del Sol* and *New America*; lives at Taos Pueblo.

ROBERT L. CONLEY — (Cherokee) — poet, short story writer, teacher, administrator; born in Cushing, Oklahoma in 1940; published in *Scree*, *The Blackbird Circle*, *Blue Cloud Quarterly*, *Pembroke*, and *Indian Voice Magazine*; book, *21 Poems* (Aux Arcs Press); taught at Northern Illinois University, Southwest Missouri State, and Eastern Montana College; now living in Tahlequah, Oklahoma and working as an assistant programs developer for the Cherokee Nation.

ELIZABETH COOK-LYNN — (Sioux, Crow Creek Reservation) — poet, short story writer, teacher; born at Fort Thompson, South Dakota; published in *Pembroke*, *South Dakota Review*, *Prairie Schooner*, *CCCC Journal*, and *The Great Plains Observer*; book, *Then Badger Said This* (Vanguard Press); teaches at Eastern Washington University; at work on a biography of Little Crow and literary criticism of several contemporary Native American poets.

LARRY EMERSON — (Navajo) — short story writer, painter, journalist; born near Shiprock, New Mexico; served in U.S. Army; wrote a column, *Red Dawn*, syndicated in several Indian newspapers; fiction published in *New America*; has had several exhibitions of his paintings in the Southwest; currently at work on a history of the Navajo Nation; lives in Albuquerque, where he works for the Albuquerque Indian School.

NIA FRANCISCO — (Navajo) — poet, teacher; born near Shiprock, New Mexico in 1952; published in *Southwest: A Contemporary Anthology* (Red Earth Press), *College English*, *Cafe Solo*, *New America* and *Southwest Women's Poetry Exchange*; teaches at Navajo Community College, Shiprock Branch.

KIRK GARCIA — (Chippewa, Turtle Mountain Reservation) — poet, journalist; born in Grand Forks, North Dakota; worked as a news reporter for Indian and underground papers; served a term in the North Dakota State Prison Farm at Bismarck where he began to write poetry; currently a law student at the University of New Mexico.

PHIL GEORGE — (Nez Perce) — poet, spent two years in Vietnam with the Army; anthologized in *The Whispering Wind* (Doubleday), *The American Indian Speaks* (Dakota Press) and *The Next World* (Crossing Press); attended Gonzaga University and the Institute of American Indian Arts; lives in Coulee Dam, Washington.

RAVEN HAIL — (Cherokee) — poet, storyteller, musician, editor, herbalist; born in Dewey, Oklahoma; edited a monthly newsletter, *The Raven Speaks,* a journal of Cherokee culture, from 1968 to 1972; published in *The State, The Cimarron Review, Mr. Cogito, Blue Cloud Quarterly,* and *The Herbalist;* has recorded songs, "A Cherokee Song" and "The Indian Christmas Carol"; lives in Dallas.

JOY HARJO — (Creek) — poet, photographer, artist; born in Tulsa, Oklahoma in 1951; studied art and writing at IAIA, the University of New Mexico, and the University of Iowa; anthologized in *Southwest: A Contemporary Anthology* (Red Earth Press), *The Indian Rio Grande* (San Marcos Press); published in *Dacotah Territory, New America,* and *Southwest Women's Poetry Exchange;* lives and teaches in Santa Fe.

SUZAN SHOWN HARJO — (Cheyenne-Creek-Pawnee) — poet, administrator; born in El Reno, Oklahoma in 1945; anthologized in *Come to Power* (Crossing Press); published in *Anteaus, The New York Quarterly, Nimrod,* and *Quest;* lives in Washington, DC, where she works as a Special Assistant in the Office of the Assistant Secretary of Indian Affairs in the Department of Interior.

LANCE HENSON — (Cheyenne) — poet; served in the U.S. Marine Corps; is a member of the Cheyenne Dog Soldier Warrior Society, and the Native American Church; books: *Keeper of Arrows, Naming the Dark* (Point Riders Press, 1976) and *Mistah* (Strawberry Press, 1977); published in many journals and anthologies; lives near Calumet, Oklahoma.

BILLY HOBSON — (Cherokee-Chickasaw) — illustrator and graphic artist; born in Desha Co., Arkansas in 1943; served in U.S. Air Force; attended electronics schools in Little Rock, Dallas, Shreveport and New York; currently lives in Dallas with his wife and son.

GEARY HOBSON — (Cherokee-Chickasaw) — poet, short story writer, essayist, editor; born in Chicot Co., Arkansas in 1941; served in the U.S. Marines and later in anti-war peace movement; published in *Sun Tracks, Y'Bird, Greenfield Review, La Confluencia, New America* and *Arizona Quarterly; The Road Where the People Cried,* a book of poems, is forthcoming from Blue Cloud Press in 1979; teaches at the University of New Mexico.

LINDA HOGAN — (Chickasaw) — poet, teacher; born in Denver in 1947; grew up in Oklahoma; published in *The Beloit Poetry Journal, Hiram Review, The Little Magazine, Greenfield Review* and *Prairie Schooner;* book, *Calling Myself Home,* forthcoming from Greenfield Review Press later this year; lives in Idledale, Colorado.

KARONIAKTATIE/ALEX JACOBS — (Mohawk) — poet, graphic artist, painter, editor; born in 1953; poetry editor of *Akwesasne Notes,* 1972-1974; published in *Come to Power* (Crossing Press) and *The Next World* (Crossing Press); book, *Native Colours* (Akwesasne Notes); taught at the Institute of American Indian Arts; currently living in Kansas City where he is studying art.

GERALDINE KEAMS — (Navajo) — poet, playwright, actress; born in Winslow, Arizona in 1951; attended the University of Arizona; has appeared in several films, including "The Outlaw Josey Wales"; will appear in television dramas this fall; author of several one-act plays; published in *Sun Tracks;* lives in Tucson.

MAURICE KENNY — (Mohawk) — poet, playwright, editor; born at Watertown, New York in 1929; one-time poetry editor of *Akwesasne Notes;* author of eight books of poetry, including *North: Poems from Home* (Blue Cloud Press) and *I Am the Sun* (Strawberry Press); co-editor of *Contact/II* and publisher of Strawberry Press; widely published in more than a hundred journals; lives in Brooklyn.

JOHN F. KERR — (Cherokee) — poet, teacher; born near Monette, Arkansas in 1930; served in the U.S. Marine Corps; published in *Southwest: A Contemporary Anthology*

(Red Earth Press) and *Blue Cloud Quarterly;* teaches at California Polytechnic State University, San Luis Obispo.

KING KUKA — (Blackfeet) — poet, painter, sculptor; born at Browning, Montana in 1946; attended the Institute of American Indian Arts, 1963-1965; anthologized in *The Whispering Wind* (Doubleday), *The First Skin Around Me* (Territorial Press) and *Voices of the Rainbow* (Viking); lives in Montana.

HAROLD LITTLEBIRD — (Santo Domingo-Laguna Pueblo) — poet, potter; born in Santa Fe in 1951; poems in *Voices from the Rio Grande* (Rio Grande Writers Association Press) and *The Indian Rio Grande* (San Marcos Press); lives in Santa Fe with his wife and daughter.

ADRIAN C. LOUIS — (Paiute) — poet, publisher; born in Lovelock, Nevada in 1946; attended University of Nevada and currently enrolled at Brown University; published in more than 50 magazines; books, *The Indian Cheap Wine Seance* (Gray Flannel Press) and *Muted War Drums* (Strawberry Press); lives in Providence, Rhode Island.

LEE H. MARMON — (Laguna Pueblo) — photographer; born at Laguna, New Mexico; has been a photographer for 30 years; works with the Indian Pueblo Cultural Center in Albuquerque; his work has appeared in *New America, Pueblo News,* and on the covers of such books as Leslie Marmon Silko's *Ceremony* and Simon J. Ortiz's *The Howbah Indians;* currently doing liasion work with Hollywood film companies and New Mexico Indian communities.

N. SCOTT MOMADAY — (Kiowa) — poet, novelist, essayist; born in Lawton, Oklahoma in 1934; novel, *House Made of Dawn* (Harper & Row); other books include *The Way to Rainy Mountain* (University of New Mexico Press), *The Gourd Dancer* (Harper & Row), and *The Names* (Harper & Row); won Pulitzer Prize in 1969 for *House Made of Dawn;* currently teaching at Stanford University.

DANA NAONE — (Hawaiian) — poet, editor, teacher; born in Hawaii in 1949; former editor of *Hawaii Review;* published in *Carriers of the Dream Wheel* (Harper & Row), *The Nation, Ironwood, Kayak, Ocean Mountain,* and *San Marcos Review;* involved in a long-term project of translating Hawaiian songs, chants, and prayers into English; teaches with the Hawaii Poets-in-the-Schools.

JEAN NATONI — (Navajo) — poet; born in Rehobeth, New Mexico; attended Fort Lewis College and Navajo Community College; lives at Tsaile, Arizona with her husband and son; "Catoni" is her first publication.

SANDIE NELSON — (Choctaw) — poet; born in Chicago in 1951; has lived in the Southwest most of her life; published in *Southwest Women's Poetry Exchange* and *A: a journal of contemporary literature;* lives in Farmington, New Mexico.

nila northSun — (Shoshoni-Chippewa) — poet, editor; born in Schurz, Nevada in 1951; co-editor of *Scree;* co-author (with Kirk Robertson) of *After the Drying Up of the Water* and *Diet Pepsi & Nacho Cheese* (Duck Down Press); published in *Wormwood Review, Vagabond, Nausea, Sun Tracks, Dacotah Territory,* and *Nitty Gritty;* lives in Carpinteria, California.

WILLIAM OANDASAN — (Yuki) — poet, journalist, editor, publisher; born at Round Valley Reservation in Northern California in 1947; founder and publisher of A Press; published in *Mississippi Valley Review, New America,* and *Akwesasne Notes;* author of chapbooks *Earth and Sky* (A Press), *Taking Off* (A Press), and *Sermon and Three Waves* (A Press); was a conscientious objector during the Vietnam War; lives in Santa Fe, but currently studying in Chicago.

SIMON J. ORTIZ — (Acoma Pueblo) — poet, short story writer, teacher; born at Acoma Pueblo in 1941; books include *Going for the Rain* (Harper & Row), *A Good Journey* (Turtle Island Foundation), *The People Shall Continue* (Children's Book Press) and *The Howbah Indians* (Blue Moon Press); published in *Pembroke, Carriers of the Dream Wheel* (Harper & Row) and *Man to Send Rain Clouds* (Viking); lives in Kentfield, California.

TED PALMANTEER — (Colville) — poet, painter, sculptor; born near Omak, Washington in 1943; attended the Institute of American Indian Arts for three years; now an instructor at IAIA; published in *The Whispering Wind* (Doubleday); book, *Man-Spirit,* forthcoming from Greenfield Review Press in 1979.

ROBERT L. PEREA — (Oglala Sioux) — short story writer; born in Wheatland, Wyoming in 1946; published in *Mestizo: An Anthology of Chicano Literature;* is half-Chicano; served in the Army in Vietnam; currently living in Mesa, Arizona.

MANUEL PINO — (Acoma Pueblo) — journalist, editor, storyteller; born at Acoma Pueblo in 1953; currently editing *Americans Before Columbus;* published in *Wassaja* and *Pueblo News;* this year he was a participant on the Longest Walk; lives in Albuquerque.

OPAL LEE POPKES — (Choctaw) — short story writer, novelist; grew up near Roswell, New Mexico; published in *The Man to Send Rain Clouds* (Viking); currently at work on a novel entitled *War Games* and a project dealing with Pre-Columbian trade routes of Native American people; teaches at Stephens College in Clearview, Missouri.

CARTER REVARD — (Osage) — poet, teacher; born in Pawhuska, Oklahoma in 1931; has taught at Amherst and Washington University; published in *River Styx, Sun Tracks,* and *Voices of the Rainbow* (Viking); lives in St. Louis.

DIANE REYNA — (Taos Pueblo) — photographer, film maker; born at Taos Pueblo; attended the University of New Mexico; works for the American Indian History Project at UNM as a film maker and editor; participated in the Longest Walk where she filmed several segments of the march, from which she hopes to edit a film; lives in Albuquerque.

VERONICA RILEY/GOWEITDUWEETZA — (Laguna Pueblo) — poet, short story writer; born at Laguna Pueblo in 1950; published in *New America;* student at the University of New Mexico; lives in Albuquerque.

RONALD ROGERS — (Cherokee) — poet, short story writer; born in Claremore, Oklahoma in 1948; published in *A: a journal of contemporary literature, New America,* and *Calvacade;* anthologized in *The Whispering Wind* (Doubleday), *Voices of Wah-kon-tah* (New World), and *The American Indian Speaks* (Dakota Press); book, *Man-Spirit* (with Ted Palmanteer), forthcoming from Greenfield Review Press in 1979; lives in Albuquerque.

ROKWAHO/DANIEL THOMPSON — (Mohawk) — poet, artist, sculptor, linguist; born at Akwesasne in 1953; author of two Mohawk language texts: *Relative Syllabics* (Recherches Amerindiennes du Quebec) and *Teiohakwente* (Indian Affairs Ontario); poetry and artwork published by Strawberry Press, Akwesasne Notes and Blue Cloud Quarterly; poems, *The Poet's Analyst,* soon to be published; lives at Rooseveltown, New York.

WENDY ROSE — (Hopi-Chowchilla Miwok) — poet, painter, anthropologist; born in Oakland, California in 1948; books, *Hopi Roadrunner Dancing* (Greenfield Review Press), *Long Division: A Tribal History* (Strawberry Press) and *Academic Squaw: Reports to the World from the Ivory Tower* (Blue Cloud Press); *Lost Copper* (forthcoming); anthologized in *Carriers of the Dream Wheel* (Harper & Row); lives in Berkeley.

NORMAN H. RUSSELL — (Cherokee) — poet, botanist; university administrator; born at Big Stone Gap, Virginia in 1921; published in hundreds of magazines; author of eleven books of poetry, including *Collected Poems* (Northwoods Press), *Indian Thoughts: I Am Old* (San Marcos Press) and *Open the Flower* (The Perishable Press); author of several textbooks on botany; currently living in Edmond, Oklahoma where he is the Vice President of Academic Affairs at Central State University.

CAROL LEE SANCHEZ — (Laguna Pueblo-Sioux) — poet, painter, teacher; born near Cubero, New Mexico in 1934; author of *Conversations from the Nightmare* (Casa Editorial), *Message Bringer Woman* (Taurean Horn Press) and *Time Warps* (Taurean

Horn Press); served as director of the California Poets-in-the-Schools program; currently teaching at San Francisco State University; has had several exhibitions of her art in California and Colorado.

JOE S. SANDO — (Jemez Pueblo) — poet, historian, teacher; born at Jemez Pueblo in 1922; author of articles on Pueblo Indian history and culture; book, *The Pueblo Indians* (Indian Historian Press); poetry published in *The New Mexico Magazine;* teaches intermittently at the University of New Mexico; member of many commissions and organizations relating to Indian affairs.

REFUGIO SAVALA — (Yaqui) — poet, short story writer, teacher; born in Sonora, Mexico in 1904; published in *Sun Tracks;* autobiography, *The Autobiography of a Yaqui Poet* is forthcoming from the University of Arizona Press; lives in Tucson where he is engaged in translating The Old Testament into Yaqui.

LESLIE MARMON SILKO — (Laguna Pueblo) — poet, novelist, short story writer, essayist; born in Albuquerque in 1948; poems, *Laguna Woman* (Greenfield Review Press); novel, *Ceremony* (Viking); widely anthologized in *Man to Send Rain Clouds* (Viking), *Voices of the Rainbow* (Viking) and *Come to Power* (Crossing Press); teaches at the University of New Mexico, though currently on leave and working in Tucson.

JAUNE QUICK-TO-SEE-SMITH — (Kootenai) — painter, graphic artist; born on the Flathead Reservation in Montana in 1940; studied art in Boston, California, and the University of New Mexico; has had several shows of her work in the Southwest; lives in Albuquerque.

LOIS SONKISS — (Maya) — artist, painter, reviewer; born in Chiapas, Mexico in 1956; grew up in northern Michigan; studied art at the University of New Mexico; published in *La Confluencia;* lives in Tijeras Canyon, New Mexico.

R.A. SWANSON — (Chippewa) — poet; born in Minnesota in 1946; author of two chapbooks, *Solemn Spirits* and *Little Warrior;* published in *Phantasm,* works as a counselor and lives in Yakima, Washington.

MARY TALL MOUNTAIN — (Koyukon) — poet, prose writer; born in Alaska in 1918; published in *Way, Poetry Northwest, Bitterroot, Northwest Passage* and *Calyx;* author of *Nine Poems* (Friars Press) and *Good Grease* (Strawberry Press); at work on a novel about her people of the Yukon to be entitled *Doyon;* lives in Phoenix.

LUCI TAPAHONSO — (Navajo) — poet, short story writer, journalist; born near Shiprock, New Mexico in 1953; has worked with various Indian newspapers; published in *Sun Tracks, A: a journal of contemporary literature,* and *Southwest Women's Poetry Exchange;* lives in Albuquerque.

JIM TOLLERUD — (Makah) — poet, jewelry maker; born at Port Angeles, Washington in 1954; published in *Akwesasne Notes, Drumbeats,* and *Seattle Indian News;* anthologized in *Voices of the Rainbow* (Viking) and *The First Skin Around Me* (Territorial Press); lives in Neah Bay, Washington.

MARNIE WALSH — (Sioux) — poet; book, *A Taste of the Knife* (Ahsahta Press); anthologized in *Voices from Wah Kon-tah* (International Publishers); published in *Dacotah Territory;* does not "give out biographical garbage; the poetry is enough;" lives in Sturgis, South Dakota.

ANNA L. WALTERS — (Pawnee-Otoe) — poet, prose writer; born in Pawnee, Oklahoma in 1946; published in *Man to Send Rain Clouds* (Viking) and *Chouteau Review;* co-author of *The Sacred* (Navajo Community College Press); taught at Navajo Community College for several years; currently living in Tsaile, Arizona where she is working on an autobiography.

LAURA WATCHEMPINO — (Acoma Pueblo) — poet, journalist; born in California in 1954; former editor of the Four Directions (UNM Kiva Indian Students Club) newspaper; published in *New America* and *Americans Before Columbus;* lives in Albuquerque.

EMMI WHITEHORSE — (Navajo) — graphic artist, sandpainter, painter, poet; born near Crownpoint, New Mexico in 1956; attends the University of New Mexico; has had several exhibitions of her art work; published in *Southwest Women's Poetry Exchange*.

AARON YAVA — (Navajo-Hopi) — artist; born at Keams Canyon, Arizona in 1946; his drawings have appeared in *Man to Send Rain Clouds* (Viking) and Simon J. Ortiz's *A Good Journey* (Turtle Island Foundation); book of drawings, *Border Towns of the Navajo Nation* (Holmgangers Press); currently living in Steilacoom, Washington.

GENEVIEVE YAZZIE — (Navajo) — short story writer; born near Fort Wingate, New Mexico in 1950; attended the University of New Mexico where she later worked with the Navajo-English Dictionary Project; published in *New America*; currently living in Anchorage, Alaska.

RAY A. YOUNG BEAR — (Mesquakie) — poet, artist; born at Tama, Iowa in 1950; widely anthologized in *Carriers of the Dream Wheel* (Harper & Row), *Come to Power* (Crossing Press) and *Voices of the Rainbow* (Viking); published in *South Dakota Review, American Poetry Review, The Phoenix,* and *Seneca Review;* lives in Cedar Falls, Iowa.